W9-BSB-127

EARLY CHILDHOOD EDUCATION

EARLY CHILDHOOD EDUCATION

An International Encyclopedia

Volume 2

E–N

Edited by

Rebecca S. New and Moncrieff Cochran

Westport, Connecticut
London

Library of Congress Cataloging-in-Publication Data

Early childhood education [four volumes] : an international encyclopedia / edited by Rebecca S. New and Moncrieff Cochran.

p. cm.

Includes bibliographical references and index.

ISBN 0-313-33100-6 (set : alk. paper)—ISBN 0-313-33101-4 (vol 1 : alk. paper)—ISBN 0-313-33102-2 (vol 2 : alk. paper)—ISBN 0-313-33103-0 (vol 3 : alk. paper)—ISBN 0-313-34143-5 (vol 4 : alk. paper)

1. Early childhood education—Encyclopedias. I. New, Rebecca Staples. II. Cochran, Moncrieff.

LB1139.23.E272 2007

372.2103—dc22 2006035011

British Library Cataloguing in Publication Data is available.

Library of Congress Catalog Card Number: 2006035011

ISBN: 0-313-33100-6 (set)
0-313-33101-4 (vol. 1)
0-313-33102-2 (vol. 2)
0-313-33103-0 (vol. 3)
0-313-34143-5 (vol. 4)

First published in 2007

Praeger Publishers, 88 Post Road West, Westport, CT 06881
An imprint of Greenwood Publishing Group, Inc.
www.praeger.com

Printed in the United States of America

The paper used in this book complies with the Permanent Paper Standard issued by the National Information Standards Organization (Z39.48-1984).

10 9 8 7 6 5 4 3 2 1

Contents

E

Early Care and Education Programs, Administration of

In keeping pace with labor market trends, the demand for child care and early education services during the past two decades has surged. Data reported by the U.S. Census Bureau in 2003 shows there are more than 2.3 million preschoolers who receive care in "organized facilities" such as child-care centers, preschools, or federally funded **Head Start** programs. These organized programs come in all shapes and sizes, and differ according to philosophy, mission, service delivery mode, and legal auspices. While most are subject to regulation at the local and state level, program-licensing standards vary widely among jurisdictions, making it virtually impossible to describe their practices with a taxonomy that can be universally applied.

Program Types

A frequently used method for classifying early care and education programs is by funding source—public or private. Examples of publicly funded programs include state-prekindergarten programs housed in public schools, federally funded Head Start programs, military-sponsored programs, and local parks and recreation programs. Privately funded programs may be sponsored by social service agencies, hospitals, independent proprietors, corporate partners, or faith-based organizations. Over the past few years, the line between public and private funding has blurred as more and more early care and education programs have blended funding from multiple sources, both public and private.

Early childhood programs may also be classified according to their legal structure—for-profit or nonprofit. For-profit programs may be independent proprietary centers, partnerships, corporate chains (e.g., KinderCare, La Petite Academy), or employer-sponsored (e.g., Bright Horizons Family Solutions). Nonprofit programs may be independent or associated with a social service agency, community organization, institution of higher education, or hospital.

Programs also differ in the nature of their services, the clientele they serve, and their philosophical orientation. They may operate part day or full day, part year or year round. They may serve infants, toddlers, preschoolers, or school-age children before and after school. And they may emphasize different educational philosophies and curricular approaches such as **Montessori**, **High/Scope**, or **Reggio Emilia**.

Administrative Roles and Functions

Because the range of program models and governing auspices is so broad, a discussion concerning the administration of early care and education programs befittingly places the program administrator as the focal point. The nomenclature referring to program administrators is varied and includes *director*, *manager*, *principal*, and *supervisor*. The most common designator is center or site director.

Just as variations in the organizational structure of early childhood programs span a wide range of possibility, program administrators likewise assume roles that encompass a spectrum of functional accountability. Generally, the breadth of roles assigned to administrators is tied to the size and governing auspice of their program. Some administrators work at a single site and are responsible for all policy and procedure decisions of their programs while others are employed in more layered settings where policy is set by a governing board, management group, or government entity.

In a large program that serves many families, the administrator may oversee the work of an administrative team including assistant directors, educational coordinators, office assistants, bookkeepers, and food service personnel. In a small program, the administrator usually has direct involvement in day-to-day tasks such as record keeping, visitor reception, meal preparation, and supervision of teachers. In fact, many directors of small programs also teach, spending a portion of their workday in the classroom.

Directing different types of programs requires varying levels of administrative sophistication, and the scope and complexity of the administrative role certainly affects the repertoire of competencies needed to ensure the efficiency and effectiveness of the early care and education organization. Administrating early care and education programs includes both leadership and management functions. Leadership functions relate to the broad view of helping an organization clarify and affirm values, set goals, articulate a vision, and chart a course of action to achieve that vision. Management functions relate to the actual orchestration of tasks and the setting up of systems to carry out the organizational mission.

Administrator Competencies

The administrator's role in an early care and education program is both central and complex. One way to understand the range of competencies needed to administrate a program is to look at the task performance areas that encompass the director's role. Core competencies identified as essential for effective early childhood program administration fall into ten knowledge and skill areas (Bloom,

2000). These are not discrete categories; there is conceptual as well as practical overlap.

Personal and professional self-awareness. Effective administrators are reflective practitioners keenly aware of the variables that impact their sense of personal and professional fulfillment. They grasp adult and career development theory and are able to apply it in their professional interactions. They also understand how to flex their leadership style to accommodate the personality typologies, dispositions, and work styles of diverse teaching and support staff.

Administrators are routinely called upon to resolve ethical and moral dilemmas. In these cases, they draw on their own awareness of the beliefs, values, and philosophical convictions on which their programs stand and evaluate different courses of action in relation to the profession's code of ethical conduct. They are able to articulate a philosophy of management, set personal goals to reduce stress and avoid burnout, and develop strategies to help staff achieve a balance between personal and professional obligations.

Legal and fiscal management. Early childhood programs are essentially businesses, and successful administrators function much like the unit managers of their corporate counterparts. They are savvy financial managers who possess skill in budgeting and cash flow management. They are knowledgeable about bookkeeping methods, accounting terminology, and bank relations. They are well informed about federal, state, and local sources of revenue and seek out grant-writing and fundraising opportunities.

Additionally, effective administrators work with legal counsel to ensure organizational compliance with the many regulations that govern early childhood programs such as licensing standards, building codes, and laws relating to health and occupational safety. They have a working familiarity of legislation relevant to contracts and negotiations, insurance liability, and labor law. In their professional relationships with families, administrators regularly encounter situations that require their facile understanding of confidentiality, child protection, and antidiscrimination laws pertaining to the services provided by their programs.

Staff management and human relations. Early childhood programs are labor-intensive operations and people are the essential ingredient in delivering high-quality services to children and their families. Successful administrators understand the importance of cultivating trusting relationships. They hire, supervise, and motivate staff to high levels of performance. They implement strategies based on their understanding of group dynamics, individual communication styles, and techniques for conflict resolution. They are adept at relating to board members and staff of diverse racial, cultural, and ethnic backgrounds.

Through their command of different supervisory and group facilitation styles, effective administrators exercise skill in consensus building and team development through shared decision making. They mentor those they lead and are committed to staff performance appraisal methods that foster program growth through an individualized model of staff development.

Educational programming. Leadership is central to the role of early childhood administrators. They must be knowledgeable about current curriculum models and **assessment** practices that are consistent with quality indices and are antibias in nature. They design and implement programs that are appropriate for the ages and developmental levels of the young children in their care. They implement grouping practices that support the inclusion of children with special needs and ensure continuity and stability for all children. Effective directors are aware of the benchmarks for high-quality programming such as program **accreditation** and are committed to meeting those standards.

Program operations and facilities management. The facilities that house early care and education programs play an important role in supporting the relationships and interactions that take place within their bounds. Effective administrators plan and design learning environments based on the principles of environmental psychology and child development. They know how to furnish and maintain safe, inviting, and developmentally stimulating environments that accommodate the diverse needs of children and adults.

The early childhood administrator's knowledge and skill in establishing program policies and procedures helps ensure their centers meet state and local regulations as well as professional standards pertaining to the general health and nutrition of children and the occupational safety of program staff. This understanding also provides for efficient inventory control systems and well-thought-out emergency and risk management procedures.

Family support. In addition to providing for young children, many early childhood programs place a parallel emphasis on **parent education** or other forms of outreach to families. Such a family-responsive approach often means that the services of a program extend beyond the walls of the center facility. To effectively carry out their responsibilities, directors must rely on their understanding of family systems, parenting styles, and cross-cultural diversity. They embrace parents as valued partners in the educational process and implement program practices that support families of diverse cultural, ethnic, linguistic, and socioeconomic backgrounds.

Marketing and public relations. Early care and education programs are business enterprises and no enterprise can be sustained without a stable clientele and a steady influx of new customers. Successful administrators are strategic marketers whose programs profit from effective promotion, publicity, and community outreach activities. Their business plans are designed to attain maximum enrollment. In all that they do, effective directors communicate their program's philosophy and promote a positive public image to parents, business leaders, public officials, and prospective funders. They conduct routine assessments to determine community needs and promote linkages with local schools. Their programs are promoted to the public on paper, through broadcast media, and over the Internet through attractive brochures, Web sites, handbooks, newsletters, press releases, and carefully placed advertising.

Advocacy. **Advocacy** is a natural outgrowth of administrative leadership, since early childhood program directors have firsthand exposure to the needs and concerns of the children, families, and the communities they serve. Effective administrators are persuasive advocates for their cause and know how to explain issues with clarity and eloquence. They are cognizant of legislative processes, social issues, and public policy affecting young children, their families, and program staff. They know how to evaluate program effectiveness by identifying organizational problems, gathering data to generate alternative solutions, and applying analytical skills to the solution of those problems. In addition, they initiate community collaborations for efficient and cost-effective service delivery and mobilize others to advocate for better child and family services.

Oral and written communication. In both writing and speaking, effective early childhood administrators know how to synthesize complex information and communicate cogently and succinctly to a variety of different audiences. This ability requires mastery of the mechanics of good writing for organizing ideas, grammar, punctuation, and spelling, as well as effective oral communication techniques for establishing rapport, active listening, and voice control. Administrators function in an environment where opportunities abound for putting their communication skills into practice, whether it be through informal and formal written correspondence, an article contributed for journal publication, a formal presentation to a board of advisors, or a workshop presented at a professional conference.

Technology. The vast majority of early care and education programs today use computer technology to streamline administrative processes. The marketplace is replete with vendors who have developed administrative software offering turnkey solutions for a wide array of applications such as monitoring child admissions data, enrollment and attendance records, and staff scheduling. They offer financial management tools to support revenue tracking, banking, payroll, disbursements, and the preparation of regular financial statements. Additionally, some third-party software programs aid marketing efforts by tracking prospect inquiries and managing a program's waiting list.

To make the most of these technology resources, effective early childhood program administrators possess a working knowledge of computer hardware and software and are skilled users of word processing, spreadsheet, data management, and presentation applications. Their use of Internet technology fosters even greater efficiency via timely e-mail communication or by availing their programs to quality-enhancing online resources that strengthen daily practices, professional development, and advocacy initiatives.

The Link—Administrator Qualifications and Program Quality

Most administrators of early care and education programs have been promoted to their positions because of exemplary performance as classroom teachers. Few have had specialized training in leadership or program management before assuming their positions. Few states require any administrative training for directors as a prerequisite for the position. For many directors, their own experience in the form of learning while doing (the "trial and error" approach) is what they rely upon to build administrative competence. Others put together a patchwork system of course work and in-service **professional development** to acquire the knowledge and skills they need. While approximately 75 percent of directors have baccalaureate degrees, directors with a specialized degree in early childhood leadership or management are rare.

Strong evidence has accumulated that directors of early care and education programs are the "gatekeepers to quality," setting the standards and expectations for others to follow (Bloom, 1992). In a number of powerful ways the director influences the climate of a center both as a workplace for the teaching staff and as an educational and nurturing environment for young children. Without quality systems in place at the organizational level, high-quality interactions and learning environments at the classroom level cannot be sustained. The knowledge and skill of the administrator and his or her commitment to ongoing professional development have a profound impact on the quality of services a program can deliver.

Not surprising, survey data support the notion that many early childhood administrators enter their administrative roles with little or no preparation for the job. Only one-half of directors indicate that their perceptions matched reality when they assumed their current job and just one-fourth say they were well prepared for their new role (MTCECL, 2003). Equally troubling, only 12 percent of programs indicate they have a formal leadership succession plan in place. Those programs were more likely to be associated with a for-profit chain or a for-profit employer-sponsored program.

A mounting body of research has confirmed that the director's level of formal education and specialized training are two of the strongest predictors of overall program quality. Years of directing a child-care center, on the other hand, is not a potent predictor of overall program quality. Pretests and posttests of teaching practices and overall organizational climate in the centers of directors who have participated in leadership training has shown significant improvement compared with directors who have not participated in such training. The evidence is compelling; leadership training not only improves administrators' self-efficacy and perceptions of themselves as leaders, it also results in demonstrated improvements in the quality in their centers (Bella and Bloom, 2003).

Current Issues Confronting Early Childhood Administrators

Historically, the field of early childhood has always been closely tied to changes in society. Like a barometer, early care and education programs respond to changes in the social, political, and economic climate of the country. In addition to growing demand, several major trends represent new challenges for today's early childhood program administrator. These trends impact the way all programs conduct their business, regardless of services provided, agency affiliation, or governing auspices.

Emphasis on quality and accountability. Greater demands for accountability are creating additional pressures for quality assurance evaluation and performance management systems that monitor, document, and report on center efficiency and quality of care.

Welfare-to-work legislation. Federal initiatives are putting more parents into the workforce. These newly employed adults not only add to the demand for quality child care but also require different kinds of support and service relationships.

Shortage of qualified early childhood staff. Staff turnover and retention issues continue to plague early childhood programs. Finding qualified staff who are caring, motivated, and committed to early childhood as a career remains a challenge.

Increased competition for financial resources. Competition for adequate levels of funding is demanding greater entrepreneurship and innovation and more intense linkages and integration between social service delivery agencies and early care and education organizations.

The increasing complexity of the external environment has elevated the need for strong leadership in the administrator's role. The trend toward blended funding streams, coordinated delivery systems, community-based planning, collaborative data collection, service delivery networks, and other systemic changes has created demands on early childhood administrators for knowledge and skills not previously needed. More than ever, the field of early childhood education needs program administrators who are willing to make a serious commitment to the profession and to their ongoing personal and professional development to achieve the goal of providing high-quality services to children and their families. *See also* Classroom Environment; Antibias/Multicultural Education; Preschool/Prekindergarten Programs; Teacher Certification/Licensure.

Further Readings: Bella, Jill, and Paula J. Bloom (2003). *Zoom: The impact of leadership training on role perceptions, job performance, and career decisions*. Wheeling, IL: The McCormick Tribune Center for Early Childhood Leadership at National-Louis University; Bloom, Paula J. (1992). The child care center director: A critical determinant of program quality. *Educational Horizons* 70 (Spring), 138–145; Bloom, Paula J. (2000). How do we define director competence? *Child Care Information Exchange* (March), 13–18; Culkin, Mary, ed. (1999). *Managing quality in young children's programs—The leader's role*. New York: Teachers College Press; Hearron, Patricia F., and Verna Hildebrand (2003). *Management of child development centers*. Upper Saddle River, NJ: Pearson Education; Kagan, Sharon L., and Barbara Bowman, eds. (1997). *Leadership in early care and education*. Washington, DC: National Association for the Education of Young Children; McCormick Tribune Center for Early Childhood Leadership (2003). Leadership transitions—what do directors experience? *Research Notes* (Fall), 1–2; U.S. Census Bureau (2003). *Who's minding the kids? Child care arrangements: Spring 1999 (PPL-168)*. Available online at http://www.census.gov/population/www/socdemo/child/ppl-168.html.

Paula Jorde Bloom and Douglas Clark

Early Child Development and Care

Early Child Development and Care is a multidisciplinary publication that serves psychologists, educators, psychiatrists, paediatricians, social workers and other professionals who deal with research, planning, education and care of infants and young children.

The journal provides English translations of work in this field that has been published in other languages, and original English papers on all aspects of early child development and care. Published eight times per year by Routledge, the journal also contains book reviews, conference reports and other items of interest. For more information, please visit http://www.tandf.co.uk/journals/titles/03004430.asp.

Roy Evans

Early Childhood Connections Journal of Music- and Movement-based Learning

Early Childhood Connections Journal of Music- and Movement-based Learning is a quarterly publication focusing on best practices, current theories, and applied research influencing the field of early childhood music education. Guided by a belief in the fundamental contributions of music and movement to healthy growth and development, this journal posits an eclectic approach that entertains multiple stances and curricular approaches. Issues are often thematic and have included topics such as Music and **Autism**, Musical Parenting, and Children at **Play**. First published in 1995 by the Foundation for Music-based Learning, *Early Childhood Connections* includes invited articles, book and research reviews, and peer-reviewed submissions from a wide variety of writers; music educators and researchers, psychologists, developmental specialists, teacher educators, professional musicians, and parents have all been featured. Worldwide views are represented in International Perspectives issues that appear almost annually, often including papers delivered at global conferences. For more information, see www.ecconnections.org.

Lori Custodero

Early Childhood Education Journal (ECEJ)

The mission of *Early Childhood Education Journal (ECEJ)* is to provide an international forum in which to share information, insights, research, and policy with implications for early childhood educators worldwide. *Early Childhood Education Journal* is a peer-reviewed, scholarly, and interdisciplinary journal that publishes original articles written by professionals with a shared commitment to the education and care of young children. Articles selected for publication in *Early Childhood Education Journal* represent a skillful blend of theory, research, and practice. Published six times per year, *Early Childhood Education Journal* is available in print format as well as electronically archived issues of the journal (full text and fully searchable). Guidelines for authors and instructions for obtaining a free sample copy are posted on the journal's homepage at http://www.kluweronline.com/issn/1082-3301. Additionally, the publication uses a sophisticated and completely electronic system of manuscript submission and review called Editorial Manager© (http://ecej.edmgr.com/). The sponsor of the journal is Kluwer Academic Publishing, the second-largest professional publisher in the fields of science, technology, and medicine in the world.

Mary Jalongo

Early Childhood Environment Rating Scales (ERS)

Among the most frequently utilized environment rating scales (ERS) in the United States are four developed by Thelma Harms, Richard M. Clifford, and Debby Cryer at the FPG Child Development Institute of the University of North Carolina at Chapel Hill. These scales, each designed for a different segment of the early childhood field, are described below.

- **Early Childhood Environment Rating Scale-Revised (ECERS-R), Updated (2005), T. Harms, R.M. Clifford, and D. Cryer:** This scale is designed to assess group programs for preschool-**kindergarten**-aged children, from 2 1/2 through 5 years of age. The total scale consists of forty-three items and is commonly referred to as the ECERS-R. The ECERS-R is also available in Spanish.
- **Infant/Toddler Environment Rating Scale-Revised (ITERS-R), Updated (2006), T. Harms, D. Cryer, and R.M. Clifford:** This scale is designed to assess group programs for children from birth to two-and-a-half years of age. The total scale consists of thirty-nine items and is commonly referred to as the ITERS-R. The ITERS-R is also available in Spanish.
- **Family Child Care Environment Rating Scale (FCCERS), (2006), T. Harms, D. Cryer, and R.M. Clifford:** This scale is designed to assess family **child-care** programs, usually conducted in a provider's home. The total scale consists of thirty-eight items. This scale is a revision of the Family Day Care Rating Scale (FDCRS, 1989).
- **School-Age Care Environment Rating Scale (SACERS), (1996), T. Harms, E.V. Jacobs, and D.R. White:** This scale is designed to assess group care programs for school-age children, 5 to 12 years of age, during out-of-school time. The total scale consists of forty-nine items, including six supplementary items for programs enrolling children with disabilities. It is commonly referred to as the SACERS.

Two resource books that provide in-depth information in text and photographs—*All About the ECERS-R* (Cryer, Harms, and Riley, 2003) and *All About the ITERS-R* (Cryer, Harms, and Riley, 2004)—are available to help with interpretation of the scales.

All four scales have the following features in common:

- They have items to evaluate: Physical Environment; Basic Care Routines (including health and safety practices); Curriculum; Interaction; Schedule and Program Structure; and Parent and Staff Support.
- The scales are suitable for use in evaluating inclusive and culturally diverse programs, half day and whole day programs.
- The scales have proven reliability and validity.
- They use the same format and scoring system, a 7-point Likert scale with indicators for (1) inadequate, (3) minimal, (5) good, and (7) excellent.

Following is a sample item from the ECERS-R.

32. Staff–child interactions*

Inadequate	*Minimal*	*Good*	*Excellent*
1.1 Staff members are not responsive to or not involved with children (e.g., ignore children, staff seem distant or cold). 1.2 Interactions are unpleasant (e.g., voices sound strained and irritable). * 1.3 Physical contact used principally for control (e.g., hurrying children along) or inappropriately (e.g., unwanted hugs or tickling).	3.1 Staff usually respond to children in a warm, supportive manner (e.g., staff and children seem relaxed, voices cheerful, frequent smiling). 3.2 Few, if any, unpleasant interactions.	5.1 Staff show warmth through appropriate physical contact (e.g., pat child on the back, return child's hug). 5.2 Staff show respect for children (e.g., listen attentively, make eye contact, treat children fairly, do not discriminate). 5.3 Staff respond sympathetically to help children who are upset, hurt, or angry.*	7.1 Staff seem to enjoy being with the children. 7.2 Staff encourage the development of mutual respect between children and adults (e.g., staff wait until children finish asking questions before answering; encourage children in a polite way to listen when adults speak).

****Notes for Clarification***

Item 32. While the indicators for quality in this item generally hold true across a diversity of cultures and individuals, the ways in which they are expressed may differ. For example, direct eye contact in some cultures is a sign of respect; in others, a sign of disrespect. Similarly, some individuals are more likely to smile and be demonstrative than others. However, the requirements of the indicators must be met, although there can be some variation in the way this is done.

1.2. Score this indicator "Yes" only if many unpleasant interactions are observed throughout the observation or during one part of the observation. If only one or two brief instances are observed, and most interactions are neutral or positive, score "No."

5.3. Sympathetic response means that staff notice and validate a child's feelings, even if the child is showing emotions that are often considered unacceptable, such as anger or impatience. The feelings should be accepted although inappropriate behaviors, such as hitting or throwing things, should not be allowed.

A sympathetic response should be provided in most, but not necessarily all, cases. If children are able to solve minor problems themselves, then teacher response is not needed. The observer needs to get an overall impression of the response of the staff. If minor problems persist and are ignored or if staff responds in an unsympathetic manner, give no credit for this indicator.

The ERS are designed to assess process quality in an early childhood or school age care setting. Process quality is defined in the ERS as consisting of the various interactions that go on in a classroom between the staff and children, among staff members, between staff and parents, among the children themselves, as well as the interactions children have with the many materials and activities in the environment. Also included are those features such as space, schedule, and materials that support these interactions. With the ERS, process quality is assessed primarily through observation and has been found to be more predictive of child outcomes than judging quality based on structural indicators such as staff to child ratio, group size, cost of care, and even type of care (e.g., child-care center or family child-care home) (Whitebook, Howes, and Phillips, 1995).

Central to these four ERS is the belief that, in order to provide care and education that will permit children to experience a high quality of life while helping them develop their physical, social/emotional, and cognitive abilities, a quality program must provide for the three basic needs all children have:

- Protection of their health and safety;
- Support in building positive relationships and social/emotional resilience; and
- Opportunities for stimulation and learning from experience.

No one component is more or less important than the others, nor can one substitute for another. It takes all three to create quality care. Each of the three basic components of quality care manifests itself in tangible forms in the program's environment, curriculum, schedule, supervision, and interaction; and can be observed. These are the key aspects of process quality that are assessed in these environment rating scales.

The ERS define environment in a broad sense and guide the observer to assess the arrangement of space both indoors and outdoors, the materials and activities offered to the children, the supervision and interactions (including language) that occur in the classroom, and the schedule of the day, including routines and activities. The support offered to parents and staff is also included. One classroom is assessed at a time, thus providing an in-depth picture of the ongoing quality of care. An assessment usually takes at least three hours of observation in a classroom, followed by a short interview with the teacher.

The scales have good interrater reliability and validity and have demonstrated in numerous studies to be good predictors of child outcomes, thus making them suitable for research and program evaluation. Since they were developed in close collaboration with realistic field-based sites, they are also widely used in program improvement efforts. Each scale has a training program; the ECERS-R, ITERS-R, and FCCERS-R training programs include an interactive videotape.

Research and program evaluation uses of the ERS have been extensive since 1980 when the original ECERS was published. Most major U.S. studies of the effects of early childhood programs on child development outcomes have used one or more of the ERS, including the *National Child Care Staffing Study* (Whitebook, Howes, and Phillips, 1989), the *Family and Child Experiences Study* (FACES) (1997), the *Cost, Quality, and Child Outcomes Study* (1995), and the *Pre-Kindergarten Study* (2005). The FDCRS was used in *The Study of Children in Family Child Care and Relative Care* (Galinsky et al., 1994). In each of these studies, a significant relationship was found between higher scores on the ERS and more positive child development outcomes in areas considered important for later school success. Children in programs scoring high on the ERS were more competent socially as well as cognitively and verbally. The effects of higher quality early childhood experiences, as indicated by high ERS scores, have now been shown to last at least through the second grade of elementary school (Peisner-Feinberg et al., 1999). Research is continuing to evaluate longer-lasting effects.

The Environment Rating Scales in Program Improvement

The ERS are used in a variety of ways in program improvement efforts, including self-assessment by center staff and family child-care providers, preparation for credentialing and accreditation, and voluntary improvement efforts by state licensing and other agencies. The following examples are from the United States:

- The state of Arkansas has trained personnel who do assessments and provide training and technical assistance so that child-care centers and homes can increase their quality scores on the ERS. The Federal money allotments for improving child care are linked to measurable program improvement on the scales. A unique feature of the Arkansas program is that parents who select child-care facilities with an average of 4.5 or higher on the ERS are eligible for two times the state child-care tax exemption. Thus both parents and providers are being rewarded for quality improvements that benefit the children.
- North Carolina has a program called "Partnerships for Inclusion" which has been effective in on-site consultation with child-care staff to include children with disabilities in programs for typically developing children. The ERS are used as a basis for their consultants. This has enabled many children who require early intervention services to be served in inclusive programs.
- Many counties involved in the state of North Carolina's quality improvement program, Smart Start, require training on and use of the scales in self-assessment before a center or family child-care home may apply for a grant. This ensures that the staff will order equipment, materials and/or request training based on needs that have been objectively substantiated.
- North Carolina currently uses scale scores as part of their 5 star Rated License System. Centers and family child-care homes are awarded either one or two stars based on compliance with licensing standards. Programs may voluntarily apply for an additional three stars based on a set of quality measures including teacher and director education, and level of process quality as measured by the appropriate environment scale. Only the lowest level of licensing is mandatory. However, an additional fee is paid to the provider of subsidized care for each additional star earned voluntarily in this tiered reimbursement program.
- Tennessee uses the ERS for a yearly program evaluation to create a "Report Card" that must be posted with the license, so child-care consumers have access to reliable information on the quality of child care they are selecting for their children. Technical assistance and training are available if requested by providers.
- Other states, including California, The District of Columbia, Delaware, Massachusetts, Montana, Mississippi, Kansas, Oregon, Kentucky, New Mexico, Georgia, Florida, South Carolina, Wisconsin, Ohio and Nebraska have also initiated quality evaluation and improvement programs using the ERS. Each state is tailoring its use of the scales to its individual needs and resources.
- All the U.S. military services have been using the ERS routinely in their child-care centers and family child-care homes for program improvement and monitoring. The military child development system was recognized by Executive Order of the President in 1998 for its high quality.
- The ERS are widely used by programs as they prepare for various national accreditation and credentialing programs. This is due to the fact that the scales use a format with indicators at four levels of quality from inadequate to excellent that provide a

blueprint for gradual change. The content of the scales is completely supportive of the various national credentialing and accreditation programs.

Use of the ERS in Other Countries

It is also interesting to note that the ERS have been used in research studies and program improvement efforts in many other countries including Canada, Germany, Italy, Sweden, Finland, Russia, Iceland, Portugal, England, Spain, Austria, Singapore, Hong Kong, Korea, Hungary, Greece, and Japan. The scales have proven reliable and valid in each country with relatively minor adaptations. No doubt there are cultural differences among these various countries, yet each of these countries adheres to a core set of child development values and early childhood practices common to most modern industrialized countries (Tietze et al., 1996). It has been shown that in England, Greece, Germany, Portugal, Spain, and Austria, higher scores on the scales are related to more positive child development outcomes (Petrogannis and Melhuish, 1996, European Child Care and Education Study Group, 1997).

- In Canada, the ERS are available in both English and French. In many of the provinces, they are used as a voluntary part of the licensing visit. The license is given for compliance with a licensing checklist, composed mainly of health and safety items. During the visit, the licensing consultant also completes one of the ERS and, with the voluntary cooperation of the caregiver, sets improvement goals for the program. The scales are used over a longer period in intensive consultation with programs that show problems during the licensing visit.
- In Sweden, several projects are using the Swedish translation of the ECERS for program improvement. For example, in Stockholm, the staff working together in a classroom independently completes one subscale of the scale each month, then discusses their scores under the leadership of their head teacher, who is a fully trained preschool teacher. The staff makes and carries out its own improvement plans. A study of this low cost program showed substantial gains in quality.
- In Germany, the translations of the ERS are presently being used in many areas to evaluate the quality of child care and kindergarten programs. Reports are provided to administrative agencies and to center staff, as a basis for program improvement. In addition, the scales are being considered as part of planning a program accreditation system.

For further information on the ERS, visit www.fpg.unc.edu/~ecers.

Further Readings: Burchinal, M. R., J. E. Roberts, R. Riggins, S. A. Zeisel, E. Neebe, and D. Bryant (2000). Relating quality of center-based child care to early cognitive and language development longitudinally. *Child Development 71*(2), 339–357; Buysse, V., P. W. Wesley, D. Bryant, and D. Gardner (1999). Quality of early childhood programs in inclusive and noninclusive settings. *Exceptional Children 65*(3), 301–314; Cost, Quality, and Child Outcomes Study Team (1995). Cost, quality and child outcomes in child-care centers: Key findings and recommendations. *Young Children 50*(4), 40–44; Cryer, D., T. Harms, and C. Riley (2003). *All about the ECERS-R—A detailed guide in words and pictures*. PACT House Publishing, Kaplan Early Learning Company; Cryer, D., T. Harms, and C. Riley (2004). *All About the ITERS-R—A detailed guide in words and pictures*. PACT House Publishing, Kaplan Early Learning Company; Galinsky, E., C. Howes, S. Kontos, and M. Shinn (1994). *The study of children in family child care and relative care: Highlights* *of findings*. New York: Families and Work Institute; McKey, Ruth (2002). *What are we learning about program quality and child development?* (FACES Study Team). *Head Start Bulletin* 74, 38–39; Peisner-Feinburg, E. S., M. R. Burchinal, R. M. Clifford, M. L. Culkin, C. Howes, S. L. Kagan, and N. Yazejian (2001). The relation of preschool child-care quality to children's cognitive and social developmental trajectories through second grade. *Child Development 72*(5), 1534–1554; Phillipsen, L. C., M. R. Burchinal, C. Howes, and D. Cryer (1997). The prediction of process quality from structural features of child care. *Early Childhood Research Quarterly 12*(3), 281–303; Pre-Kindergarten Study Team (2005). Pre-Kindergarten in the United States. *Early Developments*. FPG Child Development Inst., 9(1); Tietze, W., D. Cryer, J. Bairrao, J. Palacios, and G. Wetzel (1996). Comparisons of observed process quality in early child-care and education programs in five countries. *Early Childhood Research Quarterly 11*(4), 447–75; Whitebook, M., D. Phillips, and C. Howes (1995). National Child Care Staffing Study Revisited: Four years in the life of center based child care. Child Care Employee Project.

Thelma Harms

Early Childhood Music Education Commission (ECME)

The International Society for Music Education (ISME) was founded in 1953 through the joint efforts of the United Nations Educational, Scientific, and Cultural Organization (**UNESCO**), the International Music Council (IMC), and the U.S.-based Music Educators National Conference (MENC). With members in over seventy countries, ISME is currently headquartered in Australia and is constituted by seven special interest commissions, each of which holds individual international conferences immediately preceding the biennial ISME World Conference. The early childhood commission was chartered in 1984, and has since met every two years at locations from Capetown to Copenhagen, providing an international forum for cultural exchange. Issues examined include children's inherent musicality as manifest in their play, advances in music and neuroscience research; the roles of the family, schooling, and culture in musical development; and the preservation of cultural traditions in the light of the breakdown of cultural barriers. Proceedings are published and are often reprinted in one of three annual ISME journals. For more information, see www.isme.org.

Lori Custodero

Early Childhood Research & Practice (*ECRP*)

Early Childhood Research & Practice (*ECRP*), the first Internet-only, peer-reviewed, open-access journal in early childhood education, addresses issues related to the development, care, and education of children from birth to approximately eight years of age. The journal focuses mainly on research with clear implications for practice and contains articles on practice-related research and development.

ECRP was established in 1999 with funding from the U.S. Department of Education under the auspices of the ERIC Clearinghouse on Elementary and Early Childhood Education. When the clearinghouse system was discontinued in 2003, the editors—Lilian G. Katz and Dianne Rothenberg—explored other economic models to keep the journal available at no cost to readers. In 2004, with funding from the Bernard van Leer Foundation and institutional support from the College of Education at the University of Illinois at Urbana-Champaign, the journal became bilingual, publishing all articles in both English and Spanish. The journal is available online at http://ecrp.uiuc.edu.

Lilian G. Katz, Diane Rothenberg, and Laurel Preece

Early Childhood Research Quarterly (ECRQ)

Early Childhood Research Quarterly (*ECRQ*) is sponsored by the **National Association for the Education of Young Children** (NAEYC). The *Quarterly* publishes research and scholarship related to the development, care, and education of children from birth through eight years of age. The articles reflect the interdisciplinary nature of the field and of the National Association. Manuscripts published in the *Quarterly* are evaluated using blind peer review. The reviewers include international as well as U.S. researchers and scholars. Ad hoc reviewers, as well as Consulting Editors and Editorial Board members, provide critiques of submitted manuscripts.

The first issue of *ECRQ* was published in March 1986 with Lilian Katz at the University of Illinois as the first editor. The purpose of the *Quarterly*, described in the first issue, has been to provide a publication outlet for research and scholarship that addresses issues with important implications for policy and practice. The *Quarterly* has continued this tradition since that first issue. The *Quarterly* occasionally publishes topical issues. These issue have focused, for example, on research related **to Head Start**, to **inclusion** of **children with disabilities** in programs with their typically developing classmates, and to research related to early learning in **math** and **science**. The *Quarterly* is currently published by Pergamon, an imprint of Elsevier, Inc.

Karen Diamond

Early Childhood Special Education (ECSE)

The term Early Childhood Special Education (ECSE) embodies a field characterized by grounded theory, practices, and applied research concerned with the causes and consequences of disability in the first eight years of life. The field has evolved since its inception in the 1960s and 1970s based on increasingly more sophisticated understandings of the nature of early childhood disability and a clearer articulation of the obligations of society to **young children with disabilities** and their families. As the name itself implies, the field of ECSE can be conceptualized as a synthesis of knowledge and practice in Early Childhood Education and Special Education. But the field is more than the sum of these two components; it now represents a distinct body of professional knowledge, practice, and policy. The defining characteristics of ECSE may be found in the arenas of theory, program design (including professional preparation, credentialing, and standard-setting), state and federal social policy, and applied research.

Theoretical Foundations and Contemporary Understandings

Contributions from Early Childhood Education. Historical elements of the field of early childhood education have been incorporated into contemporary interpretations of ECSE. These include the Enlightenment and subsequent Romantic notions of childhood as a distinct time of human development in which both nature and nurture play key roles. Generally rejecting Calvinist concepts of the sinful human, Jean-Jacques **Rousseau**, Friedrich **Froebel,** and Johann **Pestalozzi**, among others, articulated a view of the child as capable, curious, innocent, active, and intentional. In addition, these early proponents particularized the early years of life as distinct from adult responses to and interpretations of the world. They suggested that there is a sequential developmental trajectory and that children have differential ways of thinking and behaving as they progress along such a trajectory.

Twentieth century writers, philosophers, and pedagogues took these ideas further, providing more complex analyses of the early years as times of psychosocial, cognitive, linguistic, and motor development. Thus, the work of John **Dewey**, Sigmund **Freud**, Arnold **Gesell**, Erik **Erikson**, and Jean **Piaget** influenced the field of early childhood in ways that have been incorporated into today's conceptualizations of ECSE. Complementing the primarily psychological orientation that these contributors offered, the work of human ecologists (Urie **Bronfenbrenner** and his followers) has also helped define the field as one that is alert to the contextual aspects of development. More recently, the social constructivist theories of Lev **Vygotsky**, as interpreted in the United States by Wertsch, Rogoff, and others, has shifted the focus from concepts of fixed stages of development to more dynamic variables associated with the developmental niche (cf. Super, 1987) and the influence of sociocognitive interactions with peers and more capable others.

Contributions from Special Education. Emerging roughly at the same time as Rousseau's Enlightenment ideas was a body of work interested in abnormal development and its amelioration. Beginning perhaps with the publication of Itard's *The Wild Boy of Aveyron* in 1801, European and American educators began to describe cases of developmental disability associated with early experiential deprivation, congenital conditions leading to mental retardation and psychomotor impairments, and chronic physical and mental illnesses. Subsequently, a significant effort was made to provide various forms of humane and not so humane treatment to individuals with disabilities. For example, in France and the United State, large-scale congregate institutions were built to house those with cognitive, sensory, and health-related disabilities (e.g., the Asylum for the Deaf and Dumb was built in 1818 in Connecticut, and the Perkins Institute and Massachusetts School for the Blind opened in the 1830s. These and similar institutions were soon expanded to serve "idiots" and "morons" whom it was believed could benefit from intensive and sheltered long-term treatment).

In the early part of the twentieth century, the field of special education began to emerge in conjunction with the rapid expansion of public schooling. Technical concerns with the diagnostic process (e.g., Alfred **Binet**'s design of **intelligence tests** that could be used to predict intellectual ability), behavioral treatment (Edgar Doll's early work in operant conditioning), and the effects of social cues and environment all became the building blocks for contemporary special education practices. Much of this work challenged Darwinian notions of purely inherited and fixed intellectual and social capacities, thus creating a rationale for the efficacy and imperative of treatment for those whose development deviated from the norm.

Converging Theory and Practice. It could be argued that Maria **Montessori**'s work in Rome, where she established the Orthophrenic School for the Cure of the Feeble-minded in 1899, was the first example of a systematic effort to work with young children with significant developmental disabilities. Her belief that "defective children were not extrasocial beings, but were entitled to the benefits of education as much as—if not more than—normal ones" (Roos, 1978) became a key principle in the practice of special education. Subsequently, she turned her attention to developmental challenges associated with early environmental constraints. Her *Casa dei Bambini* in the slums of Rome was an explicit effort to mitigate the effects of poverty in early childhood. These two strains of intervention—in response to developmental impairments as well as the social conditions of early development—can be seen as the basis for the field of ECSE as it is understood today.

By the 1960s, J. McVicker Hunt and Benjamin Bloom, among others, were leading investigations of the interdependence of innate capacity, the qualities of environment in the early years, and the role of "cultural deprivation" as it was then conceptualized. These three streams of investigation invited interdisciplinary research and practice, exemplified over the past four decades by the work of neonatologists (Brazelton), sociologists (Bronfenbrenner), developmental psychologists (Samaroff, Chandler), behavioral psychologists (Bijou, Bricker, Strain), and proponents of **family systems** approaches (Turnbull, Dunst).

These historical and contemporary interpretations of young children and early disability have created a somewhat eclectic, a-theoretical approach to Early Childhood Special Education as it is practiced today. Many practitioners remain focused on a "medical model" that embraces the clinical concepts of diagnosis and treatment aimed at the absence of pathology (normalcy) even as they incorporate **sociocultural** perspectives that take into account the **ecology of childhood**, in which the concern is with the effects of early experience and the quality of caregiving environments. Depending on both the nature of the individual child and the professional orientation of the practitioner, ECSE may draw upon behavioral, biomedical, or psychosocial/developmental models of intervention as applied in homes, child-care centers, preschool programs, public schools, or community agencies.

Programmatic Representations of ECSE

The practice of ECSE has its recent roots in compensatory early childhood programs such as Project **Head Start** (established in 1964) and more targeted, intervention-oriented programs funded by the Handicapped Children's Early Education Act of 1968. Project Head Start is significant in this light as a model of comprehensive, family-directed support aimed at both individual children's well-being and the family's economic and social development. Grounded in Hunt's observations of the link between **poverty** and early childhood disability, Head Start began as a form of primary prevention. The working assumption was that early educational support for children living in poverty, in combination with **parental education** and support provided in the context of extensive social services, would increase the likelihood of educational success and reduce the incidence of childhood disability. Responding to a concern that some young children with disabilities were not being included in Head Start classrooms, in 1972 the U.S. Congress mandated that at least 10 percent of Head Start enrollments include children with diagnosed disabilities. In this way, Head Start became an important national effort to provide direct services to young children with a wide range of disabilities, and it was intended to serve as a model for other program development in the public and private sectors.

The Handicapped Children's Early Education Program (HCEEP) was conceived by Congress in 1968 as a means to demonstrate innovative approaches to the treatment of young children with disabilities as well as those who were "at risk" for educational disability due to development that was compromised by environmental or biological conditions. Programs were required to model not only new approaches to treatment, they were also expected to involve parents intensively (like Head Start), pilot effective methods of program evaluation, and ultimately lead to local community sponsorship and funding. Dozens of new programs received three-year pilot funding under the First Chance Network, thus establishing a national context for the subsequent expansion of special education and therapy for children from birth to school entry age.

Head Start, HCEEP, and related program initiatives were growing at the same time that states were limiting admissions to or closing residential institutions for individuals with severe disabilities. This had two direct consequences. First, the financial burden for care was shifted from centralized, institutional settings, often situated in remote rural locations, to local, community-based nonprofit organizations and, later, public schools. Second, the social support burden was shifted from institutions (where little parent–child contact occurred) to families. In this way, the treatment of very young children with disabilities became a matter of family responsibility rather than a state commitment. Some states systematically developed family support measures to offset the effects of this shift. In other states, families received little help for the new demands placed on them as a result of deinstitutionalization.

Another historical development that became salient beginning in the 1970s and 1980s was a marked increase in the incidence of childhood disability. This increase was a function of improved diagnostic and reporting procedures (including greater access to local clinics and implementation of federally mandated Child Find procedures), increased survival rates for premature infants due to improved medical technologies, and measured increases in post-natal disability such as **autism** as well as cognitive, motor, and behavioral complications following maternal substance abuse. This convergence of model program development, deinstitutionalization and the shift to community-based care, and the growing incidence of early childhood disability all contributed to the ways in which the field of ECSE was defined and practiced.

Professional organizations have also played a key role in the conceptualization and standards that characterize ECSE. The two primary constituencies of professionals have been early childhood special educators and clinical specialists affiliated with the **Division for Early Childhood** (DEC) of the **Council for Exceptional Children** and early childhood teachers and program directors affiliated with the **National Association for the Education of Young Children** (NAEYC). These two groups have collaborated closely over the past ten years to articulate standards for professional practice and preparation. Following a critique of the original NAEYC's guidelines for **Developmentally Appropriate Practice** (Bredekamp and Copple, 1987) for undue emphasis on child development at the exclusion of children whose development does not follow the "normal" course (Mallory, 1992) and the standard's failure to account for variations in cultural context (Mallory and New, 1994), the guidelines were revised to include strategies for use in infant and preschool classrooms designed for typically developing children as well as those with special needs and those from minority and non-U.S. cultures. Further, the revised guidelines now include significant reference to assessment procedures, classroom adaptations, interdisciplinary therapy, and parent involvement appropriate to young children with disabilities. In complementary fashion, DEC has articulated recommended practices for **early intervention** and early childhood special education (Sandall, Hemmeter, Smith, and McLean, 2005).

In addition to describing current approaches to child assessment, family participation, program design, therapeutic interventions, and program evaluation processes, DEC has also been a strong advocate for improved **professional development** and licensure. Together the two organizations have had a significant impact on the U.S. Department of Education personnel preparation initiatives and **state licensing standards**. It is now the norm for states to require some form of early childhood special education teaching credential, often associated with a baccalaureate or master's degree in ECSE or a related field. This, in turn, has led to the rapid expansion of ECSE programs in colleges and universities nationwide, many of which are located within regular early childhood teacher education programs. However, a shortage persists of qualified teachers who are capable of working effectively with young children with disabilities and their families. The collaboration of early childhood teachers and those who specialize in working with young children with disabilities has been fostered by increased application of interdisciplinary and transdisciplinary team models. Because young children with disabilities often experience multiple challenges to their development, and because treatment is seen as most effective when provided in natural environments such as home or school (rather than isolated, clinical settings), ECSE programs often include diverse specialists who must carefully coordinate their work with individual children and families. Thus, a child with motor and cognitive impairments might receive direct support from an occupational therapist, a speech therapist, a child psychologist, and a teacher, all working in the same setting and orchestrating their interactions with the child in a way that assures her inclusion in the classroom group and effective delivery of therapies as required in an IFSP or IEP.

The final essential characteristic of ECSE to be addressed here is the role of family-centered service delivery. While the initial focus of ECSE was on individual child treatment and education, the ecological orientation that came to define special education in the 1970s and 1980s was translated into policy requirements in the 1980s and 1990s. Family-centered models emphasize full parent participation in child assessment and subsequent decision-making about program design, parent support through educational and social services, counseling for parents and families experiencing emotional stress related to raising a child with a disability, and, in some programs, specific training for parents in **advocacy** techniques to increase their ability to secure appropriate services (Dunst, Trivette, and Deal, 1988; Turnbull and Turnbull, 1986).

State and Federal Policies

The field of ECSE has been significantly affected by the implementation of federal and state laws and regulations over the past thirty years. In addition to the Head Start integration mandate mentioned above, federal special education laws beginning with the Education for All Handicapped Children Act of 1975 have had profound impacts on services for young children with disabilities. While the early versions of the law did not mandate free, appropriate public education for children below six years old, subsequent amendments did. When the law was revised in 1987, it included a requirement for educational services beginning at age 3 and allowed access to federal dollars for those states that chose to begin services at birth. Under Part C of the law, children from birth to three years of age who are deemed to be "at risk" for school failure due to developmental problems and/or environmental challenges associated with poverty or harsh living conditions may be served, in addition to those with diagnosed disabilities. Beginning in 1987, programs serving children from birth to three years may develop **Individual Family Service Plans** (rather than **Individual Education Plans**), reflecting the family-centered practices described above. The current version of the law, known since 1997 as IDEA (**Individuals with Disabilities Education Act**), preserves the requirement for free, appropriate public education in the least restrictive environment, beginning at age 3.

States have enacted laws and policies that parallel the federal legislation. Some states (e.g., Maryland, Minnesota, New York) have extended the mandatory provision of services even earlier, to the birth of a child with a known disability or condition with a strong likelihood of causing later impairment. Such services tend to be home based in the case of infants and available in day care centers and preschool programs in the case of toddlers and preschoolers. These service delivery systems are often under the jurisdiction of health and human service agencies rather than local or state educational agencies, but the nature of service tends to reflect the practice standards referred to above regardless of type of government sponsorship.

The Focus of Applied Research

Research in the field of ECSE over the past three decades has focused on four major areas of interest. First, classroom-based alternative treatment and education approaches have been extensively studied, from traditional behavior modification models to more ecologically oriented analyses that investigate the transactions between children and their social contexts. Particular therapy models have been examined, such as sensory integration techniques, **augmentative and alternative communication** strategies, and dietary and related biochemical experiments with children with presumed health-related disorders (e.g., hyperactivity, autism, seizure disorders). Second, considerable research has occurred in preschool classrooms on effective strategies for enhancing the social integration of children with disabilities and typically developing children. Again, a major orientation of this research has been on the ecology of childhood disability, with concerns for how young children establish and sustain friendships and how children use peers for problem solving and to fulfill social needs. Third, extensive research has focused on the effect on families of raising a young child with a congenital or acquired disability. **Family systems theory** has framed much of this research, and a notable shift from pathological or deficit models (child as a negative factor) to more asset-based models (child as opportunity for family growth and reorganization) has occurred in recent years. The DEC recommended practices cited earlier (Sandall et al., 2005) articulate a synthesis of research on effective practices for young children with disabilities and their families with respect to assessment, family support, interdisciplinary educational practices (including the use of **technology**), policy and systems change, and personnel preparation. Finally, policy-oriented research has emphasized the efficacy of ECSE programs and their cost-benefit to society. Much of this work has sought to illuminate the long-term developmental outcomes of children served in such programs and the long-term financial benefits associated with early prevention or intervention. *See also* Disabilities, Young Children with; Teacher Certification/Licensure.

Further Readings: Bredekamp, S. and C. Copple, eds. (1997). *Developmentally appropriate practice in early childhood programs*. Washington, DC: National Association for the Education of Young Children; Dunst, C. J., C. M. Trivette, and A. G. Deal (1988). *Enabling and empowering families: Principles of guidance for practice*. Cambridge, MA: Brookline Books; Mallory, B. L. (1992). Is it always appropriate to be developmental? Convergent practice for early intervention practice. *Topics in Early Childhood Special Education* 4(11), 1-12; Mallory, B. L., and R. S. New, eds. (1994). *Diversity and developmentally appropriate practices: Challenges for early childhood education*. New York: Teachers College Press; Roos, P. (1978). Parents of mentally retarded children—misunderstood and mistreated. In A. Turnbull and H. Turnbull, eds., *Parents speak out*. Columbus, OH: Charles E. Merrill; Sandall, S., M. L. Hemmeter, B. Smith, and M. McLean, eds. (2005). *DEC recommended practices in early intervention/early childhood special education*. Longmont, CO: Sopris West; Super, C. M., ed. (1987). *The role of culture in developmental disorder*. San Diego: Academic Press; Turnbull, A. P., and H. R. Turnbull (1986). *Families, professionals, and exceptionality: A special partnership*. Columbus, OH: Merrill.

Bruce L. Mallory

Early Head Start

Early Head Start is a federal, two-generation **Head Start** program, or low-income pregnant women and fathers, and children ages birth to three and their families. The program was created by the Head Start reauthorization legislation in 1994. The 1998 Coats Human Services Reauthorization Act increased Early Head Start funding to 10 percent of the Head Start budget. As of 2004, the program had expanded to 708 American communities serving approximately 68,000 children and their families in all states and in many Tribes and Nations.

While Early Head Start is a child development program, it has a two-generation focus. Programs can select to offer families one of four program options: home-based (in which families receive weekly home visits and the option of biweekly group socialization), center-based (in which children and families receive quality center-based services and **parenting education**), combination (in which families receive specified combinations of home-based and center-based services), and locally designed options. Program options are selected after programs complete community needs assessments every three years. Early Head Start is a distinct program within the Head Start family of programs and follows the Head Start Program Performance Standards.

Early Head Start programs serve families whose incomes are at the poverty level or below and who have greatest needs unmet by other community services. Across all Early Head Start programs approximately a fifth of families do not speak English as their primary language. At least 10 percent of enrollment must be made available to children with verified disabilities. Typically, about a third of parents are teens at the time of the birth of the Early Head Start child and typically fewer than half of the families have two resident parents.

The following notable features have been instituted during Early Head Start's brief program life:

Research. The Head Start Bureau instituted a rigorous, random assignment evaluation in 1996, carried out by Mathematica Policy Research, Columbia National Center for Children and Families and fifteen research universities. Together, the researchers formed the Early Head Start Research Consortium, which oversaw the evaluation and completed local research and cross-site studies. 3001 children and families were assessed at ages fourteen, twenty-four, thirty-six months and again before kindergarten entry. A fifth-grade follow up begins in 2007. At age 3 (at completion of the program), results from the evaluation showed that Early Head Start had a broad pattern of significant impacts across a wide array of child and parent outcomes and in nearly all program subgroups. There were relatively large effect sizes found in fully implemented programs providing both home visits and center-based services. The kindergarten follow-up study showed that a number of the program impacts remained two years after children left the program and that formal care and education during the preschool years also supported gains from the zero to three program. Many lessons for program improvement were drawn from the research findings. Subsequently, a mental health research consortium and a survey of program performance have been instituted. Research reports and Research to Practice briefs can be accessed at: http://www.acf.hhs.gov/programs/opre/.

Training and Technical Assistance. While Early Head Start is served by Head Start T/TA activities, special infant-toddler focused training has been provided by the Early Head Start National Resource Center located at **Zero to Three**, Washington DC. http://www.ehsnrc.org.

Special Initiatives. Since its inception, a number of initiatives have enabled the program to focus on areas of special need. These have included the Hilton Special Quest program to develop expertise in working with infants and toddlers with disabilities; the Child Care Partnership Initiative to build community-level expertise in Early Head Start child-care partnerships; the Child Welfare Services Demonstration for serving children in the child welfare system within Early Head Start; the Enhanced Home Visiting Demonstration to develop model programs for kith and kin care; the Fatherhood Demonstration to develop model programs for involving fathers; the Culturally Responsive and Aware Dual Language Education Project; Operation Parenting Edge, and StoryQUEST: Celebrating Beginning Language and Literacy.

Further Readings: Administration for Children and Families (2002). *Pathways to quality and full implementation in Early Head Start programs*. Washington, DC: U.S. Department of Health and Human Services; Administration for Children and Families (2002). *Making a difference in the lives of infants and toddlers and their families: The impacts of Early Head Start*. Washington, DC: U.S. Department of Health and Human Services; Administration on Children, Youth and Families (2001). *Building their futures: How Early Head Start programs are enhancing the lives of infants and toddlers in low-income families*. Washington, DC: U.S. Department of Health and Human Services; Boller, K., R. Bradley, N. Cabrera, H. Raikes, B. Pan, J. Shears, and L. Roggman (2006). The Early Head Start father studies: Design, data collection, and summary of father presence in the lives of infants and toddlers. *Parenting Science and Practice, Special Issue Early Head Start Fathers and Children* 6(2/3), 117–145; Lombardi, J., and M. M. Bogle (2004). *Beacon of hope: The promise of Early Head Start for America's youngest children*. Washington, DC: ZERO TO THREE Press. Love, J., L. Harrison, A. Sagi-Schwartz, M. H. van IJzendoorn, C. Ross, J. Ungerer, H. H. Raikes, C. Brady-Smith, K. Boller, J. Brooks-Gunn, J. Constantine, E. Kisker, D. Paulsell, and R. Chazan-Cohen (2003). Child care quality matters: How conclusions may vary with context. *Child Development* 74, 1021–1033; Love, J., E. E. Kisker, C. Ross, H. Raikes, J. Constantine, K. Boller, J. Brooks-Gunn, R. Chazan-Cohen, L. B. Tarullo, P. Z. Schochet, C. Brady-Smith, A. S. Fuligni, D. Paulsell, and C. Vogel (December, 2005). The effectiveness of Early Head Start for 3-year-old children and their parents. *Developmental Psychology* 41(6), 885–901; Peterson, C., S. Wall, H. H. Raikes, E. Kisker, M. Swanson, J. Jerald, J. Atwater, and W. Qiao (2004). Early Head Start: Identifying and serving children with disabilities. *Topics in Early Childhood Special Education* 24(2), 76–88; Raikes, H., and R. N. Emde (2006). Early Head Start: A bold new program for low-income infants and toddlers. In N. Watt, C. Ayoub, R. H. Bradley, J. E. Puma, W. A. LeBoeuf, eds., *The Crisis in Youth Mental Health: Early Intervention Programs and Policies*. Westport, CT: Praeger, pp. 181–207.

Helen Raikes

Early Intervention

"Early intervention" as applied to early childhood education refers to policies, systems, programs, services, and supports provided to vulnerable young children and/or their families in order to maximize a child's development. The concepts and practices of early intervention rely upon knowledge derived from the developmental science of normative child development as well as the developmental science of risk and disability, coupled with clinical experience and evidence-based educational and developmental strategies. Research findings and social values over the last century have led to the recognition of the unique contributions special supportive services provide to children during the early childhood years. Vulnerable children and families for whom early intervention may be valuable include children with established disabilities as well as children whose development is at risk due to a variety of biological or environmental factors.

Established disabilities include children with cognitive delays (often leading to a diagnosis of mental retardation), autism, motor disabilities, communication and language disorders, and hearing and vision impairments. Recently, attention has been paid to the importance of early intervention for children with or at risk for social/emotional disorders and challenging behavior.

Vulnerable children at risk for developmental problems such as those due to prematurity/low birth weight, infectious diseases, exposure to toxic substances and other environmental health risks, **poverty**, **violence**, abuse, or neglect can benefit from a variety of preventive intervention programs. The populations of children needing early intervention are expanding rapidly worldwide (ISEI, 2004; Olness, 2003).

The concept of early intervention implies that: (1) acting earlier rather than later results in important effects not gained if action is delayed, and (2) action is needed beyond that typically available and is based on specific circumstances and unique child and family characteristics. First, intervening early is grounded in the recognition of the impact of the early years on a child's later life. Recently, this belief has been realized in various "school **readiness**" movements. Studies of the difficulties of children with special needs have shown that developmental problems or school failure can be reduced or prevented through effective early intervention (Guralnick, 1998). Early intervention services and systems are also supported by social values; in other words, supporting families and children who are in need is considered the right thing to do. Second, early intervention refers to services beyond those typically available that are targeted to the particular needs of children and families that have been carefully assessed. This component of early intervention relates to the need to individualize interventions for the child and family.

Early Intervention Policies and Systems

Public policies and systems have been crafted to ensure that certain populations of children receive early intervention in order to optimize their development. One of the earliest of the United States federal efforts was **Head Start**, launched in 1965 with the purpose of improving outcomes for children whose development was at risk particularly related to poverty. While the Head Start program has not reached a level of funding to serve all eligible children, the program provides funding and guidance to local Head Start programs nationwide to serve low income children as well as children with disabilities. A goal of Head Start is for 10 percent of the enrollment to be children with disabilities.

Other public policies related to early intervention in early childhood education have been developed at the federal, state, and local levels. A major federal program for children with disabilities is the **Individuals with Disabilities Education Act** (IDEA) established in 1975 (as the Education of the Handicapped Act). IDEA provides funds and guidance to states to provide a free, appropriate education for children with disabilities from birth to twenty-one years of age. IDEA contains two major provisions related to early intervention for young children: (1) Part C for infants and toddlers who have disabilities and the option for states to serve children who are at risk for developing a disability or developmental delay, and (2) the preschool provisions of Part B which provide for appropriate education and related services to children ages 3–5 with disabilities or developmental delays.

Various state and local policies have been enacted over the past several years to provide early intervention to young children including an increasing number of state programs to provide early childhood education to children at risk. Included in this trend is the establishment of state Interagency Coordinating Councils (ICCs) under IDEA which recognize that young children with disabilities and their families may need coordinated services and supports provided by many state and local agencies including health, education, Medicaid, professional development institutions, social services, and mental health. There are other state cross-agency efforts focused on young children including state early education or school readiness efforts and children's **mental health** initiatives.

Early Intervention Services

Effective, highly individualized early intervention systems rely on many disciplines, including those from health and education as well as those representing social and behavioral domains. Early intervention services require specialized knowledge and skills in order to be effective (Sandall et al., 2005). National professional associations have issued guidelines for appropriately meeting children's special needs. For example, the **National Association for the Education of Young Children** (NAEYC) and the **Division for Early Childhood** (DEC) have produced joint recommendations for personnel knowledge and skills needed to effectively provide early intervention and special education to young children with disabilities, and have developed a position statement (see www.dec-sped.org) with respect to delivering early intervention and special services in typical settings referred to as "inclusion." DEC also provides recommendations for appropriate early intervention and special education services for young children with disabilities (Sandall et al., 2005). In addition, Head Start provides guidance for programs serving eligible children in the form of Head Start Program Performance Standards and issues specific guidance related to serving children with disabilities within Head Start programs.

An important development in the general field of early intervention over the past thirty years is the principle and associated practices of **inclusion**. A major feature of this concept refers to the delivery of special services or early intervention services within the context of natural environments, that is, environments where the child's peers and family typically spend time. This movement has led to delivering early intervention services in typical early childhood settings such as child-care environments, preschools, and other community settings (see DEC position on Inclusion, www.dec-sped.org). Inclusion has affected how personnel are prepared, how services are delivered, and how society views children with special needs (Guralnick, 2001b). Of importance, the services of IDEA can be provided in any location as long as they are overseen by IDEA agencies. Thus, the IDEA early intervention services are not defined by a place (e.g., special class) but rather by a child's written **individualized education plan** (IEP). Inclusion has led to the blending of programs, funding sources, children, and personnel so that all children, whether receiving early intervention or typical early childhood services, can be together. *See also* Child Abuse and Neglect; Disabilities, Young Children with; Early Childhood Special Education.

Further Readings: Division for Early Childhood (DEC). Available online at www.dec-sped.org; Guralnick, M. J., ed. (1997). *The effectiveness of early intervention*. Baltimore: Brookes; Guralnick, M. J. (1998). The effectiveness of early intervention for vulnerable children: A developmental perspective. *American Journal on Mental Retardation* 102, 319–345; Guralnick, M. J. (2001a). Connections between developmental science and intervention science. *Zero to Three* 21(5), 24–29; Guralnick, M. J., ed. (2001b). *Early childhood inclusion*. Baltimore: Brooks; International Society on Early Intervention (ISEI) (2004). Available online at http://depts.washington.edu/isei/; Meisels, S. J., and J. P. Shonkoff, eds. (2000). *Handbook of early childhood intervention*. 2nd ed. New York: Cambridge University Press; Olness, K. (2003). Effects on brain development leading to cognitive impairment: A worldwide epidemic. *Journal of Developmental and Behavioral Pediatrics* 24, 120–130; Sandall, S., M. L. Hemmeter, B. J. Smith, and M. McLean (2005). *DEC recommended practices in early intervention/Early childhood special education*. Longmont, CO: Sopris West; Smith, B. J. (2000). The federal role in early childhood special education policy in the next century: The responsibility of the individual. *Topics in Early Childhood Special Education* 20(1), 7–13.

Barbara J. Smith and Michael J. Guralnick

Early Years: An International Journal of Research and Development

Early Years: An International Journal of Research and Development is published by Routledge on behalf of Training, Advancement and Co-operation in Teaching Young Children (TACTYC). As the importance of early childhood education and care in providing the foundations for lifelong learning is now widely acknowledged, the journal aims to broaden the international debate by representing a wide range of perspectives from different countries, different disciplines, and different research methodologies.

The journal publishes papers which relate to the training, education, and continuing professional development of all early years practitioners including managers, support staff, qualified teachers, and higher education academics teaching on early childhood courses and specializms. *Early Years* is published three times per year. For more information, please visit http://www.tandf.co.uk/journals/titles/09575146.asp.

Rod Parker-Rees and Marian Whitehead

ECEJ. *See Early Childhood Education Journal*

ECME. *See* Early Childhood Music Education Commission

Ecology of Human Development

The ecology of human development, as defined by its chief architect, Uric **Bronfenbrenner**, is a scientific perspective that addresses "the progressive, mutual accommodation between an active, growing human being and the changing properties of the immediate settings within which the developing person lives." This process of accommodation is to be understood "as it is affected by relations between those settings, and [as it is affected] by the larger contexts in which the settings are embedded." In terms of early childhood education this definition contains the developing child engaged with others in several settings, interaction between those settings, and ongoing analysis of the ways that those settings "immediate" to the child are in turn shaped by settings and environmental systems more distant from the child.

Origins

In the preface to his now classic book *The Ecology of Human Development: Experiments by Nature and Design*, Bronfenbrenner credits Kurt Levin, George Herbert Mead, Sigmund **Freud**, William and Dorothy Thomas, Edward Tolman, Lev **Vygotsky**, Kurt Goldstein, Otto Rank, Jean **Piaget,** and Ronald Fisher as scholars who influenced his development of the ecological perspective. Of these thinkers, the work of Kurt Levin was especially influential, with its conception of the psychological "life space" as made up of a set of regions or territories and Levin's emphasis on the intersection between the structure of the person and of the situation encountered by that person. Basic Levinian concepts upon which the ecology of human development approach was built included the idea of differentiated regions affecting the psychological development of the child, the concept and motivational power of activities for development, the importance of the connections between people in the settings containing the child, the power of ecological transitions, and the idea of **action research**. The influence of Jean Piaget, with his interest in the child's construction of reality and perceptual constancy across situations and settings, can be seen in the ecologically oriented definition of development as "the person's evolving conception of the ecological environment, and his relation to it, as well as the person's growing capacity to discover, sustain, or alter its properties." Vygotsky's influence is found especially at the macro-level, based on his theory of the "sociohistorical evolution of the mind," the idea that the developing child's characteristics as a person depend on the options available in a particular culture at a particular time. The strong emphasis within the ecology of human development on understanding development *in context* received impetus from the psychological ecologists of the Kansas school, including Roger Barker, Herbert Wright, and Phillip Schoggen, who adapted observational strategies designed for studying other species to document the natural behavioral settings of children and the children's behaviors within them.

Key Elements

Context. The ecological perspective involves understanding the meaning that the developing child gives to experience. This meaning is found in the content of what the child perceives, or feels, or thinks about. That content is provided by the setting or settings within which the child engages in activities. These settings are the contexts in which development occurs, and development cannot be understood in the absence of an understanding of those contexts. The ecological approach to studying human development was born out of a reaction to the fact that during much of the twentieth century the study of early development had been conducted "out of context," that is, in the laboratory rather than in the environments within which children grow and develop. The careful specification of the contexts in which development takes place provides one of the primary building blocks for understanding the meaning of that development, together with the particular characteristics of the child her/himself. This interaction can be summarized with the formula D=f(PE), where development (D) is a function of the interaction of the person (P) with the environment (E).

Environmental Systems. In his "reappreciation" of the ecological point of view, Robert Glossop identifies the emphasis on immediate settings and the larger contexts in which those settings and the developing child are embedded as "the cornerstone of the ecological frame of reference." Within the ecological framework these settings and contexts are organized within four environmental systems, conceived as nested one within the next. *Microsystems* are patterns of activities, roles, and interpersonal relations that are experienced by the child directly in a particular setting, like the home or the child-care center classroom, containing other people with distinctive characteristics (temperaments, personalities, belief systems). *Mesosystems* consist of the interrelations between two or more such micro-settings; for instance, parent-caregiver relations between home and the child-care center. *Exosystems* are made up of settings that affect or are affected by the developing child, but do not involve the child as an active participant. The example often used is the world of work, the nature of which shapes the time and energy that the employed parent has available for the child but usually does not include the child as an active participant. The *Macrosystem* refers to beliefs and values found at the level of culture, society, or subculture that manifest themselves consistently as resources, opportunity structures, hazards, lifestyles, and patterns of social exchange in the form and content of the environmental systems (exo-, meso-, micro-) contained within it—a "blue-print," so to speak. For instance, a societal belief in the value of family privacy and individual responsibility for child rearing might be reflected in relatively little concern for the parental role (opportunity to parent) within the [still the same ... even the example] parent's workplace (exo-), not much discussion of child-rearing issues (social exchange) between parent and child-care center caregiver (meso-), and little help-seeking beyond the immediate family (resource) by parents even in times of acute stress or crisis.

Ecological Niches. These are regions within the larger environment (society, state) that are particularly favorable or unfavorable to the child's development, because they combine greater or fewer environmental resources with particular personal characteristics. These regions can be defined to some extent by the "social addresses" of education, income, occupation, race, and gender; and the developmental risks associated with low resource regions depend in part on the personal characteristics of the child. For instance, the developmental impacts of living in poverty conditions are likely to be greater for a shy or a physically handicapped child than they are for a child that is outgoing, engaging, and physically well coordinated.

The Active, Initiating Child. The forces propelling development, from an "ecology of human development" perspective, emanate as much from the nature of the developing organism as they do from how and with what resources the environment engages with that child. The child is seen not as a passive recipient of environmental stimulation but as innately motivated to engage actively with the surrounding world. Over time competence consists of the growing capacity to figure out how the world is organized, participate in that organization, and even restructure the world to a certain extent.

Reciprocity. Within the ecological perspective development is a function of the variety and complexity of activities engaged in with others, referred to as joint activities. When what the child does in the activity influences the behavior of the significant other, and that behavior then stimulates a response by the child, to which the other responds in turn, then the relationship is said to be reciprocal. Bronfenbrenner saw this kind of reciprocity, "with its concomitant mutual feedback," as generating a momentum that motivated the participants not only to continue the interaction but also to "engage in progressively more complex patterns of interaction, as in a ping-pong game in which the exchanges tend to become more rapid and intricate as the game proceeds." Development is seen as stimulated by the variety and complexity of the activities engaged in by the child with significant others in his or her psychological field. A distribution of power is necessarily a part of reciprocal activities, and development is seen as enhanced by the gradual shift in the balance of that power in favor of the developing child.

Ecological Transitions. A transition is a move by the developing person to a new and different context. Examples in the life of the child include moving from one place of residence to another, from home to preschool, from preschool to school, away to summer camp and home again, and into the hospital and then home once more. A significant transition of this sort involves the child in new activities, often requiring the establishing of new relationships, and may include experimenting with new roles. For these reasons such transitions are seen as placing high developmental demands on the child, offering both opportunity and risk.

More Recent Extensions of the Ecological Perspective

Later in his career, Bronfenbrenner extended his ecological theory, adding the prefix "bio" to "ecological" in recognition of his long-held view that biological resources are important to understanding human development. Important expansions included further elaboration of the "person" in the person–environment interaction, spelling out ways of understanding and measuring cognitive competence within real-life settings and as mastery of culturally defined, familiar activities. He also added "time" to his interest in context-based person-focused developmental processes, underscoring the importance of recognizing that these processes and their effects will differ at different points in the life course and in different historical periods.

In reassessing his definitions of the four environmental levels, Bronfenbrenner made additions at the micro- and macro-levels, adding greater specificity about the characteristics of the significant others in the immediate contexts containing the child and more emphasis on belief systems, resources, hazards, and opportunity structures at the level of culture and society. Although he made no changes to the definition of the mesosystem (linkages and processes taking place between two or more settings containing the developing child), others working in the tradition of human ecology have expanded the features of these linkings, proposing, for example, that greater emphasis be given to key other persons in that system as well (Cochran et al., 1990). Relations between *people* in several settings containing the child give meaning and power to this system, a dynamic that is not conveyed through simply considering linkages between settings in general terms. The literature on social networks and social support documents the nature of those meanings.

Applications to Early Childhood Education

The ecological orientation to development has had and continues to have considerable influence within the field of early childhood education, both within the United States and abroad. Within the immediate (micro) settings containing the child the emphasis on the power of reciprocal relations (adult–child, child–child) as the "engines" of development reinforces much previous and contemporary theory and practice related to early childhood education teaching and learning at the classroom level. One application of the priority given to the importance of dyadic relations has been an explicit inclusion of the parent–child dyad in the design of **early intervention** programs, thereby shifting the programmatic focus beyond the individual child to include the parent or other significant adult. This conception, supported with empirical evidence, has underscored the general importance of parent involvement in early education programs, and anticipated the shift to "two-generation" programming that has increasingly become the norm in the twenty-first century (see **Early Head Start**). Recognition of the developmental demands associated with transitions from one immediate setting to another (i.e., home to child care) has shone new light on the need to plan those transitions carefully for children, in order to insure that they are managed in a way that is developmentally enhancing rather than overly challenging.

At the meso-level the importance accorded parent–teacher relationships by the ecological perspective lends support to the ongoing programmatic interest in how to establish and sustain those connections in ways that reduce dissonance and intensify support on behalf of the developing child. With the growing recognition that over half of all American infants and toddlers in child care are being looked after by kinfolk, friends, and neighbors, there is also increased interest in ways that public supports can be used to enhance and strengthen these natural helping systems.

At the level of exo-systems (affecting the child, but indirectly), the ecological orientation provides a renewed focus on the parents' world of work, backed by financial analyses showing that the private sector contributes only 1–2 percent of the total revenues invested in early care and education each year. The absence of any federal paid parental leave from work policy in the United States makes it much more difficult for American parents to form a close, enduring relationship with their newborns than is the case in the rest of the industrialized world, and illustrates how public policies related to the workplace can impact young children in the absence of direct contact with them. Another example of exo-level impact involves the extent to which city governments invest resources in local parks and playgrounds that insure their safety and enhance their developmental potential.

At the macro-level the most unique and enduring contribution made by the ecological perspective has been in helping policymakers, practitioners, and academics track the ways that public policies developed and implemented at the national or state level shape the major institutions of society (workplaces, schools, child-care settings) to affect the development of children through interactions with significant adults and peers. By illuminating these pathways, an ecology of human development framework has brought an understanding of the "family and child impacts" of macro-level policies (both public and private sector) to the fore, insuring that such potential and demonstrated impacts become and continue to be a part of the public policy discourse. *See also* Parents and Parent Involvement.

Further Readings: Barker, R., and H. Wright (1954). *Midwest and its children: The psychological ecology of an American town*. Evanston, IL: Row, Peterson; Bronfenbrenner, U. (1978). Lewinian space and ecological substance. *Journal of Social Issues* 33(4), 199–212; Bronfenbrenner, U. (1979). *The Ecology of human development: Experiments by nature and design*. Cambridge, MA: Harvard University Press; Bronfenbrenner, U. (1992). Ecological systems theory. In R. Vasta, ed., *Six theories of child development: Revised formulations and current issues*. London: Jessica Kingsley, pp. 187–249; Bronfenbrenner, U., ed. (2005). *Making human beings human: Bioecological perspectives on human development*. Thousand Oaks, CA: Sage Publications; Cochran, M. (2006). *Finding our way: American early care and education in the 21st century*. Washington, DC: Zero to Three Press; Cochran, M., M. Larner, D. Riley, L. Gunnarsson, and C. Henderson, Jr. (1990). *Extending families: The social networks of parents and their children*. Cambridge: Cambridge University Press; Glossop, R. (1988). Bronfenbrenner's ecology of human development: A reappreciation, In A. Pence, ed., *Ecological research with children and families: From concept to methodology*. New York: Teachers College Press, pp. 1–15; Levin, K. (1935). *A dynamic theory of personality*. New York: McGraw-Hill.

Moncrieff Cochran

ECRP. *See Early Childhood Research & Practice*

ECRQ. *See Early Childhood Research Quarterly*

ECSE. *See* Early Childhood Special Education

Education 3-13

The journal *Education 3-13* is published by Routledge on behalf of the Association for the Study of Primary Education (ASPE). The journal publishes refereed articles representing and analyzing practice, research, and theory that are of relevance to those working with children between the ages of 3 and 13, both in the United Kingdom and internationally.

The journal welcomes submissions on all aspects of education in the form of articles that report classroom research, analyze practice, discuss local and national policy and initiatives, offer a comparative perspective on research and policy, and report on major research projects.

Published three times a year by Routledge, *Education 3-13* will be of interest to students, teachers, advisers, and academics who seek helpful and stimulating ways of viewing what they do, or might do. For more information, please visit http://www.tandf.co.uk/journals/titles/03004279.asp.

Mark Brundrett

Eliot, Abigail Adams (1892–1992)

Abigail Adams Eliot is best known for her contributions to the American nursery school movement. In 1922 Dr. Eliot founded the Ruggles Street Nursery Training School of Boston, where she integrated parent education and teacher training components into work with nursery age children. Her educational philosophy, formulated in 1944, outlined a set of beliefs that anticipated contemporary early childhood education in the United States. She urged teachers to help children develop "balancing traits" and, at the same time, to supply what they need for self-realization. Eliot emphasized the child's need to balance a sense of security with growing independence; self-expression with self-control; awareness of self with social consciousness; growth in freedom with growth in responsibility; and the opportunity to create with the ability to conform.

Born in Dorchester, Massachusetts, on October 9, 1892, Abigail was the third child of Reverend and Mrs. Christopher Rhodes Eliot. Reverend Eliot served as minister of the Meeting House Hill Church in Dorchester and later of Bulfinch Place Church in Boston's West End. The Eliot children attended public primary school. Abigail and her older sister, Martha May, graduated first from Boston's prestigious Winsor School and later from Radcliffe College, located across the Charles River in Cambridge.

After graduating, Eliot began a career in social work with Boston's Children's Mission to Children, an organization that placed children in foster homes. Soon disillusioned with social work, she left Boston in 1919 to study economics at Oxford

University. While abroad, Eliot determined that her ambitions lay in education—an interest she attributed in part to her experience as a young child instructed in a Froebelian **kindergarten**.

Through a fortuitous association with Mrs. Henry Greenleaf Pearson, who knew of Margaret McMillan's *The Nursery School* (1919), Eliot learned of the English nursery school movement. Mrs. Pearson, as head of the Women's Education Association's nursery committee, raised money to send Eliot to study at the **Rachel McMillan** Nursery School at Deptford, a slum district of London. Eliot left for England in 1921, eager to learn directly from **Margaret McMillan**, the crusader who first coined the term "nursery school."

Upon returning to Boston in January 1922, the Ruggles Street Day Nursery, situated in Roxbury, became the **Ruggles Street Nursery School and Training Center**. The change in name reflected a groundbreaking emphasis on "schooling" for very young children. Until that time, young children in group care benefited primarily from improved physical health and safety; educational programs were most often reserved for older children. Additionally, Eliot worked with children living in poverty, unlike colleagues who leaned toward conducting child development research in laboratory nursery schools (Braun and Edwards, 1972, p. 151).

The **Ruggles Street Nursery School** originally employed an eclectic mix of Froebelian gifts, Montessori apparatus, and McMillan materials, plus art supplies, clay, and blocks. Eliot selected soft yellow paint for the schoolroom walls, colored cloth for the tables, and soft rugs for seating. She hung pictures, set out vases of flowers, and used attractive plates and napkins for the children's meals (Eliot, no date, p. 31).

Ruggles Street teachers encouraged the children to play with materials as they chose—to the dismay of some visitors. The emphasis on imagination and creativity shocked Montessori-trained observers. Miss Eliot, in turn, described her own discomfort with the Watson-trained teachers of Teachers College, Columbia University who strove "never to touch a child," a startling departure from her own beliefs about children's needs (Braun and Edwards, 1972, p. 156).

Eliot confronted skepticism in other quarters as well. Lucy Wheelock, founder of Boston's Wheelock College, never endorsed early childhood education as practiced at the Ruggles Street Nursery School, although she did invite Eliot to teach a course on nursery education. Primary educators of the day doubted whether young children should be away from home at all, particularly as susceptibility to contagious diseases increased when children came into close contact. Social workers worried that Ruggles Street teachers lacked adequate training to work effectively with families; Eliot's parent education program was often deemed too "experimental."

In 1926, the Ruggles Street School expanded into new buildings and became the Nursery Training School of Boston. That same year Eliot earned the Master of Education degree at the Harvard Graduate School of Education, followed by the doctorate in 1930. By then, nursery education had attracted the interest and enthusiasm of middle class families through such programs as the Cambridge Nursery School, a cooperative formed and financed by a group of mothers with guidance from Abigail Eliot.

As the nursery school movement gained momentum, Eliot—with colleagues Patty Smith **Hill** of Teachers College and Edna Noble **White** of the Merrill Palmer Institute—began meeting annually with graduates of their respective schools. Dr. Eliot also assisted in founding the National Association for Nursery Education and, in 1933, served as their representative to the federal Works Progress Administration, which provided funds to nursery schools for unemployed families and jobs for teachers. These conferences evolved into the **National Association for the Education of Young Children** (NAEYC). During World War II, Eliot consulted on providing day care for the children of war workers under the Lanham Act.

By mid-century, Dr. Eliot recognized the need to offer four-year, bachelor's degree programs to students preparing to work with young children. In collaboration with Tufts University's President Carmichael, the Boston Nursery Training School became affiliated with the university in 1951. Eliot retired in 1952 and, in 1955, the school was renamed in her honor as the Eliot-Pearson School. Evelyn Goodenough Pitcher took over as director in 1959 and, in 1964, the school was reconfigured as an academic department. Today Abigail Eliot's legacy is known as the Eliot-Pearson Department of Child Development at Tufts University.

In retirement, Dr. Eliot traveled extensively with her companion of many years, Anna Holman. She continued to work on behalf of children, first by helping to found Pacific Oaks College in California and later by teaching at the Brooks School in Concord, Massachusetts.

Further Readings: Braun, S. J., and E. P. Edwards (1972). *History and theory of early childhood education*. Belmont, CA: Wadsworth Publishing Company, Inc.; Eliot, A. A. (1982). *A heart of grateful trust: Memoirs of Abigail Adams Eliot*. Transcribed and edited by Marjorie Gott Manning; McMillan, M. (1919). *The nursery school*. New York: E.P. Dutton; Pearson, E. W. (January–March 1925). The Ruggles Street Nursery School. *Progressive Education* II, 19–21; Weber, E. (1969). *The kindergarten: Its encounter with educational thought in America*. New York: Teachers College Press.

Ann C. Benjamin

Emotional Development. *See* Curriculum, Emotional Development; Development, Emotional

Environmental Assessments in Early Childhood Education

Environmental assessments in early childhood education involve a set of evaluation tools that are used to assess the quality and quantity of early childhood education environments, such as those found within classrooms, **playgrounds**, and homes. Research studies demonstrate that high-quality care in early childhood programs is associated with features of the physical and social environment; and that these quality measures are predictive of a range of positive developmental outcomes for children in their cognitive, language, social-emotional, and physical domains (e.g., NICHD Early Child Care Research Network, 2000; Peisner-Feinberg et al., 2000). A thoughtfully designed and organized setting with a positive climate is interpreted as providing a safe, secure, and instructive place for children to be inquisitive and learn—from the teacher, their peers, and their environment.

Environmental assessments have been primarily used for accreditation, licensure, or research purposes. For example, the **National Association for the Education of Young Children** (NAEYC) developed Standards for Physical Environment in 2005 for accreditation purposes to assess the quality of indoor and outdoor physical environments, including equipment, facilities, and materials to ensure that the environment is welcome, accessible, and promotes children's learning, comfort, health, and safety.

Environmental assessments are developed and utilized based on theories of child development and cultural values and beliefs. One of the more predominant theories is the ecological model developed by Urie **Bronfenbrenner** (1994). Within this model children are observed in one of their natural contexts (e.g., child-care centers, home, and classroom). It is assumed that these settings operate within a broader system (e.g., societal beliefs, state and federal laws and regulations, interactions between caregivers, educators and service systems). Many assessments focus on one or more aspects of the ecology of the setting. Based on adaptations of Carta's model (2002), for example, an environmental assessment could include one or more of the following: (a) Classroom features (e.g., **curriculum,** practices, schedule and nature of activities, materials); (b) interactions of the child with peers, teachers, and parents; (c) staff characteristics (e.g., formal preparation, experience and perceptions about their roles in relationship to their teaching; (d) classroom structures (e.g., group size, adult-child ratios, size of space and its arrangement, nature of equipment and furnishings, and hours of operation).

Environmental assessments are formatted in several ways. For example, these tools may include: (a) Inventories/rating scales and/or checklists; (b) interviews of personnel and family members directly associated with the targeted environment; and/or (c) reviews of pertinent documents. The scope of environmental assessments varies depending upon the following three factors for a child's development: (1) Purpose (e.g., safety, health, quality, or planning); (2) age/focus of child (e.g., infant-toddler, preschooler, or child with special needs); and (3) location (e.g., home setting, classroom, or playground). Individual assessments have been used in conjunction with other assessments to form a better understanding of the child. It is important to note that these assessments are only one picture of a child's surroundings within a specific period of time and should be considered within the broader context. Environmental assessments in early childhood education are developed for various reasons: (a) To ensure the safety and health of children; (b) to assess and ultimately obtain high-quality early childhood educational environments; and (c) to plan the schedule, curriculum, and/or individualized education programs (IEP) (Wolery, 2004). Assessment tools will address one, two or all three of these areas. The following sections will address each of these reasons.

Ensuring Safety, Security, and Health

Environmental assessments that address safety, security, and health issues in early childhood environments are designed to help identify any materials, conditions, and/or events that may lead to unintentional child death or injury. In addition, these assessments determine whether the responsible adults (i.e., caregivers, teachers) in these settings are engaging in precautions that will prevent any injuries. These assessments focus on areas where accidents are most likely to occur, such as on playgrounds where children may slip or fall. The Public Playground Safety Checklist (Consumer Product Safety Commission [CPSC] 2005) assesses the sturdiness of the equipment, the type of grounding to break falls and the supervision of children as they climb the jungle gym, use the slides or swings. Other assessment instruments ensure that children are safe from potential fires, firearms, weapons, toxic materials, and materials that pose danger of suffocation. For more safety issues, such as issues related to materials, toys, cribs, products, or home equipment, CPSC provides a good source of publications (available online at http://www.cpsc.gov/cpscpub/pubs/pub_idx.html).

Achieving Quality Environments for Children

Another reason for developing environmental assessment is to assess the quality of environments that will promote children's overall growth and development, and to design and implement plans to improve that quality, when appropriate. There have been different ways of defining quality of the environment and measuring it. One approach is assessing the overall quality of the classroom or day care environment by including measures of a range of characteristics associated with quality care. For example, the Day Care Environmental Inventory and Observation Schedule for Physical Space (Prescott, Kritchevsky, and Jones 1975) is one of the earlier assessments of child-rearing environments focusing on children in relation to the environment. The Preschool Environmental Rating Scale (Fromm, Rourke, and Buggey, 2000) is another environmental scale that involves physical layout, materials, basic care needs, curriculum, interrelationships, and activities in the setting. The Early Childhood Physical Environment Observation Schedules and Rating Scales (Moore 1994) consist of five types of scales (i.e., Early Childhood Center, Children, and Teacher Profiles; Early Childhood Teacher Style and Dimensions of Education Rating Scales; Early Childhood Physical Environment Scales; Playground and Neighborhood Observation Behavior Maps; Environment/Behavior Observation Schedule for Early Childhood Environments) to assess overall quality of various dimensions of children's environments. The **Early Childhood Environment Rating Scale**—Revised (ECERS-R) (Harms, Clifford, and Cryer, 2005) and the Infant/Toddler Environment Rating Scale—Revised (ITERS-R) (Harms, Cryer, and Clifford, 2003) are other assessment tools that have been the most widely used measures of the quality of care in child-care settings including both the physical structures and nonphysical features of the settings.

Many environmental assessments are developed to be used also in home settings for licensing, research, and clinical application purposes. As more families are opting to place their young children in family child-care programs, measures, such as the Family Day Care Rating Scale (Harms and Clifford, 1989), are developed to provide useful information about the quality of the provider's home environment. In addition, these assessments have been used to identify influences on children's development from their home environment. They have also been used to set goals for families who are receiving early intervention services.

Since the legislation of **Individual Family Service Plans**, professionals develop partnerships with families to provide them information in order to make their own decisions regarding what they think is best for their child and family. Examples of these assessments include the following:

- Home Observation for Measurement of the Environment (HOME) Inventory (Caldwell and Bradley, 1984), which is designed to assess physical and social aspects of home environments, such as the interaction between the mother and the child, organization of physical and temporal environment, and the learning materials.
- The Infant/Toddler (IT) HOME, the Early Childhood (EC) HOME, and the Middle Childhood (MC) HOME are three versions of the HOME Inventory used to assess early childhood home settings. More information is available online at http://www.ualr.edu/crtldept/home4.htm.

In addition to these purposes, assessments such as the School-Age Care Environment Rating Scale (SACERS) (Harms, Jacops, and White, 1996) have also been designed for not only home but other group care programs for children during out-of-school time.

Planning the Schedule, Curriculum and/or Program

Planning the schedule, curriculum, or program for either a group of children or individual children requires designing and organizing the environment according to children's diverse cultural, ethnic, and socioeconomic backgrounds as well as their varied developmental levels. To accomplish this, the assessment tools just mentioned can be used as well as some others, such as The Classroom Practices Inventory (CPI) (Hyson, Hirsh-Pasek, and Rescorla, 1990), which is based on the NAEYC Guidelines for **Developmentally Appropriate Practices** for 4–5-year-old children. CPI is a rating scale with an emphasis on curriculum, teaching practices, and the emotional climate of child-care programs.

Other instruments focus on the development of individual children, particularly those having certified disabilities (i.e., with **Individualized Education Plans** or Individualized Family Service Plans) and their **inclusion** in general education settings. Some of these instruments include the following:

- The Ecological Congruence Assessment (Wolery et al., 2000)
- Classroom Ecological Inventory (CEI) (Fuchs et al., 1994)
- The Assessment of Practices in Early Elementary Classroom (APEEC) (Hemmeter, Maxwell, Ault, and Schuster, 2001).

These assessments help parents, teachers, and other professionals plan for smooth transitions for children from more restrictive to inclusive settings as well as ensuring access for all children to the curriculum, the other children, teachers and other features of the environment. Other environmental assessments are designed to plan for specific curricula areas, such as children's literacy. The Early Language and Literacy Classroom Observation (ELLCO) Toolkit for children from 3- to 8-years-old (Smith and Dickinson, 2002) is designed as a comprehensive set of observation tools for describing the extent to which classrooms provide children optimal support for their language and literacy development. *See also* Classroom Environments; Disabilities, Young Children with; Ecology of Human Development; Grouping; Parents and Parent Involvement.

Further Readings: Caldwell, Bettye M., and Robert H. Bradley (1984). *HOME observation for measurement of the environment*. Little Rock: University of Arkansas at Little Rock; Consumer Product Safety Commission. Public Playground Safety Checklist. Available online at http://www.cpsc.gov/cpscpub/pubs/327.html; Fromm, Barbara, Michelle Rourke, and Tom Buggey (2000). Appendix C: Preschool environmental rating scale. In Richard M. Gargiulo and Jennifer L. Kilgo, eds., *Young children with special needs: An introduction to early childhood special education*. New York: Delmar Publishers, pp. 312–326; Fuchs, Douglas, Pamela Fernstrom, Stephanie Scott, Lynn Fuchs, and Linda Vandermeer (1994). Classroom ecological inventory. *Teaching Exceptional Children* 26(3), 11–15; Hemmeter, Mary Louise, Kelly L. Maxwell, Melinda Jones Ault, and John W. Schuster (2001). *Assessment of practices in early elementary classrooms (APEEC)*. New York: Teachers College Press; Hyson, Marion C., Kathy Hirsh-Pasek, and Leslie Rescorla (1990). The classroom practices inventory: An observation instrument based on NAEYC's guidelines or developmentally appropriate practices for 4- and 5-Year-Old Children. *Early Childhood Research Quarterly* 5, 475–494; Moore, Gary T. (1994). *Early childhood physical environment observation schedules and rating scales: Preliminary scales for the measurement of the physical environment of child care centers and related environments*. 2nd ed. Milwaukee: Center for Architecture and Urban Planning Research, University of Wisconsin-Milwaukee; National Association for the Education of Young Children (NAEYC). Program Standard 9—Physical Environment. Available online at http://www.naeyc.org/accreditation/performance_criteria/environment_criteria.asp; NICHD Early Child Care Research Network (2000). The relation of child care to cognitive and language development. *Child Development* 71(4): 960–980; Peisner-Feinberg, Ellen S., Margaret R. Burchinal, Richard M. Clifford, Mary L. Culkin, Carolle Howes, Sharon Lynn Kagan, Noreen Yazejian, Patricia Byler, Jean Rustici, and Janice Zelazo (2000). *The children of the cost, quality, and outcomes study go to school: Technical report*. Chapel Hill: University of North Carolina at Chapel Hill, Frank Porter Graham Child Development Center; Prescott, Elizabeth, Sybil Kritchevsky, and Elizabeth Jones (1975). An environmental inventory. Part 2 in Elizabeth Prescott, with Elizabeth Jones, Sybil Kritchevsky, Cynthia Milich, and Ede Haselhoef, eds., *Assessment of child-rearing environments: An ecological approach*. Pacific Oaks, CA: Pacific Oaks College; Smith, Miriam W., and David K. Dickinson, with Angela Sangeorge and Louisa Anastasopoulos (2002). *User's guide to the early language & literacy classroom observation toolkit*. Baltimore: Paul H. Brookes Publishing Co.; Wolery, Mark (2004). Assessing children's environments. In Mary McLean, Mark Wolery, and Donald B. Bailey, Jr., eds., *Assessing infants and preschoolers with special needs*. Upper Saddle River, NJ: Merrill, pp. 204–235; Wolery, Mark, Margaret Sigalove Brashers, Sheila Grant, and Theresa Pauca (2000). Ecological congruence assessment for classroom activities and routines in childcare. Chapel Hill: Frank Porter Graham Child Development Center.

Hatice Zeynep Inan and Laurie Katz

Environments, Classroom. *See* Classroom Environments

Environmental Health

Childhood health problems such as asthma and other respiratory diseases, neurodevelopment disorders, endocrine disruption and cancers have all been associated with environmental risk factors. Air pollutants (both indoor and outdoor) lead, pesticides, tobacco smoke, and house dust mite and cockroach allergens are important environmental contributors to childhood illnesses. Genetic and socioeconomic conditions have been shown to increase the susceptibility of children to the adverse effects of these environmental stressors. Over the past several decades there has been growing evidence of the increase in incidence rates, morbidity, and mortality for a number of these health problems (Israel et al., 2005). In developing countries additional environmental burdens to children include exposure to biologically contaminated water, poor sanitation, disease vectors such as mosquitoes, and unsafe use of chemicals and waste all of which are worsened by the effects of poverty, conflict, and malnutrition. Over 40 percent of the global burden of disease attributed to environmental factors falls on children below five years of age, who account for only about 10 percent of the world's population (WHO, 2006).

Children are more vulnerable than adults to environmental risks for the following several reasons (Landrigan et al., 2004; NAS, 1993; USEPA, 2006):

1. Children drink more water, eat more food, and breathe more air pound-for-pound than adults resulting in disproportionately heavier exposures to environmental agents.
2. Children's metabolic pathways are immature making them in most cases less able to metabolize, detoxify, and excrete environmental agents.
3. Environmental chemicals can do more harm to central nervous, reproductive, immune, endocrine and digestive systems during phases of rapid growth and development, including embryonic, fetal and early childhood life stages.
4. Young children crawl, put things in their mouths, and sometimes even eat dirt. These actions tend to put them in closer contact with some environmental agents compared with adults.
5. Children have a longer life expectancy and more time to develop chronic diseases that might be triggered by early environmental exposures. Early childhood exposure to certain carcinogens or toxicants may be more likely to lead to disease than the same exposures experienced later in life.

Ambient and indoor air pollution is associated with asthma and other respiratory disorders in children. From 1990 to 2002 over 50 percent of children lived in counties in the United States where the ground-level ozone standard was exceeded during the year; from 2000 (first measured) to 2002, between 20 and 30 percent of children lived in counties where the fine particulate standard ($PM_{2.5}$) was exceeded (USEPA, 2003). Ozone provokes airway inflammation and reactivity at low levels. Ozone levels have been related to increases in asthma emergency room visits in Atlanta, Georgia, New Jersey, and Mexico City. Fine particulates derived primarily from power plants and vehicle emissions have been associated with asthma and other respiratory conditions, low birth weight, and increased risk of birth defects (Landrigan, 2004).

Indoor air pollution consists of gases and aerosols from consumer products, allergens including dust mites, cat dander and cockroaches, pesticides, and gases and vapors from combustion sources. Environmental tobacco smoke is a common indoor pollutant associated with chronic respiratory infections and decrements in lung growth and development. In 1999–2000, 63 percent of white, non-Hispanic,

86 percent of black, non-Hispanic, and 49 percent of Mexican American children were exposed to detectable levels of blood cotinine, an indicator of tobacco smoke exposures (CDC, 2003).

Cockroach droppings or body parts play a significant role in asthma in many inner-city areas. In a study of seven U.S. metropolitan inner city areas skin test sensitization (an indicator of exposure) to cockroach was 69 percent overall and to dust mites was 62 percent. Cockroach allergens were highest in high-rise apartments, whereas dust mites allergen levels were highest in detached homes (Gruchalla et al., 2005). Other triggers of asthma include mold, animals, pollen, cold air, exercise, stress, and respiratory infections (NIEHS, 2006).

Chronic low-level exposure to lead measured in terms of blood lead levels is associated with cognitive deficits, developmental delays, behavioral problems, and diminished school performance at levels at least as low as 10 micrograms of lead per deciliter of blood (μg/dl) (CDC, 1991; WHO, 1995; USEPA, 2003). Pooled data from several studies around the world suggest the impact level may be as low as 7.5 μg/dl (Lanphear et al., 2005).

The elimination of leaded gasoline in many countries has reduced overall lead exposures, however studies of mining areas in Mexico indicate levels higher than five times the action limit of 10 ug/dl (CEC, 2006). In the United States lead-based paint in older homes is the primary source of childhood lead exposure. In developing countries, sources such as lead-oxide found in pottery glazes also represent a predominant exposure through food prepared and stored on the pottery.

Children are exposed to pesticides in soil, dust, and grass and through pesticide residues in food. Children of farm workers, pesticide applicators, and those living in agricultural areas are especially at risk. Key risks are cancer, birth defect, and damage to the nervous and endocrine systems (WHO, 2004). Organophosphate pesticides are used in the production of many foods consumed by children (USEPA, 2003). Between 1994 and 2000 the percentage of food samples in the United States with detectable levels of organophosphate pesticide residues ranged between 19 percent and 29 percent (CEC, 2006).

Childhood environmental health has become a focus of environmental research, agency initiatives, and public advocacy. Particularly in developing countries, environmental hazards and pollution are major contributors to childhood illnesses and disability. Further efforts are needed to better characterize the specific exposure mechanisms, developmental toxicity, and overall environmental risks associated with early childhood and to regulate these hazards in a manner protective of this vulnerable and precious life stage.

Further Readings: Israel, Barbara A., et al. (2005). Community-based participatory research: lessons learned from the centers for children's environmental health and disease prevention research. *Environmental Health Perspectives* 113(10), 1463–1471; Landrigan, Philip J., Carole A. Kimmel, Adolfo Correa, and Brenda Eskenazai (2004). Children's health and the environment: Public health and challenges for risk assessment. *Environmental Health Perspectives* 112(2), 257–265; Lanphear, Bruce P., Richard Hornung, Jane Khoury, Kimberly Yolton, Peter Baghurst, David C. Bellinger, Richard L. Canfield, Kim N. Dietrich, Robert Bornschein, Tom Greene, Stephen J. Rothenberg, Herbert L. Needleman, Lourdes Schnaas, Gail Wasserman, Joseph Graziano, and Russell Roberts (2005). Low-level environmental lead exposure and children's intellectual function: An international pooled analysis. *Environmental Health Perspectives* 113(7), 894–899; Gruchalla, Rebecca, Jacqueline Pongracic, Marshall Plaut, Richard Evans III, Cynthia M. Visness, Michelle Walter, Ellen F. Crain, Meyer Kattan, Wayne J. Morgan, Susan Steinbach, et al. (2005). Inner city asthma study: relationship among sensitivity, allergen exposure and asthma morbidity. *J. Allergy Clinical Immunology* 115(3), 478–485; Centers for Disease Control and Prevention (CDC) and Commission for Environmental Cooperation (CEC) Publications and Web Sites: CDC (1991). *Preventing lead poisoning in young children: A statement by the centers for disease control.* Atlanta: Centers for Disease Control and Prevention; CDC (2003). National health and nutrition examination survey. National Center for Health Statistics. Atlanta: Centers for Disease Control and Prevention; CDC (2006). National Center for Environmental Health. Avaliable online at http://www.cdc.gov/nceh/; CEC (2006). *Children's health and the environment in North America: A first report on environmental indicators and measures.* In collaboration with the governments of Canada, Mexico, and the United States. Montreal,Quebec. Available online at www.cec.org; National Academy of Sciences (NAS), National Institute of Environmental Health Sciences (NIEHS), and U.S. Environmental Protection Agency (USEPA) Publications and Web Sites: NAS (1993). *Pesticides in the diets of infants and children.* Washington, DC: National Academy Press; NIEHS (2006). Available online at http://www.niehs.nih.gov/oc/factsheets/ceh/home.htm; USEPA, Office of Children's Health Protection (2006). Available online at http://yosemite.epa.gov/ochp/ochpweb.nsf/homepage); World Health Organization (WHO) Publications and Web Sites: WHO (1995). Environmental Health Criteria 165–Inorganic Lead. Geneva: International Programme on Chemical Safety, World Health Organization; WHO (2004). Childhood pesticide poisoning: Information for advocacy and action. prepared for the United Nations Environment Programme. Chatelaine Switzerland: Chemicals Programme of the United Nations Environment Programme; WHO (2006). Children's Environmental Health Program. Available online at http://www.who.int/ceh/en/.

Christine Rioux

Environments, Playground. *See* Playgrounds

Erikson, Erik H. (1902–1994)

Child psychoanalyst Erik Homburger Erikson was born on June 15, 1902, near Frankfurt, Germany's scientific and industrial center. His parents separated before his birth, and his mother left for Germany to be closer to friends living in Karlsruhe. When he was three years old, his mother married Dr. Homburger, the local pediatrician. Young Erikson spent his childhood with his Danish mother and Jewish stepfather in a comfortable home overlooking a beautiful castle and park, with ample space to run and play, in a town that would soon become an industrial center.

Erikson attended the local primary and secondary schools in Karlsruhe, where he studied Latin, Greek, literature, ancient history, and art all subjects in which he excelled. However, with regard to formal education he was not a good student. After graduating, he traveled through the Black Forest, and on to Munich and Florence in search of answers of what to do next with his life. Although he was unsuccessful in his initial attempt to formally study art, he returned to Karlsruhe at the age of 25 and prepared to study and teach art.

It was at that time that he received a letter from his close friend Peter Blos in Vienna. Blos had been tutoring the children of Dorothy Burlingham, an American studying with Sigmund and Anna **Freud**. The ladies, Dorothy Burlingham and Anna Freud, had offered Blos an opportunity to start his own school, and he recommended that Erikson join this venture. So in 1927, Erikson moved to Vienna, where he worked with Blos to start an experimental progressive school. His subsequent work with young children was influenced by Montessori's educational philosophy, and eventually led Erikson to study psychoanalysis in children as well as adults at the Vienna Psychoanalytic Institute.

In 1929, he met and married Joan Serson, who also joined the school's faculty. By 1933, Germany and Austria were having rough economic times, Hitler had taken office, and most Jewish analysts were fleeing to America. Erikson and his family also decided to leave Vienna, and he arrived in Boston where he established himself as the city's first child psychoanalyst, opening an office on Boston's Marlborough Street. He also took a position at Harvard Medical School, living and working in Cambridge for the next three years. In addition, he was asked to consult at the Judge Baker Guidance Center which was a clinic devoted to the diagnosis and treatment of children's emotional disorders. In 1936 he accepted the position of instructor at Yale Medical School, and then moved to California in 1939 where he resumed his analytic work with children in San Francisco, and his research in anthropology and history at Berkeley. After ten years in California Erikson moved back to the east coast and to Harvard University.

Erikson's work led him to study children in different cultural contexts, specifically poor children, including those from the Sioux and Yurok Native American tribes. This work inspired his attempts to demonstrate how the customs of a given society influence childhood and child-rearing traditions. Erikson was additionally fascinated by the way people like Luther and Mahatma Gandhi could exert a psychological influence on millions. He visited India in 1962 to lead a seminar on the human life cycle, which prompted his exploration on Gandhi's life.

Erikson published a great many articles and books including *Gandhi's Truth* and *Young Man Luther*. His most important work, *Childhood and Society* (1950), in which he maps out eight stages of psychosocial development in the human life, had a profound influence on the **social-emotional curriculum in** early childhood education. In 1969, in spite of never having earned a formal college degree, Erikson was offered a professorship at Harvard where he taught until his death in 1994. *See also* Child Art; Development, Psycho-Social Theory of.

Further Readings: Coles, Robert (1970). *Erik H. Erikson: The growth of his work*. Boston: Little, Brown and Company; Crain, William (2005). *Theories of development: Concepts and applications*. Englewood Cliffs, NJ: Pearson Prentice Hall; Erikson, Erik Homburger (1950). *Childhood and society*. New York: Norton; Erikson, Erik Homburger (1958). *Young man Luther: A study in psychoanalysis and history*. New York: W.W. Norton & Company; Erikson, Erik Homburger (1969). *Gandhi's truth: On the origins of militant nonviolence*. New York: W.W. Norton & Company; Stevens, Richard (1983). *Erik Erikson: An introduction*. New York: St. Martin's Press.

Amita Gupta

ERS. *See* Early Childhood Environment Rating Scales

Ethics. *See* Professional Ethics

European Early Childhood Education Research Journal (EECERJ)

The *European Early Childhood Education Research Journal* (*EECERJ*) is the journal of the European Early Childhood Education Research Association (EECERA). EECERA is an international organization dedicated to the promotion and dissemination of research in early childhood education throughout Europe and beyond. Its principal aims are the following:

- to provide a rigorous academic forum at a European level for the development and dissemination of high-quality research on early childhood education;
- to facilitate collaboration and cooperation between European researchers working in this field;
- to encourage the clear articulation and communication of the links between research and practice in early childhood education;
- to give mutual support and offer peer group interaction to researchers in early childhood education;
- to raise the visibility and status of research on early childhood education throughout Europe and beyond.

The *Journal of the Association* was launched in 1993 and has published two volumes each year since its launch. It is based at the Centre for Research in Early Childhood (CREC) at University of Worcester in Birmingham, UK, an internationally acknowledged centre of excellence in early childhood research and practice. The director of the Centre is the journal's Coordinating Editor and manages the journal refereeing and editorial process. The journal is currently published as an independent enterprise on behalf of the Association, but from January 2007 will be published through Taylor and Francis (Routledge). The journal's unique and distinguishing features include:

- an unbroken publication record since its launch twelve years ago;
- ownership and publication by a European based and focused early childhood research association;
- promotion of a European perspective on early childhood education and care within an international field;
- a multidisciplinary and multiprofessional focus in its remit which includes, but is not exclusively, sociological or psychological in its focus;
- an intention to establish a new discipline of early childhood educational research;
- the linking of research, policy and practice in early childhood;
- the promotion of new paradigms in early childhood research;
- a cross national and highly respected editorial board;
- a cross national and established readership;
- promotion at an annual conference of the Association;
- a rigorous cross national refereeing process;
- a cross national publishing policy;
- a rolling programme of editorial comment amongst senior European early childhood researchers;

- an increasing rate of paper submissions and a subsequent decreasing acceptance rate, indicating increasing quality in published papers;
- an increasing number of international library subscriptions;
- a profit-making margin in its publication.

Christine Pascal

Even Start

The Even Start Family Literacy Program is a U.S. federally funded program serving low-income families with young children, birth through seven years of age. The long-term goal of the Even Start program is to break the cycle of poverty and illiteracy for eligible families by improving children's academic achievement and parents' literacy skills. The Even Start Family Literacy program consists of four key components: early childhood education, adult literacy, parenting education, and interactive literacy between parents and children (U.S. Department of Education, 2005). The Even Start Family Literacy Program originally initiated in 1988 as part of the reauthorization of the Elementary and Secondary Education Act. The program was then reauthorized by the Literacy Involves Families Together Act of 2000 and **No Child Left Behind Act** of 2001 (U.S. Department of Education, 2005).

The purpose of the Even Start program is to promote family self-sufficiency and improve child outcomes for targeted families. Families served by Even Start are typically extremely high need families. Even Start families have lower incomes, lower employment rates, and lower education levels than other families served by U.S. federal antipoverty programs such as **Head Start** (U.S. Department of Education, 2005). Even Start programs serve English speaking families with low literacy levels as well as low-income families who are learning English as a second language.

Even Start services are provided throughout the United States. Federal grants are awarded to states and states then award local contracts to agencies serving high need children and families. In addition to the provision of state grants, Even Start programs are also operated specifically for Migrant and Native American populations. Even Start programs use a variety of service models including home visits for children and families, center-based early childhood education, and intergenerational parent–child literacy activities. In 2003, over 1,200 local Even Start programs were funded throughout the United States serving over 50,000 families (U.S. Department of Education, 2005).

Several national evaluations have been conducted on the effectiveness of the Even Start program. The most recent evaluation conducted in 2003 suggested that the impact of the program on children's outcomes was related to the participation rates of families in the Even Start program. However, children's literacy outcomes of randomly assigned Even Start families were no higher than those in the control group (St. Pierre et al., 2003). And yet, a previous national study and other small-scale studies have found improved literacy outcomes for young children (Ryan, 2005; Tao, Gamse, and Tarr, 1998). Current legislation in the United States requires that Even Start programs use scientifically based literacy practices. *See also* Literacy; National Even Start Association.

Further Readings: Ryan, A. M. (2005). The effectiveness of the Manchester Even Start Program in improving literacy outcomes for preschool Latino students. *Journal of Research in Childhood Education* 20(1), 15–26; St. Pierre, R. G., A. E. Ricuitti, F. Tao, C. Creps, J. Swartz, W. Lee, A. Parsad, and T. Rimdzuis (2003). Third national Even Start evaluation: Program impacts and implications for Improvement. Abt Associates; Tao, F., B. Gamse, and H. Tarr (1998). National evaluation of the Even Start Family Literacy Program. 1994–1997 Final report. Alexandria, VA: Fu Associates, Ltd.; U.S. Department of Education (2005). Available online at http://www.ed.gov/about/offices/list/oese/sasa/esfacts.html.

Rena Hallam

Exchange

Exchange, formerly titled *Childcare Information Exchange*, has been a leading source of support, encouragement, and up-to-date information for leaders in early childhood programs worldwide since 1978. Each issue of *Exchange* provides practical ideas and strategies for dealing with the responsibilities and demands that directors face every day, such as the special needs of today's children, staff turnover, ever-increasing competition, uncertain public subsidies, abuse, accusations, recruitment, and training. In addition, *Exchange* helps directors prepare for the challenges they will encounter in the future, such as the changing fabric of the family unit, transformations in the workplace, the movement to find balance between work and family, and the increasing stresses placed upon our young children. Details available online at www.ChildCareExchange.com.

Bonnie Neugebauer and Roger Neugebauer

Experimental Designs. *See* Quantitative Analyses/Experimental Designs

F

Families

Early childhood educators have long embraced the idea that families are the first and foremost educational and socialization influence on children. The prevalence of this view has led to the development of early childhood programs and practices that help families promote children's well-being. Supportive assistance to families with young children historically has focused on parenting and the mother–child relationship. Since the 1980s, there has been growing interest in other types of family relationships, functions, and contexts.

Family Systems, Influences, and Contexts

Perspectives on families as contexts of early development have broadened to include more than the conventional focus on the mother–child relationship. Families are increasingly viewed as social systems because families typically are comprised of subsystems, including parent–child relationships, sibling relationships, relationships with extended family members, and marital or partner relationships. Change in one of these subsystems generally triggers a change in other systems. Marital discord, for example, is negatively associated with children's well-being (Cummings and Davies, 2002). Families are also viewed as social systems because the roles and functions of all family members are interdependent (Parke and Buriel, 1998). For example, a child's entry into an early childhood program is typically associated with shifts in the parent role, the parent–child relationship, and the child's relations with a sibling (e.g., less available as a playmate at home).

The question of whether participation in early childhood programs in the early years of life diminishes family effects on children's development has received considerable attention since the mid 1980s (Fein and Fox, 1988). Some early studies on this topic found that family factors were stronger predictors of children's outcomes when children were not enrolled in child care in the first year of their lives (Howes, 1990). More recent research with larger samples has found that the influence of family factors on children's outcomes is not weakened or altered by extensive participation in nonparental child care beginning in infancy (NICHD Early Child Care Research Network, 1998).

Although families represent many different structural forms, including single-parent families, a common theme across varying family types is the role of extended family members as a support system for young children and their parents. In the United States, for example, nearly one-half of all grandparents with young grandchildren living nearby provide some type of child-care assistance to their adult children. Slightly more than one-half of grandmothers and nearly 40 percent of grandfathers are involved in child-care roles (Guzman, 2004). Research in Sweden, the United States, Wales, and West Germany indicates that grandparents are an important part of social networks that provide information plus emotional and material assistance to parents and their young children (Cochran et al., 1990).

In addition to social networks, studies point to characteristics of parents' work environments, neighborhoods, and communities as well as socioeconomic status, race, and ethnicity as key contributors to the quality of family child-rearing environments (Luster and Okagaki, 2005).

Program–Family Relationships

In most countries today, positive relationships between families and early childhood programs are considered to be a key element of program quality. Reasons for an emphasis on parent involvement, which vary by national histories and goals, include commitments to parental rights and responsibilities, interests in strengthening ties between families and communities, community development, employment for low-income parents, and empowering women to take more control of their lives (Cochran, 1993). The early childhood field has long functioned with the expectation that frequent, two-way communication in which parents and program staff share decision-making responsibilities for children's care and development will strengthen continuity between family and program, yielding improved outcomes for young children (Powell, 2001).

Productive relationships between early childhood program staff and parents are an integral part of some program models. Many municipal early childhood programs in **Italy** (see Volume 4), for example, consider parental engagement to be central to their philosophy, practices, and success. The concept of parental engagement in **Reggio Emilia** calls for parents and citizens to become intimately involved in the educational enterprise through trusting and reciprocal relations carried out through advisory councils and meetings at individual, classroom and school-wide levels. **Documentation** of children's behaviors and understandings also are a means of connecting with families. More generally in the United States, professional guidelines for **developmentally appropriate practice** in early childhood programs emphasize reciprocal relationships between families and programs.

Research on program–family relationships is limited. Studies conducted in the United States indicate that, overall, early childhood programs fall short of realizing frequent, two-way communications with parents (Powell, 2001). Research in other nations suggests that parents tend to desire an active role in programs (e.g., classroom aide or decision-making role on a preschool board) but that teachers tend to prefer a more passive role for parents (e.g., recipients of professional advice and guidance; Boocock and Larner, 1998).

Programs to Support Families

The early childhood field has a long history of providing programs of child-rearing information and social support to families. Program models vary in the extent to which they give attention primarily to the parent or to both child and parent, and in whether the program content focuses on child development exclusively or also incorporates support for other family functions such as meeting basic needs (e.g., housing and food) and adult literacy. Programs also vary in the use of home visiting and/or groups for engaging parents.

Parenting education efforts are prominent among programs aimed at providing supportive assistance to families with young children. An example is the Home Instruction for Parents of Preschool Youngsters (HIPPY) program, which originated in Israel in the 1960s (Lombard, 1994) and has been implemented and evaluated in seven countries (Westheimer, 2003). The HIPPY curriculum emphasizes early literacy skills developed through parent–child educational interactions. Parents are trained by paraprofessionals from their own communities who use role-playing as the primary means of instruction.

The growing interest in family systems has led to the development of programs that focus on more than the mother–child relationship. Some programs address the marital or adult partner relationship as it impinges on parenting, for example, and other programs seek to strengthen parents' own literacy skills while also giving attention to the parenting role and the quality of family connections with informal and formal supports in the community (Cowan, Powell, and Cowan, 1998).

Further Readings: Boocock, S. S., and M. B. Larner (1998). Long-term outcomes in other nations. In W. S. Barnett and S. S. Boocock, eds., *Early care and education for children in poverty*. Albany, NY: State University of New York Press, pp. 45–76; Cochran, M. (1993). Public child care, culture, and society: Crosscutting themes. In M. Cochran, ed., *International handbook of child care policies and programs*. Westport, CT: Greenwood Press, pp. 627–658; Cochran, M., M. Larner, D. Riley, L. Gunnarsson, and C. Henderson, Jr. (1990). *Extending families: The social networks of parents and their children*. London/New York: Cambridge University Press; Cowan, P. A., D. R. Powell, and C. P. Cowan, (1998). Parenting interventions: A family systems perspective. In W. Damon, ed., and I. E. Sigel and K. A. Renninger, vol eds., *Handbook of child psychology. Vol. 4: Child psychology in practice*. New York: Wiley, pp. 3–72; Cummings, E. M., and P. T. Davies (2002). Effects of marital conflict on children: Recent advances and emerging themes in process-oriented research. *Journal of Child Psychology and Psychiatry* 43, 31–63; Fein, G. G., and N. Fox (1998). Infant day care: A special issue. *Early Childhood Research Quarterly*, 3, 227–234; Guzman, L. (2004). Grandma and grandpa taking care of the kids: Patterns of involvement. *Child Trends Research Brief* 2004(17). Washington, DC: Child Trends; Howes, C. (1990). Can the age of entry into child care and the quality of child care predict adjustment in kindergarten? *Developmental Psychology*, 26, 292–303; Lombard, E. (1994). *Success begins at home: The past, present and future of the Home Instruction Program for Preschool Youngsters*. 2nd ed. Guilford, CT: The Dushkin Publishing Group; Luster, T., and L. Okagaki, eds. (2005). *Parenting: An ecological perspective*. 2nd ed. Mahwah, NJ: Lawrence Erlbaum Associates, Publishers; NICHD Early Child Care

Research Network (1998). Relations between family predictors and child outcomes: Are they weaker for children in child care? *Developmental Psychology* 34, 1119-1128; Parke, R. D., and R. Buriel (1998). Socialization in the family: Ethnic and ecological perspectives. In W. Damon, ed., and N. Eisenberg, vol. ed., *Handbook of child psychology. Vol. 3: Social, emotional, and personality development.* 5th ed. New York: Wiley, pp. 463-552; Powell, D. R. (2001). Visions and realities of achieving partnership: Parent-teacher relationships at the turn of the century. In A. Goncu and E. Klein, eds., *Children in play, story and school.* New York: Guilford, pp. 333-57; Westheimer, M. (2003). *Parents making a difference: International research on the Home Instruction for Parents of Preschool Youngsters (HIPPY) Program.* Jerusalem: Hebrew University Magnes Press.

Douglas R. Powell

Family Child Care

Family Child Care is one of the diverse options for employed families in the United States for the early care and education of their children. Family Child Care refers to either nonparental or relative early care and education that is provided in a family child-care provider/educator's own home. The names kith and kin and relative care are given to family child care/educators who provide care and education for their own or relative's children. Family child-care providers/educators, in addition to offering safe and healthy environments that support the development of young children, serve as managers of their small business. Throughout the United States, a majority of families seeking out-of-home care bring their young children aged birth through five and often through school age to family home care providers. Current estimates suggest that more than 4 million children, including more than 25 percent of infants and toddlers, in early care and education can be found in family child care homes.

Advantages and Disadvantages for Families

For many families there are distinct advantages of family child-care homes in comparison with center-based care/education programs. These advantages include but are not limited to: fewer children/more individualized care/education; mixed ages of children; possibility for selecting caregivers with language and child-rearing practices similar to the family; location in a family home, thus less formal and school-like; sometimes lesser costs than center-based care; consistency of one care/educator; nutritious home-cooked food; flexible, more nontraditional hours, and possible emergency (temporary) services; possible location in family's neighborhood; care/education for multiple children in family; accessibility for children with special needs and school age children; and curriculum based on real life activities.

On the other hand, some families find disadvantages with care/education in family child-care homes that include but are not limited to: lack of consistency of quality, lack of standards (80-90 percent are nonregulated), multitasking of family care providers/educators who simultaneously care for children and engage in routine home maintenance tasks, isolation of family care providers/educators from other care/educators, lack of same supports and resources as child-care centers, care of family care provider's/educator's own or relative children, lack of public perception of family care/educators as professional and neglect by the profession, and lack of age mates for their children. Families are also concerned that family care providers/educators may lack the professional training and resources to promote the physical, cognitive, social-emotional, communication, and creative development of the children in their care.

Quality of Family Child Care Homes

Despite the increasing numbers of children in family child care homes, the early care and education profession has directed the least amount of attention to this category of child care perhaps because family child care homes are private businesses and not as much in the eye of the public as child care centers. Until the 1990s, there were fewer research studies, publications, and journal articles addressing issues relating to family child care than there were about child-care centers. Reasons for lack of research include the lack of visibility of family child care/educators, the informality of the setting as compared to educational centers, lack of willingness of family child care providers/educators to participate in research, and the turnover rate of family child care/educators. These studies that have been conducted and the publications detailing the findings of the research have focused on understanding both the context of family child care and the quality issues related to family child care.

Quality in child care for all types of programs including family child care is a continuous discussion in the early childhood profession. According to a recent synthesis of research, findings suggest that "high quality child care programs promote children's cognitive development (for example, language and math skills), foster children's social skills (interactions with other children, behavior management, for example), and encourage higher levels of school readiness." Weaver (2002, pp. 16–20) suggests that, on the basis of this research, there are numerous identified characteristics of "master providers" which significantly impact the quality of care/education in a family child care home. These factors include: regulation through licensing, a life long learning disposition, a high level of "psychological well-being," a commitment to the child-care profession, established and varied community connections, and dependable financial resources.

Family child care/educators throughout the United States have access to a variety of regulatory systems and opportunities for professional development. Some states mandate regulations and other states offer options of licensing or registering. Licensing offices, food programs, and resource and referral programs are just three of the many monitoring systems available for family child care. In addition to state regulations that typically focus on safety and health issues, family child care/educators have other tools available to review the quality of their programs. Harms and Clifford (1989) developed *The Family Day Care Rating Scale (FDCRS)* for family child care/educators themselves to rate the comprehensive quality of their home or as an instrument for an outsider to observe. Family child care/educators can also seek accreditation through the National Association of Family Child Care (NAFCC).

Many family child care/educators have not had formal training in early childhood education, child development, health, safety, and nutrition, family and community collaboration, business management, and other areas related to family child care. Options for professional development for family child care/educators include but are not limited to: resource and referral agencies, community colleges and universities, specific state training programs, and local, state, and national conferences. There may be fewer options available to family child care/educators in rural areas. In addition to enhancing knowledge and skills, professional development opportunities provide opportunities for family child care/educators to network with others. Some states/communities establish networks of family child care to diminish the isolation that family child care/educators experience by working in their homes.

Summary

As the number of working families increases and family child-care homes become the choice for many families, the early childhood profession will have to focus efforts on further understanding the context and quality of family child-care homes. In the absence of national policies to insure affordable, accessible, high-quality early care and education programs, there are efforts in many states to require higher standards and more rigorous licensing requirements for family child-care providers. Research efforts are important to learn about developmental outcomes for young children who participate in family child care/education and to influence public policy regarding family child care/education.

Further Readings: Harms, T., and R. M. Clifford (1989). *Family day care rating scale*. New York: Teachers College Press; Kontos, Susan, Carollee Howes, Marybeth Shinn, and Ellen Galinsky (1995). *Quality in family child care & relative care*. New York: Teachers College Press; Kontos, Susan, Carollee Howes, Marybeth Shinn, and Ellen Galinsky (1992). *Family day care: Out of the shadows and into the limelight*. Washington, DC: National Association for the Education of Young Children; Peters, D., and Alan R. Pence, eds. (1992). *Family day care. Current research for informed public policy*. New York: Teachers College Press; Solnit, June S., ed. (1999). *Family child care handbook*. 6th ed. California: Child Care Resource and Referral Network; Weaver, Ruth H. (2002). The roots of quality care. Strengths of master providers. *Young Children* 57(1), 16–22.

Nancy Baptiste

Family Literacy

Family literacy is a phrase that is used to describe the intergenerational development of literacy within families. Family literacy services or programs refer to sponsored programs in which more than one generation of a family participates in activities designed to promote literacy in the home, school, or community. The term was first used by Taylor (1983) to describe the meanings and uses of literacy in families. Wasik and Herrmann (2004) describe the phrase as referencing "literacy beliefs and practices among family members and the intergenerational transfer of literacy to children" (p. 3).

Family literacy appears in several federal laws, including the *Workforce Investment Act*; the *Reading Excellence Act*; the *Community Opportunities, Accountability, and Training and Educational Services Act* (**Head Start** Reauthorization); and the *Family Literacy Federal Work-Study Waiver*. The **No Child Left Behind Act** contains numerous references to family literacy and parent involvement, including articulation of the William F. Goodling **Even Start** Family Literacy Program. As stipulated in these laws, many federally funded programs, such as Head Start, Reading First, and Early Reading First are required to include a family literacy component. It is an approved expenditure for several other programs, including Title I preschool programs, education of migratory children programs, and 21st Century Community Learning Centers. The federal definition used in these statutes reads as follows:

> services that are of sufficient intensity in terms of hours, and of sufficient duration, to make sustainable changes in a family and that integrate all the following activities:
> (A) Interactive literacy activities between parents and their children.
> (B) Training for parents regarding how to be the primary teacher for their children and full partners in the education of their children.
> (C) Parent literacy training that leads to economic self-sufficiency.
> (D) An age-appropriate education to prepare children for success in school and life experiences.

Other definitions of family literacy found in the professional literature vary in their emphasis. Some scholars (Morrow, 1995) emphasize an empowerment model that expands upon the definition of what counts as family literacy. This model goes beyond an emphasis on direct parent–child interactions around literacy tasks to include parents or other caregivers working independently on reading and writing, using literacy to address family and community problems, addressing child-rearing concerns through family literacy class, supporting the development of their home language and culture, and interacting with the school system regarding children's early learning.

From a social constructivist perspective (Neuman, Celano, and Fisher, 1996), programs that support family literacy are not about changing people; rather, they are about offering choices and opportunities for families. Parents come to family literacy programs with life experiences and family stories that should be honored and used in program development. Family literacy is about providing context, resources, and opportunities for families that allow them to demonstrate what they already know and can do. To be effective, family literacy programs must be responsive to parents' needs and interests. From this perspective, family literacy is about power.

Research on family literacy has expanded understandings of the potentials of these various sources of support. For example, a recent study explored the meaning family literacy programs had for participants. Family members acknowledged its potential to improve their abilities to help, encourage, and read to their children, as one mother noted. "Before [family literacy] I thought reading was just reading. Now I know it's also talking and asking questions" (Handel, 1999, p. 135). Participants also focused on their own learning, including opportunities to interact with other adults, the quality of the materials and teaching staff. Another participant noted how willing people were to help her, describing the school "like a relative" (p. 138) to her. She eagerly responded to their offers of assistance. The women expressed the idea that the program reflected their personal values and life experiences. From the participant perspective, family literacy can replace negative educational experiences with positive educational experiences that can change parent attitudes about their children's educational opportunities.

A comprehensive family literacy model includes all four components listed in the federal definition (adult basic education, age-appropriate education for children, parenting education, and parent–child literacy activities) in a fully integrated and unified package. Adult educators collaborate with early childhood teachers and parent educators to plan and deliver the programs that are located together. Through such an integration of services, families have an opportunity to break out of intergenerational patterns of poverty to achieve economic self-sufficiency while concurrently boosting their ability to support the literacy development of their children. Comprehensive family literacy programs that have developed and served as models over the past twenty years include the Parent and Child Education Program (PACE), the Kenan Trust Family Literacy Project, and Even Start—a federally funded family literacy model program.

Family literacy services or programs generally represent a continuum of options, ranging from the fully integrated comprehensive model to programs that engage family members from multiple generations in one or more literacy activities concurrent with the services provided to individual family members (e.g., early childhood educators use parent volunteers to read books to children or adult education programs that offer monthly family picnics with oral storytelling). Programs that systematically take a family-focused approach, integrating two or more components, can typically be found in libraries, community centers, family resource centers, adult basic education programs, Head Start programs, and many other community-based programs. They can be ongoing in nature or limited to single events. Adult educators recognize that family literacy programs differ from traditional adult literacy programs in that they are designed to maximize the probability that adults who receive literacy education will actually succeed in transferring aspects of their new beliefs, attitudes, knowledge, and skills across generations to their children.

Family literacy programs can also be found within schools. The National Center for Family Literacy (NCFL) supports an initiative to develop school-based family literacy programs. In this program, school personnel can apply a gradual phasing-in approach to family literacy. In pilot projects using this model, elementary teachers began by bringing parents into their classrooms for parent–child literacy activities. They expanded these efforts so parents could attend adult education classes during the day in the elementary school building, occasionally breaking to participate in structured parent–child literacy activities. The NCFL website, http://famlit.org, offers details and information about this program.

When offered with sufficient quality, intensity, and duration, family literacy programs can be effective in breaking cycles of illiteracy. Data from more than sixty NCFL sites across fourteen states that enrolled more than 2,000 families over a five-year period indicate changes in several critical areas. Families remained active in family literacy programs longer and attended more frequently than those in typical adult-focused programs, literacy activity in the home increased, and adults showed significant gains in language and math skills (NCFL, 1996). A comparison study involving over 500 former Even Start families up to six years after program exit (NCFL, 1997) also found many positive results for both children and adults. For children, findings showed that 90 percent had earned satisfactory grades in reading, language, and mathematics. For adults, 54 percent of those seeking educational credentials had earned a GED or high school certification, 40 percent continued to make educational progress by enrolling in higher education or training programs, and 45 percent increased their self-sufficiency by reducing or eliminating their dependence on public assistance. A research synthesis on family literacy programs confirmed findings that family literacy participants have increased positive child and adult outcomes (Tracey, 1994).

Since early childhood education is a critical component of family literacy, it is important that the quality and nature of it be consistent with effective programs. Research on preschool programs for children living in poverty consistently indicates that compensatory programs isolated from strong parent components will not provide children with long-term educational benefits. More can be achieved for both children and parents by offering family literacy programs than can be achieved by traditional age-based service delivery models. Parent levels of education are closely related to child achievement in school. Drawing from research on high-quality early childhood classrooms, Dickinson, St. Pierre, and Pettengill (Wasik, 2004) conclude that increasing a family's ability to support child development produces the maximum potential impact on long-term language and literacy achievement of the children.

Family literacy programs reflect the belief that the primary source for learning continues to be the family. Families live and interact within the context of their communities. Communities provide a wide array of educational and cultural resources of varying quality that can and do contribute to the literacy of residents within the area, such as public schools, libraries, theatrical productions, and so forth. Nevertheless, the family remains the most fundamental learning environment in the lives of young children. The concept of family literacy then refers to the role the family plays in helping all its members grow and develop into educated citizens ready to contribute to the family, the community, and the nation—as members of the workforce, as leaders in the community, and as guides for the next generation.

Further Readings: Handel, Ruth D. (1999). The multiple meanings of family literacy. *Education and Urban Society* 32, 127–144; Morrow, Lesley Mandell, ed. (1995). *Family literacy, connections in schools and communities*. Newark, DE: International Reading Association; National Center for Family Literacy (1996). *The power of family literacy*. Louisville, KY: National Center for Family Literacy; National Center for Family Literacy (1997). *Even Start: An effective literacy program helps families grow toward independence*. Louisville, KY: National Center for Family Literacy; Neuman, Susan B., Donna Celano, and Robyn Fischer (1996). The children's literature hour: A social-constructivist approach to family literacy. *Journal of Literacy Research* 28, 499–523; Taylor, Denny (1983). *Family literacy: Young children learning to read and write*. Exeter, NH: Heinemann; Tracey, D. H. (1994, November). *Family literacy: Research synthesis*. Paper presented at the 44th annual meeting of the National Reading Conference, San Diego, CA; Wasik,

Barbara Hanna, ed. (2004). *Handbook of family literacy*. Mahwah, NJ: Lawrence Erlbaum Associates;

Web Site: National Center for Family Literacy (NCFL), http://www.famlit.org/ NCFL is the primary national organization for family literacy and provides basic information on family literacy, policy and research information, training and technical assistance, family literacy in the schools, and the Family Literacy Alliance. The Web site offers links to many other related Web resources.

Susan Benner

Family Systems Theory (FST)

Family Systems Theory (FST) describes principles of family functioning believed to be true for all families. It is one example of a larger **developmental systems theory** orientation that has been applied widely to the natural and social sciences. Simply put, systems theory studies the relationships of parts to wholes, parts to parts, and describes change therein. Thus, Family Systems Theory describes how various family members relate to each other and—importantly—to the whole, and describes the ways in which families accommodate change. Early childhood educators have long recognized the importance of understanding the family as the primary context for the child's development. Educators place high value on communicating with family members, particularly parents; and on fostering strong connections between home and school. Thus, early childhood education is strengthened by understanding family dynamics, and FST elucidates these dynamics.

When FST was first developed in the mid-twentieth century, "family" usually meant a mother, father, and their biological children living under the same roof. When educators examined the family, it was usually to identify the things parents—especially the mother—did to "cause" the child to behave in certain ways. Later, the field recognized that the direction of effect goes both ways: young children affect parents as much as parents affect children, and attention was directed toward these "bi-directional influences." FST became the next step in understanding families by describing the ways in which the entire family functioned. This is a critical perspective for the twenty-first century because families have become much more complex. Currently, the concept of "family" has changed to include blended families after divorce and remarriage, foster families, single-parent families, families parented by gay and lesbian couples, and homeless families. In addition, educators are teaching children of families from a vast number of cultural and religious contexts. The increasing complexity of families makes it even more important to understand how they work.

The following are six basic principles of Family Systems Theory, including their application to early childhood education:

1. **A family system is an organized whole and all parts of the whole—members of the family—are linked and interdependent.** Families have identifying traits (e.g., "Her family is very close-knit"). When something happens that affects one member of a family, the family as a whole changes and thus all family members are affected. The child cannot be understood outside the context of the family, so early childhood

educators benefit from learning as much as they can about the family structure and values of the children in their centers and classrooms.

2. **There are identifiable subsystems within the family.** Such as the parent subsystem, the sibling subsystem, or the grandparent subsystem. The young child may be a member of a number of subsystems. These subsystems also have implicit rules that govern their behavior. For example, in the early childhood setting, the sibling subsystem might be relied upon for children having trouble separating from their parents.
3. **There are boundaries around family subsystems and around the whole family, and there are rules that govern the behavior of the family and its subsystems.** These boundaries define how people interact and who is considered part of the family or subsystem. Boundaries can be strong and impermeable (e.g., "In our family the parents make the rules and the children follow them"), or weak and permeable (e.g., "In our family the older children and parents talk about family rules together"). Early childhood educators must be aware of where the boundaries are drawn; for example, the oldest sibling may have an important status within the sibling subsystem, or the grandparents may have ultimate authority. Obviously, boundaries and rules are very dependent on the cultural background of specific families.
4. **Patterns of interaction between individuals and between subsystems are circular rather than linear.** It is not useful to think about one member "causing" another member to behave in a certain way. Rather, individual members influence other members who, in turn, influence still others and the family as a whole. The family constantly changes in a spiral-like pattern. For the early childhood educator, for example, rather than blaming the father for being "too strict," it is more useful to think of the parent and child creating a system in which child behavior and father behavior influence each other which, in turn, influences the other family members and the whole.
5. **Family systems have features that maintain their stability or equilibrium, and when something happens to alter a pattern, the family tries to return to the previous stable state.** An example of this might be a family with a child identified with ADHD who requires a lot of attention. Intervention might cause the child's behavior to change and become more typical. But it may be easier to continue to think of the child as the designated "problem child" because things were more predictable that way for the parents, who had established ways of interacting with the child, and also for the child, who was accustomed to receiving a great deal of parental and family attention and resources.
6. **Families are always changing.** When something happens to one member, the entire family as a whole must also change, in addition to the individuals and various subsystems. This happens in obvious ways, such as when a new baby is born or adopted into the family or when a primary caregiver goes to work, but also in subtle and less visible ways, such as when a parent finishes a graduate program or an older sibling learns to drive. Early childhood educators must be aware of these changes because they change the place of the young child in the family and the ways in which family members relate to each other.

Many theorists have contributed to the development of Family Systems Theory, drawing upon philosophical traditions going back many centuries. It is a theory that is still changing. It is an especially well-known and useful perspective for therapists and developmental psychologists. Many credit Murray Bowen (1913–1990) with first describing FST as we know it today. Bowen, a psychiatrist, conducted a research project at the National Institute of Mental Health in the 1950s in which he examined families with a schizophrenic member longitudinally over a five-year period. He described the ways in which the family member with schizophrenia influenced other family members, and the ways in which changes in family functioning influenced the ill family member as well as other members. He explained this in a widely read book, *Family Therapy in Clinical Practice*, published in 1978. Esther Thelen was another contributor to systems theory as it relates to self and other, publishing a major work on the topic in 1989 in the *Minnesota Symposium on Child Psychology*. She was perhaps best known for applying and popularizing dynamic systems theory to the study of child development. Arnold Sameroff, a developmental theoretician and researcher, wrote about family systems in a chapter published in the first volume of the *Handbook of Child Psychology* in 1983. He is perhaps best known for explaining the impact of changes over time by describing "transactional analysis" as it relates to FST. And perhaps the most extensive contributions to our current understandings of FST (particularly as it impacts family therapy) comes from the work of Patricia and Salvador Minuchin, therapists who defined the basic principles of FST in numerous publications in psychology, beginning in the 1970s and continuing today.

Only recently has FST been applied in any detail to early childhood education. In January 2006, Linda Christian published an article in *Young Children*, the journal of the **National Association for the Education of Young Children** (NAEYC), describing some principles of FST and giving examples of how the principles can be applied to practice in the early childhood setting.

Very few cross-cultural examinations of FST have been conducted, and therefore the claim that its principles apply to all families has not been demonstrated. Yet the principles are general and common to all systems, and thus are assumed to have ecological validity. In addition, FST has been criticized for describing *what* goes on in families but not *how* change occurs; in other words, the theory lacks a way of showing mechanisms of family change. Clearly, studying the family is difficult and complex, and there will always be much to examine. Nevertheless, Family Systems Theory has added a great deal to our understanding of this critical context for the socialization and education of young children. *See also* Attention Deficit Disorder/Attention Deficit Hyperactivity Disorder; Families; Gay or Lesbian Parents, Children with; Parents and Parent Involvement.

Further Readings: Bowen, M. (1978). *Family therapy in clinical practice*. New York: Jason Aronson. Christian, L. G. (2006). *Understanding families: Applying family systems theory to early childhood practice. Young Children* 61, 12–20. Washington: NAEYC; Minuchin, Patricia (1985). Families and individual development: Provocations from the field of family therapy. *Child Development* 56, 289–302; Minuchin, Salvador (1974). *Families and family therapy*. Cambridge, MA: Harvard University Press; Parke, R. D., and R. Buriel (1998). Socialization in the family: Ethnic and ecological perspectives. In N. Eisenberg and W. Damon, eds., *Handbook of child psychology*. 5th ed. *Vol. 3: Social, emotional, and personality development*. New York: Wiley; Sameroff, A. J. (1983). Developmental systems: Contexts and evolution. In W. Kessen, ed., *Handbook of Child Psychology*. *Vol. 1: History, theory, and methods*. New York: Wiley; Thelen, E. (1989). Self-organization in developmental processes: Can systems approach work? In M. R. Gunnar and E. Thelen, eds., *Systems and development. The Minnesota Symposia on Child Psychology*. Vol. 22. Hillsdale, NJ: Erlbaum, pp. 77–117.

Martha Pott

FAS. *See* Fetal Alcohol Syndrome

Fathers

Thirty years ago, fathers were called "the forgotten contributors to child development" (Lamb, 1975). No longer forgotten, fathers today are acknowledged as competent caregivers who can play a unique role in their children's development. In the mid-twentieth century, psychoanalytic theories of child development were popular, and forwarded a view that fathers were not central to a child's development during the first years of a child's life. The father's role, it was believed, was at first indirect, in supporting mothers as primary caregivers. In the United States, fewer mothers than today were employed outside the home in the paid workforce, and were more often at-home primary caregivers. Later, beyond infancy, the father's role was seen as more direct, in encouraging children to separate from their mothers, and to develop independence. Today, we recognize that infants and their fathers form special relationships from birth. Research has shown that infants develop **attachments** to their fathers from the beginning of life, and that many men are involved in the lives of their young children in many ways.

Positive fathering behaviors that include being both available and involved are associated with favorable development in children. Fathering characterized by warmth, clear communications, and high expectations for children is often linked with more positive development in children, at least in "mainstream" U.S. families. The beneficial effects of positive fathering have been demonstrated in areas such as children's academic achievement, empathy, self-esteem, self-control, well-being, life skills, and **social competence**. Positive fathering is not just the amount of time that fathers spend with their children; it involves warmth and sensitivity, economic support, monitoring of children's activities, and the beliefs that fathers have about child development and fathering.

Fathers often are characterized as "playmates," spending a greater percent of their time with their children in **play** activities, compared with mothers. Father-child play is often physical, or "rough and tumble," especially during the early years. One feature of this kind of play is that there are "emotional highs and lows"; the play can bring shrieks of joy and laughter or, sometimes, tears. Fathers, then, may play a special role in the development of children's emotion regulation, since this kind of play provides opportunities for children to learn and practice skills or behaviors for coping with strong emotions (positive or negative). Paternal involvement in early childhood also is associated with empathy development, both in childhood and adulthood.

The development of children's social skills as successful participants in peer and other relationships beyond the family can also be affected by father involvement. Warm, face-to-face interactions can promote the acquisition of social skills necessary for peer relationships. Similar to the influence of a positive mother–child attachment, a positive father–child attachment can influence social adaptation. In general, children with secure attachments are more liked by others, exhibit higher levels of self-esteem, and have better social skills. When the father monitors his child's social relationships, as a mentor or guide, he is able to educate his child on appropriate social patterns and behaviors necessary for the promotion of peer relationships.

Fathers also seem to have a special role in children's **cognitive development.** Research shows that father involvement is associated with children's learning, cognitive achievement, and academic success in school. Children of involved fathers also are more likely to believe that they have some control over events, and may show greater verbal performance, perhaps in part due to high educational expectations when fathers are involved in children's school performance.

Becoming a father is a life-changing experience for men and contributes to a man's own development. Involved fathers have been shown to exhibit higher levels of self-esteem, self-confidence, and satisfaction, both personally and within their parental role. Men who are involved fathers also are more involved in their communities, making greater social connections. Father involvement also affects marital stability and satisfaction. The ways in which a man fathers are affected by other things in his life, including the relationship that he has with the mother of his child, his relationships with his own parents, especially his father, his employment, and other institutional supports and barriers to positive fathering.

While the average age of U.S. men at the birth of their first child has remained relatively stable in recent years (29.7 years), other trends in the changing demographics of the United States affect fathers and children. Rates of divorce and nonmarital births have risen substantially in recent decades. Subsequently, the number of children living without their fathers in residence has increased by some 14 million, from 10 million in 1960 to 24 million in 2005. Past research on nonresidential fathers shows that they have less influence over their children and child-rearing decisions, and that these fathers spend the majority of the time with their children engaging in leisure play activities. Father-headed single parent families also have steadily increased in the last half-century. The number of residential single fathers living with their children has increased from 393,000 in 1970 to 2.3 million in 2004, and men currently comprise 19 percent of single residential parents. Single-parent fathers face many of the same challenges that single-parent mothers do, and in general, prove to be as competent in the role of primary caregiver. As divorce rates have increased so has the rate of remarriage and stepfathering. Stepfathers face unique challenges, particularly with regard to establishing disciplining patterns. Stepfathers who do not have biological children tend to develop better relationships with their stepchildren; perhaps they have more time for involvement with their stepchildren. When a stepfather becomes a part of a new family system, biological fathers tend to reduce their involvement both socially and economically with their children.

Many children in the United States grow up without the stable, consistent involvement of their biological fathers. Recent surveys show that 40 percent of children with nonresidential, biological fathers have not seen their fathers in at least one year, and an estimated two-thirds of nonresidential fathers do not pay child support. The implications of this trend are substantial, as these children are more likely to experience **poverty,** perform poorly in school, engage in criminal activity, and abuse drugs and alcohol. Among men in state prisons, 55 percent are fathers of children under the age of 18. Recent studies have shown that nearly 3 percent of U.S. children (2.1 million nationwide) under the age of 18 have fathers who are incarcerated. The effects of having an incarcerated parent on children may include impaired parent-child bonding and socioemotional development, as well as reactive behaviors and an intergenerational cycle of crime and incarceration. Rates of incarcerated fathers vary across racial groups. Studies show that while 1.2 percent of non-Hispanic white children have a father who is incarcerated, 3.5 percent of Hispanic children, and 9.1 percent of non-Hispanic black children have an incarcerated father.

As we begin to recognize the complexity of paternal involvement, as well as recent changes in fathering trends, policies, and programs have been developed to support fathers' development and involvement in their children's lives. A host of programs at the federal, state, and local levels aim to support positive fathering. At the federal level, for example, the Bush Administration's Fatherhood Initiative, the Health and Human Services Department, and the Family and Youth Services Bureau have proposed programs to strengthen the role of the fathers, programs to assist noncustodial fathers become more involved in their children's lives, and programs that provide mentoring for children of prisoners. *See also* Development, Emotional; Development, Social; Incarcerated Parents, Children of; Peers and Friends.

Further Readings: Lamb, M. E. (1975). Fathers: Forgotten contributors to child development. *Human Development* 4, 245–266; Tamis-LeMonda, C. S., and N. Cabrera, eds. (2002). *Handbook of father involvement: Multidisciplinary perspectives*. Mahwah, NJ: Erlbaum; Palkovitz, R. (2002). *Involved fathering and men's adult development*. Mahwah, NJ: Erlbaum; Parke, R. D. (2002). Fathers and families. In M. H. Bornstein, ed., *Handbook of Parenting*. 2nd ed. Mahwah, NJ: Erlbaum, pp. 27–73.

M. Ann Easterbrooks and Cynthia R. Davis

Feminism in Early Childhood Education

Feminism is the worldwide struggle to end sexist oppression. Often misunderstood as a radical push to make women equal to men in our society (i.e., "women's lib"), feminism does not aim for social equity; rather, the emphasis is on ending sexist oppression for all women. Although in industrialized countries white middle-class women have made significant strides in gaining access to education and economy, most women throughout the world continue to suffer under male control. In the broadest sense, feminism is the political movement for global gender equality. It is one of the most powerful struggles for social justice in the modern world and is becoming more and more recognized and established within the educational community.

Across educational settings, sexist oppression is perhaps most visible in early childhood. The predominance of female teachers within this field is illustrative of the long-standing social belief that working with young children is women's work, and that women are instinctively good at teaching because they innately love children. Furthermore, it is widely held that women are by nature maternal beings and thus provide nurturing mother-images in classrooms; male teachers, on the other hand, provoke harsh, authoritative father-images. By juxtaposing females as maternal and soft against males who are abrasive and punishing, women are socially positioned as the weaker sex. A significant objective of feminist research in early childhood education is the deconstruction of this sexist definition of teaching. A great deal of current feminist work focuses on what being both a woman and a teacher of young children means within present-day United States society.

The work of Robin Leavitt (1994) is a hallmark example of feminist work in early childhood education. Leavitt challenges the "teacher = mother" notion, revealing sexist power structures that keep female teachers marginalized. She explains that, regardless of how instinctive or innate teaching and loving children may appear to be for women, the emotional investment that is required of teachers is not natural. Rather, she says, it is bought and sold labor:

> The emotional labor of the caregivers is complex, as they are expected to develop a sense of investment in each child that enables them to sustain caring throughout the day and over time, but also each day release children to their parents. In short, caregivers are expected to emotionally engage intensely, and disengage gracefully, and do both upon demand. (p. 61).

Feminism also challenges the gendered nature of that which is considered to be acceptable knowledge in early childhood education. Worth considerable note is that, despite the fact that approximately 98 percent of early childhood teachers are female, the predominant theories upon which most practices are based were generated by men. Friedrich **Froebel**, John **Dewey**, Lev **Vygotsky**, Jean **Piaget**, Sigmund **Freud** and Arnold **Gesell** are frequently referenced as sources for the field's knowledge base. While there are many females who have made a mark on early childhood education (e.g., Maria **Montessori,** Elizabeth **Peabody**, Patti Smith **Hill**, Constance Kamii, to name a few), the overall early childhood philosophy is dominated by male worldviews. This notion is underscored in the field's written history, such that **kindergarten** has a *father* (i.e., Froebel) but not a mother.

Feminist ideology challenges the structure of the traditional "malestream" approach to early childhood education (Coffey and Delamont, 2000) and suggests alternative classroom practices via inquiry into curriculum content and the establishment of classroom communities with democratic values—in other words, a feminist pedagogy. Feminist pedagogy is the political effort aimed at dismantling the masculine culture of power in education and building instead a society which benefits and values all students and all knowledge, not just that of males. In this approach to education, stereotypic female traits that keep women socially marginalized (e.g., care) are repositioned as strengths (e.g., an intellectual and moral relationship). Feminist teachers maintain an awareness of male privilege in education—and society in general—and work to develop an education appropriate for women. For instance, within this approach life histories and personal stories are recognized as valid ways of knowing. Within early childhood settings, feminist pedagogy is represented by supporting gender-free play zones, encouraging the boys, for example, to help take care of the babies in the dramatic play area and creating spaces that invite and support girls' efforts in the block corner. Some educators strategically move those two traditionally separate play spaces so that they are integrated, thereby discouraging easy gendered segregation of children's play activities and social relations.

A central challenge to the feminist movement in education, however, is the lack of any unified, consistent definition of, or theoretical approach to feminism; rather, there are "feminisms." Because of the broad and often misinterpreted conceptualization of feminism, teachers are discouraged from using the term as a form of personal or political identity. It is encouraged, instead, that teachers "advocate feminism" in their practice, noting that "the foundation of future feminist struggle must be solidly based on a recognition of the need to eradicate the underlying cultural basis and causes of sexism and other forms of group oppression" (hooks, 2000, p. 33). *See also* Gender and Gender Stereotyping in Early Childhood Education.

Further Readings: Belenky, M. F., B. M. Clinchy, N. R. Goldberger, and J. M. Tarule (1986). *Women's ways of knowing: The development of self, body, and mind*. New York: Basic Books; Brady, J. (1995). *Schooling young children: A feminist pedagogy for liberatory learning*. Albany, NY: SUNY Press; Coffey, A., and S. Delamont (2000). *Feminism and the classroom teacher*. London: Routledge Falmer; Gilligan, C. (1982). *In a different voice: Psychological theory and women's development*. Cambridge, MA: Harvard University Press; hooks, b. (2000). *Feminist theory: From margin to center*. Cambridge, MA: South End Press; Humm, M., ed. (1992). *Modern feminisms: Political, literary, cultural*. New York: Columbia University Press; Jipson, J. (1995). Teacher-mother: An imposition of identity. In J. Jipson, P. Munro, S. Victor, K.F. Jones, and G. Freed-Rowland, eds., *Repositioning feminism and education: Perspectives on educating for social change*. Westport, CT: Bergin & Garvey, pp. 20–35; Leavitt, R. (1994). *Power and emotion in infant-toddler day care*. Albany, NY: SUNY Press; Maher, F. (1999). Progressive education and feminist pedagogies: Issues in gender, power, and authority. *Teachers College Record* 10(1), 35–59; Noddings, N. (1984). *Caring*. Berkeley and Los Angeles: University of California Press; Weedon, C. (1997). *Feminist practice and poststructuralist theory*. 2nd ed. Oxford: Basil Blackwell; Weiler, K., ed. (2001). *Feminist engagements*. New York: Routledge.

Candra Thornton

Fetal Alcohol Syndrome (FAS)

Fetal alcohol syndrome (FAS) is one of the main threats to child health. FAS is a set of birth defects associated with prenatal alcohol exposure. This is distinguished from fetal alcohol effect (FAE), which is a less severe manifestation of the same symptoms of FAS. The pertinent questions become the etiology and the relationship between alcohol exposure during pregnancy and birth outcome. In 1968, a French article published by Dr. Paul Lemoine reported on a study of 127 children born to alcoholic parents. These children showed anomalies such as peculiar facial features, psychomotor disturbances, and a high frequency of malformations. Lemoine believed that the similarities between the children's features could help diagnose maternal alcoholism. However, it was not until five years later that the term "fetal alcohol syndrome" was coined; the credit was given to Dr. Kenneth Jones and Dr. David Smith discovering FAS since the French publication was not well known prior to the publication of their research in the United States (Armstrong, 2003).

There are four main criteria for medical diagnosis of FAS. The first of the criteria is confirmed maternal alcohol exposure. This is characterized by excessive intake of alcohol on a regular basis or episodically. Evidence of such actions can include frequent episodes of intoxication; legal problems related to drinking; development of tolerance or withdrawal from alcohol; social problems related to drinking; or alcohol-related medical problems such as hepatic disease. The second of the criteria is evidence of facial anomalies characteristic of FAS. This includes short palpebral fissures and facial anomalies in the premaxiallary zone such as flat upper lip, flattened philtrum, and flat midface. The newborn's nose may be short and upturned with a low and broad bridge. The ears may be large, low-set, and rotated posteriorly. Anomalies of the eyes may also be characteristic of FAS (e.g., ptosis, strabismus, microphthalmia, and epicanthic folds). Also, the upper and lower jawbones can be underdeveloped. The third of the criteria is evidence of growth retardation. These growth retardations includes at least one of the following: low birth weight for gestational age, disproportionately low weight for height, or decelerating weight over time that is not due to malnutrition. The final criterion is evidence of central nervous system neurodevelopmental abnormalities. This includes at least one of the following: decreased cranial size at birth, structural brain abnormalities, or neurological hard or soft signs (Armstrong, 2003).

It may not be possible to determine at-risk levels of alcohol consumption since there are other factors that affect pregnancy outcomes. Factors such as genetic susceptibility, pattern of exposure, time of embryo/fetal exposure, and type of alcohol can all affect the outcomes. Environmental and biological factors can work together to produce the effects of FAS on the newborn, which can start while in utero. In utero exposure to alcohol can produce fetal central nervous system depression, bone cell anomalies, as well as symptoms of fetal asphyxia such as decreased blood oxygen content and breathing activity; acidosis; and flattening of EEG activity. In some instances, the alcohol exposure can lead to death (Abel, 1984).

There are several risk factors that contribute to the occurrence of FAS. The pattern of alcohol consumption can affect FAS occurrence. Differences in the susceptibility to alcohol have been proposed for higher incidences of FAS. Poverty can be another major factor that contributes to FAS. Poverty can lead to adverse conditions such as poor maternal nutrition and health and increased stress (e.g., unemployment, martial instability, decreased access to prenatal care), which can interact with alcohol to produce negative pregnancy outcomes. Aside from environmental factors, biological factors such as cellular processing of alcohol can also increase risk in producing a child with FAS (Abel and Hannigan, 1996).

It has been estimated that 2,000–12,000 children are born with FAS every year in the United States. The Center for Disease Control and Prevention has identified rates ranging from nine cases per 10,000 births among whites to six cases per 10,000 births among blacks to 29.9 cases per 10,000 births among American Indians. The range varies because there is no biological marker to diagnose FAS.

Facial abnormalities, which are the most distinctive markers of FAS, may change with age, become less noticeable, and some may be harder to distinguish due to racial phenotypes (Armstrong, 2003).

Children, families, and educators can be challenged by the effects of FAS on behavioral, psychological, and cognitive processing due to abnormalities in the brain and central nervous system. Central nervous system problems can include hyperactivity, diminished intelligence (average IQ of 70, with a range from 45 to 110), learning disabilities, inappropriate social behaviors, delays in speech and language, impaired hearing, poor eating (leading to failure to thrive) and sleeping patterns, longer reaction time, and delayed developmental milestones. These various problems can be addressed through support systems in place by parents, medical professionals, and **early intervention**. Interventions can address environmental issues that may complicate matters such as organizing living environments to reduce clutter, which can relax the child. Building consistent daily routines for a child with FAS can also provide alleviations of behavioral problems. Careful, repetitive teaching of appropriate behaviors and clear, immediate rewards can also provide the child with FAS structure to learn appropriate social skills. In order to address learning issues, it may be necessary for parents to collaborate with educators to plan lessons and activities that utilize all the senses for learning (Morse and Weiner, 1996).

Prevention may need to take place on the level of the federal and state governments. The government may step in to regulate the availability of alcohol and educate the consumers of the dangers of drinking while pregnant. States may also need to take responsibility in informing the public of the dangers of drinking while pregnant. The first step to change in the United States came in 1988 in which alcoholic beverages were required to carry health-warning labels of the dangers of drinking while pregnant. Evaluation of the information and education campaigns must also take place to understand the impact of the campaigns of raising awareness of the possible dangers and whether the information had an impact on drinking practices during pregnancy.

Apart from educational campaigns, benefits can be observed from initiating counseling for pregnant women on the effects of alcohol use on the unborn child and the repercussions after the child is born. Dr. Henry L. Rosett initiated the first program of this type at Boston City Hospital in 1974. Women who attended the prenatal clinic were interviewed during their first visit to record diet, smoking, and alcohol/drug habits. Those classified as heavy drinkers were then encouraged to return to the clinic for counseling. The counseling approached the women to stress the positive side of abstaining or decreasing alcohol consumption rather than emphasizing the negative effects. As seen, it is necessary to focus prevention and intervention on the level of the family, environment, and community in order to improve recovery and abstinence (Rosett et al., 1978).

Legal issues arise in cases that surround the issue of FAS. One legal issue surrounds the idea of exposing the fetus to alcohol as a type of **child abuse and neglect**. The question arises around the issue of maternal rights in comparison to fetal rights. Questions also arise in the obligations of the obstetricians who treat pregnant patients with potential alcohol problems. Is an obstetrician obligated to advise pregnant women not to drink if he suspects alcoholism? Can the doctor be charged with negligence if he fails to warn his patient? During such difficult legal circumstances, the court may become arbiters in deciding the extent and quality of prenatal care.

Many children with FAS require **early intervention** and special education services. Children with FAS have various needs that must be met: learning disabilities, emotional problems, behavioral issues, or multiple conditions. Assessments may be needed in speech and language, occupational therapy, and cognitive functioning to measure a child's strengths and deficits. Children with the condition may have various educational issues such as hyperactivity, distractibility, poor memory, decreased cognitive abilities, and poor social skills. Up to the age of 3, early intervention services can be used by families of children with FAS. The staff works with the families to create an **Individualized Family Services Plan (IFSP)** to describe the child's needs and the services the child and family will receive in order to address those needs. Once a child becomes school-aged, educational staff works with families to develop an **Individualized Education Program (IEP)** to meet the individual needs of the child with FAS. The curriculum should include hands-on learning, multiple modes of learning, flexibility of scheduling, and consistency in teaching to promote sensory development and social and life skills development in addition to meeting academic goals agreed upon by the teacher and family.

Further Readings: Abel, E. L. (1984). *Fetal alcohol syndrome and fetal alcohol effects*. New York: Plenum Press; Abel, E. L., and J. H. Hannigan (1996). Risk factors and pathogenesis. In H. L. Spohr and H. C. Steinhausen, eds., *Alcohol, pregnancy and the developing child*. New York: Cambridge University Press, pp. 63–75; Armstrong, E. M. (2003). *Conceiving risk, bearing responsibility: Fetal alcohol syndrome & the diagnosis of moral disorder*. Baltimore: The Johns Hopkins University Press; Morse, B. A., and L. Weiner (1996). Rehabilitation approaches for fetal alcohol syndrome. In H. L. Spohr and H. C. Steinhausen, eds. *Alcohol, pregnancy and the developing child*. New York: Cambridge University Press, pp. 249–268; Rosett, H. L., E. M. Ouellette, L. Weiner, and E. Owens (1978). Therapy of heavy drinking during pregnancy. *Obstetrics and Gynecology* 51, 41–46.

Web Site: National Organization on Fetal Alcohol Syndrome (NOFAS), http://www.nofas.org/.

Sonia Susan Issac

Frank, Lawrence Kelso (1890–1968)

Over the years of a multifaceted career, Lawrence Kelso Frank sowed novel research ideas and brought these ideas to fruition by linking groups of professionals with funding. As lecturer, organizer, and disseminator of ideas, Frank escalated research in human development.

Lawrence Kelso Frank was born on December 6, 1890, in Cincinnati, Ohio. He received his bachelor's degree in economics from Columbia University in 1912 where he was strongly influenced by progressive educator John **Dewey.** As a student, Frank worked for the Bureau of Social Research in New York City, where he grew increasingly interested in human welfare. After graduation, he was a systems analyst for the New York Telephone Company, a position that brought him in contact with Wesley Clair Mitchell and his wife, Lucy Sprague **Mitchell**. Mrs. Mitchell, along with Caroline **Pratt** and Harriet Johnson, began the Bureau of Educational Experiments (BEE) in 1916, the aim of which was to bring various specialists and research together in an experimental educational environment. Frank himself believed that early investments of healthy social interactions at the nursery school level could prevent future interpersonal problems. He was impressed with the BEE and sent his own children to its City and Country School and served on its Working Council.

By 1920, Frank was business manager for the New School for Social Research and soon thereafter developed a vision for systematic research of children's developmental growth. In 1923, his dreams were realized when he was appointed associate director in charge of expending over $1,000,000 per year for the benefit of children through the Laura Spelman Rockefeller Memorial (LSRM). Under Frank's leadership, LSRM funds established the child study institute at Teachers College (1924), the child study center at the University of Minnesota (1925), and the Institute of Child Welfare at the University of California, Berkeley (1927). The existing Iowa Child Welfare Research Station, the Clinic of Child Development at Yale, and other research centers were also enhanced through the LSRM. Frank additionally gave funds to the Committee of Child Development in 1925, predecessor to the Society for Research in Child Development.

From 1931 to 1936, Frank was associate director for the General Education Board through which he supported research into the needs of the whole child. Frank believed that effective early childhood programs were founded upon the comprehensive needs of children and held tremendous potential to affect society for good. From 1936 to 1942, he was vice president of the Josiah Macy, Jr., Foundation, an agency devoted to general health research. Frank held posts during both world wars, serving on the War Industries Board of the Bureau of Planning and Statistics (1918–1919) and as Secretary of the Scientific Committee of the National Resources Planning Board and consultant to the Office of War Information in 1944.

A long-standing Progressive Education Association member, he directed the association's Caroline Zachry Institute of Human Development (1945–1950) and utilized General Education Board grants for continued study of personality development. Frank was coawarded the National Committee for Mental Hygiene's Lasker Award in 1947 for contributions to mental health and a 1950 *Parents Magazine* book award for his *How to Help Your Child in School*, coauthored with his third wife, Mary Frank. As a retiree, Frank lectured at several colleges, including the Massachusetts Institute of Technology, Merrill-Palmer, and Harvard. He served as a trustee for Wheelock College and **Bank Street College**, held numerous positions within thirteen professional associations, and authored several articles and books on the behavioral and social sciences. Frank died on September 23, 1968.

Further Readings: Lascarides, V. Celia and Blythe Hinitz (2000). *History of early childhood education*. New York: Falmer Press; *Who was who in America with world notables volume V 1969–1973*. Chicago, IL: Marquis Who's Who, Inc.; Weber, Evelyn (1984). *Ideas influencing early childhood education: A theoretical analysis*. New York: Teachers College Press.

Charlotte Anderson

Freud, Anna (1895–1982)

Anna Freud is considered to be the originator of child psychoanalysis. She was born in Vienna, the youngest of six children of Sigmund **Freud** and his wife Martha. Her mother left the children with a nanny and took a "vacation" of several months soon afterward. She had a lifetime bond with her father, who was developing his psychoanalytic theory about the basis of emotional problems.

Anna's only formal education was at Vienna's elite Cottage Lyceum, where she complained about being bored. After graduation in 1912, she visited her grandmother in Italy and became acquainted with Maria **Montessori**'s method. She taught elementary school children at the Lyceum until she developed tuberculosis in 1917. Her first experience with children from troubled homes came in 1920, when she volunteered at Vienna's Baumgarten Home for Jewish orphans.

An involvement with psychoanalysis began at age 14, when she read some of her father's books. He psychoanalyzed her from 1918 to 1922. After they attended the International Psychoanalytic Congress together in 1920, she became one of the first female members of that association. From 1927 to 1934, she was its general secretary. In 1923, when Sigmund Freud had the first operation for a malignant tumor on his jaw, she abandoned her plan to open a psychotherapy practice and devoted herself to translating and writing down his ideas. She also observed wartime effects on children and her "Introduction to the Technique of Child Analysis" was published in 1927.

Dorothy Burlingame, an American psychoanalyst who had moved to Vienna with her children, formed a lifelong relationship with her. In 1927, they organized a school utilizing the "project method" that was closed after the 1938 Nazi takeover of Austria. The Freud and Burlingame families moved to England, where Sigmund Freud died from his cancer in 1939. Anna and Dorothy became involved with programs for children who were without parents and published books and articles about children under stress. They established the Hampstead War Nursery, which soon became a training center. In 1947, this became the Anna Freud Centre, now recognized as a leading institution for studying psychotherapy.

Following World War II, Anna Freud traveled frequently to the United States and other countries. Her Yale Law School seminar series on crime and the family was published as "Beyond the Best Interests of the Child" in 1973. She received several honorary doctorates, the first at Clark University (1950) and the last at Harvard (1980).

By the 1950s, the therapeutic importance of young children's activities was incorporated into the developing preschool and **kindergarten** programs of the United States and other nations. At the painting easel, in the "housekeeping corner" or with building blocks, children could express their inner feelings. Teachers observed, interpreted, and sometimes facilitated their projects, but allowed freedom within defined boundaries. Wartime programs had demonstrated the advantages of having one nurturant adult with each small group of children, providing a theoretical basis for current staffing regulations. Parent education began to incorporate psychoanalytic principles, from the importance of breast-feeding to sex education. Even the role of fathers began to change to one of more nurturance and less corporal punishment. Many cities established child guidance clinics to help families resolve interpersonal relationships and developmental concerns. Psychoanalyic theory continues to be a controversial issue among psychologists, but the heritage of Anna Freud and her followers is such an integral part of early childhood education that its origins are rarely recognized. *See also* Preschool/Prekindergarten Programs.

Further Readings: Ekins, R., and R. Freeman (1998). *Anna Freud: Selected writings*. London: Penguin Books; Freud, A. (1967–1982). *The writings of Anna Freud*. 8 vols. Madison, CT: International University Press; Peters, U. H. (1985). *Anna Freud: A life dedicated to children*. London: Weidenfeld. Young-Bruehl, E. (1988). *Anna Freud: A biography*. New York: Summit.

Web Sites: Anna Freud Centre, www.annafreudcentre.org; Freud Museum, www.freud.org.uk/fmanna.htm.

Dorothy W. Hewes

Freud, Sigmund (1856–1939)

Arguably one of the most influential thinkers of the late nineteenth and twentieth centuries, Freud was an Austrian doctor and psychoanalyst who created a dynamic theory to explain biological and cultural influences on mental development and behavior. His work with patients suffering mental illness led him to consider the human roots of both normal and abnormal development, including the contributions of **families, culture,** gender, and **sexual abuse** to personality. According to Freudian theory, inborn biological drives (Freud's concept of the *id*, including hunger, social contact, sexuality) encounter society's limits to those drives.

Many of Freud's ideas have contemporary currency. For example, he believed that humans develop a *superego*, or conscience, to provide an internal representation of society's rules; Freud's is a seminal psychological view of moral development. The interplay of id and societal forces shapes our *ego*, or who we are as a person; Freud's interpretation of this process is an early version of self-concept. His dynamic view of personality argues that much of development is subconscious or unconscious. Childhood is the crucible where these dynamic forces emerge. A psychosocial theory from Freud's view points to early **attachment** and **play** as important for self-concept, and Freud's psychosexual theory provides connections between early development and both gender and sexual identity. While the main thrust of his work was directed to psychiatry and clinical psychology, the importance of childhood within Freud's school of thought created many opportunities for connections with early education.

In 1909 Freud gave a series of lectures at Clark University at the invitation of G. Stanley **Hall,** leader of the **Child Study Movement.** These lectures provided international legitimacy for Freud's ideas and introduced them to early leaders in child development and early education. His thinking can be seen directly in developmentally oriented early childhood programs that were emerging at that time, such as the **Bank Street** child-centered school (see also **Developmental-Interaction Approach**) and other programs that acknowledged the whole child, play-based pedagogy, and creativity as bases for early education. With connections established to child study, Freud's thinking has had continuous, if controversial, visibility within the developmental community that provides one knowledge base for early education.

Perhaps more important than Freud's direct influence on early childhood programs is the influence of his many followers. Scholars such as Erik **Erikson**, Anna **Freud**, Melanie Klein, Lili Peller, and Donald Winnicott have provided psychodynamic perspectives on children's development that have expanded conceptions of play as an avenue for expression and growth. Freud inspired others to think of play as an indicator of how each child constructs a unique life history, resolves problems, expresses feeling or affect, and helps us understand who we are as persons.

It is easy to forget how elements of Freud's thinking have become pervasive in contemporary culture (e.g., Freudian slips, ego trips, unconscious acts). His thinking also continues to guide academic studies in a variety of areas, such as attachment theory (see John **Bowlby**), feminist studies of object relations, postmodern studies on gender, life-span development, law, history, biography, motivation, and other fields of inquiry. Many consider Freud's ideas to be metaphysical and untestable, while others see in his work a way of understanding the complexities of children's early growth and learning. *See also* Psychosocial Theory; Gender and Gender Stereotyping in Early Childhood Education; Mental Health; Pedagogy, Activity-Based/Experiential; Pedagogy, Play-Based; Self-Esteem and Self-Concept.

Further Readings: Freud, S. (1949). *An outline of psychoanalysis*. New York: Norton; Freud, S. (1952). *On dreams*. New York: Norton; Freud, S. (1959). Beyond the pleasure principle. In J. Strachey, ed., *The standard edition of the complete psychological works of Sigmund Freud*. London: Insititute of Psychoanalysis; Frost, Joe L., Sue C. Wortham, and Stuart Reifel (2005). *Play and Child Development*. 2nd ed. Columbus, OH: Merrill/Prentice Hall; Gay, Peter (1988). *Freud: A life for our time*. New York: W.W. Norton.

Stuart Reifel

Friends. *See* Peers and Friends

Froebel, Friedrich (1782–1852)

Although recognized primarily as the "Father" of the **kindergarten**, Friedrich Froebel also helped change educational methods for all age levels around the world. In the early 1800s, it was assumed that school should begin at age 7, with male teachers who enforced rote memorization by strict discipline. By the end of the nineteenth century, women were accepted as classroom teachers, discipline was less punitive, and his ideas about active learning had been incorporated into kindergartens and upper grades.

Many of Froebel's innovations can be attributed to his own difficult childhood, described in detail by Bowen (1909), Downs (1978), and others. He was born in the Thuringian village of Oberweisbach, now in eastern Germany. His mother died when he was an infant, a stepmother rejected him, and his father was an overworked Lutheran minister. Because he was a "dreamer" with learning problems, Friedrich was placed in the local school for girls until age 10. After that, he lived with an uncle and attended classes with boys. At fifteen, he was a forester's apprentice for two years, where he developed an interest in nature and read scientific books.

Froebel briefly attended several universities to study philosophy and sciences. It was a period of radical ideas and social reform. At Jena, from newly translated Persian scriptures and crystallography, he redefined God to mean a spiritual element that holds everything in the universe together. In 1805, after being persuaded to teach at a Pestalozzian school in Frankfurt, he found his lifetime occupation. He said that it was like being a fish put back into water and he became determined to open his own school. He established his coeducational Universal German Educational Institution in 1816, following two years with Johann **Pestalozzi**. Its unique emphasis was upon "learning by doing" in cooperative groups, including gardening and handicrafts. Its philosophical goal was to integrate the inner spirit of students with the outer world.

When Froebel recognized that his students lacked preparation for a system of learning through doing when they entered at age 7, he began extensive correspondence and observations. Reading the long-forgotten writings of John Amos **Comenius** supported his concept of infant education with the assistance of their mothers and classrooms for those aged 3–7. When he was fifty-eight years old, despite the recent death of his wife and persistent financial problems, a kindergarten with a teacher training class and a mothers organization formally opened in Rudelstadt in 1840. It introduced the idea of "making the inner outer and the outer inner" by playful games and activities. The concept quickly spread, with his followers establishing similar schools in other locations. By 1848, 260 kindergarten supporters met at Rudelstadt to celebrate its success. However, Prussian officials became increasingly suspicious of his political affiliations. He was accused of being a pantheist and a socialist. They ordered all kindergartens closed in 1851, although most of those outside their state remained open. Support of other educators, originally negative because he supported female teachers and because he had difficulty in explaining his philosophy, had become positive. This was indicated by the standing ovation given when he entered a major European Educational Congress the following spring, but Froebel died "of a broken heart" two months later.

Although Froebel was a charismatic and persuasive speaker, he always found it difficult to express his thoughts in writing. He depended upon his wife, friends, and even former students to clarify his thoughts, but he traveled widely and maintained a prodigious output of letters, journals, and some major publications. His *Education of Man* (1826) was widely discussed throughout Europe, with its 1885 annotated translation by William **Hailmann** a major contributor to the movement in the United States that became known as **Progressive Education**. The activities of his 1844 picture book with an English title of *Mother-, Play- and Nursery Songs* are still chanted by mothers and integrated into preschool classes around the world.

At the time of his death, Froebel was still developing sequenced curriculum materials. Best known are the Gifts and Occupations, blocks and manipulative materials that were to be introduced in a logical progression from simple to complex as children became ready for them. Music was integrated into active games.

Children had garden plots and sand boxes. In these original kindergartens, individuality and creativity were encouraged by teachers who were facilitators, not disciplinarians. Mother volunteers were welcome, with teachers often addressed as "Auntie" to indicate their sisterhood.

Froebel's kindergartens, with their teacher training classes, continued after his death. He had married Luise Levin in 1851, a former pupil who successfully moved the training program to Keilhau. The Baroness Bertha von Marenholz-Bulow, a financial supporter since 1849, carried the message to England, France, and other nations until her own death in 1893. Some of his followers, particularly those who had participated in his training classes and had left Germany because of the political situation, maintained his philosophy and passed it on to their own students in the United States. They recognized that he had intended to continue modifying and improving upon his original ideas. However, there soon were varied interpretations of his methods. Manufacturers sold manuals describing rigid use of products that they attributed to Froebel. Some educators who professed to follow him had only a superficial understanding and interjected their own beliefs (Hewes, 2001, 2005).

In the United States, when the kindergartens became integrated into the public schools during the early 1900s, children under age 4 or 5 were no longer admitted. Patty Smith Hill and other Froebelians became concerned about younger children. Their 1926 Committee on Nursery Schools evolved into the **National Association for the Education of Young Children** (NAEYC), which maintains the basic kindergarten philosophy (see www.naeyc.org).

Interest in Froebel has recently revived. Brosterman (1997) described how modern art and architecture of the early 1900s derived from the Froebelian schooling of their creators. Rubin (2002) explained the relationship between Frank Lloyd Wright's architecture and Froebel's crystallography. Authentic Froebelian materials and reprints of early books are available from the Froebel Foundation (www.froebelfoundation.org). Archives and other references are in several European universities. In England, the Froebel College in Roehampton is also the location of an International Froebel Society organized in 2002 with plans for biennial conferences (www.froebelweb.org). American kindergarten archives include those of the **Association for Childhood Education International** (see www.acei.org) at the University of Maryland in College Park.

Further Readings: Bowen, H. Courthope (1909). *Froebel and education through self-activity*. New York: Charles Scribner's Sons; Brosterman, Norman (1997). *Inventing kindergarten*. New York: H. N. Abrams. Downs, Robert B. (1978). *Friedrich Froebel*. Boston: Twayne; Froebel, Friedrich (1826). *The education of man*. Translated by William Hailmann, 1885. New York: D. Appleton; Hewes, Dorothy W. (2001). *W. N. Hailmann: Defender of Froebel*. Grand Rapids, MI: Froebel Foundation; Hewes, Dorothy W. (2005). Maintaining the median. *Journal of Early Childhood Teacher Education*, 26/2(April–June); Rubin, Jeane (2002). *Intimate triangle: Architecture of crystals, Frank Lloyd Wright, and the Froebel kindergarten*. Huntsville, AL: Polycrystal.

Dorothy W. Hewes

FST. *See* Family Systems Theory

G

Gay or Lesbian Parents, Children with

A growing number of children are being brought up by one or more gay or lesbian parents in one of a variety of family constellations. Accurate statistics regarding the number of children who have one or two parents who are gay or lesbian are impossible to obtain. The secrecy required as a result of the stigma still associated with homosexuality has hampered even basic epidemiological research. The best guess is that there are at least one million children in the United States who have at least one parent who is gay or lesbian. Many of these children are participating in early care and educational programs; in some cases, teachers are unaware of the children's family circumstances.

Most children now living with parents who are lesbian or gay were conceived in the context of a heterosexual relationship. Increasing social acceptance of diversity in sexual orientation has encouraged more gay men and lesbian women to "come out" prior to forming intimate relationships or becoming parents. The majority of lesbian women who conceive a child do so using alternative insemination techniques with sperm donated by an anonymous donor who has agreed to be identifiable when the child becomes an adult, or a fully-known donor (e.g., a friend or relative). Lesbian women and gay men can become parents as well by fostering or adopting children. Growing numbers of gay men have chosen to become fathers through the assistance of a surrogate mother who bears their child. Others have made agreements to share parenting responsibilities with a single woman or a lesbian couple.

Most research regarding children with gay or lesbian parents has focused on parental attitudes and behaviors; and children's psychosexual development (and sexual orientation), social and interpersonal experience, and psychological/emotional status.

Research on Parental Attitudes, Personality, and Adjustment

Research suggests that the parenting styles and attitudes of gay and heterosexual fathers are more similar than they are different. Fathers in each group endorse a similar active, caretaking stance regarding their paternal role. Several studies have described fathers' encouragement of gender-appropriate toys, their attempts to provide a female role model for their children, and their children's generally accepting reactions to knowledge of their father's homosexuality. Gay fathers have been described repeatedly as nurturing and as having positive relationships with their children.

Lesbian and heterosexual mothers also describe themselves similarly in terms of maternal interests, current lifestyles, child-rearing practices, role conflicts, social support networks, and coping strategies. Few differences have been found over two decades of research comparing lesbian and heterosexual mothers' self-esteem, psychological adjustment, and attitudes toward child rearing. Lesbian mothers fall within the range of normal psychological functioning based on interviews and psychological assessments and report scores on standardized measures of self-esteem, anxiety, depression, and parenting stress indistinguishable from those reported by heterosexual mothers. Based on such assessments, lesbian mothers are at no greater risk for psychiatric disturbance than are heterosexual mothers.

Lesbian mothers typically endorse child-centered attitudes and commitment to their maternal roles. Lesbian mothers report making more efforts than do divorced heterosexual mothers to provide male role models for their children, and encourage their children to see their fathers more frequently after divorce than do heterosexual mothers. Lesbian mothers have also been reported to have greater knowledge of child development and more successful parenting skills, as a group, than heterosexual mothers. Lesbian partners appear to share child-care tasks more equitably than do typical heterosexual couples, and both partners are more equally involved with discipline and with their children's day-to-day activities.

Research on Children's Gender Identity and Sexual Orientation

Both environmental and genetic mechanisms might result in an increased likelihood for children who have a lesbian or gay parent to develop a homosexual orientation. Much attention has been paid to the play, playmate, and activity preferences of preadolescent children. These studies have failed to identify any differences in children's gender identification, playmates, toys, and activities based on the sexual orientation of their parents.

Only a few studies include *adults* whose parents were gay or lesbian, and the data are ambiguous. In one study of adult daughters of divorced mothers, no differences were found in gender identity, social roles, or sexual orientation based on the sexual orientation of the mother. In the most extensive study of the adult sexual orientation of the sons of gay fathers, 9 percent were bisexual or homosexual. A longitudinal follow up of adult men and women who had been raised as children in families with a lesbian mother as well as men and women who had been raised by a single heterosexual mother, found that although the former were more likely to consider the possibility of having a same-sex partner and to have been involved in at least a brief relationship with someone of the same gender, similar proportions of both groups reported feelings of attraction toward someone of the same gender or identified themselves as gay or lesbian (Tasker and Golombok, 1997).

Children's Emotional and Social Development

Children's experience in households with gay and lesbian parents varies widely, based on the origin of the parenting relationship, whether they have experienced divorce, and the subsequent partnership experience of both parents. Some children are being raised by a single parent, some by two separated parents, others by a couple, and still others by three or four adults in a newly-imagined coparent arrangement (e.g., a lesbian couple and one or two sperm donors). This diversity in family arrangements is helping to elucidate the requirements of successful parenting, but makes systematic research difficult.

Nine studies published between 1981 and 1994 compared 260 children from the ages of 3 to 11 who were living with a lesbian or gay parent after divorce, and compared them to children who lived with a heterosexual parent after divorce. These studies included reports from parents, teachers, and children themselves. They concurred in finding no meaningful differences between the groups in academic achievement, self-esteem, peer relationships, social adjustment, emotional problems, or psychiatric symptoms. Neither the subsequent partnership status of the divorced mothers nor the quality of the relationship between these mothers and their former spouses was included in the research.

One longitudinal study assessed twenty-five young adults (seventeen to twenty-five years old) who were raised by a divorced lesbian mother with twenty-one young adults who had been raised by a divorced heterosexual mother, and similarly found few differences among them in psychological or social adjustment or in family relationships (Tasker and Golombok, 1997). The young adults with a lesbian mother were no more likely to report anxiety or depression than their peers whose mothers were heterosexual, and scores on standardized inventories of psychological functioning in both groups were well within the normal range. Extensive interviews revealed that their memories of having been teased during childhood were little different from those experienced by children raised by single heterosexual mothers, and intrafamily relationships were rated as equally good.

Seven studies published from 1987 to 2003 included 208 children between the ages of 2 and 11 with lesbian mothers and 218 children with heterosexual parents. Once again, no differences were found based on the sexual orientation of the mothers in children's cognitive functioning, self esteem, behavior, peer relationships, social adjustment, emotional symptoms, psychiatric diagnoses, or relationships with grandparents (Golombok, Tasker, and Murray, 1997; Tasker, 1999; Vanfraussen et al., 2003). Some studies report that children of heterosexual parents saw themselves as being somewhat more aggressive than did children of lesbians; and parents and teachers reported them to be more bossy, negative, and domineering. Children of lesbian parents more often saw themselves as lovable and were reported by both parents and teachers to be more affectionate, responsive, and protective of younger children (Steckel, 1987; Patterson 1994; 1996; 1997).

Since all parents studied were women, the possible effects of gender cannot be separated from those of sexual orientation. Children whose parents reported greater relationship satisfaction, more egalitarian division of household and paid labor, and more regular contacts with grandparents and other relatives, were rated to be better adjusted and to have fewer behavioral problems by both parents and teachers (Chan, Raboy, and Patterson, 1998; Patterson et al., 1995, 1998).

Most of these studies report on volunteers, generally parents who are Caucasian, relatively well educated and middle class, and live in urban areas. Because the findings in many separate reports are very similar they have been presumed to reflect a more generalizable pattern. Two recent studies used community-based random samples of parents to investigate the well-being of children whose mothers were lesbian, thus strengthening the findings of smaller investigations. The importance of these two studies is that the research was planned and carried out without the intent to investigate same-sex parents. In both cases the investigations regarding same-sex (in both case lesbian) parents and their children were post-hoc analyses and thus neither the sample nor the methods were influenced by any possible bias.

Among a national sample of 12,000 adolescents in the United States, the forty-four who reported living with two women in a "marriage-like" family arrangement were found to be similar to peers whose parents were heterosexual in measures of self esteem, depression, anxiety, school functioning, school "connectedness," and the presence of school difficulties. Overall, these adolescents reported positive family relationships, including parental warmth, care from others, personal autonomy, and neighborhood integration, and there were no systematic differences between the same-sex and the opposite-sex parent families. There was no difference between the two groups in the proportion of adolescents who reported having had sexual intercourse, nor in the number who reported having a "romantic relationship" within the past eighteen months (Wainright, Russell, and Patterson, 2004).

Another study reported data from a cohort study that enrolled all children born within a particular county in England during one year (14,000), comparing the well-being of the 39 7-year-old children whose parents self-identified as lesbian to the well-being of peers whose parents were heterosexual. No differences were found in maternal warmth, emotional involvement, enjoyment of motherhood, frequency of conflicts, supervision of the child, abnormal behaviors of the child reported by parents or teachers, children's self esteem, or psychiatric disorders. On the other hand there were significant differences in warmth, parenting quality and enjoyment, emotional involvement, imaginative play activities, severity of conflicts, supervision of the child, maternal stress, and abnormal child behaviors reported by teachers—all favoring two-parent families (lesbian *or* heterosexual) over single parent families (Golombok et al., 2003).

Summary

Lesbian and gay parents appear to have parenting styles and quality of relationships with their children similar to those of heterosexual parents. A large and growing professional literature demonstrates that parental sexual orientation has no measurable effect on children's mental health or social adjustment. Children whose parents are lesbian have been reported to be affectionate, nurturing toward younger children, and accepting of diversity.

These changing family constellations suggest numerous implications for early childhood educators. It is important to emphasize that considerable diversity exists among the population of children whose parents are not heterosexual. The life of a child who lives alone with her divorced gay father is surely different from that of a child born to a well-functioning lesbian couple, and different as well from one who lives with his divorced lesbian mother and lesbian stepmother. The roles of the sperm donor or surrogate mother, and the child's gender, are likely also to affect family relationships and life experience. Teachers should ensure that the diversity in family constellations present in their classrooms and schools is discussed and valued. School libraries should include books for children of all ages about families with gay or lesbian parents.

Further Readings: Benkov, L. (1994). *Reinventing the family*. New York: Crown Publishers; Chan, R., B. Raboy, and C. Patterson (1998). Psychosocial adjustment among children conceived via donor insemination by lesbian and heterosexual mothers. *Child Development* 69(2), 443–457; Flaks, D., I. Ficher, F. Masterpasqua, and G. Joseph (1995). Lesbians choosing motherhood: A comparative study of lesbian and heterosexual parents and their children. *Developmental Psychology* 31(1), 105–114; Gartrell, N., A. Banks, N. Reed, J. Hamilton, C. Rodas, and A. Deck (2000). The national lesbian family study, 3. Interviews with mothers of five-year-olds. *American Journal of Orthopsychiatry* 70(4), 542–548; Golombok, S., F. Tasker, and C. Murray (1997). Children raised in fatherless families from infancy: Family relationships and the socioemotional development of children of lesbian and single heterosexual mothers. *Journal of Child Psychology/Psychiatry* 38(7); Golombok, S., B. Perry, A. Burston, C. Murray, J. Mooney-Somers, M. Stevens, and J. Golding (2003). Children with lesbian parents: A community study. *Developmental Psychology* 39(1), 20–33; Patterson, C. J. (1992). Children of lesbian and gay parents. *Child Development* 63, 1025–1042; Perrin E. C. (2002). *Sexual orientation in child and adolescent health care*. New York: Kluwer/Plenum Publisher; Tasker, F., and S. Golombok (1997). *Growing up in a lesbian family: Effects on child development*. New York: Guilford; Tasker, F. (2005). Lesbian mothers, gay fathers, and their children. *Journal of Developmental and Behavioral Pediatrics*, 26, 224–240; Wainright J., S. Russell, and C. Patterson (2004). Psychosocial adjustment, school outcomes, and romantic relationships of adolescents with same-sex parents. *Child Development* 75(6), 1886–1898.

Ellen C. Perrin

Gender and Gender Stereotyping

Background

Gender issues in U.S. early childhood education began to be addressed in the early 1970s largely in concert with the rise of the third phase of the Women's Movement. At that time, the focus was on freeing girls from gender stereotyping perceived as limiting their physical, cognitive, and social/emotional development.

Early research carefully differentiated gender identity—that is, the self-awareness and acceptance of being male or female—from gender roles—that is, the acceptance and adoption of socially defined behaviors and attitudes associated with being male or female. We now know that gender identity develops very early. By age 2 children know if they are a girl or a boy. Gender roles also begin to develop very early. Most children enter preschool with well-defined knowledge of whether they are a girl or a boy, and also which toys and play activities are considered suitable for their sex.

Studies conducted in the 1970s and 1980s pointed to the ways that nature and nurture intersect to create very different socialization experiences for girls and boys. Some studies documented the different reactions and behaviors of parents based on the sex of their child. In one study (Fagot, 1978), parents were shown an infant dressed first in girl's clothing and then in boy's clothing and their initial reactions were recorded. The "girl" baby was described as tiny, delicate, precious. The "boy" baby was a bruiser, big, a future football player. In fact, there was only one infant involved in this study, alternately dressed in different clothing. Another study (Bridges, 1993) analyzed baby congratulation cards to document the role that societal expectations play in gender stereotyping from the moment of birth (or before). Greeting cards to welcome the birth of a child conveyed their messages through color-coding—pink for girls, blue for boys; boy cards showed boys (usually older than an infant) engaged with balls, sports equipment, vehicles and other objects suggesting action. Illustrations on girl cards typically showed girls immobile in cribs or baskets surrounded by rattles, flowers, and mobiles. The written messages were as stereotyped as the illustrations. Boys could be anything, girls were forever small, precious, little girls, and inactive. Unfortunately, the same study could have been conducted in the twenty-first century with very similar results.

Researchers in the 1970s also examined the effects of gender differentiated teacher interactions with girls and boys, and the role that toy preferences play in the development of cognitive, physical, and social/emotional skills. Some wrote about the importance of appropriate teacher intervention to ensure that girls and boys engage with variety of toys and activities to help them develop a broad range of skills. Others demonstrated the teacher's crucial role in helping girls move beyond typical play patterns to enter spaces such as the block area that had been almost exclusively the realm of boys. Also in the 1970s, the Non-Sexist Child Development Project was turning research into practice by providing staff development, parent workshops, and curriculum to help the adults who work with children and to free children, both girls and boys, from the limits imposed by rigid sex-role expectations (Sprung, 1975).

The purpose of the large body of early gender identity and gender-role literature was to first document the ramifications of stereotyped play in terms of children's development, and then help teachers and parents understand how the perpetuation of rigid roles limited the potential development of both girls and boys. In a review of the research on the gender divided learning attributes (Greenberg, 1985), honed in the home and preschool, that girls and boys bring with them as they enter kindergarten, there were several findings of significance. For girls these include verbal, small motor acuity, nurturance, social ability, and impulse control; for boys the attributes include spatial ability, large motor skills, inventiveness, self-worth. These attributes follow closely the sex differences described by Eleanor

Maccoby and Carol Jacklin in their 1974 landmark book *The Psychology of Sex Differences*.

Awareness Made a Difference

The research studies, the work with teachers and parents, research reports in professional journals, articles in the popular press, and the passage in 1972 of Title IX (the federal legislation barring sex discrimination in programs receiving Federal funding) all converged to bring about changes in early childhood education regarding gender roles and gender stereotyping. For the most part, attention focused on freeing girls from the limits of sex-role stereotyping. Parents were encouraged to dress girls in pants that allowed them to run and climb freely and to get dirty with abandon instead of worrying about messing their dresses or scraping their knees. Teachers made a concerted effort to enlarge the scope of girl's activities, encouraging block building and other large motor games that built physical strength. Researchers helped teachers understand the ways in which their unconscious interactions with girls and boys helped to perpetuate sex-roles. Classroom videotapes and observations documented that teachers called on boys more often than girls, praised boys' strengths and accomplishments, and complimented girls on their appearance and clothes.

Other factors highlighted the damaging effects of sex-role stereotyping on girls. Books and articles urged parents to encourage their daughters to break out of sex-typed play. Sexist language became an issue, and guidelines for gender neutral terms were issued by most educational publishers, for example, fireman became firefighter, repair man became repair person, the generic *he* was avoided by using the plural *they* or, if necessary, he and she. Pressure from activists groups of parents and educators convinced toy manufacturers to reduce stereotyping in their packaging. As a result, toy boxes began to show both boys and girls, and girls were no longer relegated to the background watching the boy use the toy.

In the movement to free girls from sex-role stereotyping, some early childhood educators and parents also looked at how rigid roles limited boys' potential. Efforts were made to help boys develop and express a full range of emotions and their nurturing side. The Non-Sexist Child Development Project, a national effort to reduce sex-role stereotyping beginning in early childhood, worked with teachers and parents to free *both* boys and girls from the limitations imposed by rigid role divisions. "Free to Be You and Me," books, records, and videotapes gave teachers and parents enjoyable tools to work with. Publishers of children's trade books came out with many books that showed boys and girls and men and women in a variety of nonstereotyped roles. The more open view of what children could be was apparent at the annual conferences of the National Association for the Education of Young Children. The exhibit hall displayed early childhood materials and toys that were nonsexist, multicultural, and even began to be inclusive of children with disabilities.

Backsliding

As in all movements, a period of real progress is followed by a plateau or backsliding, and this happened in the efforts to free children from gender-stereotyped roles. Starting in the mid-1980s and into the 1990s war toys and cartoon-type action figures geared to boys became resurgent and even LEGO became color-coded, with pink and lavender sets for girls and primary color sets for boys. Violence in society and depicted in television shows, in cartoons, and in movies seemed ubiquitous. Critics put forth that boys were being feminized and more conservative attitudes began to emerge. Of course, not all gains were lost, and girls continued to close the gap in areas where they had not been expected to achieve, for example, sports, mathematics and science. For boys, however, the backsliding led to gender problems that urgently needed to be addressed.

Emerging Gender Issues

Beginning in the late 1990s books such as *Real Boys: Rescuing Our Sons from the Myths of Masculinity* (Pollack, 1998); *Raising Cain: Protecting the Emotional Life of Boys* (Kindlon and Thompson, 1999); and *Bad Boys: Public Schools in the Making of Black Masculinity* (Ferguson, 2000) began to appear that illuminated concerns about boy's social/emotional development and school performance. The research showed that on both levels boys were not faring well. Boys lag behind girls in reading and writing; are more likely to be referred to a school psychologist; are more likely to be diagnosed with **Attention Deficit Disorder/Attention Deficit Hyperactivity Disorder**; represent 70 percent of students with learning disabilities and 80 percent of those with social/emotional disturbances; represent 70 percent of school suspensions, particularly minority males in urban schools; and commit 85 percent of the school violence and comprise the majority of victims of that violence.

Research shows that boys are especially vulnerable during their first ten years with respect to social/emotional development and academic achievement, particularly in the area of **literacy**. Many of the statistics cited above have been prevalent in schools for many years, but until recently little attention was paid. Teachers and parents alike seemed to assume that boys were okay.

The academic and social well-being of boys, however, is becoming a key gender issue. The literature has just begun to examine the difficulty schools face in adequately supporting the developmental needs of many boys. Since boys' problems emerge in the primary grades, it is imperative that early childhood educators become aware of the issues and develop strategies to address them. This does not mean that attention should turn away from girls; it means that educators must look at gender issues in the preschool years in terms of *all* children.

Addressing teasing and *bullying* behavior in the early childhood years became another emerging issue in the1990s, with gender-related implications. Educational Equity Concepts and the Wellesley College Centers for Research on Women conducted a study in grades K–3 in New York City and Framingham, Massachusetts, to determine the extent and the nature of this behavior. Methods included classroom observations throughout the school day, one-on-one interviews with children, and focus groups with teachers and parents. Findings, which agreed with those of other researchers, showed that boys initiated incidents three times as often as girls, that girls and boys were equal recipients, and that adults did not intervene in over 70 percent of observed incidents. Children were well aware of the fact that teachers usually did nothing to stop the teasing. In interviews they remarked, "Boys usually chase girls because that's what boys do—boys chase" "Teachers don't do anything." "Kids won't stop until the teacher makes them." The gender message in children's reactions is subtle. If adults don't intervene, boys learn that it's okay to behave in ways that upset others, and girls learn that they have to put up with this behavior and usually won't be helped by adults.

Based on a growing body of research on the harmful effects of teasing and bullying, and the fact that it is a pervasive problem in schools nationally and internationally, many programs have been developed to address the need for school wide intervention. At the early childhood level, the Quit it! Model, Don't Laugh at Me, the Bullying Prevention Model, and the Second Step Model all take a school-wide approach that involves all the adults who work with children (see Web sites).

Conclusion

Understanding the role of gender in early childhood education has come a long way—and there is an even longer road ahead. The learning gap for girls has significantly narrowed and their options and opportunities, despite some backsliding, have been greatly enhanced. Gender issues regarding the development of young boys need to be addressed much more directly than in the past, and attention must be paid in preschool.

The early childhood classroom is the place where all the building blocks for later learning are put in place, which presents a challenge and opportunity for curriculum and a learning environment that addresses the individual needs of boys and girls and is free from teasing and bullying behavior.

To meet the challenge, more attention needs to be paid to gender issues in teacher education, both at the preservice and inservice level. Research on gender issues in child development needs to be continuous, and teachers need be exposed to research findings and practical applications. At the present time, there is a push to make early childhood education more academic as a way to make children more "ready" for primary school. If their early childhood teachers create a learning community that meets the physical, cognitive, and social/emotional needs of each child and frees him or her from the limits of gender stereotyping, children will truly be "ready" for the challenges ahead.

Further Readings: Bridges, S. B. (1993). Pink or blue: Gender stereotyped perceptions of infants as conveyed by birth congratulations cards. *Psychology of Women Quarterly* 17, 193–205; Fagot, B. (1978). The influence of sex of child on parental reactions to toddler children. *Child Development* 49, 459–465; Greenberg, S. (1985). Educational equity in early childhood environments. In S. Klein, ed., *Handbook for achieving sex equity through education*. Baltimore, MD: Johns Hopkins University Press; Honig, A. (1983). Research in review: Sex role socialization in young children. *Young Children*. Washington, DC: National Association for the Education of Young Children; Koch, J., and B. Irby, eds. (2002). *Defining and redefining gender equity in education*. Greenwich, CT: Infoage Publishing; Maccoby, E. Eleanor and C. Jacklin (1974). *The psychology of sex differences*. Stanford, CA: Stanford University Press; Sprung, B. (1975). *Non-sexist education for young children: A practical guide*. New York: Citation Press (Scholastic).

Web Sites: Bullying Prevention Program: www.wcwonline.org/bullying; Operation Respect: Don't Laugh at Me, info@operation respect.org; Quit it! School-Wide Model, www.edequity.org; Second Step: Cfc.org/program.

Barbara Sprung

Gesell, Arnold (1880–1961)

Arnold Gesell was a pioneer in the child study movement, best known for his belief in the genetic blueprint that he called "maturation." Gesell was born in 1880 in Alma, Wisconsin, and studied psychology at Clark University in Worchester, Massachusetts, where he received his doctorate in 1906. While attending college, Gesell was influenced by the work of one of his professors, G. Stanley **Hall**, who was one of the first psychologists to study child development. After graduation, Gesell was invited to teach at the State Normal School in Los Angeles, California. There he met and married a child psychology professor, Beatrice Chandler. In the summer of 1909, Gesell and his wife spent time at the Pennsylvania Training School for Feeble Minded Children. While working with these "backward" children, he became aware of a need to better understand normal development. In 1911, Gesell went to Yale as head of the Yale Clinic of Child Development. It was during this period of his life that he became convinced that medical training was critical to his study of young children. Gesell completed a medical degree at Yale in 1915.

Gesell began his work by studying retarded development in children, but soon concluded that it was first necessary to understand normal development. Gesell used novel methods for studying young children, including recording children on movie film while using controlled environments and specific stimuli. Using the technique of filming through a one-way mirror, Gesell amassed data on over 12,000 children. From this information, he concluded that children go through specific and ordered stages in their development. His research eventually led to the creation of a set of behavioral norms for infant development. Gesell charted behavior in the areas of motor development, language, adaptive behavior, and personal habits.

Gesell believed that development of the child begins at conception, and that development is under the control of basic biological systems, or a genetic blueprint that Gesell called "maturation." The rate of this development may vary but the development itself unfolds in a set sequence. Environment and socialization have some effect over development, but it is the maturational process that takes primacy. Gesell felt that each child was unique and that teaching should be child centered to reflect these differences. He also believed that there were optimal times when a specific learning was most effective: when the child was "ready to learn." Teaching should take place within this optimal period that is directed by the child's maturational schedule. A failure on the part of the teacher or caregiver to correctly interpret the "readiness" of the child could lead to wasted effort on the part of the teacher, and also lead to unjustified punishment.

Gesell's concept of **readiness** for learning has come under attack on many occasions. Some theorists feel that the environment and the activities that a child is exposed to can lead development into new areas and it is this interaction that spurs on the development. Gesell would argue that it is a waste of time to pursue new challenges in development before the child is ready, that new learning could not proceed without the maturity necessary to further that development. Frustration in learning is caused by children being exposed to new ideas before they are ready. Instead, children should be given "the gift of time" and allowed to wait until they are mature enough to be ready to learn. Many public school systems are presently basing their entry to school on Gesell's behavior norms and maturational theory.

Gesell's most noted work centered upon establishing "norms" for typical development in children. These norms were used to educate parents and caregivers of young children and help them become more aware of typical behaviors in children. His work also guided the development of supportive programs for young children. Gesell died in 1961, after publishing over 400 items, including books, articles, monographs, and films.

Further Readings: Gesell, A. (1930). *The guidance of mental growth in infant and child*. New York: Macmillan; Gesell, A. (1940). *The first five years of life: A guide to the study of the preschool child*. New York: Harper & Brothers; Peltzman, B. R. (1998). *Pioneers of early childhood education: A bio-bibliographic guide*. Westport, CT: Greenwood Press; Pitcher, E. G. (1975). *Guidance nursery school: A Gesell Institute book for teachers and parents*. New York: Harper & Row.

Martha Latorre

Gifted and Talented Children

Recognizing the gifted and talented children in the United States has long been an ill-defined process. Lewis Terman (1916) was one of the first researchers to identify children of superior intellectual ability. According to Terman's study, students were recognized as gifted if they exhibited functioning at or above an **Intelligence Quotient** (IQ) of 140 and they were superior to others in physique, health, science, morality, and adjustment factors (Reid and McGuire, 1995). Whereas Terman's definition is extremely focused, others interpret giftedness more broadly as a "general ability . . . a multidimensional construct that includes both potential and performance" (Harrison, 2004, p. 78). Nonetheless, Terman's definition of a gifted and talented student has remained the widely accepted picture of a superior child. Because of the definition's emphasis on the physical characteristics of a person, individuals with disabilities, including emotional and behavioral, have often been overlooked for possessing gifted traits (Reid and McGuire, 1995).

In the United States, twenty-five states have legislation that defines who is gifted and talented, twenty-one states have mandated that the state board of education define the gifted and talented education, and in four states, no legislative body has defined the population. The lack of clarity surrounding the definition of giftedness, combined with a nonuniversal view of this subject, has resulted in the lack of comprehensive data pertaining to this group of students. Educational responses to the complex social, emotional, and academic needs of gifted children are as uncertain and controversial as the definition. Many parents and teachers complain that basic prescribed curriculum and instruction is not challenging for gifted learners.

Programs for children who are identified as gifted range from achievement classes, enrichment and acceleration programs, grade skipping, or "services beyond the basic programs provided by schools" (Bathon, 2004). Acceleration refers to "raising the level and/or pace of instruction to be commensurate with students' achievement levels and capacity or rate of learning" and "[e]nrichment . . . refers to qualitatively different sorts of programs and effects on achievement" (Feldhusen, 1991, p. 133). Acceleration programs can be traced to the early twentieth-century American system of the tracking hierarchy, which separated children who exhibited a much greater capacity for learning and creative expression from others in a typical classroom. This practice often involved removing gifted and talented children from the classroom at a prescribed time during the week and allowing them to use different resources from the rest of their typical classroom peers (Oakes and Lipton, 1994). Starting in the 1990s, this tracking practice came under scrutiny, particularly in public schools, due to the uneven distribution of resources and opportunities. School choice and private schools were seen as viable options for children who fell into the state's definition of gifted and talented (Oakes and Lipton, 1994). Enrichment programs also redirect potentially limited resources to only a small population of children.

There is little long term research on the benefits of acceleration versus enrichment programs, primarily due to a lack of federal, state, or foundation funding. The little data available suggested that acceleration programs offered more in terms of skills for independent study, research, and creative thinking (Feldhusen, 1991). Tracking this data and making academic recommendations for the gifted and talented remains a challenge and source of debate in the educational system.

Among the concerns about the effects of gifted programs is the generally narrow focus on intellectual growth at the expense of the social, emotional, and behavioral elements of development. Some scholars (Feldman, 1986) suggest that such a singular focus can contribute to anxiety and social isolation due to lack of adequate personal and social coping skills. Others (Lubinskiet al., 2001) suggest that these emotional, behavioral, and in some instances, social difficulties, interfere with the gifted children's capacity to use the full potential of their skills, particularly when they are put into accelerated courses or opt to skip a grade level. Some suggest that the indifference to the emotional/behavioral disability that some children identified as gifted and talented experience is related to the mindset that the gifted and talented "appear to be doing fine" (Plucker and Levy, 2001, p. 75). Research suggests the contrary, however; with gifted children approximately twice as likely as nongifted students to exhibit social and emotional difficulties (Winner, 2000). The gifted child's level of socioeconomic status and ethnicity also play a role; the social pressures on many gifted African American students, including economic pressures, may lead to the adoption of negative behaviors that camouflage their giftedness (Dillard and Brazil, 2002). This research indicates a strong need for programs designed for the gifted and talented that support the emotional and social needs of the children as well as maximize their academic potential.

Mara Sapon-Shevin (2003) offers another critical appraisal of gifted education programs in the United States, arguing that, by focusing on this elite population, schools and communities are less inclined to work to improve the overall general education programs. Sapon-Shevin suggests, as an alternative, that the educational system work to improve classroom settings, teaching, and curriculum for all children, not just a select few. She argues, further, against the idea that the gifted population is homogenous; and that educating this population should focus on promoting challenges for each student, as it should be with all academic talents. Sapon-Shevin couches her critic of gifted education within a larger context of advocacy for political and economic justice such that improved educational opportunities are created for the full range of students, from the poor to the gifted.

Critics of Sapon-Shevin challenge the political and socioeconomic arguments against gifted education, and emphasize the need to focus on the educational aspect of the gifted and talented programs and services (Gallagher, 1996). Such advocates of gifted education are especially resistant to the idea that "[e]xcellence can only be considered once equity is reached (for all children)" (p. 245), both because this premise is highly unrealistic and unfair, given the implication that the gifted population would be excluded from quality programs because the rest of the educational system does not offer superior programs for all children (1996). As an alternative, Gallagher challenges the gifted education field to engage in a self-critical reflection that does not offer excuses for wanting to extend the boundaries for knowledge for superior, intellectual children (1996).

These differences in perspectives converge around the need for a rich debate over gifted education, bringing this population to the forefront of the education discussion in the United States. Few deny that the gifted and talented are an important population because of their potential contributions to society, and thus, need to be supported as such in their learning and development.

Further Readings: Bathon, J. (2004). ECS state notes gifted and talented: State gifted and talented definitions. *Education Commission of the States*; Dillard, J., and N. Brazil (Winter 2002). Improving the selection process for identifying gifted ethnic minority children: Race, ethnicity and public education. *Trotter Review* 14(1). Boston: University of Massachusetts Boston. William Monroe Trotter Institute. (ERIC Documentation Reproduction Service No. ED465838); Feldhusen, J. (1991). Effects of programs for the gifted: A search for evidence. In W. Thomas Southern, and Eric D. Jones, eds., *The academic acceleration of gifted children*. New York: Teachers College Press; Feldman, D. H. (1986). *Nature's gambit: Child prodigies and the development of human potential*. New York: Basic Books, Inc.; Gallagher, J. J. (1996). A critique of critiques of gifted education. *Journal for the Education of the Gifted* 19(2), 234–249; Harrison, C. (Winter 2004). Giftedness in early childhood: The search for complexity and connection. *Roeper Review* 26(2), 78–84; Lubinski, D., R. M. Webb, M. Morelock, and C. Benbow (2001). Top 1 in 10,000: A 10-year follow-up of the profoundly gifted. *Journal of Applied Psychology* 86(4), 718–729; Oakes, J., and M. Lipton (1994). Foreword. In Mara Sapon-Shevin, *Playing favorites: Gifted education and the disruption of the community*. Albany, NY: State University of New York Press, pp. ix–xvi; Reid, B., and M. McGuire (1995). Square pegs in round holes—these kids don't fit: Bright students with behavior problems (Report No. RBDM-9512). Storrs, CT: University of Connecticut, The National Research Center on the Gifted and Talented. (ERIC Documentation Reproduction Service No. ED402701); Sapon-Shevin, M. (2003). Equity, excellence and school reform: Why is finding common ground so hard? In James Borland, ed., *Rethinking gifted education. Education and psychology of the* *gifted series*. New York: Teachers College Press; Terman, L. (1916). *The measurement of intelligence: An explanation of and a complete Guide for the use of the Stanford revision and extension of the Binet-Simon intelligence scale*. Cambridge, MA: Houghton Mifflin Company; Winner, E. (2000). The origins and ends of giftedness. *American Psychologist* 55(1), 159–169.

Sarah A. Leveque

Good Start, Grow Smart

Good Start, Grow Smart is a new reform initiative to improve low-income **Head Start** children's academic readiness for school, as well as to improve accountability and quality in Head Start, and preschool education more generally. Under the George W. Bush administration, new reforms (most notably known as **No Child Left Behind** [NCLB]) have been directed at improving educational achievement at the elementary and secondary levels of schooling. Good Start, Grow Smart is aligned with the No Child Left Behind initiative but with a focus on low-income 3–4 year olds enrolled in Head Start. Announced by the Bush administration in 2002 (White House, 2002), Good Start, Grow Smart focuses on greater accountability, increased qualifications of teachers, and more frequent assessment of four-year-old children on academic readiness outcomes.

Head Start is the longest lasting social program remaining from the 1960s Kennedy-Johnson era program. After the implementation of NCLB, the Bush administration (White House, 2002) announced that it would begin a new reform at the preschool level, aimed at the federally funded Head Start program. *Good Start, Grow Smart* is aligned with the NCLB in that it focuses on greater accountability, increased qualifications of teachers, and more frequent assessment of four-year-old children on academic readiness outcomes.

The Purposes of Good Start, Grow Smart

President Bush announced the Good Start, Grow Smart initiative at the White House in 2002. He emphasized the following key aim of the reform:

- To continue Head Start's emphasis on the "whole child" by focusing on health, social, emotional, cognitive, language, and academic development (White House, 2002).

In addition, the Good Start, Grow Smart initiative addresses the following three major areas (White House, 2002, p. 1):

- Strengthening Head Start: Through the Department of Health and Human Services (HHS), the Administration will develop a new accountability system for Head Start to ensure that every Head Start center assesses standards of learning in early literacy, language, and numeracy skills.
- HHS will also implement a national training program with the goal of training the nearly 50,000 Head Start teachers in early literacy teaching techniques.
- Partnering with States to Improve Early Childhood Education: The Administration proposes a stronger Federal-State partnership in the delivery of quality early childhood programs, *Key Debates related to Good Start, Grow Smart Reforms from 2002–2006.*

Access and Funding

Good Start, Grow Smart envisioned adding funds to Head Start for teacher training, enhancing teacher salaries, and to pay for assessments and new accountability measures. But the amount of funding provided, given social cuts to the federal budget over the past four years, has resulted in a slight reduction in number of children funded, and the funding of programs more generally. In addition, while Good Start, Grow Smart focused on improving the credentials or "quality" of its teachers and programs by having 50 percent of its teachers with bachelors degrees in education or early education, 2006 legislative records suggest this aim may be reduced or eliminated as a mandate, as there is too little funding available federally to adequately increase teacher salaries as envisioned (National Head Start Association, 2006).

Assessment and Accountability

Since 2002, a new form of "managerialism" in welfare state discourses (Clarke- and Newman, 1997) appears to be leading toward a renewed emphasis on a variety of managerial and accountability standards in Head Start, with one child development researcher even suggesting that Head Start could be likened to a factory where efficiency and accountability standards must be met. These shifts have resulted in multiple new developments as part of Good Start, Grow Smart reforms and suggested reforms. These include the following:

- Renewed emphasis on academic readiness, especially in early literacy and numeracy outcomes, with new summative or high stakes assessments of child outcomes.
- Renewed emphasis on accountability and management standards, with more professional management and program accountability assessments.
- Recompetition for Head Start contracts based on determination of "noncompliance."
- New faith-based hiring initiatives.
- New emphases on paternal, as well as maternal involvement programs.
- New ways to collaborate or form partnerships with state-based preschool (prekindergarten) initiatives.

New Outcomes. Head Start, from its inception, was organized around comprehensive outcomes related to health and child development, child care, and educational programming. The Good Start, Grow Smart reform focuses more narrowly on preacademic readiness skills in literacy and numeracy. These shifts follow the lead of No Child Left Behind, and the scientific reports that suggest young children are "eager to learn" (National Research Council, 2001), and that reading failures can be prevented by earlier attention to a rich literacy-oriented curriculum (Snow, Burns, and Griffin, 1998). There is significant debate about a too narrow curriculum for Head Start, as well as an inappropriate interpretation of what an effective early literacy and numeracy curriculum should be for young children, although there is support in the Head Start and early childhood education community for additional emphases in curriculum related to appropriate early literacy and numeracy activities, and developmentally appropriate assessments (Zigler and Styfco, 2004).

Assessments. As suggested above, there is still great debate about how much emphasis should be placed on early literacy and numeracy, their definition, and how to teach these skills in a developmentally appropriate way to the nation's children (Delpit, 1995; National Research Council, 2001; Snow, Burns, and Griffin, 1998). The new national assessment of Head Start four year olds first implemented in the Fall of 2003 as part of the Good Start, Grow Smart reform is called the National Reporting System or NRS. It is oriented toward testing early academics, especially language comprehension, vocabulary acquisition, early letter and number recognition, phonetic awareness, word recognition, and early numeracy skills. Since its first national implementation, the NRS has been administered twice a year in English to all children, and in Spanish and then English to children whose primary language is Spanish. The test has been criticized as an inappropriate high stakes assessment of young children that is unreliable as well as lacking in validity, particularly for children whose first language is Spanish (GAO, 2005; Meisels and Atkins-Burnett, 2004). It has also been judged to be culturally biased (GAO, 2005; Meisels and Atkins-Burnett, 2004). The 2005 GAO report found that teachers reported that the Head Start curriculum was beginning to change to a more narrow range of academic skills, and that some were "teaching to the test." This refocusing of the curriculum toward more academic readiness outcomes was a primary goal of the 2002 Good Start, Grow Smart reform (White House, 2002). The GAO report (2005) recommended revising the NRS to increase reliability and validity for all children, and adding a socioemotional outcomes assessment. Despite continuing debate, in 2006, new revisions and an additional socioemotional assessment are being piloted for addition to the NRS.

Accountability and Management. The legislative proposals in Good Start, Grow Smart have shifted oversight from advisory and/or parent councils for making important policy decisions about their own children's programs (hiring/firing, curriculum orientation) to management councils that would implement accountability performance standards. These would include determination of *noncompliance*, fraud, and when grantees should be involved in recompetition of federal funds and grantee status. Head Start grantees throughout the United States have accepted the need for oversight and accountability standards throughout the history of Head Start, but are concerned about the loss of powers by parent–community councils, as well as the specter of being judged noncompliant. There is concern that the recompetition of federal Head Start grants might result in greater state or private control of Head Start funds, and potentially greater inequalities across the states compared to the current federally guided and managed program (Clarke and Newman, 1997).

Increased Encouragement of "Faith-based" Hiring and Curricular Practices. While Head Start has frequently had programs in religious-sponsored building sites over its history, Good Start, Grow Smart proposes an increase in federal funding for private faith-based contractors, with an allowance that these contractors can hire and fire employees based on religious background. Some suggest that the new proposed provisions use public funding to allow for discriminatory hiring practices based on religion, and also would allow different Head Start community-based grantees to fire long-term employees, even those highly credentialed, in favor of assistant and full-time staff that conform to the religious beliefs of the sponsoring program.

New Emphases on Paternal as well as Maternal Involvement Programs. Definitions of marriage and family, as well as support for nuclear two parent families, have been an important part of recent welfare legislation since the 1990s, and have been stressed under the Bush administration reforms related to a variety of policy initiatives. There has been greater support for the traditions of marriage, family, and father-as well as mother-support programs. Good Start, Grow Smart reforms and proposed legislation encourage marriage over single parenthood, and also provide the framework for new fatherhood programs to educate fathers about their responsibilities and possibilities for involvement with their preschool-age children through Head Start programs. Although this has been implicit in Head Start since its inception, and fathers and other relatives have often been involved in their children's education and in Head Start programs, the Good Start, Grow Smart reforms provide new funding and policy recommendations aimed at father involvement, education, and support. Because these initiatives are also part of a broad new welfare policy aimed at enhancing maternal employment outside the household, increased emphasis on marriage, and maternal/father individual responsibility, the new reforms in Good Start, Grow Smart are one part of a larger debate related to changing discourses about family and marriage, personal responsibility, and employment (Bloch et al., 2003).

Increased Collaboration and Partnership with the States. Good Start, Grow Smart (White House, 2002) encouraged partnerships with states enabling more efficient use of Head Start funds in combination with funds for child-care and early childhood programs at the state level. Good Start, Grow Smart proposes more integrated partnerships that would use federal, state, and local funds and programming more effectively and efficiently to enhance the ability of states and localities to provide 4-K programs for children "at risk" as well as to provide more full-day child-care services for children of low-income single mothers who must find employment under the new welfare-to-work regimes. Despite the efforts of the Bush Administration to devolve federal Head Start funding to the states, two specific attempts to experiment with state block grants to selected experimental states have failed to be approved by Congress after resistance from Head Start lobbyists, parents, and key legislators. The current emphasis on integration and collaboration of Head Start funds with other state and local funds is aimed at making a better "system" of early education and child care, though no new funding is provided (Zigler and Styfco, 2004; National Head Start Association, 2006). *See also* Families; Fathers.

Further Readings: Bloch, M. N., K. Holmlund, I. Moqvist, and T. S. Popkewitz, eds. (2003). *Governing children, families, and education: Restructuring the welfare state*. New York: Palgrave Press; Clarke, J., and J. Newman (1997). *The managerial state: Power, politics and ideology in the remaking of social welfare*. London: Sage Publications; Committee on Health, Education, Labor, and Pensions (2005). S.B. 1107-*Full* *committee report on Head Start improvement for school readiness act of 2005*. Available online at http://www.whsaonline.org/senatecommitteereport.pdf; Delpit, L. (1995). *Other peoples' children: Cultural conflict in the classroom*. New York: The New Press; Government Accountability Office (May, 2005). *Head Start: Further Development Could Allow New Test to Be Used for Decision-Making*. Report 05-343. Washington, DC: U.S. Accountability Office; Meisels, S., and S. Atkins-Burnett (2004). The Head Start national reporting system: A critique. *Young Children* 59(1), 64–66; National Head Start Association (2006). Special report: The Bush administration's fiscal year 2007 budget proposal would slash Head Start and Early Head Start program enrollment. Available online at http://www.nhsa.org/download/advocacy/PresidentFY2007Budget.pdf; National Research Council (2001). *Eager to learn: Educating our preschoolers*. Washington, DC: National Academy Press; Snow, C. E., M. S. Burns, and P. Griffin, eds. (1998). *Preventing reading difficulties in young children*. Washington, DC: National Academy Press. Available online at http://books.nap.edu/html/prdyc/; White House (2002). *Good Start, Grow Smart: The Bush administration's early childhood initiative*. Available online at http://www.whitehouse.gov/infocus/earlychildhood/earlychildhood.pdf; Zigler, E., and S. J. Styfco, eds. (2004). *The Head Start debates*. Baltimore: Paul Brookes Publishing Co.

Marianne Bloch and Ko Eun Kim

Gordon, Ira J. (1923–1978)

Ira Gordon is best known for his groundbreaking work in parent education and home visiting. He was a native of New York City and received his advanced education in the city of his birth: his bachelor's degree from City College of New York and his master's degree and doctorate from Teacher's College at Columbia University. He wrote twelve books and cowrote three others. He taught at Kansas State College, the University of Florida, and the University of Maryland. He ended his career at the University of North Carolina in 1978 after moving there in 1977 to become Kenan Professor and Dean of the School of Education.

Dr. Gordon was equally proficient in research, programmatic innovation, public speaking, and social action. He was a pioneer of action research and one of the first university-based psychologists to develop home visiting programs for the educational and social enrichment of infants and toddlers from poor families. His first such effort in that area was the Parent Education Program (PEP). Developed in 1966, PEP was the beginning step in a series of intervention research efforts that engaged paraprofessionals as home visitors to demonstrate home-learning activities to parents (usually the mother) so that they in turn would engage in broadly defined instructional interaction with their children. This series of interventions, which he based on sound developmental theory and research, continued through 1974 and included such variations on PEP as the Early Childhood Stimulation Through Parent Education Program (ECSPEP), the Home Learning Center Approach to Early Stimulation (HLC), Instructional Strategies in Infant Stimulation (ISIS), the Social Roots of Competency Project, and the Effect of Reinforcement on Infant Performance Project.

From its beginning in rural northern Florida, his parent intervention model spread throughout the country. His "Florida Model" influenced the design of the "Follow Through Program," the "Head Start-Planned Variations Program," the

"Parent Child Centers," and the "Teacher Corp." As a frequent consultant to the Department of Health, Education and Welfare and private foundations, he helped to turn the nation's attention to the needs of very young children.

Dr. Gordon was a firm believer in the importance of longitudinal research and with the support of the Department of Health, Education and Welfare organized a group of over fifty researchers involved in early intervention efforts. The group, nicknamed "Upstart" by Irving Lazar, met twice a year for five years in the 1970s. Its members were many of this country's early intervention pioneers, including Kuno Beller, Bettye Caldwell, Sybille Escalona, Susan Gray, Jerome Kagan, Ronald Lally, Phyllis Levenstein, Howard Moss, Frank Palmer, Earl Schaefer, Jean Watts, David Weikart, and Leon Yarrow. Dr. Gordon worked tirelessly to keep the focus of "Upstart" discussions on the sharing of ideas, strategies, and research that could be used in the service of bettering educational opportunities of children from poor families. His efforts with this group led to the development and funding of the *Consortium for Longitudinal Studies*, a cluster of carefully designed research studies that provided evidence of the lasting effects of early intervention.

Ira Gordon was a brilliant synthesizer who worked best in a room full of bright creative thinkers. He would take the research reports, theories, guesses, and opinions of his peers and weave them into sophisticated meta-ideas that were more wise than any previously stated, yet inclusive enough of the essence of those thoughts to be immediately accepted by the group. He stands out as one of the first American academicians to harness the power of developmental research as a vehicle for social change. He was dedicated to learning how to assist, and then actually assisting, poor and undereducated parents make life better for their children.

J. Ronald Lally

Grade Retention

Whether it is called *nonpromotion*, *flunking*, *failing*, *being held back*, *the gift of time*, or *being retained*, grade retention refers to a child repeating his or her current grade level again in the following year. Despite a century of research that fails to support the effectiveness of grade retention, its use has increased over the past twenty-five years. Reasons for its dramatic increase as a contemporary educational practice include a renewed emphasis on educational standards and accountability (e.g., **No Child Left Behind Act** of 2001), increased use of grade level tests determining promotion or retention, and the call to end "social promotion" (i.e., the practice of promoting students with their same age-peers although they have not mastered current grade level content). In spite of its current status as an acceptable educational practice, grade retention remains a controversial intervention strategy.

Who Is Retained and Why?

It is estimated that at least 2 million American students are retained each year, and 30–50 percent of students in some schools in the United States are retained at least once before ninth grade. While the specific factors involved in the decision to retain an individual student vary, several individual, family, and demographic characteristics are associated with an increased risk of retention. For example, research has found that black or Hispanic male students are more likely to have been retained than their peers. Additional characteristics associated with an increased likelihood of grade retention are: (1) late birthdays, delayed development, and/or attention problems, (2) living in poverty or in a single-parent household, (3) frequent school changes and/or chronic absenteeism, (4) low parental educational attainment and/or parental involvement in education, (5) behavior problems and/or aggressive behavior or immaturity, (6) difficulties with peer relations and/or low self-confidence/self-esteem, and (7) reading problems—including those of English Language Learners.

Some children are recommended for retention when their academic performance is low or if they fail to meet grade level "performance standards" established by a school district or state. Some children may be recommended for retention if they seem socially immature, display behavior problems, or are just beginning to learn English.

Retention Outcomes

Too often, anecdotal evidence, clinical experience, and folklore overshadow the results of empirical research when discussing the merits and limitations of grade retention. Research indicates that neither grade retention nor social promotion alone is an effective strategy for improving educational success. To the contrary, most studies indicate that grade retention is not effective for addressing academic or social/emotional concerns, and, further, that retention is perceived negatively by students and is associated with negative long-term consequences. These research results are not easily understood, however, perhaps because many studies emphasize short-term gains and fail to take into account the long-term consequences of retention.

Research demonstrates that initial academic improvements may occur during the year the student is retained. However, numerous studies reveal that achievement gains decline within two to three years of retention. This means that over time, children who were retained either do not show higher achievement, or sometimes show lower achievement than similar groups of children who were not retained. For most students, the research suggests that grade retention has a negative impact on all areas of academic achievement (e.g., reading, math, and oral and written language) and social and emotional adjustment (e.g., peer relationships, self-esteem, problem behaviors, and attendance).

There is evidence of negative effects of retention on long-term school achievement and adjustment. Research demonstrates that during adolescence, the fact of having previously experienced grade retention during elementary school is associated with health-compromising behaviors such as emotional distress, low self-esteem, poor peer relations, cigarette use, alcohol and drug abuse, early onset of sexual activity, suicidal intentions, and violent behaviors. Furthermore, students who were retained are much more likely to drop out of school. Indeed, a recent review of research indicates that grade retention is one of the single most powerful predictors of high school dropout, with retained students being five to eleven times more likely to drop out. In addition to lower levels of academic adjustment in eleventh grade and a greater likelihood of dropping out of high school, retained students are also less likely to receive a diploma by age 20. As adults, individuals who repeated a grade are more likely than adults who did not repeat a grade to be unemployed, living on public assistance, or in prison. Finally, grade retention is perceived negatively by students. In a recent study, sixth-grade students rated grade retention as one of the *most* stressful life events.

Individual Considerations

While there may be individual students who benefit from retention, there is currently no systematic means to predict accurately which children will benefit from being retained. Under certain circumstances, retention may be an appropriate educational response that can yield positive effects. For example, students who have difficulty in school because of lack of opportunity for instruction rather than lack of ability may be helped by retention. However, this assumes that the lack of opportunity is related to attendance/health or mobility problems that have been resolved and that the student is no more than one year older than classmates. Considering that research during the past century has failed to support the practice of grade retention, educational professionals must carefully weigh the evidence that potentially supports retention as the preferable choice for a particular student rather than promotion to the next grade.

Alternative Intervention Strategies

In contrast to the negative effects associated with grade retention, research provides evidence supporting other educational interventions that promote the cognitive and social competence of students. Yet neither grade retention nor social promotion is likely to enhance a child's learning without the presence of other supporting features. Research and common sense both indicate that simply having a child repeat a grade is unlikely to address the problems a child is experiencing. Likewise, simply promoting a student who is experiencing academic or behavioral problems without additional support is not likely to be an effective solution. When faced with a recommendation to retain a child, a more effective solution is to identify specific intervention strategies to enhance the cognitive and social development of the child and promote his or her learning and success at school. A combination of grade promotion and utilization of evidence-based interventions ("promotion plus") is most likely to benefit children with low achievement or behavior problems.

It is important to note that there is no single "silver bullet" intervention that will effectively address the specific needs of low-achieving students. However, the application of evidence-based interventions, selected to meet the diverse needs of individual students, will have a greater chance of facilitating the academic and socioemotional development of students at risk for school failure. It is important to note that effective practices for students at risk tend not to be qualitatively different from the best practices of general education. (See Algozzine, Ysseldyke, and Elliott, 2002, for a review of research-based tactics for effective instruction; and see Shinn, Walker, and Stoner, 2002, for a more extensive discussion of interventions for academic and behavior problems.) The following programs and strategies are examples of evidence-based alternatives to grade retention and social promotion:

- **Parental Involvement:** Parents should be involved in their children's schools and education through frequent contact with teachers, supervision of homework, and continual communication about school activities to promote learning.
- **Early Reading Programs:** Developmentally appropriate, intensive, direct instruction strategies have been effective in promoting the reading skills of low-performing students.
- **Early Developmental and Preschool Programs:** These programs enhance language and social skills. Implementing prevention and early intervention programs is more promising than waiting for learning difficulties to accumulate. Effective preschool and kindergarten programs develop language and prereading skills using structured, well-organized, and comprehensive approaches. Research suggests that optimally programs follow students and their parents beyond kindergarten and provide support services through the primary grades.
- **Age-Appropriate and Culturally Sensitive Instructional Strategies:** Such strategies accelerate progress in the classroom.
- **Systematic Assessment Strategies:** Such strategies, including continuous progress monitoring and formative evaluation, enable ongoing modification of instructional efforts. Effective programs frequently assess student progress and modify instructional strategies accordingly.
- **School-Based Mental Health Programs:** These programs are valuable in promoting the social and emotional adjustment of children. For instance, addressing behavior problems has been found to be effective in facilitating academic performance.
- **Behavior Management and Cognitive-Behavior Modification Strategies:** These strategies reduce classroom behavior problems.
- **Student Support Teams:** These teams should include appropriate professionals to assess and identify specific learning or behavior problems, design interventions to address those problems, and evaluate the efficacy of those interventions. Effective programs tend to accommodate instruction to individual needs and maximize direct instruction.
- **Extended Year, Extended Day, and Summer School Programs:** Such programs should focus on facilitating the development of academic skills.
- **Tutoring and Mentoring Programs:** Whether with peer, cross-age, or adult tutors, these programs should focus on promoting specific academic or social skills.
- **Comprehensive School-Wide Programs:** These programs promote the psychosocial and academic skills of all students. Too often, remedial and special education services are poorly integrated with the regular education program, and, therefore, collaboration and consistency between regular, remedial, and special education are essential.

Other alternatives include mixed-age groupings and multiyear programs where students may stay with the same teacher for more than one year, thereby giving children more time before they must demonstrate "readiness" for a subsequent classroom.

Conclusion

Neither grade retention nor social promotion is an effective remedy to address the needs of children experiencing academic, emotional, or behavioral difficulties. Parents, teachers, and other professionals committed to helping all children achieve academic success and reach their full potential must discard ineffective practices (such as grade retention and social promotion) in favor of "promotion plus" specific interventions designed to address the factors that place students at risk for school failure. Parents and teachers are encouraged to actively collaborate with each other and other educational professionals to develop and implement effective alternatives to retention and social promotion. Identifying school problems early can help students to develop skills before children begin to feel like failures and improves students' chances for success. Incorporating evidence-based interventions and instructional strategies into school policies and practices will enhance academic and adjustment outcomes for all students. *See also* Parents and Parent Involvement.

Further Readings: Algozzine, B., J. E. Ysseldyke, and J. Elliot (2002). *Strategies and tactics for effective instruction*. Longmont, CO: Sopris West; Jimerson, S.R. (1999). On the failure of failure: Examining the association of early grade retention and late adolescent education and employment outcomes. *Journal of School Psychology* 37(3), 243–272; Jimerson, S.R. (2001). Meta-analysis of grade retention research: Implications for practice in the 21st century. *School Psychology Review* 30(3), 420–437; Jimerson, S.R., G. Anderson, and A. Whipple (2002). Winning the battle and losing the war; Examining the relation between grade retention and dropping out of high school. *Psychology in the Schools* 39(4), 441–457; Jimerson, S.R., and A. M. Kaufman (2003). Reading, writing, and retention: A primer on grade retention research. *The Reading Teacher* 56(8), 622–635; McCoy, A.R., and A. J. Reynolds (1999). Grade retention and school performance: An extended investigation. *Journal of School Psychology* 37(3), 273–298; Shinn, M.R., H. M. Walker, and G. Stoner eds. (2002). *Interventions for academic and behavior problems II: Preventive and remedial approaches*. Bethesda, MD: National Association of School Psychologists.

Shane R. Jimerson, Kelly Graydon, and Sarah Pletcher

Grouping

Grouping in early childhood education refers to the ways in which young children are organized for **play**, learning, and instruction. How to group children is an important consideration for early childhood caregivers and teachers who aim to provide environments and interpersonal experiences that most effectively and appropriately support children's optimal growth and development. In the United States, three common grouping schemas are traditional groupings, multiage or mixed-age groupings, and grouping for instruction.

Age Grouping

The traditional method for grouping children in schools, early childhood programs, and child-care centers is chronological grouping or grouping by age. This method of grouping is evidenced in institutional structures (such as schools and grade levels within schools), statutory requirements (such as licensing regulations for child-care centers), and individual teacher and caregiver practice. Rationales for grouping by age are based upon the assumption, drawn from the maturationist perspective, that age is or should be the single most important factor in promoting developmental progress and positive learning outcomes. A number of common beliefs about children seem to underlie this grouping method. One belief is that children prefer to be with others their own age. A second belief is that all children of the same age have the same capabilities and the same interests. A third belief is that young children learn best when grouped chronologically because they are not intimidated by the behaviors and competencies of older children, and their developmental needs will not be ignored in favor of those of the older children.

Research aimed at providing evidence for the effectiveness of grouping by age in early childhood programs is sparse at best. Children in fact grow up in multiage groups (families) and are for the most part quite comfortable there. Further, it is well known and well documented that children, even those of the same age, have very diverse personal and cultural experiences, capabilities, and interests. And finally, a child's potential feelings of intimidation by the presence, behavior, or skills of older children can be and indeed are ameliorated by the effective strategies employed by competent, caring, and qualified teachers.

Chronological grouping of children in early education settings appears to be of benefit to teachers and caregivers. This grouping practice allows teachers and caregivers to limit their knowledge of children and child development to the specific-age group in their charge. In addition, this practice limits both the content knowledge base required of teachers and the breadth and depth of the curriculum and experiences to be planned and implemented for the children.

Multiage Grouping

Multiage grouping is known by a number of different names: family grouping, vertical grouping, heterogeneous grouping, **mixed-age grouping**, and ungraded or nongraded classrooms. This method of grouping is commonly found in family child-care homes and, to a lesser extent, in programs or classrooms for preschool-age children. It is rarely found in infant and toddler care or in kindergarten and primary classrooms. In a multiage group, the age-range of the children typically exceeds one year and the curriculum is not constrained by particular grade-level parameters. The practice of multiage grouping is based on several assumptions about its benefits to children. One assumption is that in such a group, which is characterized by a wider range of personalities and competencies, there are more opportunities for each child to form positive and meaningful relationships. A second assumption is that the multiage group offers a greater likelihood that children will have access to more and appropriate models of behavior and learning. These potential outcomes are particularly advantageous given that children's development in all domains tends to be uneven, and it is unlikely that any given child can serve as an effective model in every developmental domain. In addition, children who may be struggling with a particular developmental task or within a particular domain are less likely to be ostracized and/or feel belittled by peers in a multiage group where the broad range of development and skill acquisition is evident, expected, and accepted.

It is further assumed that children in multiage groupings will advance in social development as a result of an increased expectation for and occurrence of prosocial behaviors. Children do adjust their behaviors and language when interacting with other children they perceive as younger or less competent. Prosocial behavior fosters the development of community and serves as a deterrent to unruly and aggressive behavior. As a result, there is a reduced need for disciplinary actions and enhanced opportunities for sustained engagement in valuable learning experiences.

Finally, there are assumed benefits to cognitive and language development in the multiage grouping. Opportunities to experience more challenging cognitive tasks, to hear and use more advanced language, to receive support from a more skilled peer, and to offer support in the way of teaching a less-skilled peer are more likely to be routinely found in a multiage group. These types of opportunities provide all participants valuable support for learning.

The benefits of multiage grouping are not inherent in the grouping itself but are directly related to the knowledge, skill repertoire, and actual work of the teachers and caregivers. Teachers and caregivers must create the physical, social, and cognitive structures within the **classroom environment** that will promote and support the desired outcomes. Children will need to be guided toward the interpersonal relationships and prosocial behaviors that are associated with the anticipated social benefits. The **curriculum** needs to be conceptualized and structured so as to provide a broad range of possibilities and activities that can accommodate children at various levels of interest and competence. Younger- or less-advanced children need to be taught how to recognize when assistance is truly needed and how to seek such assistance. Older or more competent children need to be taught how to provide appropriate assistance without doing everything for the less-skilled peer. Teachers and caregivers need to be alert to the potential for learned helplessness as well as the potential for overburdening the more competent child with the expectation of providing assistance whenever requested.

There are other pitfalls that may serve as potential obstacles to realizing the benefits of multiage groupings. The actual age span represented in the group must be thoughtfully determined. If too large, the benefits may be lost. In addition, teachers and caregivers should avoid creating single-age groupings within the multiage group or separating children into their respective traditional grade levels. The advantages of the multiage grouping for children's development and learning are in large part the result of an engaging, multidimensional curriculum and meaningful interpersonal relationships and interactions.

Grouping for Instruction

Within the broader frameworks of traditional and multiage groupings is a set of options for other short-term instructional grouping practices. These options include whole class, large group, small group, pairs and triads, ability groups, and cooperative learning groups. The choice of a grouping pattern should be based on the individual needs of the children and the purpose of instruction. It is generally acknowledged that whole class and large group instruction are rarely developmentally appropriate for children in the early childhood years (birth to eight years). Small groups, pairs and triads are potentially more appropriate and effective especially when they are constructed purposefully around children's interests, competencies, and needs, and when they are flexible as well as changeable.

Ability grouping is generally considered to be an inappropriate practice, as it runs the risk of fostering unnecessary competition in the learning environment. Ability grouping also tends to stigmatize children in terms of their (low especially) abilities and to create undesirable social barriers and attitudes. Further, ability grouping seems to be rooted in the assumption that development in all domains is simultaneous and even, and deprives all children of the rich learning opportunities inherent in diverse grouping, cooperative learning, and collaborative interactions. However, occasionally, several children have very similar instructional needs with respect to specific concepts or skills. In these cases, a short-term, ability grouping may be very appropriate as a means for meeting the individual but shared specific instructional needs of those children. In these instances, the grouping should be temporary, purposeful, and focused on a specific learning outcome.

Cooperative learning groups, whether formal or informal, provide the occasion for collaborative inquiry and effort. These types of groups can be very effective instructional strategies when they are organized around specific concepts to be learned or projects to be completed, and when attention is given to identifying the membership of each learning group. The cooperative learning group should not be an ability group, but rather a mixed group where all the children can make a contribution and benefit from the contributions of others. *See also* Development, Language; Development, Social.

Further Readings: Balaban, Nancy (1991). Mainstreamed, mixed age groups of infants and toddlers at the Bank Street Family Center. *Zero to Three* (February), 13–29; Goodlad, John I., and Robert Anderson (1990). *The nongraded elementary school.* 2nd ed. New York: Teachers College Press; Katz, Lilian G., Demetra Evangelou, and J. A. Hartman (1990). *The case for mixed-age grouping in early childhood.* Washington, DC: NAEYC.

Stephanie F. Leeds

Guidance. *See* Behavior Management and Guidance

Hailmann, Eudora Lucas (1835–1904)

Eudora Hailmann (nee Lucas) was born into a politically liberal family that valued the education of girls. This oriented her toward improving the status of women through organizations, by professional training for kindergarten teachers, and in parent education programs. Her studies in music and art, at Miss Guthrie's School in Louisville, Kentucky, prepared her for development of methods, materials and activities used for decades in preschool and primary classes.

In 1856, Eudora married William **Hailmann**, a Swiss immigrant who was teaching at the Girls High School in Louisville. They had a daughter and three sons. When William was asked to develop a German-American Academy in 1865, he included the first **kindergarten** classroom built in the United States. As a volunteer mother, working with its Froebelian teacher from Germany, Eudora became so interested in the system that she studied it in Europe in 1866 and 1871. The Hailmann marriage then became a dual-career partnership as they promoted the humanist philosophy of Friedrich **Froebel**. Willliam's focus was upon the elementary grades and Eudora's upon kindergarten children under the age of 7, their mothers, and their teachers.

During a period in which married women were supposed to devote themselves to maintaining the household, Eudora had unique freedom to travel and to carry out professional activities. The family moved to Milwaukee in 1873 and to Detroit in 1880 when William administered public schools and Eudora established private kindergartens with training programs. After William became Superintendent of Schools in LaPorte in 1883, they developed a nationally acclaimed curriculum from kindergarten through all grades to teacher training. Eudora also helped establish two of the first normal schools in the nation, in Oshkosh and Winona. Her speeches at the summer Chautauqua circuit and other institutes were often reprinted as bulletins for wider distribution. From 1884 until the Columbian Exposition of 1893, she coordinated displays of creative work done by kindergarten children and held demonstration classes for educational conferences and world's fairs. Between 1876 and 1893, the Hailmanns published the bimonthly

New Education as the major communication medium for the nation's Froebelian kindergartens. They established the Froebel Institute, with its first national conference in 1882. It became the Kindergarten Department of the National Educational Association (NEA) in 1884. As president of that department in 1888, Eudora was the first woman to sit on the NEA governing board. She spoke on kindergarten topics at each year's convention from 1885 until 1892.

From her studies in Europe, Eudora recognized that Froebel had developed his "gifts and occupations" with the expectation that they would be expanded by his followers. She developed wooden beads, based upon the cube, ball, and cylinder of his Second Gift, and popularized the sandbox, modeling clay, dollhouses, and small tables for group projects. With daughter Elizabeth, she wrote *Songs, Games, and Rhymes* in 1887.

President Cleveland, a Democrat, appointed William as Superintendent of Indian Schools in 1894. Because the department was severely underfunded, his entire family became unpaid staff. Eudora developed three normal schools and forty reservation kindergartens with training programs for aides and parents. William's position was terminated in 1897, after a Republican became president. Shortly afterward, Eudora had "an attack of nervous prostration" that caused her to be a housebound invalid until her death in 1905. The heritage she left includes major universities that evolved from her kindergarten training schools. Her egalitarian marriage demonstrated that wives can have successful careers. Through promoting self-directed education of young children and their teachers, Eudora Hailmann helped establish the early care and education of today.

Further Readings: Archival collection of W. N. Hailmann. Department of Special Collections, University of California, Los Angeles; Hewes, Dorothy W. (2001). *W. N. Hailmann: Defender of Froebel.* Grand Rapids, MI: Froebel Foundation; International Kindergarten Union. (1924). *Pioneers in the kindergarten.* New York: Century; Vandewalker, Nina C. (1908). *The kindergarten in America.* New York: Macmillan.

Dorothy W. Hewes

Hailmann, William Nicholas (1836–1920)

William Nicholas Hailmann facilitated the introduction of Froebelian methodology into American schools. Hailmann could understand Friedrich **Froebel**'s underlying concepts and adapt them to educational methods in a different time and culture because he was fluent in both German and English.

William Hailmann grew up in a German-speaking Swiss village, encouraged to visit the nearby carpenter shop and to play in the woods. His education, based upon Johann **Pestalozzi**'s active learning model, enabled him to graduate from the Zurich Cantonal College when he was fifteen.

He emigrated to the United States in 1852, settling in Louisville. His fluency in Italian, French, and German led to positions at the Henry Female College and the new public high school. He married Eudora Grover in 1857 and they had four children (see **Hailmann, Eudora Lucas**). When he visited his parents in 1860, he became intrigued by Froebel's philosophy of helping students at all educational levels connect the outer world and their own inner life through a process of active learning. After brief service with the Union army during the Civil War, he developed a new German-American Academy with a Froebelian curriculum. It included one of the first **kindergartens** in the United States. In recognition of the academy's quality, he was granted an honorary master's degree from the University of Louisville in 1864.

William and Eudora Hailmann worked together as egalitarian partners to promote Froebel's controversial educational system after studying Swiss kindergartens in 1866 and 1871. This included publication of an influential newsletter, *The New Education*, from 1876 until 1893. "Although Eudora concentrated upon kindergartens, their work often merged so that it was impossible to tell whether the ideas were his or hers" (Hewes, 2001, p. 24).

After directing German-American schools in Milwaukee and Detroit, Hailmann became Superintendent of Schools in LaPorte in 1881, hired to design a model Froebelian curriculum. It included kindergartens and a teacher training institute supervised by Eudora and was soon acclaimed not only for student accomplishments but for community involvement (Rice, 1893). He received an honorary doctorate from the University of Ohio in 1885. President Cleveland appointed Hailmann as Superintendent of Indian Schools in 1894. Despite a meager budget, he devised a Froebelian system with appropriate textbooks and activities for the Indian boarding schools. Reservation kindergartens were opened with teacher training for tribal members (Hewes, 1981). After this political appointment terminated in 1898, he held several academic positions, concluding in 1914 at the Broadoaks Kindergarten Training School in Pasadena. Until his death in 1920, he continued to be professionally active.

The potential influence of organizations, especially the National Education Association (NEA), was recognized early in Hailmann's career. He gave presentations at most annual NEA meetings from 1872 until 1915. In 1872, he successfully campaigned to include women as members. He organized the Froebel Institute in 1882 and was its president when it became the Kindergarten Department of the NEA in 1885. He also coordinated a kindergarten conference during the 1883 Columbian Exposition in Chicago, and was a regular presenter at summer Chautauqua tent events.

Hailmann wrote thirteen books, including *Kindergarten Culture in the Family and Kindergarten* in 1873 and *Primary Methods and Kindergarten Instruction* in 1887. In his extensively annotated 1889 translation of Froebel's *Education of Man*, Hailmann explained the original intent of such phrases as "Come, let us live for our children" as having meant living *with* them. Because he emphasized that Froebel saw self-activity as essential for education at all levels, this book became a foundation for the movement known as **Progressive Education**. His enthusiasm was for Froebel's underlying philosophy, not the manufactured products or carefully sequenced activities that characterized "traditional" kindergarten practice.

The legacy of William Hailmann has many facets. While he was in Indiana, he was instrumental in its becoming the first state to formally incorporate kindergartens into the public schools. He mentored Patty Smith Hill and other "progressive" educators who developed nursery schools and laid the foundation for today's early care and education. He promoted manual training for "hand-minded" high school students. He spoke out vigorously in favor of equal pay for women and retirement benefits for all teachers. In his own personal life, he demonstrated the egalitarian principles that he advocated for others. "William and Eudora Hailmann took kindergarten and primary education and teacher training into a new era. Their inventive, dynamic, theoretical and practical work serves as an excellent model for early education professionals" (Lascarides and Hinitz, 2000, p. 215).

Further Readings: Hewes, Dorothy W. (1981). Those first good years of Indian education. *American Indian Culture and Research Journal* 5(2), 63–82; Hewes, Dorothy W. (2001). *W. N. Hailmann: Defender of Froebel*. Grand Rapids, MI: Froebel Foundation; Lascarides, V. Celia, and Blythe F. Hinitz (2000). *History of early childhood education*. New York: Falmer Press; Peltzman, Barbara Ruth (1998). *Pioneers of early childhood education: A Bio-bibliographical guide*. Westport, CT: Greenwood Press; Rice, Joseph M. (1893). *The public school system of the United States*. New York: Century.

Dorothy W. Hewes

Hall, G(ranville) Stanley (1844–1924)

Although best known as the founder of organized psychology in the United States, G. Stanley Hall should also be recognized as a major contributor to child development research and preschool methodology.

G. Stanley Hall was born on February 1, 1844. Little is known about his family or his childhood on a farm near Ashfield, Massachusetts. With financial assistance from various sources, he graduated from the Williston Academy (1862) and Williams College (1867). Study for his divinity degree from the Union Theological Seminary in New York City (1871) included several months at the University of Berlin. He taught at Antioch College (1872–1876) before concluding his formal education at Harvard University, where he was awarded America's first Ph.D. in psychology. With further financial assistance, he returned to Germany. He had met Cornelia Fisher at Antioch and in 1879 they were married in Berlin. Upon their return from Europe, his Saturday morning lectures at Harvard presented European philosophies to Boston's educational leaders. These led to a teaching position at John Hopkins University and to his appointment in 1888 as first president of Clark University. Hall's seminars, held from 7:30 p.m. until midnight, were so stimulating that his graduate students claimed they couldn't sleep afterward. Within ten years, however, Clark had awarded thirty of the fifty-four psychology doctorates in the United States.

In 1888, Hall coordinated establishment of the Child Study Association of America, popularizing the questionnaire research method that he had learned in Germany. In 1892, initial plans for the American Psychological Association were developed in his office and he became its first president. His efforts led to the 1894 organization of a Department of Child Study within the National Education Association and his many presentations at its conferences oriented teachers and administrators to his viewpoint. His extensive writings in a wide variety of publications are documented by Ross (1972) and others.

Hall's introduction to the **kindergarten** was in Germany, where popular training programs were based upon Friedrich **Froebel**'s belief that children learn through self-activity. This is reflected in the positions taken by John **Dewey**, Arnold **Gesell**, and others who were his students. It is sometimes stated that he was an opponent of the Froebelians. However, it was the symbolism and "mechanical depersonalized instruction" that he deplored. He made his position clear in such statements as "I believe heart and soul in the kindergarten as I understand it, and insist that I am a true disciple of Froebel, but that my orthodoxy is the real doxy which, if Froebel could now come to New York, Chicago, Worcester, or even to Boston, he would approve" (Hall, 1911, p 16).

While in Germany, Hall also studied Haeckle's theory that "ontology recapitulates phylogeny" as an explanation for developmental stages. This means that individuals replicate progression of the human race from simians to an integrated society. Accordingly, formal education should not begin until about age 8. Although highly controversial when first proposed, this fits into the philosophy of the liberal Froebelians and is similar to stages later described by Jean **Piaget** and others.

The introduction of psychoanalysis into the United States came when Hall invited Sigmund **Freud** and Carl Jung to a conference in 1909. Activities for self-expression and "acting out" of inner emotions were incorporated into preschool classrooms by the 1940s. This supported the original Froebelian concept of "making the inner outer and the outer inner" through interpreting children's activities.

Hall's most direct influence upon today's early childhood education resulted from an 1894 summer session at Clark University. Thirty-five kindergarten leaders accepted his invitation. All dropped out after the first day except Anna Bryan and Patty Smith **Hill**. They developed a developmentally appropriate curriculum that was not implemented until 1926, when Hill's Committee on Nursery Schools convened. This group became today's **National Association for the Education of Young Children** (NAEYC), which maintains much of that original 1894 plan in its mission statement and the criteria for accreditation. *See also* Preschool/Prekindergarten Programs.

Further Readings: The G. Stanley Hall Papers are in Archives and Special Collections, Goddard Library. Worcester, MA: Clark University; Hall, G. Stanley (1911). *Educational problems*. New York: Appleton; Hall, G. Stanley (1923). *The life and confessions of a psychologist*. New York: Appleton; Rosenzweig, Saul (1992). *Freud, Jung, and Hall the king-maker: The historic expedition to America, 1909*. St. Louis, MO: Rana House Press; Ross, Dorothy (1972). *G. Stanley Hall: The psychologist as prophet*. Chicago, IL: University of Chicago Press.

Dorothy W. Hewes

Hawkins, David (1913–2002) and Hawkins, Frances Pockman (1913–)

Philosopher, mathematician, historian, physicist, educator, essayist, David Hawkins was a man of many talents. Together with his wife, Frances P. Hawkins, an early childhood teacher and writer, he made many contributions to the fields of early childhood and elementary education. David studied philosophy, physics, and mathematics, and earned a Ph.D. in probability theory at University of California in Berkeley. For most of his career, he was a professor of philosophy, science, and mathematics. He served on the faculty of the University of Colorado at Boulder for thirty-five years. While at Boulder and in forays elsewhere, he frequently turned his attention to the education of children and teachers. He was the recipient of numerous awards, including a MacArthur Award in 1986 for his work in philosophy and childhood science education.

Frances P. Hawkins studied education at San Francisco State College. She taught **kindergarten** and preschool classes for many years, with children of diverse economic and cultural backgrounds in a range of settings. A thoughtful and passionate observer of young children in action, Frances wrote articles and two books about her experiences as a teacher.

During the early 1960s, David worked on a curriculum development and science education reform project called the Elementary Science Study (ESS) in Watertown, Massachusetts. Frances accompanied him as a consultant to this project while also helping start a kindergarten in the South End of Boston, at that time a very poor section of the city. The ESS project drew together a diverse and talented group of scientists, university educators and classroom teachers (including, among others, Jerrold Zacharias, Philip Morrison, and Eleanor Duckworth), who came together to create science education materials for the young.

The idea that guided the ESS project was the notion that children could actually *do* science, that science was a matter of inquiry and investigation in which children could meaningfully participate. Influenced by the ideas of John **Dewey** and the work of Jean **Piaget**, Jerome **Bruner**, and others, the ESS group created materials that were innovative in their time for their focus on investigation and inquiry in the immediate contexts of daily life. With titles like "Peas and Particles" and "Kitchen Physics," ESS brought real science and scientific method, observation, inquiry, exploration, and analysis into the everyday environments of children and teachers. The science curriculum plans and activities were notable also for their playful, interdisciplinary approaches that built on and fostered an exploratory approach to learning with materials designed to engage children's curiosity across a range of subject matters. Children were seen as capable investigators rather than as recipients of rote knowledge. Although the ESS units have not been in print since the 1980s, the work served as a foundation for decades of curriculum development materials in science and other disciplines, and its perspectives continue to be valued among some constituencies in ongoing debates about curriculum and instruction for the young.

ESS took place during a fertile and optimistic time in education not only in the United States but elsewhere. David and Frances served as consultants to related curriculum reform initiatives in science education in schools in Nigeria, Kenya, and Uganda, and in schools supporting inquiry-oriented learning for children in Leicestershire, England.

In the 1970s, David and Frances founded and directed a center at the University of Colorado for the professional development of teachers, The Mountain View Center for Environmental Education. This Center provided workshops and advanced learning experiences for teachers of elementary and preschool children, and for sixteen years published a journal, *Outlook* (1970–1986), notable for its inclusion of the voices of teachers writing about teaching and learning in their classrooms.

Later Frances and David also visited the preprimary programs of **Reggio Emilia**, Italy, where David became friendly with Loris **Malaguzzi**. Malaguzzi references Hawkins as a source of his understandings about teaching and learning (in Edwards, Gandini, and Forman, 1998, pp. 78, 86).

Both David and Frances wrote extensively. Frances' first book, *The Logic of Action* (1969, 1986), vividly recounts her learning encounters with six deaf children. Her second book, *Journey with Children* (1997) is her memoir about her lifelong work and dedication to the education of young children.

David wrote numerous essays about teaching and learning. Collected in several volumes (Hawkins, 1974, 2000), the essays are rich with insights about the human capacity to learn. Among the most famous, "I, Thou and It"(1967, 1974) addresses the relationship between teacher and learner and also of a third entity in this triangular relationship, the "it" of the content of learning, in which the teacher-learner relationship is focused and defined. Resonant with sociocultural theory, the essay eloquently communicates the importance of subject matter as a defining context for the teacher-child relationship. In "Messing About in Science" (1965, 1974) David was an early proponent of the value of free **play** as a significant element of scientific exploration. Deeply committed to the value of exploration in learning, Hawkins said of curriculum development, "You don't want to cover a subject; you want to uncover it" (quoted in Duckworth, 1987, p. 7).

In addition to their work in education, David and Frances were both lifelong peace activists. David served as historian to the Manhattan project in 1945–1946, but turned away from its focus on weaponry. Both Frances and David were called upon to testify before the House Committee on Un-American Activities in 1950, during its anti-Communist investigations. Both refused to name any names of people they had known to be Communists unless these names had already been cited by the committee (*New York Times*, March 4, 2002).

Frances' activist stance was also embedded in her teaching and throughout her writing, as she eloquently fought for the opportunities that teachers have to make a difference in the lives of young children whom society has rejected or neglected. In "the Eye of the Beholder" (1979), for example, Frances addresses the failure of schools and society to adequately serve children with special needs. At the root of her approach as a teacher is her affirmation that "within the child, within the classroom, and within myself, seen altogether, there exists the potential and promise of new growth and development" (pp. 11–12).

Throughout their careers, and grounded in their experiences, both David and Frances Hawkins retained their hope for what schools can provide. They maintained their belief in the role that thoughtful teaching can play in the lives of children when combined with observation, inquiry, curiosity about children and subject matter, and, especially, joy. *See also* Curriculum, Science; Preschool/Prekindergarten Programs.

Further Readings: Duckworth, E. (1987). *"The having of wonderful ideas" and other essays on teaching and learning*. New York: Teachers College Press; Hawkins, D. (2000). *The roots of literacy*. Boulder, CO: University Press of Colorado; Hawkins, D. (1974). *The informed vision: Essays on learning and human nature*. New York: Agathon Press; Hawkins, F. P.L. (1997). *Journey with children: The autobiography of a teacher*. Niwot, CO: University Press of Colorado; Hawkins, F. P. (1979). The eye of the beholder. In

S. J. Meisels ed. *Special education and development perspectives on young children with special needs*. Baltimore, MD: University Park Press, pp.11–31; Hawkins, F. P. (1969, 1986) *The logic of action: Young children at work*. New York: Pantheon Press; Lehman-Haupt, C. (March 4, 2002). David Hawkins, Manhattan Project historian, dies at 88 [Obituary]. *New York Times*; Malaguzzi, L. (1998) History, ideas, and basic philosophy: An interview with Lella Gandini. In C. Edwards, L. Gandini, and G. Forman, eds. *The hundred languages of children—Advanced reflections*. 2nd ed. Greenwich, CT: Ablex Publishing Corporation, pp. 49–99.

Mary Eisenberg

Head Start

Head Start is a comprehensive child development program that serves families with children from birth to five years. It is the longest lasting social program remaining from the 1960s Kennedy–Johnson era. Its primary goal has been to increase school **readiness** of young children in low-income families. All Head Start programs must adhere to federal Program Performance Standards. These standards define the services that Head Start Programs provide and identify the seven program components. This program has served 23 million children and their families since its inception.

Head Start began in 1965 as part of the War on Poverty program launched by President Lyndon Johnson. The program was conceived by a panel of child development experts who were invited by President Johnson to draw up a model to help communities meet the needs of disadvantaged preschool children. Project Head Start was initially launched as an eight-week summer program for children aged three to five and their families. It was designed to help break the cycle of **poverty** by providing preschool children of low-income families with a comprehensive program to meet their emotional, social, intellectual, language, health, nutritional, and psychological needs. Head Start was developed in response to specific political, economic, and social pressures in the 1960s (Elkind, 1986) as well as new understandings about child development. From the start the program has been affected by politics, budget allocations, differing expectations about its purpose, and questions about its impact on children and their communities (Bee, 1981; Clemitt, 2005; Collins, 1989; McKey et al., 1985).

In 1965, Head Start enrollment was 561,000 and had a budget of $96.4 million. By fiscal year 2005, enrollment had grown to 906,993 and by fiscal year 2006 the budget appropriation had increased to more than $6.5 billion for programs, and an additional $231 million for training and technical assistance, research and demonstration projects, and monitoring and program reviews. This works out to an average cost per child of $7287 (2005).

During the 2004–2005 Head Start program year, 12.5 percent of the Head Start enrollment consisted of children with disabilities, nearly 49,000 children participated in home-based Head Start program services, and 91 percent of Head Start children had health insurance. Over 890,000 parents volunteered in their local Head Start program, more than 207,000 fathers were involved in regularly scheduled program activities, and 27 percent of Head Start program staff members were parents of current or former Head Start children.

In 1994, a reauthorization of the Head Start Act established a new **Early Head Start** program for low-income families with infants and toddlers. In Fiscal Year 2005, $684 million was used to support more than 650 programs to provide Early Head Start child development and family support services in all fifty states and in the District of Columbia and Puerto Rico. These programs served nearly 62,000 children under the age of 3. A historical strength of Project Head Start is its emphasis on family and community participation, as Head Start mandates parent involvement, including parent and community participation on parent governing councils. Because Head Start was conceived as part of the Community Action Programs in the Office of Economic Opportunity, community empowerment was a goal. However, over the years, Head Start programs have received praise as well as criticism for their flexibility of programming and involvement of the community in management. Over its forty-year history, Head Start has been consistent in its focus on a comprehensive developmental program that has included academic, health, and social initiatives for preschool age children, as well as parent and community involvement.

Head Start programs have focused, since the beginning, on children's health and dental care, **parent involvement**, parent councils, employment opportunities for children's parents, **family literacy** programs, **inclusion** of children with, special needs and programs for English Language Learners. Despite many debates, the most consistent framing of goals and recommended pedagogical approaches for children has been in terms of a comprehensive approach toward health and child developmental goals, or the "whole child"—physical, socioemotional, language, cognitive, and academic development were all considered important in the education of young children (see debates in Vinovskis, 2005; Zigler and Muenchow, 1992; and the most recent debates summarized in Zigler and Styfco, 2004). While Vinovkis' (2005) history of Head Start shows that academic aims have been an important part of the debate related to curriculum in Head Start since its inception, fostering the development of the "whole child," including preventive health and dental care, has been a long-term belief in Head Start, bolstered by evidence that this was an educational and cost-effective approach to quality early education for low-income children (see debates and evidence for and against this point in Zigler and Styfco, 2004). National guidelines focusing on developmentally appropriate" practice (see Bredekamp and Copple, 1997) reinforced the "whole child" curricular approach as "best practice" for *all* children. Therefore, until recently Head Start has emphasized a curriculum that fostered socioemotional development through play, the fostering of positive self-esteem, peer as well as adult relationships, and an integrated developmental approach to language development, cognitive development, and early literacy and numeracy knowledge (Zigler and Muenchow, 1992).

Late twentieth and early twenty-first century research on cognitive learning (National Research Council, 2001) and children's eagerness to learn, as well as research on prevention of early reading failures (Snow, Burns, and Griffin, 1998) focused attention on children's capacity for greater cognitive and academic learning in Head Start programs, and in preschool programs, more generally. Recent research (see the synthesis by the National Research Council, 2001) focused attention on the importance of teacher training and teacher qualifications in early childhood education for delivery of a "high quality" program and desired child development and academic outcomes. Therefore, the low number of "qualified" Head Start teachers and teaching aides with bachelor's degrees or associate degrees in early childhood related fields has been highlighted as one reason Head Start children continued to have academic problems compared to middle-income peers when entering school (see National Research Council, 2001; Zigler and Styfco, 2004). It is argued that Head Start teachers were also insufficiently trained in early **literacy**, numeracy, or even in **socioemotional development** to produce sufficient, desirable long-term effects comparable to other experimental high-quality programs for young children (all of which had much higher costs per child and per teacher than the federally funded and much larger national Head Start program).

At its inception in the 1960s there were also debates about whether Head Start should be administered by the Office of Education, the Department of Health, Education, and Welfare (HEW), or by the Office of Economic Opportunity, where it eventually was situated as part of the Community Action Program. In 1970, Head Start was moved to HEW's Office of Child Development, directed by Edward Zigler. By the 1990s, Head Start had become part of the Administration on Children, Youth and Families in the Department of Health and Human Services (DHS). Arguments continue as to whether it should be moved to the Office of Education and become more focused on readiness for school, and school academics. In the spring of 2006, Head Start, still in DHS, was moved to the section focusing on welfare policies, which administers federal funds for **Temporary Assistance to Needy Families** (TANF). This move reinforces a federal welfare policy that focuses on the *temporary* nature of federal assistance to low-income working families and their children for assistance to find and maintain employment, and for child-care or preschool education. It also integrates the Head Start program with other federally and state funded programs focused on low-income and "working poor" families.

Head Start began as a large-scale program that involved a large number of children from its first summer in 1965, and has continued to be a large social program throughout its forty-year history. Though Head Start has increased its coverage of children over the years, it has included from one-third to one-half of all eligible low-income children, in largely half-day programs. By beginning quickly and targeting many children and through involvement of community and parent members, including employment of parents as teacher aides or assistants, Head Start built a large community support-base, potentially at the cost of the "quality" of the teachers and their training to teach certain skills to children (see debates on these points in Delpit, 1995; Zigler and Styfco, 2004). The decisions to move quickly, to be comprehensive in aims, and to involve parents and community in multiple ways had many perceived advantages and positive effects. They also had some perceived disadvantages that are part of continuing debates and reforms (Vinovskis, 2005; Zigler and Muenchow, 1992; Zigler and Styfco, 2004). *See also* Child Development Group of Mississippi; National Head Start Association.

Further Readings: An annotated bibliography of Head Start research and a list of ongoing research studies on Head Start is available online at www2.acf.dhhs.gov/programs/hsb/research/resources.htm; Bee, C. K. (1981). *A longitudinal study to determine if Head Start has lasting effects on school achievement*. Unpublished doctoral dissertation, University of South Dakota; Bredekamp, S., and C. Copple, eds. (1997). *Developmentally appropriate practice in early childhood programs*. Washington, DC: National Association for the Education of Young Children; Clemmitt, M. (2005, August 26). Evaluating Head Start: Does it help poor children and their parents? *CQ Researcher* 15(29), 687–694; Collins, R. (1989). *Head Start research and evaluation: Background and overview*. Vienna, VA: Collins Management Consulting; Delpit, L. (1995). *Other peoples' children: Cultural conflict in the classroom*. New York: The New Press; Elkind, D. (1986). Formal education and early childhood education: An essential difference. *Phi Delta Kappan* 67, 631–636; McKey, R. H., L. Condelli, H. Ganson, B. J. Barrett, C. McConkey, and M. C. Plantz (1985). *The impact of Head Start on children, families, and communities. Final report of the Head Start Evaluation, Synthesis, and Utilization Project*. Washington, DC: CSR Inc. for the Head Start Bureau, Administration for Children, Youth and Families, U.S. Department of Health and Human Services; National Research Council (2001). *Eager to Learn: Educating our Preschoolers*. Washington, DC: National Academy Press; Snow, C. E., M. S. Burns, and P. Griffin, eds. (1998). *Preventing reading difficulties in young children*. Washington, DC: National Academy Press. Available online at http://books.nap.edu/html/prdyc/; Vinovskis, M. A. (2005). *The birth of Head Start: Preschool education policies in the Kennedy and Johnson administrations*. Chicago: The University of Chicago Press; Zigler, E., and S. Muenchow (1992). *Head Start: The inside story of America's most successful educational experiment*. New York: Basic Books; Zigler, E., and S. Styfco, eds. (2004). *The Head Start debates*. Baltimore: Paul H. Brookes.

Michael Kalinowski, Marianne Bloch, and Ko Eun Kim

High/Scope

High/Scope Educational Research Foundation is an independent nonprofit organization that was founded by David P. Weikart in 1970 in Ypsilanti, Michigan. High/Scope's mission is to lift lives through education and its vision is a world in which all educational settings use active, participatory learning so everyone has a chance to succeed in life and contribute to society. The Foundation engages in curriculum development, research, training, publishing, and communication. In the High/Scope educational model, learners plan, do, and review their actions; engage in activities at their own developmental levels; and receive support and respect from others. High/Scope has developed and spread its educational model for young children in preschool programs, infants and toddlers in home visit programs and child-care settings, children in elementary schools, and teenagers in summer camps. Studies by High/Scope and others have confirmed the short-term and long-term effectiveness of these applications. The organization's periodical *High/Scope ReSource* is available upon request from High/Scope Educational Research Foundation, 600 North River Street, Ypsilanti, MI 48198-2898, phone 734-485-2000, fax 734-485-0704. For further information, see its website at www.highscope.org. *See also* High/Scope Perry Preschool Study.

Further Readings: Hohmann, Mary, and David P. Weikart (2002). *Educating young children: Active learning practices for preschool and child care programs*. 2nd ed.

Ypsilanti, MI: High/Scope Press; Schweinhart, Lawrence J., Jeanne Montie, Zongping Xiang, W. Steven Barnett, Clive R. Belfield, and Milagros Nores (2005). *Lifetime effects: The High/Scope Perry Preschool Study through age 40*. Monographs of the High/Scope Educational Research Foundation, 14. Ypsilanti, MI: High/Scope Press.

Lawrence J. Schweinhart

High/Scope Perry Preschool Study

The High/Scope Perry Preschool Study is regarded as one of the pioneering studies of the long-term effects of high-quality preschool programs for young children living in poverty. This study was begun by David P. Weikart and colleagues in 1962, at a time when people had started thinking about the possibilities of fighting poverty through early childhood education. The design of the study builds on random assignment of 123 children to one of two groups—one that received a high-quality preschool program at ages 3 and 4 or one that did not. Data have been collected annually from ages 3 to 11, and at 14, 15, 19, 27 and 40, with only 6 percent of data missing. The program maintained high quality with systematic use of an educational model, certified teachers each serving 5–6 children, and weekly home visits. Compared to those without the program, program participants were more ready for school, required fewer placements for mental impairment, and later achieved greater school success. Beyond schooling, compared to the no-program group, the program group committed only half as many crimes, and had higher employment rates and earnings at ages 27 and 40. Taken together, these findings add up to a substantial economic return of $17 per dollar invested, including $13 to taxpayers. The study has served as a model for other studies, and the program has served as a model for other programs. Results of the study have been disseminated widely and have been used to advocate for high-quality early childhood education. *See also* High/Scope.

Further Readings: Schweinhart, Lawrence J., Jeanne Montie, Zongping Xiang, W. Steven Barnett, Clive R. Belfield, and Milagros Nores (2005). *Lifetime effects: The High/Scope Perry Preschool Study through age 40*. Monographs of the High/Scope Educational Research Foundation, 14. Ypsilanti, MI: High/Scope Press.

Lawrence J. Schweinhart

Hill, Patty Smith (1868–1946)

Patty Smith Hill was a well-known figure in the **Kindergarten** Movement of the late nineteenth century and an advocate of progressivism within the International Kindergarten Union. In the first decades of the twentieth century, as Head of the Department of Kindergarten Education at Teachers College Columbia, she became a leader in efforts to professionalize early childhood education and improve the status of teachers.

Hill was born in 1868 in Anchorage, a small town outside Louisville, Kentucky, where her parents Mary Jane Smith Hill and William Wallace Hill had founded the Bellewood School for Young Ladies in 1861. During her early years, her family lived a prosperous and untroubled life at Bellewood. Their security ended in

1874 when her father decided to pursue his career in the West. The Hills and their six children moved to Missouri and then to Texas. William suffered a series of financial setbacks, his health failed, and he died in 1879. Mary Jane and the children returned to Kentucky and spent the next several years struggling with poverty and recurrent illness. Support from her grandparents finally enabled Hill to attend Louisville Collegiate Institute and complete Kindergarten training.

In 1888, Hill became the Head Teacher at the Holcombe Mission Kindergarten in Louisville and began to introduce innovations within a traditional Froebelian context. Influenced by her studies at summer institutes with Colonel Francis **Parker** and G. Stanley **Hall**, she designed a sequence of classroom activities tied to child development. She published her observations in *The Kindergarten Review*, became the Director of the Louisville Free Kindergarten Association, and demonstrated her successful classroom methods at the 1893 Columbian Exposition. Educators from across the country came to Louisville to see Hill's classroom. John **Dewey** visited in 1893 and Hill went to study with him at the University of Chicago the following summer.

By the turn of the century, Hill's challenges to Froebelian orthodoxy had become well known and were threatening to split the Kindergarten Movement. Within the International Kindergarten Union, in contrast to the "Uniform Plan" advocated by traditionalist Susan **Blow**, Hill was urging teachers to adopt an experimental approach and adjust their curricula to the special needs and social circumstances of the child. The controversy continued when Hill, "that young radical in the South," and Blow were invited to offer a joint course in Kindergarten practices at Teachers College Columbia (TCC). In the "friendly warfare" that followed, Hill's engaging style and more up-to-date views won over the students and faculty in attendance.

Hill was appointed to the TCC faculty in 1905, was elected president of the **International Kindergarten Union** (IKU) in 1908, and became Head of TCC's Department of Kindergarten Education in 1910. At Columbia, she developed a rigorous course of study for early childhood students, built a highly respected graduate program, and maintained strong connections with the public schools. During the final years of her career, she worked with colleagues to establish an experimental college and, as part of that effort, directed a community-based nursery school program in the impoverished Manhattenville neighborhood. She was awarded an honorary doctorate from Columbia in 1929 and retired in 1935.

During her long career, Patty Smith Hill established model classrooms, teacher training institutes, and cooperative community centers that drew national and international attention. She authored stories and songs for children, including "Good Morning to You" and "Happy Birthday to You," designed child-appropriate classroom furniture and learning equipment, and conducted observational studies of young children at play. She wrote extensively on curricula and pedagogy. Her collaborations with other educators resulted in two collections that defined the early scholarship within the field of early childhood education: *Experimental Studies in Kindergarten Education* and *A Conduct Curriculum for the Kindergarten and First Grade*. *See also* Froebel, Friedrich.

Further Readings: Hill, Patty Smith, ed. (1915). *Experimental studies in kindergarten education*. New York: Teachers College Press; Hill, Patty Smith, ed. (1923). *A conduct* *curriculum for the kindergarten and first grade*. New York: Charles Scribner's Sons; Snyder, Agnes (1972). Patty Smith Hill: Dynamic leadership in new directions. In *Dauntless women in childhood education*. Washington, DC: Association for Childhood Education International.

Susan Douglas Franzosa

History of U.S. Early Childhood Care and Education

Multiple histories can be written of early childhood education—for example, histories based on those individuals whose leadership helped advance the availability and quality of early childhood programs; histories based on significant, defining events; histories of the field's disparate delivery systems (kindergartens, child care, preschools); and histories that chronicle the evolution of public policies on behalf of young children and their early education. None of these approaches, however, individually or collectively, could be adequately captured by an encyclopedia entry. This entry responds to this quandary by providing an overview of the history of early childhood care and education; it targets two elements of the field that have fashioned its history and are shaping its future: (1) the ebb and flow of public interest in young children's early education and (2) continuity of professional values.

Historical Overview

The U.S. history of early childhood education spans from the nation's beginning. Its emergence as a distinct professional interest in the late 1800s is tied to the beginning of the child study movement and the first systematic studies of children; efforts to develop the world's first system of "common schools"; and onset of a scientific approach to education.

Early childhood education as an area of professional interest began to solidify in the early 1900s. Yet it remained a relatively small and obscure area of interest marked by intermittent spurts of federal attention in response to national events such as the Great Depression in the 1930s, World War II, White House Conferences on Children each decade between 1909 and 1980, and efforts to reduce welfare dependency by families in need of child care because of requirements to enter the workforce. These periods of attention reflect our nation's crisis orientation to policymaking. Early childhood education issues tend to be viewed as important during national emergencies, times of economic stress, and in response to perceptions of family dysfunction.

Further, the pervasive national culture has held—and still holds—that families should care for their own children. Child rearing, including child care and early education, were, and are, viewed as a private responsibility. When President Richard Nixon vetoed comprehensive child development legislation in 1972, he asserted that "for the federal government to plunge headlong financially into supporting child development would commit the vast moral authority of the National Government to the side of communal approaches to child rearing and against the family-centered approach" (Washington, 1984, p. 256).

This orientation has meant that public interest in issues related to early education has ebbed and flowed, sporadically called forth by issues of sufficient concern to overcome the nation's reticence to "interfere" with families' child-rearing responsibilities and obligations. It has also severely limited the creation of public policies that recognize early childhood education as a public good.

Defining characteristics of the early childhood profession. Two overarching characteristics help define the early childhood field: the gender of its members and the delivery system for services. First, from its inception, the history of early childhood care and education has been shaped by the fact that it has been viewed as a profession for women. Women have been perceived as naturally inclined to be early childhood teachers because the knowledge required for this role seems so similar to—if not duplicative of—the mother's role. To the extent that women's roles in U.S. society have been marginalized and the belief prevails that the ability to mother is innate, recognition and respect for the expertise required to work effectively with young children has been absent. It follows that limited support has existed to require formal credentials or to expect compensation comparable to other professionals doing similar work. This circumstance has made it difficult to build a professional image for early childhood education that resonates with the general public as worthy of its support and respect.

Second, and also from its inception, the field's history has been shaped by distinct, even though somewhat overlapping, histories of its disparate systems for delivering early childhood programs: kindergartens, child care (formerly called day nurseries), and preschools (formerly called nursery schools). More than just differences in program type and purpose are involved; these programs have been delivered by different sponsors and, until recently, have served different children. As a result, the early childhood field is an amalgam of different cultures, purposes, professional expectations, governance structures, and funding mechanisms whose specifics are often shaped by issues of race and class.

The presence of distinctive genealogical lines and developmental histories for its component parts has challenged the field of early childhood care and education to function in an unified way on behalf of children and the early childhood profession. The fragmented character of the field also has influenced its ability to manage the ebb and flow of public interest in early childhood education.

Mobilizing sustained public support. During the 1960s, a confluence of factors once again energized public interest in early childhood education. Early childhood programs expanded exponentially, propelled by newfound recognition of the important contribution of the environment to the first years of development, the explosion of women into the labor force, the "discovery" of poverty in the United States, and movements for social justice. This expansion, driven largely by the birth of Head Start and growing demand for child care, built on the early childhood field's history of creating programs for children with distinctive auspices or sponsors and different sources of funding. Perpetuating previous patterns of growth, the field's various components grew in parallel fashion, including childcare, preschool programs, and **Head Start**.

By the 1970s, the principle of public responsibility for children's positive development and school readiness gained greater credence, though still far from universal acceptance. A series of national reports, including a prominent 1977 Carnegie Council on Children publication, helped promote increased awareness of the consequences associated with the historical disposition to insulate family matters from public policy. Child development specialists and other advocates used the opportunity to argue for a universal and developmental philosophy of care for children.

In practice, though, access most often has been accorded to families based on their income level, with children's and families' personal characteristics also being key to defining eligibility for publicly funded programs. These programs largely have been viewed as interventions for transforming the lives of poor children or of their families.

The ongoing creation of separate early childhood programs and funding streams—in this instance based on race and class—congealed the fragmented base that undergirds the delivery of early care and education programs in the United States. The framing of publicly funded early education as compensatory intervention for "at risk" children and/or as support for the employment of low income parents thwarted advocates' efforts to promote optimal human development as an overriding purpose and function of early childhood education. It also directed attention away from development of the systems needed to nurture and sustain the field's capacity on behalf of young children.

In the 1980s, momentum around early childhood issues stalled despite the landmark creation of several Congressional organizational structures to observe, report and act on the status of children (the Select Committee on Children, Youth and Families; the Senate Children's Caucus; and the Senate Family Caucus). Diminished by federal priorities that shifted public investments away from early childhood care and education, it would be almost twenty years after Nixon's 1972 presidential veto of the Comprehensive Child Development Act before Congress enacted new federal legislation focused solely on child care: the 1990 Comprehensive Child Care and Development Block Grant.

As the 1990s progressed, congressional focus on welfare reform legislation redirected attention to the needs of working women, especially low-income women who lacked the resources to pay for good child care. This deliberation helped place a spotlight on the field's issues of program availability, quality, and supply (especially for infants and toddlers). At about the same time, public awareness of research on early brain development, accompanied by new studies on the positive impact of high-quality early childhood programs (especially for children from impoverished environments) sparked renewed public interest in children's earliest years of development. A rush of new public and private investments in early childhood programs and initiatives ensued.

Perhaps most prominent of these is the current movement to make prekindergarten programs universally available for all children, thus harking back to the field's targeted efforts in the late 1800s and early 1900s to expand the availability of kindergarten. Similarly, the emphasis is on state-level activity on behalf of early care and education, and many states have increased their investments in services for young children. This activity has occurred, in part, in response to growing appreciation for the importance of the first five years of children's lives and its relationship to school **readiness**.

By the year 2000, forty-three states had invested state dollars in prekindergarten programs. Additionally, thirty-one states had invested state funds for child development and family support programs for infants and toddlers. Importantly, these new programs are increasingly blurring historical distinctions between child care and preschool. This latest surge of interest in early childhood issues is being dampened, however, by an economic downturn and changing political landscape.

Continuity of Professional Values

Throughout the fluctuations of public attention to early care and education, the early childhood field has evolved its own cultural framework. From its earliest beginnings, the early care and education field has operated from a core set of values that have become embedded in its professional culture and helped shape its historical trajectory. These values currently are being scrutinized publicly to an extent never before experienced. This scrutiny reflects both changing circumstances and expectations for public accountability tied to escalating public investment in early childhood programs.

The core values in the early care and education profession can be captured under two headings: holistic approach to child development and collaborative relationships with families. The continuity of these values has led both to stability over time of professional perspectives and to resistance to external calls for change, creating on the one hand a sense of cohesion among members of the field and, on the other hand, perceptions of intransigence by nonmembers.

Holistic approach to child development. The early childhood field has valued an integrated focus on children's physical, social, emotional, and cognitive development—what is called a "whole child" approach. Articulating this holistic focus as a respect for children, the founding pedagogies of the Froebelian kindergarten and progressive education have had an enduring impact on the field.

The ideas of Friedrich **Froebel**, recognized as the father of kindergarten, came to the United States from Germany in the mid-1880s. At this time in the history of early childhood education, nursery schools did not yet exist. These programs did not emerge until the 1920s and even then they were laboratories for child study. In the mid- to late 1800s and early 1900s, the field was focused on expanding the availability of kindergartens based on the idealistic pedagogy of Friedrich Froebel, building on the successful launch in 1893 of the first public school kindergarten in St. Louis. Froebel's approach to early education dominated until the early 1900s when interest in a more scientific and less-philosophical approach to education spawned a greater focus on children as individuals. This "new approach" to early education was informed by scientific study of the child rather than on the child's embodiment of universal features of humanity that were to be carefully nurtured. The field's intense internal debate on Froebel's approach to early education and what became the progressive approach to early education—heralded today under the banner of developmentally appropriate practice—is captured in a defining report authorized by the International Kindergarten Union in 1913. Despite their differences, however, both approaches to early education viewed the child holistically and as the center of the educational enterprise—a value that has endured to the present.

This holistic approach to children's early education has been challenged on numerous occasions and often placed early childhood leaders on the defensive. In the 1960s, new research on the environment's impact on early development, in conjunction with growing awareness of poverty and interest in ameliorating it, led to experimental interventions. A diverse array of newly constructed early childhood program models proposed to alter the direction of children's early development and support their school readiness. Many of these approaches focused on curriculum content the model's designer—often an individual from outside the early childhood field—thought children should learn or on specific instructional practices.

These new program models frequently ignored the field's focus on the whole child, often touting their own approaches by contrasting them with the "traditional" (i.e., old-fashioned) child-centered and developmental approach long associated with early childhood education. It was argued that traditional early childhood programs were too focused on **play**, and not sufficiently focused on learning outcomes, to eliminate the educational gaps presented by poor children. Early childhood educators bemoaned the way their knowledge base and experience were being ignored by relatively new entrants into the field.

Support for the field's child-centered and developmental approach to early education emerged, however, in the early 1980s from research on the long-term positive impact of child-centered approaches to early education. These research findings deflected—for the time being—criticisms of early childhood educators' views on best practice. The **National Association for the Education of Young Children**'s (NAEYC) successful 1987 publication on **developmentally appropriate practice** further helped the early childhood field reclaim the validity of its child-centered approach and reinforced its historical reliance on developmental theory as the primary informant for educational decision-making.

By the 1990s, the success of NAEYC's publication ignited new challenges to the early childhood field's holistic approach to early education. A group of researchers known as reconceptualists challenged the field's over reliance on theories of child development and successfully opened the field's reception to the impact of factors such as race, class, and gender on children's development. Simultaneously, the nation became increasingly aware of and concerned about racial achievement gaps. In response, the centrality of literacy development—versus the "whole child"—was established in prominent federal legislation called the **No Child Left Behind Act** of 2001.

In contrast to the 1960s, when limited evidence existed to confirm the validity of the field's focus on the whole child, strong evidence now exists to support essential linkages between children's emotional, social, and intellectual capabilities. Yet given current political circumstances and a focus on child outcomes, sustainability in its current form of the field's long-standing commitment to a child-centered developmental approach may be at risk.

Families as collaborators in promoting children's development. Just as early educators value the whole child, they also highly value the child's integral relationship with his or her family. Early childhood educators always have viewed families as central to the successful development of young children and as essential partners to the success of early childhood education. Early expressions of this partnership were seen in efforts to share newly emerging scientific knowledge of children's development with mothers so they could use this knowledge in their child rearing, thereby optimizing children's developmental potential.

To advance what was a novel idea in 1923, Lawrence Frank, of the New York-based Laura Spelman Rockefeller Memorial, launched an extensive parent education campaign. Similarly, nursery school programs, the majority of which served as lab sites for campus-based developmental psychologists, partnered with mothers in using the new research on child development to foster children's positive growth. Recognizing the importance of the home environment to children's development, and parents' unique knowledge and understanding of their own child, nursery and kindergarten teachers also routinely visited children in their homes to learn more about them and identify ways they could incorporate children's interests into the classroom setting.

Given differences in their formal knowledge of child development, the nature of the teacher–parent relationship often became one in which the early childhood teacher was the source and giver of knowledge, and the parent the recipient. The imbalance in this relationship intensified during the 1960s and beyond when parent education was elevated as an intervention strategy to help low-income preschoolers—most often poor black children—develop social and cognitive skills needed for school readiness.

Simultaneously, however, in conjunction with the 1960s Civil Rights movement, low-income parents were recognized as important allies in promoting the importance of early childhood education. Further, in acknowledgment of new insights on child development informed by the fields of sociology and anthropology, plus a retreat from assumptions of parental ignorance, parents' central roles in their children's development began to be recast. This updated view of parental importance was captured in 1965 with the launch of Project Head Start, the country's first federally funded early childhood program. Head Start's emphasis on families' centrality to child development and reliance on family members as decision makers, as well as implementers, in important program issues, reaffirmed the early childhood field's commitment to families and raised its commitment to a new level.

It must be noted, though, that parents' value as collaborators is facing extensive pressure as an ideal not easily accomplished in practice, considering the expense, time, skill, and commitment required. And, the increasing number of parents in the workforce, along with public policy changes requiring poor parents to work to receive public support, has lessened the availability of parent time and energy for parent involvement in their children's education.

Conclusion

No longer a small and obscure field, early childhood education programs now face increased scrutiny. Rising public expectations for consistent, high-level performance place new demands on early childhood education as a field, present new challenges, and offer new opportunities to integrate high-quality early childhood care and education into the national landscape. The growth of public interest and expanded investments in early childhood education is accompanied by increased expectations for program accountability. Based on research on early brain development and evaluation studies of early childhood education, increased pressure exists for children to come to kindergarten prepared to be successful with academic demands.

Major gains have been accomplished with significant new investments by federal and state governments as well as by increased private sector support. Nevertheless, despite more than a century of effort to elevate the importance of early childhood care and education, the United States still lacks a comprehensive system of services to ensure that all young children receive the high quality of programs they need and deserve. Seizing future opportunities will require advocates to find ways to engage and sustain public interest and commitment to early care and education.

Further Readings: Copple, Carol, ed. (2001). *NAEYC at 75: Reflections on the past, challenges for the future*. Washington, DC: National Association for the Education of Young Children; DeVita, Carol J., and Rachel Mosher-Williams, eds. (2001). *Who speaks for America's children?* Washington, DC: The Urban Institute Press; Finkelstein, B. (1988). The revolt against selfishness: Women and the dilemmas of professionalism in early childhood education. In B. Spodek, O. N. Saracho, and D. Peters, eds., *Professionalism and the early childhood practitioner*. New York: Teachers College Press, pp. 10–29; Goffin, S. G. (2001). Whither early childhood care and education in the next century. In Lyn Corno, ed., *Education across a century: The centennial volume*. Part I. Chicago: The University of Chicago Press, pp. 140–163; Grubb, W. N., and M. Lazerson (1988). *Broken promises: How Americans fail their children*. Chicago: The University of Chicago Press; Keniston, K., and the Carnegie Council on Children (1977). *All our children: The American family under pressure*. New York: The Carnegie Council on Children; *The Kindergarten. Report of the Committee of Nineteen on the Theory and Practice of the Kindergarten*. Authorized by the International Kindergarten Union. (1913). Boston, New York, Chicago: Houghton Mifflin and Co.; Washington, V. (1984). Social and personal ecology surrounding public policy for young children: An American dilemma. In D. Gullo and D. Craven, eds., *Ecological perspectives on the development of the young child*. Springfield, IL: Charles Thomas Publishers, pp. 254–76.

Stacie G. Goffin and Valora Washington

Hunt, Joseph McVicker (1906–1991)

Joseph McVicker Hunt, a developmental psychologist best known for his work with infants and young children, was born in Nebraska in 1906. He received his BA (1929) and MA (1930) degrees from the University of Nebraska and a Ph.D. from Cornell University in 1933. He went on to pursue post-doctoral work at the New York Psychiatric Institute and Worcester State Hospital in Massachusetts. He was on the faculty of Brown University from 1936 to 1946. His final faculty appointment was at the University of Illinois (1951–1974) where he taught psychology and education courses. He received numerous awards for his work through psychological and mental health foundations, including two awards for excellence in research from the American Personnel and Guidance Association, the **G. Stanley Hall** award from Division 7 (APA), and the Gold Medal for lifetime achievement from the American Psychological Foundation.

Throughout his career, Hunt pursued his two most enduring interests—psychopathology, and the study of the long-term effects of early experience on later development. His interest in psychopathology began during his undergraduate and graduate work as he researched the effects of abnormal psychology on intellectual development. Hunt was intrigued by **Freud's** contention that early experience had a deep impact on development. Building upon these ideas, Hunt proceeded to design a series of feeding-frustration experiments using rat pups. He put the young pups on a feeding deprivation schedule for a few days followed by normal feeding into adulthood. He found that when he placed the adult rats on a feeding depravation schedule, they began to hoard food pellets, a behavior that was uncharacteristic in normal rats. He postulated that this was the effect of the early experiences of depravation. This finding lead Hunt to expand his thinking into the effects of such negative environments on the development of young children.

At about this same time, Hunt was asked to teach a course on infant development, which prompted his interest in the work of Jean **Piaget**. Through his rat studies, Hunt had recognized the impact of early experiences on personality development. He expanded his thinking into the development of intellect and began to doubt the prevailing view of the static and predetermined nature of the intellect. When Hunt moved to the University of Illinois in 1951, he began investigating factors that might influence the development of the intellect, such as child-rearing practices, poverty, and the accessibility of educational stimulation. *Intelligence and Experience*, published in 1961, was the result of this work. In this book, Hunt suggested that intelligence was an information-processing system effected by environmental influences during development. The ideas presented laid the foundation for such educational movements as Project **Head Start** and the later Follow Through Project for school-aged children. Based on his research, Hunt was selected to chair the Presidential Task Force on Child Development that produced "A Bill of Rights for Children" in 1967.

Hunt strongly believed in the relevance of research in supporting theoretical assumptions, so he set forth on a number of projects to further his understanding of early development. He evaluated the development of infants placed in orphanages in both Greece and Iran who were being raised with only minimal attention to psychological needs. During these examinations, Hunt began to doubt the relevance of norm-referenced tests to the information he desired. In order to better understand the influence of different environmental stimuli, Hunt felt that new methods of evaluating development were needed. Working with one of his students, Ina C. Uzgiris, he developed the Ordinal Scales of Psychological Development (1975) based on the particular abilities that develop during the sensori-moor stage as defined by Piaget.

Hunt retired from his position at the University of Illinois in 1974, but remained an active professor emeritus until his death in 1991. At the time of his death he was still at work on a book that was to be called *Behavior Science and Child Rearing*, a summary of what his research could offer as advice to parents and teachers. He also had started another work to be titled *Motivation and Experience*, describing his work in the area of intrinsic motivation and its effect on development. Both of these works detailed his belief that psychological science should be used to influence public policy and individual practices for the education of young children.

Further Readings: Haywood, H. C. (1992). Joseph McVicker Hunt (1906–1991). *American Psychologist*, 47(8), 1050–1051; Hunt, J. McV. (1961). *Intelligence and Experience*. New York: Ronald Press; Hunt, J. McV. (1979). *Early Psychological Development and Experience*. Worcester, MA: Clark University; Uzgiris, I. C., and J. McV. Hunt (1975). *Assessment in Infancy*. Urbana, IL: University of Illinois Press.

Martha Latorre

Hymes, James L., Jr. (1913–1998)

James L. Hymes Jr. was an avowed developmentalist committed to addressing children's social, emotional, and physical needs as a means of enhancing children's cognitive growth. Hymes believed that healthy socioemotional relationships with children were the starting point for effective education and constructive social change. James Lee Hymes, Jr., was born August 3, 1913, and grew up in New York City. After graduating from Harvard University in 1934, he subsequently earned his Master's and Doctorate in Child Development and Parent Education from Teachers College, Columbia University in 1936 and 1946, respectively. In 1936, he was Assistant State Supervisor of the Works Progress Association Nursery Schools in New York under Ruth Andrus (Hymes Personal Papers). He then worked as Assistant Executive Secretary for the Progressive Education Association (1937) and later as editor of *Progressive Education* (1940–1942) and *Frontiers of Democracy*.

As World War II escalated, the need for child care for the children of working mothers increased. Shipyard owner Edgar Kaiser hired Hymes as Director for two 24-hour child-care facilities in Portland, Oregon. The Kaiser Child Service Centers opened in November 1943 and were groundbreakers on several fronts. The Centers had quality indoor and outdoor play equipment and all teachers were degreed. An on-staff nutritionist developed meals and snacks and shipyard medical staff administered immunizations. Hymes collaborated with former Teachers College Professor Lois Meek Stolz to lead the Centers and much of his future philosophy sprung from his Kaiser experience. After the war, Hymes worked with Caroline Zachry and Lawrence **Frank** at the Caroline Zachry Institute of Human Development in New York City. Hymes' work was to develop a means of sensitizing teachers to the emotional needs of children entering schools.

Hymes wrote *A Pound of Prevention* and not only used the pamphlet for his doctoral dissertation but also founded with it the simplistic writing style that became his hallmark. Hymes continued to write prolifically over the years, producing *How to Tell Your Child About Sex* (1949), *Being a Good Parent* (1949), *Teacher Listen, the Children Speak* (1949), *Understanding Your Child* (1952), *Effective Home-School Relations* (1953), *Behavior and Misbehavior* (1955), and *A Child Development Point of View* (1955).

Hymes held several organizational posts, serving as Vice-President representing Nursery Schools for the Association for Childhood Education (now the **Association for Childhood Education International** [ACEI]) from 1949 to 1951 and working to establish the Southern Association for Children Under Six (now the **Southern Early Childhood Association** [SECA]). He served as the President of the National Association for Nursery Education (now the **National Association for the Education of Young Children** [NAEYC]) from 1945 to 1947 and buoyed the association at its nadir, the postwar years. Beginning in 1946, Hymes held three different university posts as Professor of Early Childhood Education: New Paltz State Teachers College (1946–1949), George Peabody College for Teachers (1949–1957), and the University of Maryland (1957–1970). Students noted Hymes for his informal yet challenging and inviting teaching style. During his time at Maryland, Hymes took a six-month leave to serve on the National Planning Committee for President Johnson's War on Poverty program, **Head Start**. Hymes and D. Keith **Osborn** were the only two early childhood professionals on the National Planning Committee. Both emphasized educational goals and teacher training for those preparing to teach in Head Start. Through Hymes' persistence, a teacher-to-child ratio of one teacher to fifteen children was additionally secured. Upon his return to the University of Maryland, Hymes became increasingly frustrated with the diminishing emphasis upon children's total development. He retired early, began speaking and writing full-time, and opened Hacienda Press in Carmel, California. His popular works written after 1970 include *Early Childhood Education: Living History Interviews* (1978, 1979) and *Early Childhood Education: Twenty Years in Review* (1991). Hymes died March 6, 1998.

Further Readings: Anderson, Charlotte Jean (2003). Contributions of James Lee Hymes, Jr., to the field of early childhood education. Doctoral dissertation. Austin, TX: The University of Texas; Graham, Patricia Albjerg (1967). *Progressive education: From arcady to academe, a history of the progressive education association, 1919–1955*. New York: Teachers College Press; Hymes, James L., Jr. (1979). *Early childhood education: Living history interviews Book 3*. Carmel, CA: Hacienda Press; James L. Hymes, Jr., Personal Papers. *Talking Over Old Times-Up to 1976*. Unpublished manuscript. Pasadena, CA: Pacific Oaks College.

Charlotte Anderson

I

IDEA. *See* Individuals with Disabilities Education Act

IEA Preprimary Project

The IEA Preprimary Project is an unprecedented multinational study of preprimary care and education sponsored by the International Association for the Evaluation of Educational Achievement (IEA). **High/Scope** Educational Research Foundation served as the international coordinating center, and High/Scope staff, working collaboratively with researchers in seventeen countries, were responsible for sampling, instrument development, data analysis, and the writing of five published reports and one in press. The purpose of the study is to identify how process and structural characteristics of community preprimary settings affect children's language and cognitive development at age 7. The study is unique because many diverse countries participated, using common instruments to measure family background, teachers' characteristics, setting structural characteristics, experiences of children, and children's developmental status.

The study is rooted theoretically in the ecological systems model of human development, which views children's behavior and developmental status as being influenced by multiple levels of the environment, some direct and proximal to the child, such as the child's actual experiences in an education or care setting, and some indirect and distal, such as national policy. The study findings focus on the influence of young children's experiences in community preprimary education and care settings on their language and cognitive development at age 7, controlling for family and cultural influences. Both proximal and distal variables are examined within that context.

The target population consisted of children in selected community settings who were approximately 4½ years old. Data for the longitudinal project were collected in early childhood care and education settings in ten countries: Finland, Greece, Hong Kong, Indonesia, Ireland, Italy, Poland, Spain, Thailand, and the United States. Each country's research team chose to sample settings that were used by large numbers of families in the community or important for public policy reasons. With expert assistance, each country's research team developed a sampling plan, using probability proportional to size to select settings and systematic sampling procedures to select four children within each classroom. The age-4 sample included over 5,000 children in more than 1,800 settings in 15 countries. Ten of the initial fifteen countries followed the children to age 7 to collect language and cognitive outcome measures. The median retention rate across countries was 86 percent, ranging from 41 percent to 99 percent. The number of children included in the longitudinal analyses varied from 1,300 to 1,897, depending on the particular analysis.

Working with High/Scope researchers, measures used in the study were developed collaboratively by members of the international team. At age 4, data were collected with three observation systems and three questionnaire/interviews. Children's cognitive and language developmental status was measured at age 4 and age 7. The observation systems collected time-sampled information about how teachers schedule and manage children's time, what children actually do with their time, and the behaviors teachers use and the nature of their involvement with children.

Interviews were conducted to collect family background information and gather information regarding teachers' and parents' expectations about what is important for preschool-aged children to learn. A questionnaire that focused on the structural characteristics of the settings was administered to teachers and caregivers.

The children were followed until age 7, an age across countries when they had all entered primary school. At that time, cognitive and language measures developed by an international team were administered to assess developmental status.

Based on the structure of the data, with individual children nested within settings and settings nested within countries, a hierarchical linear modeling approach was used for the analysis. Accurate estimation of impacts for variables at different levels was especially important for this study because effects at two levels—settings and countries—were often confounded with one another. Although the relationship between setting variables and children's later development was of primary interest, any such findings would have been hard to interpret if country effects had not been accurately estimated and adjusted for. A 3-level approach enabled decomposition of variation of child outcomes into three parts—variation among children within settings, among settings within countries, and among countries. As a result, relationships between care setting variables and children's outcome scores are free of substantial influence from country-level effects.

To date, the project has produced a series of reports on parent beliefs, characteristics of early childhood settings, and how these characteristics relate to children's cognitive and language performance at ages 4 and 7. Among its findings are the following:

- The world over, mothers spend 8 to 12 hours a day with their 4-year-olds, while fathers spend only 6 to 54 minutes.
- In almost all types of group settings around the world, adults interacting with children use adult-centered teaching strategies more often than child-centered strategies.
- Children's language performance at age 7 improves as the predominant types of children's activities that teachers propose are free (which teachers let children

choose) rather than personal/social (personal care, group social activities, discipline). From greatest to least contribution, activity types were as follows: free, physical/expressive, preacademic, and personal/social.

- Children's language performance at age 7 improves as teachers' years of full-time schooling increase.
- Children's cognitive performance at age 7 improves as they spend less time in whole group activities (the teacher proposes the same activity for all the children in the class—songs, games, listening to a story, working on a craft, or a preacademic activity).
- Children's language performance at age 7 improves as the number and variety of equipment and materials available to children in preschool settings increase.

These findings show that teaching practices matter; how teachers set up their classrooms and the activities they propose for children make a difference. Across diverse countries, child-initiated activities and teachers' education appear to contribute to children's later language performance; and minimization of whole group activities and a greater number and variety of materials in preschool settings appear to contribute to their later cognitive performance. Although more research is necessary to establish a pattern of cause and effect and explore the learning mechanisms involved, those in the early childhood field can use these findings to examine local policies and practices and consider if changes are advisable.

Further Readings: Olmsted, Patricia P., and Jeanne Montie, eds. (2001). *Early childhood settings in 15 countries*. Ypsilanti, MI: High/Scope Press; Olmsted, Patricia P., and David P. Weikart, eds. (1989). *How nations serve young children: Profiles of child care and education in 14 countries*. Ypsilanti, MI: High/Scope Press; Olmsted, Patricia P., and Weikart, David P., eds. (1994). *Families speak: Early childhood care and education in 11 countries*. Ypsilanti, MI: High/Scope Press; Weikart, David P., ed. (1999). *What should young children learn? Teacher and parent views in 15 countries*. Ypsilanti, MI: High/Scope Press.

Lawrence J. Schweinhart

IEP. *See* Individualized Education Plan

IFSP. *See* Individualized Family Service Plan

IJEC. *See International Journal of Early Childhood*

IKU. *See* International Kindergarten Union

Immigration

Immigrant children make up the fastest growing sector of the U.S. child population and represent about 20 percent of all children in the United States. Some immigrants plan to stay for a lifetime, others hope to return to the home nation when economic or political change occurs, and still others will decide to move again because of upward mobility in the business world.

The United States and some other nations favor the term *immigration* for the act of people entering from other nations to settle and use *immigrants* as a term for the people. The term *migrants* is reserved for those who move about within the national borders. European nations usually refer to new arrivals from other nations as *migrants*. Canadian terms for immigrants include *newcomers*, a general term used for all new arrivals from other nations. *Transnational migration* is an increasingly recognized international term for those who move from one nation to another.

The semantics used to describe the phenomenon are not as important as the recognition of the enormity of the global phenomenon of movement from one nation to another and the impact on societies, communities, and schools. The transnational displacement of peoples is endemic, with some 12 million people worldwide seeking to move from their home country to a different country each year.

The thrust behind the movement of people from one nation to another can be for such reasons as seeking a better way of life, joining family, or for a work assignment. Unfortunately much of the movement of families and individuals is not by choice. Refugees leave their home country because of well-founded fears that they will be persecuted due to their religious beliefs, political opinion, or membership in a given group, or because they are affected by civil war or armed conflict.

Today's transnational migrants are from many different countries and varied socioeconomic backgrounds. While immigrant families are more likely to have limited skills and income, an increasing number of those who move from one nation to another are highly skilled and well-educated workers, managers, and entrepreneurs (Fix and Passel, 2003). The trend toward global movement among the skilled workers, while it represents a small percentage of the overall numbers engaged in transnational migration, illustrates one aspect of global change, and the individuals may consider themselves to be global citizens, comfortable almost anywhere (Friedman, 2002). Even for those who have firmly planted themselves in the new host community, communication with friends and family in the sending nation may remain strong, partly because today's technology offers swift communication across boundaries and distances. However, children of such families may have no clear concept of their familial or societal culture, identifying instead with two or more unlike cultures, but not sensing a personal identity with either one.

Although four-fifths of children living in immigrant families are U.S.-born citizens, their childhoods are shaped by their parents' experiences as immigrants. Of the California children from birth through eleven years of age who live in immigrant families, 45 percent have parents who speak no English or do not speak it well (Children Now, 2004). While children in immigrant families are more likely to be poor and live in crowded housing, research shows that life is difficult for all immigrant children (Suarez-Orozco and Suarez-Orozco, 2001). School may be fragmented for immigrant children, with time lost for moving, getting settled, and getting documents or whatever is necessary to enroll the child. Immigrant children's preparation for life and schooling in the new host nation varies widely. Those who have come from societies where early education is valued, and whose parents have invested time and effort into helping the child with the transition, may enter with excellent preparation and support. Others may have little or no firm preparation for dealing with the many stressors of relocation, lacking any prior schooling or experiences outside of the family.

Two frequent problems are that the child, regardless of socioeconomic status of the parents, lacks facility with the language of the school and, because of that lack of language, is confronted with the inability to forge new peer relationships. The multiple losses the children and their families experience from the move, the fears, confusion, sadness, loneliness, and alienation they feel, are carried with the children to their new schools (Kirova-Petrova, 2000).

Debates over the education of immigrant children include issues associated with language, training teachers to address the specific needs of immigrant children, developing instructional materials, and developing assessment instruments in language other than English. The prevailing impression is that immigrant children, regardless of their country of origin, do not adjust well to school and perform poorly academically, draining resources from an already overburdened educational system. However, there is evidence that in spite of often difficult circumstances some immigrant and refugee children perform at least as well academically and may stay in school longer than their U.S.-born native English speaking peers of similar class backgrounds. They may even exceed the native peers' academic norms (Board NRC/IOM, 1995).

Although there are agencies committed to assisting new immigrants and supporting families in beginning their life in their new country, the school or child-care setting serves as the central resource for these families. In addition to educating children, child-care programs and schools today also attend to children's health and mental health needs and to the needs of their parents by providing or identifying various forms of assistance essential for people who are learning a new language, culture, and customs. Some of the problems faced in this process are related to cultural barriers to parental involvement, including linguistic and academic issues as well as practical concerns concerning parents' work schedules, child care and fear of detection. Teachers are sometimes resistant to involving newly arrived parents because of all those challenges. Overcoming the challenges calls for child-care and school settings, and the host communities at large to be accepting and supportive of newly arrived families. Creating innovative ways to work with families may include meeting parents at their workplace, developing family resource centers, hosting classes, activities, and workshops within the school, and building a network of relationships with local businesses and community-based organizations. The strong commitment on the part of the teachers, administrative, and support school personnel is needed to help immigrant children regain a sense of mastery and pride. Strategies implemented may include having the new arrivals teach other students their own language or about their home nation and involving children in a variety of activities that do not require language as the sole means of communication (Yale, 2003).

Roughly one in six children in the United States lives in an immigrant-headed household, and the languages spoken in those households are as varied as the cultures represented. Transnational migration adds to the nation's diversity and complexity and to its hopes and directions of the future. Immigrants are a vital source of human capital that expands and strengthens the social, cultural, and economic fabric of the host society. In respect to early childhood education, meeting the complex and diverse needs of immigrant children challenges educators to examine their own policies and practices and to pursue culturally competent pedagogy. Providing an on-going and effective support to promote academic success and well-being of all children reflects teachers and administrators' abilities to respond optimally to all children, understanding both the richness and the limitations reflected by their own sociocultural context, as well as the sociocultural contexts of the children.

Further Readings: Board on Children and Families, National Research Council, Institution of Medicine (NRC/IOM) (1995). Immigrant children and their families: Issues for research and policy. *The Future of Children* 5(2; Summer/Fall). Washington, DC: Author, pp. 72–88. Available online at http://www.futureofchildren.org/pubs-info2825/pubs-info.htm?doc_id=; Children Now (2004). *California Report Card 2004: Focus on Children in Immigrant Families*. Oakland, CA: Author. Available online at http://www.childrennow.org/publications.cfm; Fix, Michael and Jeffery S. Passel (January 28–29, 2003). U.S. immigration—Trends and implications for schools. Presented at the National Association for Bilingual Education NCLB Implementation Institute. New Orleans, LA; Friedmann, John (2002). *The prospect of cities*. Minneapolis, MN: University of Minnesota Press; Kirova-Petrova, A. (2000). Researching young children's lived experiences of loneliness: Pedagogical implications for language minority students. *Alberta Journal of Educational Research* XLVI(2), 99–116; Suarez-Orozco, Carola and Marcelo M. Suarez-Orozco (2001). *Children of immigration*. Cambridge, MA: Harvard University Press; Yale Center of Child Development and Social Policy (2003). Portraits of four schools: Meeting the needs of immigrant students and their families. New Haven, CT: Author. Available online at http://www.yale.edu/21C/report.html.

Leah Adams and Anna Kirova

Incarcerated Parents, Children of

The Problem

Because of the large numbers of Americans arrested for drugs in recent years and many draconian plans for imprisonment ("three strikes" laws, to mention but one), the numbers of children impacted by their parent's incarceration has skyrocketed. 1,500,000 children in the United States had a parent in prison in 1999, up by more than 500,000 since 1991. By 2004, there were 2.3 million (Mumola, 2000). The needs of these children regularly go unmet, and they are in our classrooms, family child-care homes, and after school programs.

In 1999, 2.1 percent of American children had one or two parents in prison. This number has increased substantially by publication, probably to above 4 percent and, for children of color, into double digits. Black children were at 7 percent in 1999, nearly 9 times more likely to have a parent in prison than white children (0.8 percent) or Latino children (2.6 percent, 3 times as likely as white children to have an inmate parent). More than 22 percent of children with a parent in prison were under five years of age. And about half of the inmate parents were living with their child(ren) at the time of arrest (Mumola, 2000).

Early educators will likely meet these children in the course of their work. Since having a parent in prison is an enormously stressful experience, one that usually impacts a child for the rest of his or her life, adults who are with the child have the opportunity to help the child develop resilience. Children in families impacted by imprisonment suffer emotional stress, social isolation, difficulties in school, mood changes, regression, and health problems (notably asthma). Boys tend to explode, becoming anxious and aggressive, and girls to implode, becoming silent, anxious, withdrawn, and depressed. The arts can help them to mediate their pain. Offering open-ended art activities and dance and movement, giving children time to express what is inside them, can be a major support to children who are carrying any heavy burden.

After the arrest of a mother, children are most often sent to live with relatives, and sometimes into foster care. If the father is arrested, children generally stay with their mother. These new homes are usually far from the prison, making visiting rare. Regular visiting almost never happens, threatening the relationship between the parent and child. Prisoners from Hawaii are now often incarcerated on the mainland, meaning that visits are generally out of question. Our society has not been making provision for minimizing the upheaval in the lives of children whose parents are removed. And the huge increase (more than 100% since 1996) of women in prison has meant a doubling of the number of children with a parent in prison, and much more use of the foster care system to see to the needs of these children.

What Is Needed?

According to the *Bill of Rights for Children of Incarcerated Parents*, children with parents in prison have eight rights that should be written into the laws and social practices of our communities. These rights are as follow:

1. To be kept safe and informed at the time of my parent's arrest.
2. To be heard when decisions are made about me.
3. To be considered when decisions are made about my parent.
4. To be well cared for in my parent's absence.
5. To speak with, see, and touch my parent.
6. To support, as I struggle with my parent's incarceration.
7. Not to be judged, blamed or labeled because of my parent's incarceration.
8. To have a lifelong relationship with my parent.

The early childhood teacher can help children of incarcerated parents in the following two ways:

1. Working to change social policy so that children's outcomes are part of what is considered in arrest, trial and sentencing of parents (political help).
2. Making many connections with the child and offering to talk about the problems (direct help).

Political Help for Children

Early childhood educators are shocked by society's neglect of children under so many and varied stresses can become active in their public policy organizations, working to implement the *Bill of Rights* and also working on alternatives to locking up mothers and fathers in prison. Many of these parents would be able to care for their children from home if they were sentenced to do their time there, and their children would be the ones who would benefit most from this change.

There is almost no public outcry on behalf of these children, and public information programs are essential. If small-model programs such as the one begun in 2004 at the office of San Francisco Public Defender Jeff Adachi were brought to the attention of policymakers, more attempts to serve this community must come into existence. Keeping these (and all) children safe, comfortable and whole must become a national priority. Young school-aged children of prisoners often fear disclosing their story to others because of the shame and difference that attach to their status. They may surround themselves with an aura of secrecy.

Direct Help for Children in Educator's Care

It is important for early childhood educators to help these children feel valued and let them know that having a parent in prison isn't what defines them. If a child feels there is someone who is interested and nonjudgmental, who will listen and talk about the difficulties s/he is facing, that will help.

An adult can say to the child: "It must be hard to have your daddy (mommy) in jail." And then continue the discussion if the child wishes. If the child doesn't have anything to say at that time, it's a good idea to repeat the remark in a few weeks. It lets the child know that she or he isn't being judged and excluded, but only offered help or comfort.

Early childhood educators can be sensitive to the fact that children have different families, and approach holiday gift making or Mother's or Father's Day with language that includes this child. "Mother's Day is coming and you may want to make cards for your mom or your grandmother or your foster mother or any other woman you love very much." Or, "Here are materials to make something for your grownups."

The adult who has assumed care for the child may be angry at the incarcerated parent for leaving the parenting to be done by others, or for the crime itself. It is important that the child shouldn't find himself or herself in the midst of such anger between parent and caregiver. Sometimes the early childhood provider can help find counseling or other support systems for the caregiver, or can listen and point out what the child needs in this situation . . . a sense of being valued and protected, and a continuing connection with all the people important to him or her. Small services can make a difference in the tension levels of these families—someone to shop for groceries or take the child to visit in prison.

The teacher might have discussions with the whole group of children about *people we miss*. Children with parents in prison will be interested to hear of others missing people who have died, moved away, gone off to work in a far-off place, are in rehabilitation programs or are in the armed forces. There is a companionship among those with loved ones who aren't close by.

The teacher can invite children to draw or paint people they miss. This work should be supported and given a place of honor in the classroom. The teacher can invite the children to make a play about people they miss. Such activities benefit all children, and don't point a finger at the child with a parent in prison, but include him/her in the human story.

The teacher will also want to read and discuss books on this subject. While there are many titles, some may too wordy or too judgmental for young children. A few good ones are the following:

- Maury, Incz (1978). *My mother and I are getting stronger*. In English and Spanish. Volcano Press, P.O. Box 270, Volcano, CA 95689. Available online at http://www.volcanopress.com/cbindex.shtml.
- Woodson, Jacqueline (2002). *Our Gracie Aunt*. Hyperion. Two African American children react differently to their change in circumstances. Also by the same author is the book *Visiting Day*.
- Williams, Vera B. (2001). *Amber was brave, Essie was smart*. New York: Greenwillow. This book offers poetry and drawings about two sisters who react very differently to their father being in prison. The significance of the two children having different reactions is that conversations with children can begin, "would you feel like Amber or like Essie?" and that's a good start for exploring what children might feel. If you have a child or children with parents in prison, *don't require that the child come forth with his or her opinions*; let the others do the work and let the child with the real situation listen to the concern and sympathy that these books evoke for the children in them.

Starting in 2004 the 125,000-member **National Association for the Education of Young Children** (NAEYC) formed an Interest Group for Children with Incarcerated Parents (CHIPS), which meets annually at the NAEYC conference. Up-to-date information can be obtained from that Interest Group by telephoning the NAEYC headquarters at 800-424-2460 and asking for contact numbers or calling cochair Sydney Clemens at 415-586-7338.

Further Readings: *Bill of Rights for Children of Incarcerated Parents* (November 2003). Available free by request from gnewby@friendsoutside.com, online at http://www.norcalserviceleague.org/images/billrite.pdf, or by calling Friends Outside at 209-938-0727; Child Welfare League of America has a current bibliography available online at www.cwla.org; Legal Services for Prisoners with Children (2001). *Incarcerated Parents Manual: Your Legal Rights and Responsibilities*. Revised ed. Contact the LSPC at 100 McAllister Street, San Francisco, CA 94102; 415-255-7036, ext. 310; lspc@igc.org www.prisonactivist.org/lspc; Mumola, Christopher J. (August 2000) *Special Report: Incarcerated Parents and their Children*. United States Department of Justice, Bureau of Justice Statistics.; Seymour, C., and C. F. Hairston, eds. (2000). *Children with parents in prison: Child welfare policy, program, and practice issues*. New Brunswick, NJ: Transaction Publisher; Yaffe, R. M., L. F. Hoade, and B. S. Moody (2000). *When a parent goes to jail: A comprehensive guide for counseling children of incarcerated parents*. Windsor, CA: Rayve Productions.

Sydney Gurewitz Clemens

Inclusion

In 1975, Congress passed a law, the Education for All Handicapped Act (now the **Individuals with Disabilities Education Act** [IDEA]), which specified that children with disabilities were entitled to a free and appropriate education in the least restrictive environment. This law ended the isolation of students with disabilities who were denied access to public schools or attended isolated settings. This meant that students with disabilities were to be educated in the general education classroom.

Through the 1970s, the term *mainstreaming* was used to describe the placement of children in classrooms with typically developing children. This meant that students with disabilities who were placed in special classes should be exposed to the general education classroom for at least part of the day. For instance, they could participate in art and music with their typically developing peers. Advocates for children with disabilities set the goal that exposure to and engagement with typically developing peers for at least part of the day be interpreted as a positive educational experience for *all* children, not just those with disabilities. As concerns grew about the need to be more mindful of environmental and curriculum decisions as they might better support the learning of all children, the term *integration* began to replace the term and concept of mainstreaming. Although attitudes were changing about children with disabilities, sometimes there was an expectation that children with disabilities needed to demonstrate their abilities and skills, thereby convincing others that they could earn the right to be in the general education classroom at least some of the time.

During the 1980s, "inclusion" became the term used to describe the education of children with disabilities in the general education classroom. Along with this change in vocabulary was a significant change in attitude regarding children's rights and teachers' responsibilities. Although students could receive some instruction in other settings, their education would be the responsibility of the general education teacher. One of the major differences between contemporary practices and those associated with mainstreaming is that the general education classroom is now considered the placement for the student with disabilities. In other words, students with special needs are not assigned to a special education classroom; rather, their placement home is the general education classroom.

The term "full inclusion" (also known as the Regular Education Initiative of the 1980s) is used to refer to the practice of serving students with disabilities entirely within the general education classroom. Special educators and other specialists may provide services, but the child would be present in the general education classroom at all times. During this period there were also proponents of the concept of a continuum of services by those who believed that full inclusion would unnecessarily cause some services and special education classes to be eliminated. Such a constriction of special education programs would, they feared, limit options for parents who might wish to choose some placement other than an inclusive setting.

Stainback and Stainback (1994) articulate a number of goals for inclusive schools. Chief among them is that they "... meet unique educational, curricular, and instructional needs of all students within the general education classes." In addition, IDEA now asks that **Individualized Education Plan** (IEP) teams explain clearly the reasons why a child should not be placed in the regular education classroom, thus, favoring the notion of inclusion.

Inclusive schools emphasize valuing each community member, equitable community participation, a sense of belonging for all children. A strengths/needs approach to education is taken as opposed to a deficit orientation. This approach represents more than mere compliance with the law. It can mean improved education for all children. These principles are reflected in the endorsement of a position statement by the **National Association for the Education of Young Children** (NAEYC) and the **Division for Early Childhood** of the **Council for Exceptional Children**. Tensions remain around issues of placement, finance, and social inclusion.

Further Readings: Anderson, Peggy L. (1997). *Case studies for inclusive schools*. 2nd ed. Austin, TX: Pro-ed Publishers; Bauer, A. M., and T. M. Shea (1999). *Inclusion 101: How to teach all learners*. Baltimore: Paul H. Brookes Publishing Co.; Clough, P. and J. Corbett (2000). *Theories of inclusive education*. London: Paul Chapman Publishing Ltd.; Mastropieri, M. A., and T. E. Scruggs (2007). *The inclusive classroom*. 3rd ed. Upper Saddle River, NJ: Pearson Merrill Prentice Hall; Stainback, S., and W. Stainback (1990). Inclusive schooling. In W. Stainback and S. Stainback, eds., *Support networks for inclusive schooling*. Baltimore: Brookes Publishing Co., pp. 3-23; Wolery, M., P. S. Strain, and D. B. Bailey (1992). Chapter 7: Reaching potentials of children with special needs. In S. Bredekamp and T. Rosengrant, eds., *Reaching potentials: Appropriate curriculum and assessment for young children*. Vol. 1. Washington, DC: NAEYC, pp. 92-111.

Web Site: NAEYC/DEC, http://www.naeyc.org/about/positions/pdF/PSINC98.

Betty N. Allen

Individualized Education Plan (IEP)

An Individualized Education Plan (IEP) represents specially designed instruction and related services that meet the unique needs of a student. When a child who is eligible for special education services reaches the age of 3 years, those services are provided under the **Individuals with Disabilities Education Act** (IDEA). The IEP is the central jointly constructed document that provides for the implementation of the special education laws in the United States. It is considered a legally binding document for all signatories (parents and representatives of the local education agency) under the provisions of IDEA.

The concept of an IEP was first stipulated nationally in the Education for All Handicapped Children Act of 1975 (Public Law 94-142, which became IDEA in 1990. The IEP is one of the key provisions of the law; it guarantees a Free and Appropriate Public Education (FAPE) in the Least Restrictive Environment (LRE).

Parents or professionals (e.g., nurse, teachers, pediatricians) may make the referral to special education. The eligibility determination is made by a thorough nondiscriminatory evaluation that requires prior written parental consent. Parent input and teacher observation are desirable parts of the evaluation. All evaluation information is confidential and should be seen only by people who are directly involved. The evaluation process must be completed in a timely fashion (within thirty school days of the parent's written permission), and forms the basis for the development of the IEP.

The IEP sets out the unique strengths and needs of the student as well as the current levels of performance. The needs become the basis for student goals. The IEP allows for parents to include their concerns and vision for the child.

After evaluation and the determination of eligibility for services, the child's team is responsible for developing the IEP. IDEA specifies that parents must always be members of any team that makes decisions about their child. The child's teacher is also a vital member of the team. A member of the local education agency (LEA) who is knowledgeable about the agency's resources and general education program must also be a member of the team. The IEP must spell out the service provider, the frequency and duration of services, as well as the place where the services will be delivered. An IEP must be reviewed and rewritten each year, and students are revaluated every three years.

The team participates in the determination about how the student will participate in any mandated-testing program. Once the IEP is signed by all parties, parents are provided a copy and services can be delivered. If the parents refuse to sign the IEP, the state appeals process is set in motion.

Parents are guaranteed due process that provides procedural safeguards for students with disabilities. These timelines are associated with referral, evaluation, the development of the IEP, the signing of the IEP, and student placement. When parents and school systems disagree, there is an appeals process that can be accessed by either party.

Funding has been and continues to be controversial. Many refer to IDEA as an unfunded mandate. Meeting the testing requirements under the **No Child Left Behind Act** is also a source of difficulty. Minority and ESL students continue to be overrepresented in the special education population. *See also* Individualized Family Service Plan.

Further Readings: Bauer, A., and T. Shea (1999). *Inclusion 101*. Baltimore: Paul Brookes Publishers; Kostelnik, M. J., et al. (2002). *Children with special needs*. New York: Teachers College Press; MA/DOEd and the Federation for Children with Special Needs (2001). *A parent's guide to special education*. Boston.

Betty N. Allen

Individualized Family Service Plan (IFSP)

An Individualized Family Service Plan (IFSP) is a written document that provides the foundation for intervention for children with disabilities or at risk for having a substantial delay, aged birth through three years, and their families. The IFSP should be a broad portrait of what is desirable for the child and family. It should specify all the services that are needed by the family and the child and who will provide the service.

The authorization for the IFSP is through the **Individuals with Disabilities Act** (IDEA), formally the Education of the Handicapped Act (EHA). PL 94-142, the EHA, passed in 1975 by the U.S. Congress, was amended in 1983 through PL 98-199 to provide financial incentives to states to expand services for children from birth to three years and their families. Eleven years after the original EHA, Part H of PL 99-457 (1986), also known as the Early Intervention Amendments to

PL 94-142, supported services to all infants, toddlers, and preschoolers with a disability or at risk of having a substantial delay and required the development of an IFSP for each child/family served. In 1990, the EHA laws under PL 101-476 were renamed IDEA. The term "handicapped" was replaced with "disabled" and services were expanded. Part H, which addresses **early intervention** services, became Part C under IDEA. Part C describes the most current required components of the IFSP.

Children and families are identified through a mandated child find system, which is the responsibility of each state's designated lead agency for Early Intervention (EI) services. Primary referral sources are hospitals, including prenatal and postnatal facilities; physicians; parents; child-care programs; local education agencies; public health facilities, other social service agencies; and other health care providers.

Each state has an EI program, which is responsible for delivering IFSP services. EI eligibility is determined through a timely, comprehensive evaluation of the needs of the child and family and the current level of functioning. If found eligible, the IFSP is developed by a transdisciplinary team including the family, EI providers, other specialists, and individuals invited by the family. The IFSP includes specific components such as initial and periodic multidisciplinary assessments, a description of the strengths of the child and family, a statement of the current level of performance, measurable child and family goals, articulation of the frequency, duration, and method of service delivery, and a description of appropriate transition services when a child leaves EI or the IFSP is terminated. While there are similarities to an IEP, the plan for educational services for children aged 3–21 years, a major difference is that the IFSP is family centered and includes information and goals about the family as well as the child. Additionally, the IFSP names a service coordinator, includes a statement describing the natural environments (playgrounds, child care, library) in which early intervention services will be received, and includes activities undertaken with multiple agencies. The IFSP is intended to be a dynamic, flexible document that must be revised periodically and is supportive to families and envisions children in the natural inclusion environments within their communities.

Challenges in providing IFSPs include identifying children and families in need of services, insuring adequate funding to support the children who have identified disabilities as well as children at risk, providing services in natural settings, scheduling home visits or service delivery, intensity of services, program models, recruiting qualified staff, insuring that children's strengths as well as their needs are addressed, writing objectives in easily understood jargon-free language, insuring family needs are included in the IFSP, including technology needs, and transitioning children and families from an IFSP to an **individualized education plan** (IEP).

Further Readings: Bruder, Mary Beth (December 2000). The ERIC Clearinghouse on Disabilities and Gifted Education (ERIC EC) Digest #E605, The Council for Exceptional Children. Available online at http://ericec.org/digests/3605.html; Florian, Lani (Fall 1995). *Part H Early Intervention Program: Legislative history and intent of the law*. Topics in Early Childhood Special Education 15(3), 247–262; Gallagher, James (Spring 2000). The beginnings of federal help for young children with disabilities. *Topics in Early Childhood Special Education* 20(1), 3–6; Sandall, Susan, Mary Louise Hemmeter, Barbara J. Smith, and Mary E. McLean (2004). *DEC (Division for Early Childhood) Recommended Practices in Early Intervention/Early Childhood*. A publication of the Council for Exceptional Children; Wright, Peter W. D., and Pamela Dorr (1999). *Wrightslaw: Special Education Law*. Hartfield, VA: Harbor House Law Press.

Maryann O'Brien

Individuals with Disabilities Education Act (IDEA)

Congress enacted the Individuals with Disabilities Education Act (IDEA) in 1975 to govern the education of children with disabilities. In the years that followed, IDEA was amended a number of times, including the 2004 revisions through P.L. 108-446, the Individuals with Disabilities Education Improvement Act. Over the years since it first enacted IDEA in 1975, Congress has expanded the group of students who have a right to special education beyond the first group of students, ages 6 to 18, to include infants and toddlers, young children ages 3 through 5, and older students ages 6 through 21.

Because the needs of and services provided to infants and toddlers are so different from the needs and services for older students, IDEA is divided into two parts. Part B of IDEA contains the requirements for providing special education and related services to children with disabilities from 3 through 21 years of age. Part C authorizes grants to states to develop and maintain **early intervention** programs for infants and toddlers with disabilities (birth to three years) and their families. Part C, the infants and toddlers program, has parallels with the provisions and requirements of Part B; however, these provisions and requirements differ in a number of important respects. For example, while Part B eligibility is based on categories of disabilities, eligibility for Part C programs are often based on a diagnosis of "**developmental delay**" that requires early intervention services. Instead of an **individualized education plan** (IEP), Part C programs have **individualized family service plans** (IFSP) in recognition that services must be provided to the family as well as to the infant or toddler. Since very young children are served in a variety of locations (including the home), Part C services are to be provided in "natural environments" which are the types of settings in which infants and toddlers without disabilities would participate. IDEA 2004 now gives states the option to develop a joint system that would permit parents of children receiving Part C early intervention services and are eligible for preschool services to continue in Part C until they are eligible to enter kindergarten.

This law started into motion a movement that even today continues to impact the lives of children with disabilities and their families. This legislation was designed to ensure that all children with disabilities receive an appropriate education through special education and related services. This law established six major components that have a direct effect on children with disabilities: (1) Right to free and appropriate public education, (2) Nondiscriminatory evaluation,

(3) Procedural due process, (4) Individualized education program, (5) Least restrictive environment, and (6) Parental participation.

All children with disabilities are entitled to a free appropriate public education (FAPE) regardless of the nature or severity of their disabilities. That is, parents or family members cannot be asked to pay for any special education services. With this law, children with disabilities have a right to attend a local school as well as receive services that support their education in general education classes or most natural settings. To accomplish this, each state has in place what is called a child find system, a set of procedures for alerting the public that services are available for children with disabilities and for distributing print materials, conducting screening, and completing other activities to ensure that children are identified. The child find procedures include children with disabilities attending private and religious schools and highly mobile children with disabilities (such as migrant and homeless children) regardless of the severity of their disability.

Nondiscriminatory evaluation attempts to eliminate discrimination in the classification and placement of children suspected to have disabilities. The fundamental intent is to eliminate discrimination based on cultural background, race, or disability. The law requires that children be evaluated by trained professionals who must administer validated tests in the child's first language or other mode of communication (Braille, sign language). The evaluation must not consist of only a single general intelligence test but must be tailored to assess specific areas (language, cognitive, motor, etc.) of education. Professionals cannot use a single procedure as the sole criterion for determining a special educational program for a child. Most important, a multidisciplinary team (team of professionals from various specialties) must assess the child in all areas related to the suspected disability.

Procedural due process guarantees safeguards to children with disabilities and their parents. IDEA ensures that any decisions made concerning children with disabilities are done so with parent input and in compliance with clear procedures. Parents must give written consent for their children to be assessed to determine if they have a disability. Similarly, parents must be invited to attend any meetings regarding their child, and they must give written permission for the child to receive special education. Further, written notice must be made prior to any change in placement. All records are confidential, and if parents do not agree with any evaluation or special education placement, they have the legal right to go to court. If disagreements occur between parents and school professionals related to placement or any other part of special education, mediation is an informal strategy that must be offered to parents to try to resolve the disagreement. If mediation is not successful, a due process hearing occurs.

The key to appropriate special education is individualization. IDEA requires that an IEP or an IFSP be developed for each child with special educational needs. The plan for students ages 3 through 21 is called an IEP. IEPs are intended to serve as planning guides for students with special needs, not as mere paperwork. IFSPs are created for infants and toddlers and their families when eligibility for early intervention is established. This requirement underscores the significant role of the families.

The least restrictive environment (LRE) clause refers to the physical placement of the student. The LRE is the setting most like that of nondisabled children that also meets each child's educational needs. It is now presumed that the general education setting is the LRE for the majority of children with disabilities, and educators must justify any instance in which a child with a disability is not educated there. Young children with disabilities receive special education and related services in a variety of school and community sites. The team developing the child's IEP or the IFSP determines the appropriate placement based upon the child's needs. However, a full continuum of educational services must be available for children with disabilities. This continuum of services ranges from the general education classroom to a special day school or residential facility.

The IDEA is a remarkable law filled with very specific prescriptions (dictates) and proscriptions (prohibitions). The IDEA envisions specific roles for the federal, state, and local levels of government, as well as for parents. The most important roles, however, are reserved for parents and local government. IDEA explicitly calls for the active involvement of parents in all aspects of educational programming for their children with disabilities. When the provisions of IDEA are fully implemented, both letter of the law and the spirit of the law are protected. When this is the case, there is a supportive and mutually respectful relationship between families and professionals from the start. *See also* Disabilities, Young Children with.

Further Readings: Council for Exceptional Children (CEC) (February 2005). Available online at http://www.cec.sped.og; DeBettencourt, Laurie (2002). Understanding the differences between IDEA and Section 504. *Teaching Exceptional Children* 34(3), 16–23; Lerner, Janet W., Barbara Lowenthal, and Rosemary W. Egan (2003). *Preschool children with special needs*. Boston: Pearson Education; Turnbull, H. Ruderford, and Ann Turnbull (2000). *Free appropriate education: The law and children with disabilities*. 6th ed. Denver: Love Publishing.

Sharon Judge

Infant Care

Infant care generally refers to the nonparental care of children during the time period from just after birth to thirty-six months of age. Infant care options include care provided inside the child's home by a family member, friend, or child-care provider; and care outside the home provided by a family member, friend, family care provider, or center-based child-care provider. A good percentage of the world's infant care is unlicensed and unregulated and dependent upon informal arrangements between families and providers. The licensing of programs and providers varies widely and does not insure quality. Low quality is consistently linked with low salary, few benefits, little status, minimal training, and high adult to child ratios. When these factors are present, turnover in the field is high.

When the care they received is left unregulated or unplanned, started too early, provided by untrained caregivers or done in groups too large, or in environments unhealthy or unsafe, babies are put at developmental risk. Unfortunately, at least in the United States, this is most often the type of care provided. A recent study of infant care in the United States found that only 8 percent of infant–toddler care was judged as developmentally appropriate and 40 percent was judged as harmful (Cost Quality and Child Outcomes Study Team, 1995). This study was done in licensed centers.

Only sixty years ago most industrialized nations, including the United States, had similar visions with regard to the care of infants. Babies were cared for in the home of the parent or other family members and the family was responsible for the quality of care the child received. In the United States in 1940, 67 percent of all married couples had a wage-earning dad and a stay-at-home mom and this family-based system of care seemed to work (Oser and Cohen, 2003). But in the 1970s and 1980s family work and child-rearing patterns changed dramatically. Twenty four percent of mothers with children under one year were in the workforce in 1970, and by 1984 forty seven percent worked outside the home (Bureau of Labor Statistics, 1994). Most industrialized societies saw these risks as unacceptable and stepped in to protect infants and toddlers with paid parental leave during early infancy, liberal sick leave policies to care for sick children, and regulated and partially subsidized child-care services provided by trained workers. Few of these social adaptations happened in the United States, however, or in much of the nonindustrialized world.

Although much of the nonparental infant care provided throughout the world is of questionable quality, leaders in the field of early childhood education have identified conditions of high-quality care, including the acknowledgement that good infant–toddler care is not babysitting and not preschool. It is a special kind of care that looks like no other. For it to be designed well and carried out appropriately, all features—including lesson plans, environments, routines, staffing, group size, and relationships with families, supervision, and training—must have an infant care orientation. Because infants and toddlers have unique needs, their care must be constructed specifically to meet those needs.

Unfortunately, there is wide variation in how infant needs are interpreted. In the United States, for example, infant care has developed in two extreme directions. One orientation is guided by the conviction that all that infants and toddlers need are safe environments and tender loving care and that intellectual activity is unnecessary. Another interpretation of infant development and the role of infant-care argues that infants need to be intellectually stimulated by adult-directed and developmentally appropriate activities for them to grow cognitively. In many other nations infant learning is interpreted differently. In government-sponsored programs in Italy and Germany, for example, caregivers study the children in their care and keep detailed records of their interests and skills in order to find ways to facilitate the child's learning. They are trained to search for ways to use the children's natural interests and curiosity to develop appropriate curriculum activities and environments. In these settings, a good portion of what might be called lesson planning for infants and toddlers involves caregivers seeking to understand each child's development and how to relate to it. Observation, **documentation,** analysis, and adaptation happen daily. What results is a program approach that combines loving relationship-based care as the essential prerequisite of intellectual development; attention to the child's interests, curiosity, and motivation as the beginning point for curriculum planning; and adults who play the role of facilitator of the child's learning.

In the United States, program policies that reflect child-focused infant care can be found in the **Head Start** Program Performance Standards and are being used as the base for **Early Head Start** operation. These polices, described in the Program for Infant–Toddler Caregivers literature, are being endorsed widely as foundational polices for quality infant care (Lally et al., 1995); and are outlined below.

Primary care

In a primary care system each child is assigned to one special caregiver who is principally responsible for that child's care. When children spend a longer day in care than their primary caregiver, a second caregiver is assigned to also have a primary relationship with the child. Primary care works best when caregivers team up and support each other and provide a back-up base for security for each other's children in primary care. Primary care does not mean exclusive care. It means, however, that all parties know who has primary responsibility for each child.

Small groups

Every major research study on infant and toddler care in the United States has shown that a small group size *and* good ratios are key components of good-quality care (Cost, Quality, and Child Outcomes Study Team, 1995; Kagan and Cohen, 1996). The Program for Infant–Toddler Caregivers in California recommends primary care ratios of 1:3 or 1:4 in groups of 6–12 children, depending on their age (Lally, 1992; WestEd, 2000). The guiding principle is: *The younger the child, the smaller the group*. Small groups facilitate the provision of personalized care that infants and toddlers need, supporting peaceful exchanges, freedom and safety to move and explore, and the development of intimate relationships.

Continuity

Continuity of care is the third key to providing the deep connections that infants and toddlers need for good-quality child care. Programs that incorporate the concept of continuity of care keep primary caregivers and children together throughout the three years of infant–toddler period or for the entire time during that period of the child's enrollment in care.

Individualized care

Individualized care is interpreted as following children's unique rhythms and styles, and is believed to promote well-being and a healthy sense of self. This principle discourages the use of embarrassment if a child's biological rhythms or needs are different from those of other children. Responding promptly to children's individual needs is assumed to support their growing ability to self-regulate, that is, to function competently in personal and social contexts. An individualized infant-care program adapts to the child, rather than vice versa, and the child receives the message that he or she is important; that her or his needs will be met; and that choices, preferences, and impulses are respected.

Cultural continuity

Children develop a sense of who they are and what is important within the context of the family and the larger cultural context. Traditionally, the child's family and cultural community have been responsible for the transmission of values, expectations, and ways of doing things, especially during the early years of life. As more children enter child care during the years of infancy, questions are raised about their cultural identity and sense of belonging. Consistency of care between home and child care, always important for the very young, becomes even more so when the infant or toddler is cared for in the context of cultural practices that vary from those of the child's family. Because of the important role of culture in development, caregivers who serve families from diverse backgrounds need to (a) heighten their understanding of the importance of culture in the lives of infants, (b) develop cultural competencies, (c) acknowledge and respect cultural differences, and (e) learn to be open, responsive to, and willing to negotiate with families about child-rearing practices. In this way, families and caregivers, working together, can facilitate the optimal development of each child.

Inclusion of children with special needs

Inclusion means making the benefits of high-quality care available to all infants through appropriate accommodations and supports in order for each child, including those with disabilities, to have full, active program participation. Strategies already embraced above—that is, a relationship-based approach to the provision of care that is responsive to the individual child's cues and desires to learn—are as important for children with disabilities or other special needs as for children without these challenges.

For further information see the Program for Infant-Toddler Care Web site at www.pitc.org. *See also* Culture; Developmentally Appropriate Practice(s); Disabilities, Young Children with; Families; Teacher Certification/Licensure.

Further Readings: Cost, Quality, and Child Outcomes Study Team (1995). *Cost, quality, and child outcomes in child care centers.* Denver, CO: University of Colorado at Denver, Department of Economics; Head Start Bureau (1996). *Head Start performance standard and program guidance;* Code *of Federal Regulations, Title 45, Parts 1301-1311.* Washington, DC: U.S. Department of Health and Human Services, Administration for Youth and Families, Kagan, S. L., and N.E. Cohen (1997). *Not by chance: Creating an early care and education system for America's children.* New Haven, CT: The Bush Center in Child Development and Social Policy; Lally, J. R. (1992). *Together in care: Meeting the intimacy needs of infants and toddlers in groups* (videotape). Sacramento: California Department of Education and WestEd; Lally, J. R., A. Griffin, E. Fenichel, M. Segal, E. Szanton and

B. Weissbourd (1995). *Caring for infants and toddlers in groups: Developmentally appropriate practice*. Washington, DC: Zero to Three, National Center for Infants, Toddlers, and Families; Oser, C., and J. Cohen (2003) *America's Babies: The Zero To Three Policy Center Data Book*. Washington, DC: Zero to Three Press; WestEd (2000). *The Program for Infant-Toddler Caregivers: Group care*. 2nd ed. Sacramento: California Department of Education.

J. Ronald Lally

Intelligence

What is intelligence? Laypeople generally include practical problem solving, verbal behavior, and social competence in their definitions. Psychologists, however, do not agree on how to define the concept of intelligence. While most Western definitions have emphasized cognitive competence, many traditional societies have emphasized social competence. There is widespread agreement that intelligence is a person's capacity for goal-directed adaptive behavior (Sternberg 1994, p. 1135). Most formal and implicit theories regard language as playing an important role in the definition and measurement of intelligence. Psychologists representing the psychometric approach have defined intelligence as whatever intelligence tests measure. In the 1920s and 1930s, many equated **intelligence quotient** (IQ) with native ability. In the 1950s and 1960s, constructivist theories introduced into the United States portrayed intelligence as being constructed by children through interaction with their physical and social environments. Contemporary psychologists think of intelligence as a variety of attributes influenced by genetic makeup, prenatal environment, postnatal environment, encouragement and opportunities, and cultural beliefs and practices.

The study of intelligence has been controversial since its inception. In his early studies of intelligence, Sir Francis Galton (1822–1911) concluded that the major differences among babies were hereditary. On the other hand Alfred **Binet** (1857–1911), a French psychologist, believed that the capacity to learn could be increased by stimulation. Binet became interested in studying child development following the birth of his two daughters in 1885 and 1887. His observations of his daughters led him to formulate a conception of intelligence. In 1904, the French Ministry of Education asked Binet and his student and collaborator, Theophile Simon, to devise a method to identify children who would benefit from slower-paced instruction in public school classrooms. Binet and Simon's original measure consisted of test items that assessed memory, good judgment, and abstraction and were arranged according to the year at which the majority of children mastered each skill or ability. Binet and Simon's test was so successful at predicting school success that it was adapted for use by other countries. In the United States, compulsory school attendance laws, child labor laws, and large numbers of immigrants had caused the school population to change in the early 1900s. To address the wider range of individual abilities present in school classrooms, Louis Terman (1877–1956) at Stanford University revised Binet and Simon's scale, renaming it the Stanford-Binet Intelligence Scale in 1916.

Over the last century one of the primary questions about intelligence has been whether it is a unitary or multifaceted construct. In 1927, British psychologist Charles Spearman, using factor analysis, developed the two-factor theory of intelligence, where *g* represented a primary general intelligence (abstract reasoning) and *s* represented specific related abilities. Spearman believed that the general factor was the essential foundation from which the specific related abilities emerged. American psychologist, Louis Thurstone (1938) disagreed with Spearman, advancing his theory of seven unrelated primary mental abilities which he believed operated independently: verbal meaning, perceptual speed, reasoning, number, rote memory, word fluency, and spatial visualization. Extending factor analytic research, Raymond Cattell (1971) described two types of intelligence in addition to a general factor: (1) crystallized intelligence (i.e., accumulated knowledge and skills) which depends on culture and learning opportunities; and (2) fluid intelligence (e.g., the ability to see relationships), which depends on brain function. Recent research has shown that even fluid intelligence test items (spatial and performance tasks) depend on learning opportunities.

In the 1950s and 1960s, J. McVicker **Hunt**, Benjamin Bloom, Jerome **Bruner**, and Kenneth Wann, influenced by the interactionist theory of Jean **Piaget**, amassed evidence on and argued for the influence of early experience on intelligence. They succeeded in focusing attention on the idea that intelligence is a highly complex process, not explained by the simplistic notion of fixed genetic endowment. Hunt, in particular, became a strong advocate for early childhood enrichment programs, which he believed would maximize children's intellectual potential during its period of greatest malleability.

More recently several theories have emerged that portray intelligence as multifaceted. In 1983, Harvard psychologist, Howard Gardner introduced his theory of **multiple intelligences** (MI). Based on his studies of stroke victims, savant syndrome, and lower animals, Gardner originally posited seven distinct domains of intelligence, each of which he believed had separate neural circuitry. He included linguistic, logical-mathematical, musical, spatial, interpersonal, intrapersonal, and bodily-kinesthetic intelligences, later adding naturalistic and existential intelligences. Although Gardner's MI theory has not yet been supported by research evidence, it has been widely embraced by educators, who design curriculum, lesson plans, and classrooms to address multiple intelligences in the children they teach.

In 1985, Yale psychologist Robert Sternberg introduced a triarchic theory of intelligence, which included three subtheories of intelligence: componential, experiential, and contextual. According to this theory, individuals with high *componential* intelligence think analytically and critically and therefore, achieve high scores on standardized tests; persons with high *experiential* intelligence process information more skillfully in novel situations, demonstrating creativity; and persons with high *contextual* intelligence are intelligent in a practical way, adapting to and shaping their environment. Sternberg believes that for most people contextual or practical intelligence may be more important for success in life than are the other two subtheories of intelligence.

Definitions of intelligent behavior vary according to culture. Some researchers have found that European American parents named cognitive abilities as most important to their conception of an intelligent child, whereas Mexican American parents rated social skills, and Asian parents rated motivation—the drive to do well—as highest in importance. In Brazil, the Flecheiros or Arrow People teach their sons to become deft archers to keep intruders away; a skilled archer is considered an intelligent person. In the United States, a child who is good at academics is considered intelligent. Sternberg addresses the different contexts of intelligent behavior in his triarchic theory.

Poverty severely depresses the intelligence scores of ethnic minority children in the United States. The longer children remain in impoverished environments, the greater the negative effects on their intelligence test scores. Early intervention programs such as **Head Start** were initiated in response to research on the importance of early experiences on children's intellectual and social experiences. Other early intervention programs such as the Carolina **Abecedarian** Project have demonstrated that providing continuous high-quality early childhood experiences for the first five years of life is an effective way to help children avoid the declines in intelligence that come from being reared in impoverished environments.

Although the concept of intelligence is slippery, the study of intelligence is important to the field of Early Childhood Education for a number of reasons. First, the initial five years of life is the period of most rapid human development outside the womb. Early **assessment** allows professionals to identify infants and young children who may be at risk for developmental problems and to design and implement **early intervention** to maximize children's potential while their brains are still plastic. Second, although we know that genetics contributes to intellectual potential, we have learned that the early caregiving environment is a powerful influence on intelligence and academic success. Appropriate early stimulation increases the number of synaptic connections in the cerebral cortex. In other words, early experiences grow the brain. Third, as teachers of young children become aware of the newer theories of intelligence, they can provide experiences to foster all the domains of intelligence. Fourth, the study of intelligence has prompted an appreciation for the diversity of intelligence existing in groups of young children, from those described as slower learners to the very gifted. Such understandings of intelligence have supported critics of a "one size fits all" standardized curriculum that does not meet the needs of young children. Fifth, the ability to reliably measure cognitive abilities has enabled researchers to conduct longitudinal studies of cognitive development. *See also* Intelligence Testing.

Further Readings: Berk, Laura E. (2003). Intelligence. *Child development*. 6th ed. Boston: Allyn and Bacon, pp. 310–351; Braun, Samuel J., and Esther P. Edwards (1972). *History and theory of early childhood education*. Belmont, CA: Wadsworth. Gardner, Howard E. (1999). *Intelligence reframed: Multiple intelligences for the 21st century*. New York: Basic Books; Sternberg, Robert J., ed. (1994). *Encyclopedia of human intelligence*. New York: Macmillan; Sternberg, Robert J. (2000). *Handbook of intelligence*. New York: Cambridge University Press; Storfer, Miles. D. (1990). *Intelligence and giftedness: The contributions of heredity and early environment*. San Francisco: Jossey-Bass.

Carol S. Huntsinger

Intelligence Quotient (IQ)

The term *intelligence quotient* refers to an estimation of one's cognitive ability or **intelligence**, and is derived by **intelligence testing.** An *intelligence quotient,* or *IQ*, then, is a number estimating an individual's global or overall intellectual or cognitive ability. In the early 1900s, a French psychologist, Alfred **Binet**, first used the term *intelligence* to "refer to the sum total of the higher mental processes" (Wasserman and Tulsky, 2005, p. 7).

With Theodore Simon, Binet completed the first modern-day intelligence test, the Binet-Simon Scale, in 1905; the purpose was to efficiently and accurately evaluate children's intellectual abilities. Specifically, the goal was to identify children with mental retardation who would need special educational programming. Subsequently revised and renamed, the Stanford-Binet was the first major test to yield an intelligence quotient, in which mental age is divided by chronological age. The Stanford-Binet has undergone several revisions, and is currently in its fifth revision, extending downward to age 3 (currently published by Riverside Publishing).

The intelligence quotient or IQ was initially based on calculation of *mental age*, determined by the presumed age level at which certain cognitive tasks are typically accomplished. These early calculations of IQ were based on the following formula (Wasserman and Tulsky, 2005):

Mental age (MA) in months divided by chronological age (CA) in months $\times$ 100

For example, a child aged 6 years (72 months) who performed tasks at the 5-year-old level would earn a mental age of 60 months and an IQ of 83, according to the following the formula:

60 divided by $72 = .83 \times 100 = 83$

From this formula, the practice was established—the average IQ was set at 100. Although the formula is no longer used, 100 is still typically used as the average IQ in most formalized intellectual measures.

By the middle of the twentieth century, the Wechsler scales had surpassed the Stanford-Binet in popularity in the United States. David Wechsler, who had some experience with the early U.S. Army Alpha and Beta cognitive tests for selection and placement of soldiers, published the Wechsler-Bellevue Scale in 1939, followed by several other scales, including scales for school-age children, preschoolers, and adults. All Wechsler scales (published by Psychological Corporation) include a combination of verbal (language-based) tasks and performance (visual and visual-motor) tasks that are combined to generate a full-scale IQ (Wasserman and Tulsky, 2005).

IQ Scores

Wechsler's scales were among the first to use the deviation IQ, which provides "rankings of performance relative to individuals of the same age group" (Wasserman and Tulsky, 2005, p. 13). In this way, an individual's performance is expressed as a standard score that shows how far his or her performance is from the typical performance for other individuals of his/her age. For the Wechsler and most other contemporary IQ tests, the population average score is set to 100 and the standard deviation is set to 15. Thus, a child earning an intelligence quotient of 115 exhibits performance better than average for his/her age. About 68 percent of the population scores within one standard deviation on either side of the mean (85–115). Another 13–14 percent score within an additional standard deviation (70–85 and 115–130). Only 2–3 percent of the population scores more than three standard deviations above or below the mean. Interestingly, many American schools use scores falling at the two standard deviation mark as cutoff scores. That is, the typical cutoff for students to be identified as having mental retardation is 70 or below while the typical cutoff for students to identified as intellectually gifted is 130 or above.

Nature of Intelligence

The field of intelligence testing has been controversial since its inception. Theorists have offered various definitions and certainly the nature of the specific tasks included in a given intelligence test reflect the theoretical orientation of the authors. Most current intelligence tests include measures of the following abilities or skills: abstract reasoning, problem solving, verbal facility, mathematical facility, creativity, processing speed, memory, and the ability to learn and store new information (Sattler, 2001). Intelligence and intelligence testing continue to be the focus of much research. Most recent IQ tests tend to yield global scores or composites, essentially an IQ score, but also yield scores on various abilities, such as those listed above. These scores can yield information about an individual's particular intellectual strengths and weaknesses. Individuals identified with **learning disabilities** tend to have weaknesses in one or more of these areas and strengths in others.

Despite differences in the way various IQ tests assess intelligence, scores on most IQ tests are highly correlated for most people; in fact, IQ scores correlate more highly with other mental measures than do all other types of psychological measures (Sattler, 2001). Thus, an individual who scores well above the average on one IQ test tends to perform similarly on another IQ test. Also, typically IQ is relatively stable over time. That is, measures of one's IQ at an early age tend to be highly correlated with measures later in life. Measures of IQ at ages 5 and older tend to be fairly stable, with research yielding correlations of .50 and higher (Sattler, 2001). Note that correlations between .70 and 1.00 are very large; correlations between .50 and .69 are large (Rosenthal, 2001).

Factors Influencing Development of Intelligence

There is an ongoing debate about how much of intelligence is due to heredity versus how much is subject to environmental influences. People do not inherit IQ. They inherit genes that influence the development of their intelligence; about 50 percent of intelligence is due to heredity (Sattler, 2001). Heredity determines the range of a person's abilities and interacts with environmental factors to determine a person's intelligence. Studies show that the IQ scores of identical twins (with the same genetic makeup) are more similar than those of fraternal twins (with genetic makeup of brothers/sisters). Studies indicate an increase of about 10–12 IQ points for the identical twin adopted into an enriched environment (Sattler, 2001). Other research indicates considerable change is possible (up to twenty points) in a given child's IQ scores over time. Access to the following can influence development of intelligence: stimulating and enriching experiences, language-rich environment, adult guidance with problem solving, teaching and reinforcing skills and concepts, medical care, nutrition, social support, safety, stability, parental level of education, and infant birth weight. Evidence indicates that intelligence is more malleable in infants and toddlers, when **brain development** is very rapid, providing support for the importance of prevention and intervention services for young children with cognitive impairments or in at-risk environments (Lerner, Lowenthal, and Egan, 2003).

IQ tests have been criticized as being culturally biased. However, attempts to be culturally fair in IQ testing date back to the early twentieth century when the U.S. Army developed the Alpha tests for literate candidates and the Beta tests for nonreaders and candidates who did not have a good command of English (Wasserman and Tulsky, 2005). Nonetheless, some still consider IQ tests to be culturally biased because certain ethnic or racial groups tend to perform less well than other groups. Others argue these differences are likely socioeconomically based. To guard against misidentification of individuals (i.e., incorrect identification as mentally retarded), currently in the United States, IQ test scores alone cannot be used to identify mental retardation; measures of adaptive or functional behavior must also be gathered. Another important criticism of IQ tests is that they may not yield educationally meaningful information. That is, while they provide estimates of a child's cognitive ability compared to same-age peers, they do not give precise information on how best to instruct the child. In other words, these instruments tend to have good diagnostic value but limited treatment utility (Bell and Allen, 2000). IQ tests are most useful for estimating an individual's range of capabilities and whether or not he or she will be able to achieve educational goals expected of same-age peers; the scores tend to correlate significantly with measures of academic achievement (Sattler, 2001). What IQ scores cannot do is give parents or teachers information that would help them to enhance a child's learning or development.

Preschool Assessment

Early childhood measures of IQ tend to be somewhat less reliable than measures used with older children. Uneven and rapid brain development, shortened attention span, limited and idiosyncratic language skills, and unfamiliarity with the testing context all contribute to the lower reliability (Sattler, 2001). For very young children, **assessment** of IQ is challenging; measures of infants tend to assess perceptual and motor skills and to be only weakly correlated with measures taken later in life. Starting at age 12 months, measures tend to be correlated with measures taken later. As might be expected, the measures become more reliable as children get older. The last fifteen years have seen considerable improvement in the psychometric properties of norm-referenced assessment of cognitive abilities of young children (Ford and Dahinten, 2005). Also noteworthy are the recent development of nonverbal tests of intelligence, such as the Leiter International Performance Scale-Revised (Roid and Miller, 1997, Stoelting) and the Universal Nonverbal Intelligence Test (Bracken and McCallum, 1998, Riverside). Developed to assess students with no or limited language skills and/or who do not speak or understand spoken English, these tests are designed to provide fair assessments of cognitive abilities.

Current Practices in IQ Testing

Most IQ tests are individually administered and take an hour or longer to administer. Qualified examiners undergo extensive training, using standardized test procedures. IQ testing is part of most assessment batteries for special education in the United States. In particular, IQ testing may be used in determining if a child meets criteria for mental retardation, intellectual giftedness, learning disabilities, **developmental delay**, and traumatic brain injury. Following passage of U.S. federal special education legislation in 1975 (Education for All Handicapped Children Act [EHA], Public Law 94-142), the field of IQ testing grew dramatically. IQ testing is less common for preschoolers and students in kindergarten than for students in older grades. Nonetheless, IQ testing may be part of a preschool or early primary student's assessment battery. U.S. federal legislation passed in 1986 (Education of the Handicapped Children's Act Amendments, Public Law 99-457) established mandatory **early childhood special education** services for children from ages 3 to 5; in 1991, services were extended to children from ages birth to three (Early Childhood Amendments to the **Individuals with Disabilities Education Act** [IDEA], Public Law 102-119). IQ tests can provide useful diagnostic information about a child's capabilities and relative areas of cognitive strengths and weaknesses and can also help determine appropriate educational programming. Further, the scores can help determine if the child is exhibiting significant developmental delays and may be used as a baseline measure to gauge progress and effectiveness of intervention programs.

Summary

The intelligence quotient is an estimate of an individual's overall intellectual or cognitive abilities. IQ is typically measured via an individually administered IQ test by a trained examiner. Intelligence tends to be heavily influenced by heredity but environmental factors also influence development of IQ. Recent trends in intelligence testing include development of more accurate preschool measures and measures that are more culturally fair. IQ scores are most appropriately used to yield diagnostic information about an individual child's capabilities relative to peers and, when used in combination with other information about a child, can inform important educational decisions.

Further Readings: Bell, Sherry Mee and William Allen (2000). Review: Bayley Scales of infant development. 2nd edition. *Journal of Psychoeducational Assessment* 18, 185–195; Bracken, Bruce A., ed. (2000). *The psychoeducational assessment of preschool children*.

3rd ed. Boston: Allyn and Bacon; Flanagan, Dawn P. and Patti, L. Harrison, eds. (2005). *Contemporary intellectual assessment: Theories, tests, and issues*. New York: Guilford Press; Ford, Laurie, and V. Susan Dahinten (2005). Use of intelligence tests in the assessment of preschoolers. In Dawn P. Flanagan and Patti L. Harrison, eds., *Contemporary intellectual assessment: Theories, tests, and issues*. New York: Guilford Press, pp. 487–503; Kamphaus, Randy W. (2001). *Clinical assessment of child and adolescent intelligence*. 2nd ed. Boston: Allyn and Bacon; Lerner, Janet W., Barbara Lowenthal and Rosemary W. Egan (2003). *Preschool children with special needs: Children at risk and children with disabilities*. 2nd ed. Boston: Allyn and Bacon; Rosenthal, James A. (2001). *Statistics and data interpretation for the helping professions*. Belmont, CA: Wadsworth/Thomson Learning; Sattler, Jerome (2001). *Assessment of children: Cognitive applications*. 4th ed. San Diego: Jerome M. Sattler, Publisher, Inc.; Wasserman, John D., and David S. Tulsky (2005). In Dawn P. Flanagan and Patti L. Harrison, eds., *Contemporary intellectual assessment: Theories, tests, and issues*. New York: Guilford Press, pp. 3–22; Wechsler, David (1939). *The measurement of adult intelligence*. Baltimore: Williams and Wilkins.

Sherry Mee Bell

Intelligence Testing

The measurement of **intelligence** in children began with the Binet-Simon scale. Because Alfred **Binet** and Theophile Simon viewed intelligence as a holistic phenomenon, their test resulted in one score called the mental age (MA). A child who scored at the level of a six-year-old had a mental age (MA) of 6. In the first version of the Stanford-Binet, Lewis Terman took German psychologist William Stern's suggestion to express the child's performance as an **intelligence quotient** (IQ). It was calculated using the following formula: *IQ = MA/CA x 100*. A child who was 6-years-old chronologically, but whose score was equivalent to that of an 8-year-old would have an IQ of 133 (8/6 x 100 = 133). The current formula for calculating IQ is more mathematically sophisticated.

The Fifth Edition of the Stanford-Binet Intelligence Scales (SB5) (2003) is an individually administered test suitable for 2 year olds through adults. It includes comprehensive coverage of five factors: fluid reasoning, knowledge, quantitative reasoning, visual-spatial processing, and working memory, and the ability to compare verbal and nonverbal performance. Items range from the very easy to the very difficult. Scores are figured by comparing a child's score to scores of other children the same age. When a child performs at the average for her/his age, her/his IQ is 100. For the youngest children (2–7 years) professionals can use the Stanford-Binet Intelligence Scales for Early Childhood (Early SB5), which combines a Test Observation Checklist and software-generated Parent Report with the subtests from the SB5.

David Wechsler (1896–1981), a clinical psychologist at Bellevue Hospital in New York, developed the Wechsler Intelligence Scale for Children (WISC) for 6- to 16-year-old children in 1949 and the Wechsler Preschool and Primary Scale of Intelligence (WPPSI) for 3- to 8-year-old children in 1967. He was dissatisfied with the single IQ score derived when using the Stanford-Binet. The Wechsler tests, designed for the normal population with IQs from 70 to 130, offer a general

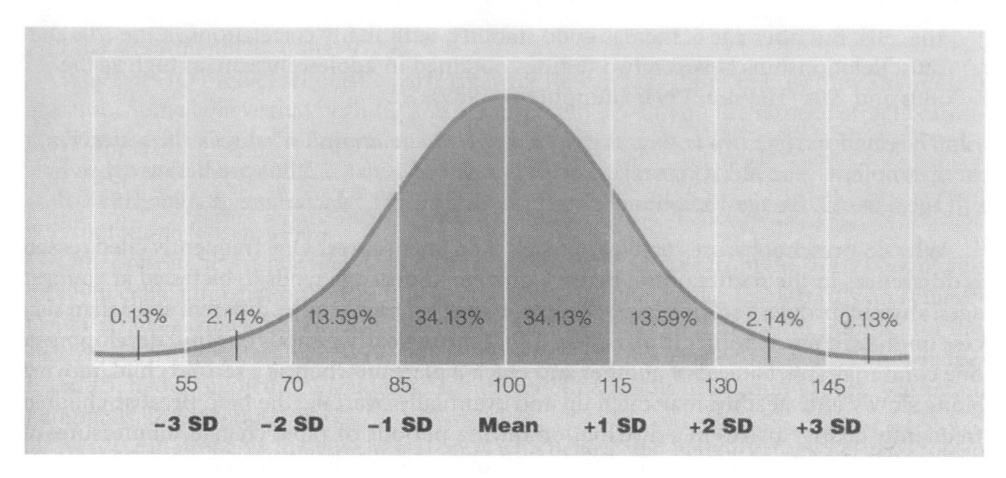

Figure 1. The normal curve. Scores on intelligence tests tend to form a normal, bell-shaped curve. Taken from Berk, L. E. (2003). *Child development*. Boston: Allyn and Bacon, p. 323.

intelligence score, as well as verbal and performance scores. The tests, downward extensions of the Wechsler Adult Intelligence Scale, are now more widely used by psychologists than the Stanford-Binet. Both the Stanford-Binet and the WISC are useful for predicting children's academic success. Neither the Wechsler tests nor the Stanford-Binet is sensitive enough to identify learning difficulties in preschool children, but the Stanford-Binet LM (1972) is most successful at identifying exceptionally gifted young children.

Measuring the intelligence of infants and toddlers is a difficult task because infants cannot sit to answer questions or follow directions to perform certain tasks. The Bayley Scales of Infant Development (1993), based on the normative work of Arnold **Gesell,** is considered the best measure of infant development from 1 to 42 months. The mental scale includes sensory perceptual acuity, discriminations, learning and problem solving, verbal ability, and concept formation. The motor scale includes muscle control as well as gross and fine motor abilities. The testing professional also rates attitude, interest, emotion, energy, activity, and responsiveness using the Behavior Rating Scale. The Bayley Scales which assess sensorimotor skills are poor predictors of later intelligence scores because different aspects of intelligence (language, thinking, and problem solving) are assessed at later ages. Infant tests are helpful for identifying for further observation and intervention, infants who are likely to have developmental problems. The Fagan Test of Infant Intelligence, which measures habituation/recovery to visual stimuli, predicts childhood IQ better than do the Bayley Scales.

Intelligence test scores tend to be distributed normally among the population. Most intelligence tests convert their raw scores so the mean (average) score is 100 and the standard deviation (average variability) is 15. As you can see in the figure above, 68 percent of individual scores fall into the average range (IQs between 85 and 115); 13.59 percent of scores fall between 70 and 85 and 13.59 percent fall between 115 and 130. Only 2.27 percent of people score higher than 130 and 2.27 percent score lower than 70. The Stanford-Binet and the Wechsler tests are periodically restandardized to keep the mean at 100. Since 1930, intelligence test performance has been rising worldwide, a phenomenon called the Flynn effect in honor of New Zealand researcher, James Flynn, who first calculated the extent of the effect.

Further Readings: Black, Maureen M., and Karen Matula (1999). *Essentials of Bayley Scales of Infant Development II Assessment*. Hoboken, NJ: Wiley; Cole, Michael, Shelia R. Cole, and Cynthia Lightfoot (2005). *The development of children*. 5th ed. New York: Worth, pp. 505–516; Feldman, Robert S. (2007). *Child development*. 4th ed. Upper Saddle River, NJ: Pearson Prentice Hall, pp. 338–345; Plucker, Jonathan A., ed. (2003). *Human intelligence: Historical influences, current controversies, teaching resources*. Available online at http:///www.indiana.edu/-intell.

Carol S. Huntsinger

Interagency Education Research Initiative (IERI)

The Interagency Education Research Initiative (IERI) is concerned with the generalizability of evidence regarding the effectiveness of interventions designed to improve preK–12 student learning outcomes in reading, mathematics, and science. A main emphasis is on understanding the impacts of interventions implemented in a variety of contexts with diverse populations and the prospects that can be successfully scaled-up to similar effect with larger numbers of students. Since its inception in 1999, IERI has supported hundreds of projects across the United States, including many early childhood projects that address early development of reading and other literacy skills, scaling up preschool mathematics curricula, and using technology to support at-risk children's development and learning and preschool teachers' professional development. IERI is a collaborative effort of the National Science Foundation, the U.S. Department of Education, and the National Institute of Child Health and Human Development. The three agencies developed the program building on recommendations contained in a 1997 report of the President's Committee of Advisors on Science and Technology. Information on IERI-supported projects can be found online at http://drdc.uchicago.edu/community/main.phtml. The number and complexity of these projects prevents simple summarization, but a wealth of information on how teachers can improve teaching skills, change the way math, science, and reading are taught, or both, is contained in the individual project descriptions at that Web site.

Further Readings: Office of Science and Technology Policy (n.d.). Interagency Education Research Initiative. Washington, DC. Retrieved from http://clinton3.nara.gov/WH/EOP/OSTP/Science/html/ieri.html; President's Committee of Advisors on Science and Technology (1997). *Report to the President on the Use of Technology to Strengthen K–12 Education in the United States*. Washington, DC.

Douglas H. Clements, Julie Sarama, and Sarah-Kathryn McDonald

International Journal of Early Childhood (IJEC)

The *International Journal of Early Childhood* is one of the oldest scientific journals in the field of Early Childhood Education, with a history of thirty-seven years. This journal is published by OMEP (Organisation Mondiale pour l'Éducation Préscolaire), a nongovernmental organisation that has about seventy member countries from all continents of the world. Children's life and education in different cultures are therefore central to this journal. The scope of the journal is on key issues in the field of early childhood education and care as they pertain to children ages 0–8 years.

The journal has two issues per year, of which one has a specific theme and the other has mixed articles. Themes of specific interest are those focused on multicultural issues, children's learning and sustainable development, infants and toddlers in ECE, children's rights, and **curriculum**. Articles about making children in different cultures visible and cross-cultural studies within ECE are especially welcome. All articles are peer reviewed and may be written in English, French, or Spanish.

Ingrid Pramling Samuelson

International Journal of Early Years Education

The *International Journal of Early Years Education* offers a comparative perspective on research and major new initiatives in the care and education of young children. The journal, published three times per year, is a forum for researchers and practitioners to debate the theories, research, policy, and practice that sustain effective early years education worldwide.

The journal carries a regular book review section, and has recently published articles from the United Kingdom, India, Zimbabwe, and Hong Kong covering subjects such as phonological awareness, the effects of food and nutrition on learning, classroom noise, and cultural diversity awareness amongst children.

The *International Journal of Early Years Education* is published by Routledge. For more information, please visit http://www.tandf.co.uk/journals/titles/09669760.asp.

Iram Siraj-Blatchford

International Journal of Special Education

The first volume of the *International Journal of Special Education* appeared twenty-one years ago at the University of British Columbia. Its purpose was to connect all special educators around the world and to provide a channel for exchange of ideas to facilitate provision of appropriate education to all children with special needs. However, the editors soon discovered that teachers in the Third World do not have funds for subscribing to professional publications nor to pay fees to professional organizations abroad. The journal is today readily available to all special educators at the Web site given below.

Today, the increasing number of manuscripts submitted to the *Journal* from countries where special education is being offered for the first time seems to indicate that more and more children with special needs are being served. The

Journal grants permission to copy articles for educational purposes. The editorial board represents many countries and helps promote mutual professional understanding. Teachers in training, practicing teachers, university personnel involved with the preparation of special educators, and parent organizations in special education form the main readership.

Web Site: *International Journal of Special Education*, www.internationaljournal ofspecialeducation.com.

Marg Csapo

International Kindergarten Union (IKU)

The International Kindergarten Union (IKU) was established in 1892, during the annual conference of the National Kindergarten Union (NEA) at Saratoga Springs, New York. Members of a committee appointed by its Kindergarten Department to plan exhibits for the next year's Columbian Exposition in Chicago were concerned about the departure from Froebelian kindergarten philosophy of "learning through play" being expressed at the conference. Their goals were to promote establishment of **kindergartens**, to unite the various kindergarten groups, to disseminate information about proper education of children aged 3–7, and to elevate the status and level of professional training of teachers. In addition to kindergarten teachers, IKU membership included women without formal training who had been supporting the early kindergartens. For example, the first president was Sarah B. Cooper, a philanthropist who supported San Francisco kindergartens.

As IKU members tried to express their philosophy, they attempted to reconcile basic internal disagreements. By 1907, these were categorized by the degree of adherence to the system introduced by Friedrich **Froebel** and his followers in the 1830s and 1840s. There was general agreement about the importance of self-activity, the relationship between children and the environment, and the idea of development as guided growth, but disagreements remained. By 1913, their Committee of Nineteen, chaired by Lucy **Wheelock**, published a final compromise representing three subcommittees instead of a summary statement of goals and objectives. In it, the Progressives, chaired by **Patty Smith Hill**, followed Froebel's instructions to continue developing his system by utilizing new psychological and philosophical research. The Conservatives, led by Susan **Blow**, believed in loving but authoritarian dictated use of the play materials and activities that they attributed to Froebel. A Conservative-Liberal group included those who would not commit to either position.

The organization grew from its original thirty members. In 1924, a national office was established in Washington, DC, and they began publication of *Childhood Education*. Annual conferences brought further discussions about preferred practices, with testing instruments becoming a major concern in the 1920s. As kindergartens became part of the public educational system by the 1920s, the English concept of nursery schools for younger ages gained attention. A further split in membership took place. In 1926, Patty Smith Hill initiated the Committee on Nursery Schools, precursor of today's **National Association for the Education**

of Young Children (NAEYC). By 1930, the IKU adopted a new constitution and merged with the National Council of Primary Education, becoming the Association for Childhood Education. From its inception, the IKU had fostered linkages with other countries, and in 1946, after World War II, the organization became the **Association for Childhood Education International** (ACEI).

Further Readings: IKU papers are in ACEI Archives, Special Collections, McKeldin Library. College Park, MD: University of Maryland; International Kindergarten Union (1913). *The kindergarten: Reports of the committee of nineteen*. Boston: Houghton Mifflin; Snyder, Agnes (1972). *Dauntless women in early childhood education*. Washington, DC: ACEI; Weber, Evelyn (1969). *The kindergarten: Its encounter with educational thought in America*. New York: Teachers College, Columbia University.

Dorothy W. Hewes

International Reading Association (IRA)

The International Reading Association promotes high literacy levels by focusing on improvements in reading instruction, reading research and information, and the importance of a lifetime reading habit. Diverse reading professionals, including teachers, reading specialists, faculty, and researchers, are among the IRA's 80,000 members. With councils and affiliates in a hundred countries, the International Reading Association network extends to 300,000 people worldwide.

The resources and activities of the International Reading Association further the following five goals:

- *Professional Development* to advance knowledge of the field by reading educators worldwide
- *Advocacy* for policy, practices, and research that improve instruction and promote the best interests of all learners and reading professionals
- *Partnerships* with national and international governments, nongovernmental organizations, community agencies, and business and industry to strengthen and support literacy efforts
- *Research* that informs the decisions made by professionals, policymakers, and the public
- *Global Literacy Development* that identifies and focuses leadership and resources on significant literacy issues worldwide

IRA Programs

Advocacy and global outreach. Members seek influence in policy, curriculum, and education reform initiatives that affect literacy, reading, and reading instruction. IRA recommendations in these areas are disseminated through position statements. Government relation reports reflect advocacy by the legislative action team related to U.S. policy.

Global projects, like Pan-African Reading for All, encourage professional communication and collaboration across borders. Educators' needs are met by region through international development committees. Teacher education and professional standards development are examples of IRA initiatives that increase awareness and recognition of reading professionals.

Awards and grants. IRA grants and awards honor teaching, service to the profession, research, media coverage, and writers and illustrators of children's books. Grants support professional development, graduate studies, and action research. Some awards and grants are only available for international programs and achievement.

Councils and affiliates. IRA councils and affiliates facilitate direct and immediate access to educators. Through this network, IRA's community extends to more than 300,000 reading professionals in hundred countries.

Meetings and events. The Association's meetings and events include large and small conferences and gatherings across the globe. A weeklong annual convention, held each spring in a North American city, represents a premiere professional development opportunity. A one-day research conference precedes this meeting. World Congresses are held biennially, and the cosponsored Pan-African Conference is also a biennial event. National, regional, and state/provincial meetings occur throughout the year.

Publications. The Ira publishes more than one hundred print and nonprint resources, with twenty-five to thirty new titles added each year. The professional journals affiliated with IRA include the following:

- *The Reading Teacher*, directed toward preschool, primary, and elementary school educators
- *Journal of Adolescent & Adult Literacy*, directed toward middle school, secondary, college, and adult educators
- *Reading Research Quarterly* for those interested in reading theory and research
- *Lectura y Vida*, a Spanish-language journal based in Latin America
- *Reading Online*, an electronic journal with a special focus on literacy and technology
- *Thinking Classroom* (also available in Russian, as *Peremena*), that focuses on the ways students acquire, create, question, and apply knowledge responsibly

IRA's bimonthly newspaper, *Reading Today*, is received by all members and contains news and features about the reading profession, as well as information about Association activities.

Beth Cady

IQ. *See* Intelligence Quotient

IRA. *See* International Reading Association

Isaacs, Susan (1885–1948)

Susan Isaacs was a British educator and psychologist influenced by John **Dewey** in early education and Sigmund **Freud** in psychoanalysis. Her positions as Head of the Department of Child Development at the University of London's Institute of

Education and the Head of the Malting House School in Cambridge effectively combined her dual interests. Two books about her Malting House School experiences continue to influence early childhood educators worldwide. *Intellectual Growth of the Young Child (IG)* (1930) and *Social Development of the Young Child (SD)* (1972) capture Isaac's educational thought and practice. A third volume of case histories explaining her observations of children was never published.

Isaacs addresses the range of children's development from infancy through young childhood, emphasizing the infant's acute sense of touch and the belief that very young children have feelings that reflect positive and negative attitudes and events. Isaacs' psychoanalytic training supported her belief that even infants have a "mental" life, that they experience fear and rage from the earliest days of life.

Children possess a need for social exchange as members of a team and a family as they learn to interact and communicate. They experience and share disappointment and joy. Today, early educators discuss brain development and appropriate practices; Isaacs was among the first to describe these concepts and their practical aspects. Isaacs believed that schools are intended to stimulate the active inquiry of the children themselves, rather than to "teach" them. Children want to "find out" about the things in their world—not to be taught, but to discover by searching. Her theoretical aims were to find suitable ways of giving satisfaction to "finding out" among all the other educative impulses of children; and to discover the beginnings of the scientific spirit and method in the thought of young children.

In *Social Development in Young Children,* Isaacs shuns quantitative measurements of young children. This study, like the earlier volume, *Intellectual Growth,* is based upon the spontaneous behavior of children in the real situations of their daily life. The books' primary aim is the direct qualitative study of the individual children's feelings and doings as they interact with others.

Isaacs states that she "was a trained teacher of young children and a student of Dewey's educational theories long before [she] knew anything about Freud" (Isaacs, 1972, p. 19). She emphasized, as follows, the distinctions between analysis and education, the overlap that must reflect both analysts and educators recognizing, valuing, and understanding the basic characteristics of each field.

1. The analyst must accept all feelings. . .of love and hate, acceptance and aggression, and address them all appropriately. The educator must focus primarily on the good and positive aspects of the child's feelings.
2. The analyst must focus on the child's therapeutic progress and how well he is handling aggression. The educator must use the unconscious only as it appears naturally as interests of the child at the moment.
3. The analyst plays various roles as he/she works with the child to uncover fears and negative feelings. The teacher mainly acts as . . . the wise parent figure, thinking positively (Isaacs, 1972, p. 456).

Further Readings: Isaacs, Nathan. AIM25: Institute of Education available online at http://www.air25.ac.uk/cgi-bin/search2?coll_id=2316&inst_id=5; Isaacs, Susan. AIM25: Institute of Education available online at http://www.air25.ac.uk/cgi-bin/search2?coll_id=

2316&inst_id=5; Isaacs, Susan (1966). *Intellectual growth in young children*. New York: Schocken Books. Originally published 1930; Isaacs, Susan (1972). *Social development in young children*. New York: Schocken Books. Originally published 1933; Isaacs, Susan (1968). *The nursery years: The mind of the child from birth to six years*. Introduction by Millie Almy. New York: Schocken Books. Originally published 1929; Lascarides, V. Celia, and B. F. Hinitz (2000). *History of early childhood education*. New York: Falmer Press, a member of the Taylor and Francis Group.

Edna Ranck

J

Journal of Children and Media

The *Journal of Children and Media* is an interdisciplinary and multimethod peer-reviewed publication that provides a space for discussion by scholars and professionals from around the world and across theoretical and empirical traditions who are engaged in the study of media in the lives of children. It is a unique intellectual forum for the exchange of information about all forms and contents of media in regards to all aspects of children's lives, and especially in three complementary realms: children as consumers of media, representations of children in the media, and media organizations and productions for children and by them. It is committed to the facilitation of international dialogue among researchers and professionals, through discussion of interaction between children and media in local, national, and global contexts; concern for diversity issues; a critical and empirical inquiry informed by a variety of theoretical and empirical approaches; and dedication to ensuring the social relevance of the academic knowledge it produces to the cultural, political, and personal welfare of children around the world. In addition to research articles, the journal also features a Review and Commentary section which includes book reviews, suggestions for new directions in theory and research, notes on work-in-progress, commentary on developments within the field of children and media, responses to past journal articles, contributions to pedagogy and informal education practices, commentary on media production for children and media literacy programs, and reflections on ways to bridge the concerns of academia and activism. The current editor of the journal is Dafna Lemish from Tel Aviv University and the journal is published by Routledge, Taylor & Francis Group. For more information, see http://www.tandf.co.uk/journals/titles/17482798.asp.

Dafna Lemish

JECTE. *See Journal of Early Childhood Teacher Education*

JEI. *See Journal of Early Intervention*

Journal of Early Childhood Research

The *Journal of Early Childhood Research* provides a major international forum for the dissemination of early childhood research, crossing disciplinary boundaries and applying theory and research within a multiprofessional community. This journal's focus reflects a worldwide growth in theoretical and empirical research on learning and development in early childhood and the impact of this on services provided.

The journal's overarching aim is to promote high quality, international early childhood research findings that are at the forefront of current theory and practice and that generate new knowledge to enhance the lives of young children and their families. This will be achieved by doing the following:

- providing access to the expanding multidisciplinary knowledge base;
- exposing and stimulating debate on current controversies in the field—methodological and ethical;
- considering the implications and applications of such findings for the improvement of life chances of young children and their families;
- establishing a means for collaborative links between early childhood research centres in the international context.

Given these aims, the journal is interdisciplinary, drawing, for instance, from anthropology, epidemiology, education, health and medicine, law, neurology, paediatrics, philosophy, psychology, social policy and welfare, and sociology.

Since the intention is to disseminate international research germane to the area of early childhood and foster an international research culture, the primary audience is established academics and researchers, as well as new researchers, postgraduate students, and undergraduates, completing final-year projects and dissertations. The journal's role in bringing new knowledge on early childhood into the field will appeal equally, however, to the growing range of multiprofessional teams working on behalf of young children and their families.

Carol Aubrey

Journal of Early Childhood Teacher Education (JECTE)

The *Journal of Early Childhood Teacher Education (JECTE)* is the professional journal of the **National Association of Early Childhood Teacher Educators (NAECTE).** *JECTE* evolved from the NAECTE newsletter, the *Bulletin* (1979-1989), and was established in 1989 as the official journal of NAECTE. In 1990, the NAECTE Governing Board appointed an editor and editorial board that developed manuscript review criteria and implemented a blind review process. The first refereed issue of the journal was published in Spring 1990. The journal was first produced by university desktop publishing. Publication was shifted in 1997 to commercial publishers.

The purpose of the journal reflects the purposes of NAECTE: to provide an issues forum, a means of communication, and an interchange of information and ideas about practice and research in early childhood teacher education. *JECTE* publishes original manuscripts, book reviews, research reports, position papers, letters to the editor, information on association activities, essays on current issues, and reflective reports on innovative early childhood teacher education practices. The journal is a membership benefit of NAECTE and is published quarterly including one-theme issue. For additional information, contact NAECTE at www.naecte.org.

Kathryn Castle

Journal of Early Intervention (JEI)

The *Journal of Early Intervention* (*JEI*) is a peer-reviewed journal related to research and practice in **early intervention**. Early intervention is defined broadly as resources, supports, and procedures that support the development and early learning of infants and young children with special needs, their families, or the personnel who serve them. *JEI* is the official research journal of the **Division for Early Childhood** (DEC) of the **Council for Exceptional Children** (CEC). Six individuals have served terms as editor since the journal was first published in 1979 as the *Journal of the Division for Early Childhood*: Merle Karnes (1981–1988), Samuel Odom (1988–1991), Donald Bailey (1991–1994), Steven Warren (1994–1997), R. A. McWilliam (1997–2002), and Patricia Snyder (2002–2007). In 1989, the journal was renamed the *Journal of Early Intervention*. *JEI* is annotated and indexed widely. Additional information about the journal, including editorial policies and author guidelines, is located at www.dec-sped.org.

Patricia Snyder

The Journal of Special Education Leadership

The Journal of Special Education Leadership provides both practicing administrators and researchers of special education administration and policy with relevant tools and sources of research on recent advances in administrative theory, policy, and practice. *The Journal of Special Education Leadership* is a refereed journal that directly supports the main objectives of The Council for Administrators of Special Education, a division of the Council for Exceptional Children, to foster research, learning, teaching, and practice in the field of special education administration and to encourage the extension of special education administration knowledge to other areas of leadership and policy. Articles for the *Journal* should enhance knowledge and contribute to a body of research about the process of managing special education service delivery systems, as well as reflect on techniques, trends, and issues that are significant. Preference is given to articles that have a broad appeal, wide applicability, and immediate usefulness to administrators, other practitioners, and researchers.

Mary Boscardin

Jumpstart

Jumpstart is a national organization that believes early literacy is a fundamental building block of success. Founded in 1993 by college students, parents, and **Head Start** staff, Jumpstart launched its first school-year program at Yale University. Jumpstart has since expanded to twenty-four states and Washington, DC.

Jumpstart's preschool goal is to enhance the literacy, language, social, and emotional development of children through positive adult–child interaction and family involvement. Jumpstart's philosophy and research-based approach incorporate recommendations from recent best practices from the field of early education, including the **National Association for the Education of Young Children** (NAEYC), the **High/Scope** Educational Research Foundation, and the Stony Brook Reading and Language Project's dialogic reading method.

Jumpstart partners with higher education institutions and early learning programs that share a commitment to the basic tenants of **developmentally appropriate practice** and quality early childhood education. Jumpstart's intensive enrichment program trains a college student, called a Jumpstart Corps member, to work one-to-one with a 3–5-year-old child in Head Start or similar early learning programs. During the eight-month school year, Corps members hold twice, weekly, two-hour Jumpstart sessions, structured-classroom sessions set aside for a team of nine or 10 Corps members to devote attention to children following the traditional school day. Corps members spend additional time in their child's classroom supporting the classroom teacher and other students.

Jumpstart Corps members receive sixty hours of training in early childhood education and learn to facilitate children's development following four key principles:

1) Utilize developmentally appropriate practices,
2) engage children in active learning,
3) strike a balance between adult and child-initiated learning, and
4) support children's early or emergent reading and writing.

Corps members implement these principles during Jumpstart sessions through *One-to-One Reading* with each child; *Circle Time* to foster socialization and to build a sense of community through active group learning; *Choice Time* to foster independence, curiosity, and self-esteem; and *Small Group Activity* to introduce common, self-paced activities, focusing on a beginning, middle, and end.

Using a pre- and post-assessment of language and literacy, social, and initiative skills, Jumpstart tracks children's progress, measures program impact, and continuously improves content and delivery. Annual assessments conducted by independent consultants show that Jumpstart children begin the school year with skills rated lower than their peers but make greater progress than their peers in language and literacy, social, and initiative skill areas by the end of the year.

During the 2004–2005 school year, Jumpstart served more than 8,000 children by partnering with 66 higher education institutions and 200 early learning programs. The organization averages 30 percent annual growth and is evaluating several expansion opportunities, including expanding its program to partner with more colleges and universities across the country, expanding existing programs by enrolling more college students, and exploring different volunteer populations that could deliver the Jumpstart program to preschool children.

Kim Davenport and Alison Pitzer

K

Kindergarten

The term "kindergarten" in the United States traditionally refers to the year of school that precedes "formal" schooling in first grade. In other countries, the term "kindergarten" often designates group settings for young children that precedes the beginning of formal schooling, and encompasses children from three- to six or seven years of age. In Israel, for example, children between five and six years of age attend "compulsory kindergarten" and younger children are educated in "recompulsory kindergarten" (Micholwitz [sic], 1992, p. 307). Kindergartens in the United States are universally available and most young children attend them. The age for entry into kindergarten is set by individual states. As expectations have escalated for what children will learn and be able to do during this year of schooling, children's entry age has changed.

The term "kindergarten" originated with Friedrich **Froebel**'s nineteenth-century notion of a children's garden in Germany. Spiritually based, his kindergarten included the development of many new child-centered materials. Robert **Owen**, a Scottish contemporary of Froebel during the Industrial Revolution, offered kindergarten as an on-site service to young children and their families as an alternative to child labor in factories. Kindergarten came to the United States in the mid-1800s and quickly spread through the efforts of individually committed women and philanthropists. The first public school kindergarten was offered in St. Louis, Missouri. It has since become a mainstay of public education in the United States.

Government oversight of kindergarten programs in the Unites States occurs primarily at the state level. Individual communities, though, have a great deal of latitude in setting rules and standards for their schools, including kindergartens. Kindergarten programs also are sponsored by private and community-based organizations such as religious institutions, community centers, and industrial settings. These privately sponsored programs often operate with fewer regulations than public school-sponsored programs.

Brief History of Kindergarten

Since Froebel's time, the kindergarten has undergone a number of transformations. The growth of the **child study movement** in the United States at the end of the nineteenth century and the **progressive education** movement in the beginning of the twentieth century influenced a child-oriented alternative to what had become a lockstep **curriculum** format. Kindergarten became increasingly viewed as a program concerned with children's overall development and with assisting children's acclimation to the more structured instructional environment of formal schooling. Its curriculum was characterized by a tradition of "free play" during which children might select sociodramatic play in a housekeeping center or block building or drawing or puzzles or table top manipulative materials. There also was time for outdoor (or indoor gymnasium) play, which might mean recess with children choosing from among balls, climbing equipment, wagons, or tricycles; or it might also mean group games organized by the teacher for the whole group; or a combination of these activities.

Over time, however, kindergartens have been viewed less and less as a year of transition to formal schooling and more and more as a child's first year of official schooling. This trend has been exacerbated by the onset of formalized state enforced content and early learning standards (what children should know and be able to do), driving many kindergartens to focus more intently on the provision of structured curricula.

Contemporary Issues

The development of kindergarten programming has been and continues to be influenced by a variety of cultural, social, political, and economic contexts. These particular cultural contexts and values influence how policymakers interpret the outcomes desired from children's participation in kindergartens, what they will experience, and when they will attend. They also influence parents' expectations and what and how adults teach during the kindergarten year. A clear connection exists between a community's philosophical stance on how young children develop and learn, and their expectations for kindergarten education. Communities and the cultures they represent often emphasize in different degrees the values of cooperation or individualism, achievement of technical skills or social skills, an emphasis on contemporary experience or future work life.

High-Stakes Tests

In recent years, with the advent of the accountability movement, there has been an increasing incursion into the kindergarten of academic thrusts. There now are many kindergartens that require children to sit with worksheets and workbooks, to finish teacher-directed required work, with reduced time available for play. Many early childhood educators express concern over the loss of child-directed learning and the growing focus on isolated skills, drills, and rote learning of letters, numbers, colors, and shapes with the use of paper and pencil formats.

Retention and Redshirting

When kindergarten children do not achieve sufficiently high grades or test scores by the conclusion of the kindergarten year, some schools are requiring their retention in kindergarten or in a "transitional" first grade for an additional year.

Despite research evidence suggesting that these practices do not produce measureable differences in children's success with learning or later grades (Shepard and Graue, 1993; Crosser, 2004), a trend exists to increase the age of kindergarten entry. Thus, children in some communities might enter kindergarten if they turned five years of age before December while in other communities they might need to have turned five years of age by September, or earlier. This practice of postponing entry into a program with the expectancy that children will develop sufficiently over the ensuing months is called redshirting. This policy reflects growing pressure for children to do more, sooner.

Instructional Framework

With changing expectations for what children will achieve during the kindergarten year, the focus and implementation style of the kindergarten curriculum is receiving increased scrutiny. Research studies tend to support approaches that involve a combination of direct instruction in conjunction with more open-ended approaches to teaching and learning.

A cross-cultural study of kindergarten children's academic achievement and cognitive ability concluded that "the kinds of academic information and skills taught in kindergarten may be conveyed more effectively by indirect than by direct forms of teaching and by informal example than by formal instruction" (Stevenson, Lee and Graham, 1993, p. 529). A comprehensive review of research further suggests that the **direct instructional** model alone appears to reflect short-term achievement gains but the "child-initiated" programs tended toward long-term academic advantages (Crosser, 2004, p. 138).

A research study on **literacy** instruction in kindergarten concluded that a combination of integrated language arts instruction as well as direct phonics instruction resulted in improved achievement measures when compared with either single method of instruction (Xue and Meisels, 2004). The preponderance of research on children who had engaged in whole language instruction indicated that they considered themselves to be good readers and had positive attitudes toward reading as compared with children schooled with a main focus on phonics skills.

Full Day Kindergarten

Kindergarten children are in school between two and a half and six hours each weekday. Until recently, it was considered developmentally inappropriate for young children to be in extended-day early learning settings. This point of view has largely shifted. In the United States, public schools increasingly are offering full day kindergartens, moving from half-day to full school day programming. There have been reviews of research concerning the efficacy of the full-day program (Entwhistle and Alexander, 1998; Gullo, 2000; Kauerz, 2005). In general, children from low-income families or second-language homes appear to reap the greatest benefits of a longer kindergarten day.

Conclusion

The educational role of kindergarten is under extensive review. A year of school caught between the educational worlds of early childhood education and elementary schooling, it increasingly is being recognized as a pivotal year of learning and transition. Given changing social, political, and economic contexts—including our nation's focus on reducing the achievement gap between lower- and higher-income children and ensuring children are well-prepared for a global economy—kindergartens are increasingly being recognized as an opportunity for forging better alignment between the K-12 and early childhood education systems (Collaborating Organizations, AFT and CCW/AFTEF, CSSO, ECS, NAESP, NEA and NAEYC, 2005). *See also* Preschool/Prekindergarten Programs.

Further Readings: AFT and CCW/AFTEF, CCSSO, ECS, NAESP, NEA, and NAEYC (2005). Why we care about the K in K-12. *Young Children* 60(2), 54–56; Crosser, S. (2004). *What do we know about early childhood education? Research based practice*. Albany, NY: Thomson Delmar Learning; Entwhistle, D. R., and K. L. Alexander (1998). Facilitating the transition to first grade: The nature of transition and the factors affecting it. *Elementary School Journal 98*(4), 351–364; Fromberg, D. P. (1995). *The full day kindergarten*. 2nd ed. New York: Teachers College Press; Gullo, C. F., ed. (2006). *Kindergarten today: Teaching and learning in the kindergarten year*. Washington, DC; Gullo, D. (2000). The long-term educational effects of half-day vs. full-day kindergarten. *Early Child Development and Care* 150, 17–24; Kauerz, K. (2005). *Full-day kindergarten: A study of state policies in the United States*. Denver, CO: Education Commission of the States; Micholwitz [sic], R. (1992). The preschool educational network in Israel. In C. A. Woodill, J. Bernhard, and L. Prochner, eds., *International handbook of early childhood education*. New York: Garland, pp. 307–309; Shepard, L. (1992). Retention and redshirting. In L. R.Williams and D. P. Fromberg, eds., *Encyclopedia of early childhood education*. New York: Garland, pp. 278–279; Shepard, L. A., and M. E. Graue (1993). The morass of school readiness screening: Research on test use and test validity. In B. Spodek, ed., *Handbook of research on the education of young children*. New York: Macmillan, pp. 283–305; Stevenson, H. W., S. Lee, and T. Graham (1993). Chinese and Japanese kindergartens: Case study in comparative research. In B. Spodek, ed., *Handbook of research on the education of young children*. New York: Macmillan, pp. 519–535; Xue, Y., and S. J. Meisels (2004). Early literacy instruction and learning in kindergarten: Evidence from the early childhood longitudinal study—kindergarten class of 1998–1999. *American Educational Research Journal* 41(1), 191–229.

Doris Pronin Fromberg

Kohlberg, Lawrence (1927–1987)

Lawrence Kohlberg founded the cognitive developmental position on moral development and moral education. Born in Westchester County, New York, he was the son of a wealthy businessman and the youngest of four children. Brilliant even as a child, he decided not to go to the university and instead went off to wander the country, living without money and learning firsthand about the tougher side of life. He then joined up with the Merchant Marines as World War II was drawing to a close and signed on to a ship that was smuggling Jewish refugees out of war-torn Europe through the British blockade into Palestine. Moved by his experiences, he attended the University of Chicago, where he earned his B.A. in one year and received his Ph.D. in Clinical Psychology in 1958.

The war had presented issues of moral duty and social justice. After studying moral philosophy and psychology, he conducted highly original research in which he posed moral dilemmas to ninety-eight boys aged 10–16 and developed a system of coding to analyze the logical structure of their qualitative arguments. His theory challenged the dominant socialization model of moral development based on social-learning theory and posited a structural model that was a major extension and elaboration of Piaget's writings about children's conceptions of rules, games, and fair punishment.

Kohlberg set forth six stages of moral judgment stretching from early childhood to adulthood, and he presented empirical and theoretical arguments for their invariance and universality across history and cultures. Recognized immediately as a major theorist and researcher, Kohlberg went on to brief stays at Yale and the Center for Behavioral Sciences at Stanford University before he was appointed Professor of Psychology and Education at Harvard University in 1968. He set forth the major outlines of his theory in *Stage and Sequence: The Cognitive Developmental Approach to Socialization* (1968), and many other publications. In *Development as the Aim of Education* (1971), he and Rochelle Mayer stated that education should be democratic and nonindoctrinative and should stimulate children's thinking in a direction of development, which is universal for all children.

Kohlberg taught at the Harvard Graduate School of Education for almost twenty years, where he established an influential circle of students and colleagues, many of whom contributed to the expanding research base on the theory and applications. Much of Kohlberg's energy in later years was devoted to envisioning a just community approach to education, implemented in school and prison settings. These democratic communities had the goals of fostering moral reasoning and empathy development, creating a moral atmosphere of mutual respect and caring, and being models for institutional change. In 1973, Kohlberg's health was badly damaged by a chronic parasitic infection he caught on a research trip to Guyana, and he was eventually overwhelmed by physical pain and mental suffering and he died at age 59. Kohlberg was recognized for his lifetime contributions by the Society for Research in Child Development. He left two sons by his former wife.

Further Readings: Fowler, J. W., J. Snarey, and K. DeNicola (1988). *Remembrances of Lawrence Kohlberg*. Atlanta, Georgia: Center for Research in Faith and Moral Development; Kohlberg, L. (1984). *Essays on moral development, volume 2. The psychology of moral development*. San Francisco: Harper & Row, Publishers; Kohlberg, L. (1987). *Child psychology and childhood education: A cognitive-developmental view*. New York: Longman Publishers; Power, F. C., A. Higgins, and L. Kohlberg (1989). *Lawrence Kohlberg's approach to moral education*. New York: Columbia University Press; Schrader, D., ed. (1990). *The legacy of Lawrence Kohlberg. New Directions for Child Development, No. 47*. San Francisco: Jossey-Bass.

Carolyn Pope Edwards and Alison Rogers

L

Laboratory Schools

The earliest American laboratory schools, frequently referred to as child development laboratories (CDLs), started to appear in the late 1800s, and were initially sites that reflected best practices in public schools. Today, most child development laboratories are on college and university campuses and they provide settings for research, teacher education, and early care and education for young children.

In 1883, Colonel Francis Wayland Parker, superintendent of schools in Quincy, Massachusetts, became principal of the Cook County Normal School in Chicago, and later opened the Francis W. Parker School in 1901. At his "practice school," visiting teachers and even persons outside the teaching profession could observe his ideas in operation. His published Course of Study, which included descriptions of materials, devices, and methods, had wide circulation and affected the classroom practices of hundreds of public school teachers.

In 1894, John **Dewey** joined the University of Chicago as Chairman of the Department of Philosophy, Psychology, and Pedagogy. His "Dewey School" opened in January 1896 with about twelve students aged six to nine years of age, two teachers, and an instructor who was listed as "in charge of manual training." His school was a laboratory, in the sense of an experimental place where one's theory of education could be put into practice, tested, and scientifically evaluated.

The concept of practice, experimentation, and research became integrally linked to the first wave of laboratory schools at Columbia University and Bank Street College. Campus nursery schools made their appearance in the early 1920s, when several universities, colleges, and research centers established them as experimental schools for training very young children. Still other laboratory schools began as settings where teachers could be trained to work with young children—one of the first was the **Ruggles Street Nursery School and Training Center** established in Boston in 1922.

By 1930 laboratory nursery schools had been established at several institutions of higher education including Iowa State, the University of Minnesota, the

University of Wisconsin, Wellesley College, Vassar, and the University of New Hampshire. Over the next two decades, child development laboratories became a popular method of training university students about young children (Osborn, 1991). The Ruggles Street Nursery School eventually became a department of child development at Tufts University with its own laboratory school, renamed the Eliot-Pearson Children's School.

Throughout this period, child development laboratory schools were identified by a particular constellation of purposes. The first was to provide a high-quality early childhood program to young children and their families, and many campus programs are considered exemplary models, although difficult to replicate in "real world" settings. As such, they provided an important university and public service to their communities. CDLs also served important campus instructional needs, serving as a location to introduce students to young children, and to train undergraduates and in some cases graduate students strategies for working effectively with young children. On some campuses, CDLs involved students from many departments interested in observing how children develop. A third purpose has been to provide a location where students can learn how to conduct research involving children and/or their families, and to support faculty research.

In the 1960s and 1970s, some laboratory schools were closed as a result of budget shortfalls and space limitations, but also because there was lack of clarity about the value of the existing models. Many were perceived as "country clubs," serving primarily white, upper-class university faculty members and administrators, and only available to mothers who could afford to be at home during the day. Often, CDLs served as the only location for a student's teacher preparation, raising concerns about preparing future teachers for the "real" world. Some questioned the usefulness of research results based on a narrow pool of children utilizing such programs. Finally there was an increasing demand by students, and to a lesser degree by faculty members, for full and also flexible day care. As a result, there was a reduction in campus-based nursery school programs and an increase in full-day programs (McBride, 1996), only some of which also served as laboratory settings.

Today, there are estimated to be over 2100 programs serving young children in all types of college settings, about half of which are CDLs housed in academic departments. At least three issues remain (Bowers, 2000): the cost of (and need of subsidy for) campus-based CDLs, the increasing popularity of early childhood majors to undergraduates, and the possible impact of new technology on training future teachers. These issues are reflected in the considerable variation in the function, administrative unit, and parent population of CDLs. A study of NCCCC members (Thomas, 1995) found that 52 percent described their function as laboratory school and child-care service. A majority (39%) of campus children's centers were housed in academic departments, with student services (29%) the next most likely administrative unit. Most campus centers enrolled children of students, faculty and staff, and over half (64%) also accepted children from the community-at-large. Campus centers typically enrolled children from infancy (38%) to preschool age (98%), with some offering kindergarten (28%) and before and after school programs (20%).

In spite of the financial pressures (Kalinowski, 2000) and concerns about elitism, future prospects for laboratory schools remain positive. Parents' interest in high-quality child care, employer interest in attracting and retaining strong, and younger faculty with impending baby boomer retirements, a greater and more sophisticated understanding of resource centered management (RCM), and an increased interest in the value of high-quality programs for teacher training should result in an increase in campus child-care variations, and also an increase in the number of campus CDLs in the coming decade. There will be a growing need to explore new ideas in early childhood education, for example, in translating principles and practices from **Reggio Emilia** into effective educational experiences and learning environments for U.S. children, preservice teachers, and members of the community. It is essential that laboratory schools return to the cutting edge of innovation and experimentation regarding the design and implementation of exemplary services to children and their families for many reasons, including the political ones of balancing the effects of the **No Child Left Behind Act** and high stakes testing of children. CDLs were initially programs that demonstrated best practices and served as experimental places where theories could be tested, and innovative approaches to education analyzed and evaluated. They should take on, once again, the mantel of creative, productive, and valuable laboratories.

Three national organizations promote the work of CDLs, including the National Coalition of Campus Children's Centers (NCCCC), the National Organization of Child Development Laboratory Schools (NOCDLS), and the National Association of Laboratory Schools (NALS). The Council for Child Development Laboratory Administrators (CCDLA) has been an important regional organization in the Northeast.

Further Readings: Bowers, S. (March 2000). Are campus child development laboratories obsolete? *College Student Journal*. Available online at www.findarticles.com/p/articles/mi_m0FCR/is_1_34/ai_62839410; Kalinowski, M. (2000). Child Care. In National Association of College and University Business Officers. *College and university business administration*. Washington, DC: Author, pp. 20–55; McBride, B. (1996). University-based child development laboratory programs: Emerging issues and challenges. *Early Childhood Education Journal* 24(1), 17–21; Osborn, D. K. (1991). *Early childhood education in historical perspective*. 3rd ed. Athens, GA: Education Associates; Thomas, J. (1995). *Child care and laboratory schools on campus*. Fact Sheet No. 3. Cedar Falls, IA: National Coalition for Campus Child Care. Available online at www.campuschildren.org/pubs/cclab/cclab1.html; University of Chicago (2004–2005). *History of the University of Chicago Laboratory Schools*. Available online at www.ucls.uchicago.edu/about/history/chapter1.shtml.

Michael Kalinowski and Maria K. E. Lahman

Language Development. *See* Development, Language

Language Diversity

Language use in early childhood classrooms is of growing interest and concern in the United States, where increasing numbers of children speak languages not spoken by their teachers. According to popular wisdom, there are over 6,000 languages in use today around the world. Educators know that speakers of a large proportion of these languages populate schools around the globe. Thus an understanding of linguistic diversity is key to understanding young learners of language and other skills and understandings, whether or not a classroom is designated "monolingual," "bilingual," or "multilingual." To better understand and support language in the multicultural classroom, it is necessary to understand language development as it characterizes children's engagement with the social and physical world and demonstrates the inherent sociolinguistic diversity of early childhood.

How Language Begins

Language, broadly defined, is a system that relates symbols—spoken, gestured, or written—to meanings. Its components include sounds or gestures; morphemes, the building blocks of words; grammatical rules that children eventually use to build sentences; and pragmatic rules that underlie the structure of conversations. Language is also a social phenomenon that begins well before children utter their first words. Imagining infants in or out of the home setting, then, we can think of them learning a symbol system in the company of others. Caregivers respond in varied ways to sounds, facial expressions, laughter, movements, and gestures as elements of early communication—infants' first use of symbols to communicate meanings. Sociolinguists, researchers who focus on the social aspects of language, have demonstrated how differences among groups of infants and their caregivers emerge early in development, so that diversity and not uniformity becomes the norm in human interactions (Heath, 1983). Put another way, when any aspect of an interactive situation changes, a change in communicating can be obvious (for example, switching languages) or subtle (changing posture or facial expression). Young children are attuned to such situational differences well before they can talk about them.

For example, adults and children within the same family or social group become attuned to the patterns of particular "melodies," high pitched or lower pitched, softer or louder, orchestrated with a range of movements, along with other aspects of communication. However, a major difference between infants learning language at home versus in a group setting is that in the latter there are always *infants*, more than one, who interact with caregivers and each other before they utter their first words. The infants may or may not belong to the same social and linguistic groups as their caregivers and peers. Thus the possibility for difference or variation in ways of communicating across groups may be present from life's start.

Language as Play

With or without words, a key component of children's interactions with each other is their playfulness. Through **play** with sounds, gestures, and, for most children, words, children participate in conversations about the physical and social worlds. They engage in varied forms of interaction and eventually transform gestures and movements into meanings in an imagined world. Through play—and the language that is a part of play—children first exercise control over the everyday world.

Play and storytelling often intertwine. When the curriculum of early childhood classrooms contains space for both, children's language is frequently heard and can be documented by teacher researchers. Paley (2004), for example, has fashioned her nursery school and kindergarten classrooms into stages for children to dramatize their own stories. Children's views on issues such as fairness and exclusion emerge in the language of stories and the play that is always embedded in them.

Sociolinguistically Diverse from the Start

Once children's communicative symbols resemble the sounds or gestures of specific dialects or languages, the potential for exercising control over the everyday world grows. At the same time there are more opportunities for communication to occur across symbol systems—from nonverbal to spoken, and from one oral linguistic system to another. (See also the entry on **Symbolic Languages** as they have been interpreted and supported in **Reggio Emilia.**) In these cross-system situations there are challenges to participants who know only one system of communication. Teachers who know only English, for example, may feel disadvantaged next to a teacher who is bilingual; a teacher who knows ASL (American Sign Language) has an advantage when working with children who use ASL or are deaf or hard of hearing. (See also the entries on **bilingual education** and **second language acquisition.**)

In the diverse settings that support second-language learners, adults work to bridge the linguistic systems. In the observation that follows, a public school prekindergarten teacher, Ms. Chan, is alert to the meanings of children's nonverbal and verbal ways of communicating. Her classroom is seldom quiet, as talk in any language is encouraged in a range of situations, from dramatic play to singing to whole-group read-alouds. Ms. Chan also knows both English and Cantonese, the language spoken by many of the children in her room:

> As the teacher begins to read [a book about butterflies], Andy calls out "*Butterflies!*" followed by some Cantonese. As she reads about the egg and the hatching of a tiny caterpillar, James and Andy both talk excitedly in Cantonese in response to Ms. Chan's translation into Cantonese. They both look intently at the pictures that the teacher is showing the class. Once the caterpillar in the book hatched, Andy begins predicting.
>
> *Andy:* (some Cantonese) . . . *Gonna turn butterfly!*
> *Ms. Chan:* *Yes, it's going to turn into a butterfly.*
> *Kenneth:* *You, you, you gonna open it gonna open and let the butterfly, school . . . out and fly!*
> *Ms. Chan:* *Yeah, we are going to let the butterfly out!*
> *Andy:* (some Cantonese) *Butterfly! Big butterfly!* (Genishi, Yung-Chan, and Stires, 2000, p. 74)

Ms. Chan's ability to understand what Andy and his friends knew and were excited about allowed her to make a small space in her **curriculum** for communicating across languages; that is, her bilingualism and attention to what engaged the children made the **read-aloud** of a book in English accessible to children just beginning to learn English. That piece of the curriculum became both permeable and informative to teacher and children.

This teacher's curriculum makes learning accessible to her English language learners at the same time that it enhances learning in general. Although her bilingualism is a clear advantage for the Cantonese speakers in her class, it is not suggested that only teachers who know the children's languages can be instrumental in their learning. (See Fassler, 2003, for an example of a teacher who knows only English in a classroom made up entirely of English language learners.) Moreover, linguistic differences exist across both languages and *dialects*, varieties of a language that differ in the components of sound, syntax or grammar, meaning system, and rules of use.

"Best Practices"?

The history of language arts education in the United States has shifted periodically in terms of policy regarding children who use languages and dialects other than the "standard," with respect to languages other than English and African American Vernacular English (also referred to as Black English or Ebonics) (Baugh, 2000). With the passage of the **No Child Left Behind Act** of 2001, the shift for children whose schools rely on federal funding has clearly been toward prescriptive methods of teaching standard forms to all learners, particularly as they relate to **literacy** (Dyson, 2003).

Much has been written about the need for evidence-based research to help educators identify "best practices" in language and literacy education. Unfortunately the chief measure for what is "best" has become a student's score on a **standardized achievement test**. Thus practices that improve schools' collective test scores in schools receiving federal funding are favored. Regardless of this fixation on test scores, researchers who look for evidence of what children and teachers do in real classrooms over time portray complex practices that cannot be reduced to packaged programs for teaching standard English or to the test scores the programs are intended to raise. Instead classroom researchers find highly specific practices that vary according to the linguistic and cultural characteristics of learners and their teachers. In classrooms where teachers use their knowledge of the children to support their diverse language and literacy learning, researchers note the following general characteristics:

- Teachers are skilled observers and listeners who look and listen for children's own ways of communicating.
- The teachers' daily schedules show flexibility within a predictable framework.
- The curriculum is adapted to allow for group preferences and for individual variation. In other words the teachers adjust to variation and do not expect uniformity.

- These teachers appear to have high expectations. They expect every child learner, whether or not she or he is a second (or multiple) language learner, eventually to enter the community of communicators—speakers or signers, listeners, readers, and writers—in short, to become master learners.

Effective teachers of children in classrooms characterized by language diversity cherish communication and connection. They accept and celebrate everyone's need to be social, to have intentions and ideas and to communicate them freely, and often, to others. *See also* Development, Language.

Further Readings: Baugh, John (2000). *Beyond Ebonics: Linguistic pride and racial prejudice*. New York: Oxford University Press; Dyson, Anne Haas (2003). Popular literacies and the 'All Children': Rethinking literacy development for contemporary childhoods. *Language Arts* 81(2), 100–109; Fassler, Rebekah (2003). *Room for talk: Teaching and learning in a multilingual kindergarten*. New York: Teachers College Press; Genishi, Celia, Donna Yung-Chan, and Susan Stires (2000). Talking their way into print: English language learners in a prekindergarten classsroom. In Dorothy S. Strickland and Lesley Mandel Morrow, eds., *Beginning reading and writing*. New York: Teachers College Press, pp. 66–80; Heath, Shirley Brice (1983). *Ways with words: Language, life, and work in communities and classrooms*. New York: Cambridge University Press; Paley, Vivian Gussin (2004). *A child's work: The importance of fantasy play*. Chicago: University of Chicago Press.

Celia Genishi

LD. *See* Learning Disabilities

Leadership. *See* Advocacy and Leadership in Early Childhood Education

Learning Disabilities (LD)

Incidence and Characteristics of Learning Disabilities

Children with learning disabilities (LD) represent over half of those students in the United States identified for special education services during their elementary or secondary school years. International research shows this disability to be a cross-cultural phenomena, a universal problem found among individuals across all languages, nations, and cultures in the world (Lerner and Chen, 1992). Learning disabilities are evident among children learning an alphabet-based system of written language (e.g., English), as well as among children learning a logo-graphic or pictorial system of language as found in Chinese or Japanese (Tsuge, 2001). "Specific learning disabilities" are considered indicative of an underlying neurological disorder. This should not be confused with learning "differences" among children or simple learning "difficulties" which all children likely experience at one time or another.

Most children with learning disabilities are identified and officially diagnosed *after* they enter school and have received several years of academic instruction. Most students are identified between ages 9 and 14 according to data from the

U.S. Department of Education. These disorders in learning become more obvious because of a student's failure to acquire expected skills in reading, writing, spelling, arithmetic, and other subjects associated with the use or understanding of language/language symbols and their meaning. A cumulative history of failure (in one or two areas of academic achievement), along with a discrepancy in performance compared to a student's overall ability, often serve as the catalyst leading to an evaluation and formal diagnosis of LD.

Boys are about four times more likely than girls to be diagnosed with LD. Research suggests, however, that incidence rates for males versus females do not differ significantly. Plausible explanations for this higher frequency of diagnosis among boys include: (a) *cultural factors* (i.e., males may be identified more frequently because they tend to be more aggressive and exhibit disruptive behaviors that adults consider more troublesome), (b) *biological factors* (i.e., males may be more genetically and biologically vulnerable to learning disabilities), and (c) *academic expectations* (i.e., expectations and pressures for school success may be greater for boys than girls, particularly during the higher grades when adolescent priorities may shift regarding academic achievement).

Characteristics or symptoms of learning disabilities (LD) vary from person to person. In fact, LD is a generic label representing a heterogeneous group of conditions that can range from mild to severe. Most individuals with this disability have average or near-average intelligence although LD can occur at all intelligence levels. Some children may even be intellectually gifted or talented in some specific area of achievement yet manifest a learning disability in another area.

Although work in the field of LD has focused primarily on elementary and middle school students, we know this disability can become evident at many stages of life. Manifestations of LD among children or adults at various ages can take a different form. For example, symptoms among school-age students are manifested most often through unexpectedly low levels of achievement in areas such as reading and associated skill areas (e.g., spelling and writing) and/or mathematics. Reading is the most common area of difficulty. Disabilities in math are second most common. In comparison, preschoolers or kindergarten-age youngsters may manifest emerging problems via developmental delays or irregular/abnormal behaviors that cause concern with parents or teachers. Characteristics often noted in young children before a diagnosis of LD is made include: slowness in acquiring age-appropriate speech/language skills, hyperactivity, attention and concentration deficits, poor coordination, poor fine/gross motor skills, difficulties in auditory or visual processing, poor perceptual-motor integration, and a lack of crucial pre-literacy skills. During late elementary and early-middle-school grades, learning difficulties in other academic areas may appear as the curriculum becomes more difficult (e.g., science, social studies, foreign languages). Frustration, anxiety, and tension may accelerate as these students experience repeated failure and become increasingly self-conscious of their learning difficulties compared to peers. This can lead to additional emotional/behavior problems as students attempt to cope with their inability to perform as expected. These secondary outcomes of LD can further complicate diagnosis as well as educational processes and become add-on impediments to successful learning.

Definition of Learning Disabilities

The most widely accepted definition of learning disabilities is contained in U.S. federal law, the **Individuals with Disabilities Education Act** and its regulations (IDEA). IDEA specifies that the term "specific learning disability" means the following:

> a disorder in one or more of the basic psychological processes involved in understanding or in using language, spoken or written, which disorder may manifest itself in imperfect ability to listen, think, speak, read, write, spell or to do mathematical calculations. Such term includes conditions such as perceptual disabilities, brain injury, minimal brain dysfunction, dyslexia, and developmental aphasia. Such term does not include a learning problem that is primarily the result of visual, hearing, or motor disabilities; of mental retardation; of emotional disturbance; or of environmental, cultural, or economic disadvantage.

This definition of LD has been controversial. Modified definitions are offered by the National Joint Committee on Learning Disability (NJCLD—representatives from several professional organizations and disciplines involved with learning disabilities) and by the Interagency Committee on Learning Disabilities (ICLD-a committee commissioned by the U.S. Congress to develop a definition of learning disabilities). Although slight differences appear across these definitions, there is general agreement on the following five elements that define a learning disability:

1. A neurological disorder or central nervous system dysfunction.
2. A disorder in one or more of the basic psychological processes involved in using or understanding language (which includes perception or input of language and its meaning, the cognitive processing of language, and finally the expressive output or communication of thoughts/ideas in spoken or written language or other modes of communication).
3. A disorder manifested in an individual's difficulties in academic and learning tasks (e.g., listening, thinking, speaking, reading, writing, spelling, or doing mathematical calculations).
4. A disorder manifested by a discrepancy between a student's potential and his/her achievement in one or more of these areas (Note: Many professionals continue using this discrepancy concept. However, it is highly controversial including how "discrepancy" should be measured, what criteria apply, and whether this discrepancy model is valid.)
5. A disorder that is *not* the primary result of other disabilities (e.g., mental retardation, emotional disturbance, hearing or vision loss, motor disabilities, or cultural/environmental or economic disadvantage). It is suggested that LD may coexist or be manifested concurrently with other disabilities. However, it is often difficult to determine which condition is primary and which is secondary.

Identification of Learning Disabilities during the Early Childhood Years

The high incidence of LD among school-age students has brought greater urgency to early identification of young children who are at risk for this disability.

Obviously, earlier treatment might minimize the impact of LD upon a student's academic achievement. This is a better strategy than attempting remediation after a student's learning problems/failures have compounded and academic performance has fallen significantly below expected grade level. Formal diagnosis of LD in young children (i.e., birth to eight years), however, is somewhat complicated and presents issues frequently described in the professional literature.

Given the official definition of LD and underlying concepts about what constitutes a "specific learning disability," formal diagnosis of this condition in young children is difficult for several reasons. First, the official definition of learning disabilities focuses upon deficiencies or irregularities in cognitive processes, thinking, and academic performance expected of older children. Young children are early in the process of acquiring these particular skills or cognitive functions. It is difficult to designate behavior as "deficient or indicative of cognitive disability" when a child has no exposure or only limited exposure to formal academic training. One can question whether it is possible to accurately determine the presence of a neurological, cognitive/language-based disability when a child is in the midst of acquiring the very behaviors by which we infer those cognitive processes are functioning normally or abnormally. Yet to identify LD in children during their preschool or early elementary years obviously requires a diagnosis based on behaviors/symptoms that come before cognitive/academic skills are learned and through which learning disabilities are manifested (e.g., reading, writing, spelling, math, etc.). The criteria for diagnosis implied in this accepted definition of LD simply do not apply to young children.

Second, young children develop and learn at different rates. Therefore, development considered "within the normal range" shows considerable variation from child to child. Children reflect this variation not only in their rate or speed of learning but in their level of mastery and quality of performance across the various developmental domains. Educators are well aware of these intra-individual differences (variation within a single child across developmental domains) as well as inter-individual differences (variation across youngsters of the same chronological age), which make each child unique and distinctive from his/her peers. The dilemma here is that some differences in children's learning/developmental characteristics, which elicit concern about potential disabilities, may only reflect this normal developmental variation. They may not be actual symptoms or warning signs of learning disabilities that will persist. It is well understood that many environmental variables, as well as genetic/biological factors, contribute to these intra- and inter individual differences among children. For example, some variation may result from differences in the early stimulation and learning opportunities children receive during their formative years. Quality of the home environment and parent–child interactions, differences in parenting skills and styles of childrearing, parent education and family resources all affect how children develop and learn. Educational opportunities available to young children at home and in their surrounding community environment (such as exposure to preschool education) also affect kindergarten **readiness**, preliteracy skills, and later academic achievement.

These individual differences among all children, added to the fact that students diagnosed with LD are an exceedingly diverse, heterogeneous population, further complicate the task of formal early diagnosis. No two students with LD are alike nor do they manifest exactly the same symptoms or performance profile. Educators and diagnosticians often find it difficult to separate what is merely normal developmental variation/individual differences in young children from deviations that signal a true neurologically based learning disability. It is also difficult to distinguish between young children with a "learning disability" from those who should simply be characterized as "slow-to-develop" or slow learners with generally low achievement.

A third factor complicating formal diagnosis of LD in young children is the fact that certain learning problems or developmental delays can be precursors of other cognitive, behavioral, sensory, or developmental disorders, not just a "learning disability." Learning disabilities are not the only potential outcome of symptoms described here. To suggest that such deviations or limitations provide a basis for a conclusive, formal diagnosis of LD in a young child may be a presumptuous, premature conclusion. Educators are reluctant to apply the LD label to infants, toddlers, preschoolers, or even primary school-age students.

Early Indicators of Risk for Learning Disabilities among Young Children

Current regulations under U.S. federal law (IDEA) allow the use of a noncategorical diagnosis of "developmental delay" for young children (from birth to nine years) to qualify them for special education services. This general diagnostic label offers greater flexibility and perhaps a more useful alternative for identifying many children needing **early intervention**, including those at risk for learning disabilities. Thus children can be evaluated for indicators of risk and delayed development that are correlated with the later diagnosis of LD. Educators can move ahead with timely treatment and intervention without getting caught up in cumbersome issues surrounding an early formal diagnosis of "learning disability." The dangers of imposing a potentially inaccurate, premature diagnosis with potentially damaging labels can be avoided.

Precursors or indicators of risk that may be useful in identifying children needing early intervention include developmental delays and/or irregularities in areas described below.

Communication, speech and language skills. Difficulty acquiring speech and in using/understanding language or language symbols are among the most common precursors of LD. Some children may be slow in acquiring vocabulary. Word memory may seem poor. They may appear confused and slow to understand or to execute instructions from an adult. Oral speech may be delayed. When these children do talk, their communications may be unclear and fail to offer a coherent expression of what they are trying to say compared to other kids of the same chronological age. Word usage may be incorrect or seem strange. Children who should be talking in sentences may only be delivering disjointed words or short phrases. They may seem more immature compared to age-mates in initiating a conversation, engaging in interactive dialogue, explaining something, or using appropriate words to express a concept.

Fine/gross motor skills. Slowness in acquiring motor skills, poor coordination, and awkwardness in the performance of fine/gross motor skills also are common precursors of learning disabilities in some children. Parents of children diagnosed with LD often describe their child's clumsiness in learning to walk, run, jump, skip, ride a tricycle, catch or throw a ball, and simply move around their environment without stumbling or bumping into things. Delayed fine motor control may be manifested as difficulty in learning to dress and undress, handle buttons or zippers, manipulate eating utensils, or handle a pencil or crayon. These problems become more evident in school-related activities as children have difficulty with working puzzles, building objects, or completing art projects that require cutting with scissors and coloring with crayons or paint brushes. It shows up as slowness in learning to print letters accurately. Handwriting may seem laborious, sloppy, and nearly illegible due to poorly formed alphabet letters and spacing between characters. However, it should be emphasized again that LD is only one of several possible diagnoses to consider when a child exhibits these problems.

Visual and auditory perception or processing. Students with learning disabilities often exhibit limitations in auditory and/or visual perception and processing skills. These modalities are important avenues for learning and academic success. These are not deficits in the ability to hear or in auditory acuity. Neither are these problems with eyesight and visual acuity. These students can see and hear, but the problem lies in the actual neurological processing of input from one or both sensory modalities.

Phonological awareness is a particularly crucial skill related to reading. This involves the ability to recognize that words are composed of individual sounds blended together. Some children with LD have great difficulty recognizing and isolating these separate distinctive sounds in a word. Other key auditory perception/processing subskills affecting reading ability include: (a) auditory discrimination (ability to hear differences in sounds), (b) auditory memory (ability to store and recall what one has heard), (c) auditory sequencing (ability to remember the order of items in a sequential list such as the alphabet, numbers, days of the week, etc.), and (d) auditory blending (combining single phonic elements or phonemes into a complete word). Children who show deficits in these auditory functions may be at risk for learning disabilities.

Visual perception involves the identification, organization, and interpretation of sensory input, which are important processes as children learn to read. Problems with visual perception processes may be another indicator of risk for a diagnosis of LD and/or difficulties in acquiring literacy skills. This includes: (a) visual discrimination of letters, words, and other visual images, (b) figure-ground discrimination (difficulty distinguishing an object from its surrounding background), (c) visual closure (ability to recognize or identify an object when the total stimulus is not presented), (d) letter or object recognition (ability to recognize or distinguish geometric shapes, alphabet letters or other entities such as a square versus triangle, letter c versus g, dog versus cat, or a particular face), and (e) visual memory (the ability to remember information that was received via the visual modality). Abilities of kindergarten-age children in these prerequisite skills are strong predictors of later reading achievement.

Attention and ability to concentrate. Some children diagnosed with LD also manifest behaviors related to attention deficit hyperactivity disorder. ADHD may be concurrent with LD, but it is not considered a problem directly caused by learning disabilities. While young children are expectedly very active and energetic, excessive activity and an inability to quiet down sufficiently for a story or focused activity may be warning signs. Such behaviors are especially disruptive to learning if they are continuous, extreme, and do not seem to lessen when the environment or activity changes. These are children whose parents complain that they don't listen or pay attention. When parents or other caregivers find it difficult to get a child to settle down or sit quietly long enough to complete an age-appropriate task, there is cause for concern. This is especially true if the behaviors do not change over time, even accelerate in frequency and severity, and the child actually seems unable to focus upon a task or shift from an active to a quiet activity requiring more concentration.

Acquisition of pre-literacy skills. A lack of appropriate kindergarten readiness skills and verbal **language** abilities when children enter school can be indicators of risk for disorders that affect academic progress and achievement including a learning disability. Limitations in the developmental areas previously described all affect **literacy** and contribute to learning problems that affect a child's ability to read, write, spell, or do **mathematical** calculations. The relationship of language skills to reading achievement and reading disabilities is well established. Strong oral vocabulary skills (both expressive and receptive) are crucial skills for both reading and general academic success. Key readiness skills that reliably and robustly predict reading failure or success for most children include phonological awareness and manipulation skills (e.g., rhyming, blending, segmenting, letter knowledge, vocabulary, short-term memory for language, knowledge-related information, and rapid automatic naming). Other predictors of reading ability include letter knowledge and identification, word recognition, story recall, sentence imitation, and overall verbal ability. In fact, verbal abilities at ages 2–4 years have been well correlated, not only with eventual reading achievement itself, but also with the set of kindergarten skills shown to differentiate at risk from not-at-risk kindergarteners. Preschoolers with early language impairments are very likely to exhibit reading difficulties in their school years. Research also suggests that youngsters exhibiting delays or weaknesses in one or more of these skills described above at the end of the first grade are unlikely to become good readers. First grade reading ability has been shown to be a strong predictor of a variety of eleventh grade measures of reading ability even when measures of cognitive ability are all partialled out. Such children may be candidates for a later diagnosis of learning disability. Reading difficulties, of course, are the most frequent type of LD found in school-age students (Conference on Emergent and Early Literacy:

Current Status and Research Directions, 2001; McCardle, Scarborough, and Catts, 2001).

In summary, research clearly shows the benefits of early identification and **early intervention** with young children who are at risk for disability, poor academic performance, and school failure. The challenge is identifying these children so interventions can be initiated to address their difficulties. Parents or other primary caregivers who spend significant time with these children also need support so they can facilitate their child's learning and promote optimal development. Some argue against spending time pursuing an illusive and perhaps difficult formal diagnosis such as "learning disabilities" if this prevents timely interventions from occurring. Others caution against waiting until a formal and accurate diagnosis can be made, using the "wait and see approach" (sometimes called "wait and fail approach"), since withholding interventions until problems increase can compound into significant skill deficits. It is especially important to focus attention on the developmental delays and irregularities that are potential risk indicators known to be correlated with the disability or other learning problems. What children need during their early childhood years are early childhood professionals, including but not limited to those from the field of **early childhood special education,** who can work together with children's families to identify environmental conditions and forms of instruction that are responsive to these specific problems. Young children identified with learning disabilities may need specific therapeutic interventions in their natural everyday routines couched in age-appropriate activities that help them progress developmentally and acquire essential skills for emerging **literacy** and academic success. *See also* Academics; Attention Deficit Disorder/Attention Deficit Hyperactivity Disorder; Kindergarten; Parents and Parent Involvement.

Further Readings: Conference on Emergent and Early Literacy: Current Status and Research Direction (2001). *Learning Disabilities Research and Practice* (Special Issue) 16(4), 183–258; Committee on the Prevention of Reading Difficulties in Young Children (1998). *Preventing reading difficulties in young children*. Washington DC: National Academy Press; Lerner, J. W., and A. Chen (1992). The cross-cultural nature of learning disabilities: A profile in perseverance. *Learning Disabilities Research and Practice* 8, 147–149; Lerner, J. W. with F. Kline (2006). *Learning disabilities and related disorders: Characteristics and teaching strategies*. 10th ed. New York: Houghton Mifflin Company; McCardle, P., H. S. Scarborough, and H. W. Catts (2001). Predicting, explaining, and preventing children's reading difficulties. *Learning Disabilities Research and Practice* 16(4), 230–239; Scruggs, T. E., and M. A. Mastropieri (2002). On babies and bathwater: Addressing the problems of identification of learning disabilities. *Learning Disability Quarterly* 25(3), 155–168; Swanson, H. L., K. R. Harris, and S. Graham, eds. (2003). *Handbook of learning disabilities*. New York: Guilford Press; Tsuge, M. (2001). Learning disabilities in Japan. In D. Hallahan and B. Keogh, eds., *Research and global perspectives in learning disabilities: Essays in honor of William M. Cruickshank*. Mahwah, NJ: Erlbaum, pp. 255–272.

Web Sites: Learning Disabilities (LD), http://www.ldonline.org; International Academy for Research on Learning Disabilities (IARLD), http://www.iarld.net. See IRLD journal *Thalamus*

Nancy L. Peterson

Literacy

Emergent Literacy—Theory, Practice, and Policy

With the introduction and widespread acceptance of literacy standards and goals starting in the 1990s, young children's literacy development has garnered a great deal of attention on the part of policymakers, researchers, educators, and families. The majority of states across the United States, and some countries internationally (such as the United Kingdom), have adopted early literacy expectations and goals for children at discrete age levels during the preschool and primary grade years. For example, California recently adopted preschool literacy standards that are aligned with the state's **kindergarten** language arts standards. These standards cover early literacy elements such as oral language development, phonological awareness, literary analysis, and concepts about print. They are designed to increase teachers' attention to the forms and functions of print during children's earliest years of formal schooling, and to give children a head start on early literacy development in the primary grades.

Emergent literacy is the most widely used term for young children's beginning literacy learning and development (Teale and Sulzby, 1986). The term pertains to children's first efforts to make sense of, use, and create written language in and out of early childhood settings. The term emergent literacy most powerfully conveys the idea of literacy instruction in early childhood as tailored to children's emerging linguistic, social, cultural, and personal needs and talents. In this view of early literacy development, teachers adjust literacy materials, goals, and strategies to foster children's curiosity, discovery, play, and development in literacy-related activities. This view of literacy development is most strongly associated with the long-standing tradition in the field of early childhood of valuing a play-based and developmentally appropriate curriculum guided by caring, reflective practitioners.

Developmentally Appropriate and Culturally Responsive Literacy

Developmentally appropriate language and literacy education honors the role of play, self-discovery, children's individual interests, and individual rates of development (Bredekamp and Copple, 1997). As children's emergent literacy learning has gained attention as a critical focus in early childhood, influential researchers and teachers have argued for a developmentally appropriate early literacy framework and set of teaching practices. It is argued that young children benefit from literacy goals, materials, and strategies that are developmentally appropriate in the following ways: children's natural sense of discovery and curiosity are valued, activities are meaningful and authentic, children are encouraged to explore and play with literacy materials, children's individual rates of maturation and development are respected, and teachers are expected to play a critical role in selecting early literacy materials, curriculum, and adapting standards to match their particular children's needs and talents.

As early childhood settings both in the United States and internationally have become more culturally and linguistically diverse, the idea of developmentally appropriate practice continuously needs to be expanded to include the ways that diversity of the world's children may approach and understand the forms and functions of written language. In terms of emergent literacy development, it is argued that conceptual frameworks and teaching practices need to be both developmentally appropriate and culturally responsive (Meier, 2000). In seeking common ground between these two ideas, emergent literacy goals and practices are grounded in young children's cultural and linguistic ways of looking at the world and using oral and written language (Delpit, 1995; Soto, 2002). For example, the selection of children's literature used in children's early literacy experiences must address children's cultural lives; children need opportunities for literacy performance that honor cultural traditions (Dyson, 2003); children benefit from literacy learning that relies on home/community literacy practices involving older siblings; and literacy needs to be tied to issues of social action and social justice.

Interplay between Literacy, Social Interaction, and Thought

Children's emergent literacy development involves an intricate interplay between thought, language, and social interaction (Vygotsky, 1978). In a Vygotskian framework, young children experience and learn about themselves and their worlds through playful and meaningful interactions with others and objects. As young children use and explore written language (such as books, reading, writing, dictation, poems, language experience activities) with others, both peers and adults, they learn about critical forms and functions of literacy through collaboration with others. This social process of interaction and collaboration, which can occur both in home and educational settings, fosters sophisticated mental activity involving the forms and functions of written language. In a public forum of literacy learning, children learn to work with others, understand another's point of view, and explain and describe a feeling or an experience to someone else. In this melding of social interaction and literacy, emergent literacy becomes a culturally valued activity for children within a certain group, community, or setting and thus gains in social and personal currency. Literacy learning and education becomes part of the culture of the educational setting and part of a community of speakers, readers, and writers. In this socially constructed use of literacy, children benefit from scaffolded literacy activities in which they have conversational partners (peers and adults) for talking about books, stories, writing, and other shared literacy experiences.

How children learn about the forms and functions of literacy is also tied to children's general cognitive and developmental growth. An important element of this growth involves experiencing and understanding literacy as a symbol system. Since alphabetic letters or characters in written languages symbolize or represent objects and phenomena in the world, there is an important interplay between children's ability to decode and understand these symbols and their general cognitive growth and development. Both processes reinforce and support the other. Children's literacy development progresses as children understand and use letters, words, and sentences to express and represent their ideas, feelings, observations, and experiences. This is a developmental journey that usually begins in preschool and continues on through the primary grades. In terms of literacy practice, young children's understanding of literacy as a symbol system is supported by involvement in familiar social and language contexts grounded in talking, interacting, and playing with others.

The Oral and Written Language Transition

Emergent literacy views young children's oral and written language as intricately linked, and young children move back and forth between the two as they talk, read, and write. This often starts off with a transition for children in which they move from mostly oral language experiences to increased exposure to written language activities and materials. This involves a movement away from primarily contextualized language use (i.e., oral language in familiar settings with familiar conversational partners) to more decontextualized language use (i.e., primarily written language activities in school settings without familiar social and language supports). Before entering formal schooling, many children communicate and express themselves primarily through oral language in familiar home and community contexts and with familiar conversational partners. Traditionally, though, school and educational settings have asked young children to focus on language without the familiar oral language and social supports of home and community. In an emergent literacy framework, children are afforded access to their oral language powers and talents in order to contextualize their early literacy activities and experiences in early childhood settings. It is this very process of contextualizing language use that helps children become more familiar and successful with decontextualized language use around literacy activities.

There are several key factors that support the oral to written language transition. For instance, children need access to familiar forms and functions of nonverbal communication (gesture, face-to-face interactions, holding of objects, turntaking) and oral language (conversations, stories, narratives, jokes, riddles) as supports for understanding more distant and unfamiliar forms and functions of written language in school settings. Narrative is one important avenue that children can use to bridge oral to written language use. For example, when teachers emphasize narrative for children with disabilities, it has a strong positive influence on the meaningful literacy learning of these children (Kliewer et al., 2005). Through storytelling and interactions with stories, children use their oral language talents to make sense of books and other forms of school-valued literacy. Varied forms of social interaction is another factor that influences the transition to literacy, as peer-peer and child–adult collaboration provide an oral language foundation and scaffold for early literacy learning (Cazden and Michaels, 1986).

Summary

Young children's literacy learning is a significant international focus in early childhood as countries seek to provide a solid foundation for children's early literacy learning, later school success, and to raise overall rates of literacy achievement. Increasingly, lawmakers and policymakers have turned to literacy standards and expectations to provide this foundation for young children's literacy learning. The framework of emergent literacy, though, cautions against a "one size fits all" approach to early literacy theory, practice, and policy. Emergent literacy advocates goals, materials, and teaching practices that support and guide the diversity of children's natural talents and abilities to talk, discover, play, and imagine as they engage in literacy activities. Children need a developmentally and culturally responsive literacy education, an integration of oral language and written language activities, and literacy practices that promote integration of children's cognitive, social, cultural, and literacy learning. The current challenge for the international early childhood community is to meld literacy theory, practice, and policy to meet the needs of all children in all learning communities. *See also* Vygotsky, Lev.

Further Readings: Bredekamp, S., and C. Copple, eds. (1997). *Developmentally appropriate practice in early childhood programs*. Rev. ed. Washington, DC: National Association for the Education of Young Children; Delpit, L. (1995). Other people's children: Cultural conflict in the classroom. New York: The Free Press; Dyson, A. H. (2003). *The brothers and sisters learn to write: Popular literacies in childhood and school cultures*. New York: Teachers College Press; Kliewer, C., Fitzgerald, L, Meyer-Mork, J., Hartman, P., English-Sand, P., and Raschke, D. (2005). Citizenship for all in the literate community: An ethnography of young children with significant disabilities in inclusive early childhood settings. In L. I. Katzman, A. G. Gandhi, W. S. Harbour, and J. D. LaRock, eds., *Special education for a new century*. Cambridge, MA: Harvard University Press, pp. 373–403; Meier, D. R. (2000). *Scribble scrabble: Learning to read and write*. New York: Teachers College Press; Soto, L. D., ed. (2002). Making a difference in the lives of bilingual/bicultural children. New York: Peter Lang; Teale, W. H., and E. Sulzby, eds. (1986). *Emergent literacy: Writing and reading*. Norwood, NJ: Ablex; Vygotsky, L. S. (1978). *Mind in society*. Cambridge, MA: Harvard University Press.

Daniel Meier

Literacy and Disabilities

Despite a rich knowledge base on how children learn to read and write and how best to teach them, an alarming number of children with disabilities will reach adulthood having not attained literacy (Saint-Laurent, Giasson, and Couture, 1998). Factors influencing this disturbing phenomenon include home literacy environments, caregiver and teacher expectations for literacy, cognitive skills, language skills, severity and type of disability, as well as the educational curriculum. As literacy development is a lifelong process that begins at birth, even for individuals with a wide range of disabilities, is important to understand the relationship between literacy and disability.

National data on literacy for young children with disabilities are not readily accessible. Few literacy specialists have opened the door to that investigative possibility. The research available suggests that children with disabilities are arriving in the classroom having had less rich literacy experiences—both in quantity and quality—than their nondisabled peers (Saint-Laurent, Giasson, and Couture,

1998). All children with disabilities appear to be given limited access to reading, drawing, and writing materials as well as literacy instruction or intervention across the lifespan (Weikle and Hadadian, 2004). And yet, research does not support the supposition that children are "too physically, too cognitively, or too communicatively disabled to benefit from experiences with written language" (Koppenhaver et al., 1991).

The type and severity of the disability play a role in placing limitations on early and later literacy experiences. A child's sensory, physical, cognitive, or communicative differences may limit their opportunities to explore print or engage in literacy-rich activities with family. Children with severe physical impairments, for example, have greater difficulty accessing and using print devices, such as writing instruments and keyboards. Children with visual impairments experience difficulty attending to print, and children with hearing impairments have trouble connecting sounds to that print. Intellectual impairments may also serve to slow the response to literacy events and the understanding and use of print. The presence of one or more impairments may lead some parents to lower their expectations for their children's future reading proficiency and overall academic achievement. Others may simply lack the knowledge and resources with which to stimulate their child's literacy skills.

Regarding the emergence of **literacy** in early childhood, children with disabilities tend to acquire emergent literacy skills at a slower rate than their same age peers (Boudreau and Hedberg, 1999). Emergent literacy delays are prevalent in children exhibiting language impairment—either as a primary disability or as a secondary disability to other conditions, such as **autism** or mental retardation. For these youngsters, delayed emergent literacy typically exists in all key areas of emergent literacy, including print awareness, phonological awareness, alphabet knowledge, and metalinguistic as awareness (1999). Thus, it is widely recognized that early intervention goals for these children should address emergent literacy in the context of overall developmental goal setting. Results of emergent literacy intervention programs reveal that children with mild impairments who are enrolled prior to six months of age achieve better outcomes than those who enter programs at later ages. Children with severe disabilities, however, exhibit consistent gains regardless of age initiation in a literacy intervention program (Weikle and Hadadian, 2004).

Children with speech and language impairments appear to be at risk for having difficulties using written language, because oral language lays the foundation for all subsequent language learning, especially reading (Boudreau and Hedberg, 1999). Children with language impairments when compared to their typically developing peers have demonstrated poorer performance on tasks measuring knowledge of rhyme, letter names, and concepts related to print. While the nature of the speech and language impairment appears to be an important factor in predicting later reading achievement, there is wide variability in reading achievement among these children. For example, some children with phonological impairments in preschool have developed reading disabilities and some have not. Children exhibiting language deficits in the areas of vocabulary and grammar are placed at highest risk for reading disabilities; at a lower risk are children exhibiting only articulation disorders (Catts, 1993). Boudreau and Hedberg (1999) found deficits in **narrative** discourse related to syntax and semantics, supporting an earlier finding that vocabulary and grammar measures at age 4 are predictive of reading achievement at age 8 (Catts, 1993). Measures of metalinguistic abilities, including phonological awareness skills, are the best predictors of reading achievement (1993), which puts children with a variety of communication disorders at high risk for reading disability.

Weikle and Hadadian (2004) report that children with disabilities experience literacy at a much lower level than their nondisabled peers, suggesting that the needs of their disability may compete for primary therapeutic and educational focus. For instance, a child with severe **cerebral palsy** (CP) may require increased assistance with gross motor and fine motor tasks, decreasing caregiver or teacher attention on the child's need for improvement in literacy skills. Research also reports that home reading and writing experiences of kids with severe speech impairments is limited and that children with disabilities are exposed to less books than their nondisabled peers (2004). Marvin (1994) found that children with single disabilities are equally as likely to have limited contact with print materials, reading episodes, and writing events as those children with multiple disabilities.

Among individuals with cerebral palsy (CP), between 50 and 100 percent are illiterate, depending upon the degree of physical and communicative impairment. Research reveals that individuals with severe physical disabilities may not have as many opportunities to develop literacy skills. They may lack appropriate accommodations for literacy learning opportunities. For example, body positioning equipment and **augmentative and alternative communication** (AAC) devices, such as buttons, switches, or computers, may allow an individual with severe physical disabilities to interact more appropriately with a reader or a book. Additionally, they may lack literacy instruction due to a focus on therapeutic needs. Teachers and caregivers may inadvertently place curricular focus on physical needs, gross or fine motor skills, and related activities of daily living, involuntarily limiting overall opportunities for text production in authentic literacy contexts (Weikle and Hadadian, 2004). When comparing AAC users to their nondisabled peers, there are significant differences found in the quality and quantity of literacy materials and activities. Parents of AAC users place greater priority on communication, mobility, and feeding than on literacy, while the parents of the nondisabled peers rank communication, peer relationships, and literacy as their highest priorities (Light and Kelford-Smith, 1993).

In children with hearing loss, literacy development frequently is delayed in the early years; but in later years, these children tend to develop basic levels of literacy. Children with hearing loss were once supposed to need to develop reading readiness through an oral or sign language. Teachers once focused primarily on these aspects of their **curriculum**. However, that fallacy is now being addressed in U.S. classrooms. Teachers are recognizing that good speaking and or signing skills are not necessarily a prerequisite to literacy learning and that reading and writing can be an effective means of communication as well as an efficient facilitator of overall language growth in all children, particularly those with disabilities (Weikle and Hadadian, 2004).

Early and ongoing home experiences with literacy also play a critical role in literacy outcomes for children with disabilities. Parents' perceptions and expectations of future literacy may be lower for these children than for their nondisabled peers. Additionally, children with disabilities may not respond to reading activities in the same manner that their nondisabled peers do. For example, a one-year-old girl who has limited upper body movement may not consistently point to the pictures in a book as her parent reads to her. One would expect a child at her age to be able to listen to simple stories, participate in rhymes and finger plays, and point to pictures in a book when named. However, when this child fails to respond like her typically developing peers, parents will unintentionally reduce regular interactions with books. Lowered expectations combined with reduced responsiveness to literacy events may unwittingly engage families in a cycle of less frequent book exposure, lowered literacy expectations, self-doubt, and a pattern of learned helplessness with regard to literacy and overall achievement (Weikle and Hadadian, 2004).

Children with disabilities who have achieved high levels of literacy relate several shared characteristics among their parents. Foremost, their parents believed themselves to be important teachers in their child's life. These parents frequently served as literate models, reading aloud regularly to their children. As adults, these children with disabilities reported that their parents created time to interact with them as literate individuals, providing reading and writing materials for the children to use. The priorities that parents hold with regard to their child's needs play a significant role in determining literacy outcomes. Parents who rank physical priorities high, such as mobility and feeding, place a lower priority on communication and literacy. Parents of nondisabled children rank communication, making friends, and literacy experiences as their highest priorities (Light and Kelford-Smith, 1993).

Older children with disabilities have traditionally been excluded from the literate community of classroom learners, due much in part to teacher expectations and curricular focus. Kliewer (1998) described the three literacy participation styles imposed by teachers within both inclusive and self-contained classrooms—citizens, squatters, and aliens in the literate community. Citizens in the literate community have two things in common: first, "they are valued as symbolic beings, not devalued as intellectually deficient, and secondly, it was recognized that they needed a tool for connecting symbolically with the wider community" (Kliewer, 1998, p. 177). Kliewer's study revealed that teacher practices in literacy inclusion play a significant role in either encouraging or limiting literacy attainment for students with disabilities. Most of the students observed in his ethnographic study were relegated to either the position of the *squatter* or the *alien*. The "squatter's" classroom participation in literacy events was limited to remedial practices that focus on low-level concepts or diminished subskills. The "alien," however, is separated from the literate community altogether due to idiosyncratic behaviors interpreted by the teacher as cognitive incompetence. These disturbing practices led the Center for Literacy and Disability Studies to formulate a "Literacy Bill of Rights" (see below), which states that "all persons, regardless of the extent or severity of their disabilities, have a basic right to use print" (Yoder, Erickson, and Koppenhaver, 1997).

A Literacy Bill of Rights

All persons, regardless of the extent or severity of their disabilities, have a basic right to use print. Beyond this general right, there are certain literacy rights that should be assured for all persons. These basic rights are:

1. The right to an opportunity to learn to read and write. Opportunity involves engagement in active participation in tasks performed with high success.
2. The right to have accessible, clear, meaningful, culturally and linguistically appropriate texts at all times. Texts, broadly defined, range from picture books to newspapers to novels, cereal boxes, and electronic documents.
3. The right to interact with others while reading, writing, or listening to a text. Interaction involves questions, comments, discussions, and other communications about or related to the text.
4. The right to life choices made available though reading and writing competencies. Life choices include, but are not limited to, employment and employment changes, independence, community participation, and self-advocacy.
5. The right to lifelong educational opportunities incorporating literacy instruction and use. Literacy educational opportunities, regardless of when they are provided, have potential to provide power that cannot be taken away.
6. The right to have teachers and other service providers who are knowledgeable about literacy instruction methods and principles. Methods include but are not limited to instruction, assessment, and the technologies required to make literacy accessible to individuals with disabilities. Principles include, but are not limited to, the beliefs that literacy is learned across places and time, and no person is too disabled to benefit from literacy learning opportunities.
7. The right to live and learn in environments that provide varied models of print to use. Models are demonstrations of purposeful print use such as reading a recipe, paying bills, sharing a joke, or writing a letter.
8. The right to live and learn in environments that maintain the expectations and attitudes that all individuals are literacy learners (Yoder, Erickson, and Koppenhaver, 1997).

The National Adult Literacy Survey (Kirsch et al., 2002) included questions requiring respondents to categorize any illness, disability, or impairments. Twelve percent of the sample population reported some illness, disability, or impairment, and when comparing their literacy proficiency levels to those of the total population, the evidence was clear. Adults with any type of disability were more likely to perform in the lowest literacy levels, and some categories of illness, disability, or impairment appeared to have a stronger correlation with very low literacy levels. For instance, adults with mental retardation exhibited the most deficient literacy levels and were four times more likely than peers to perform in the lowest level of a literacy scale. Conversely, respondents with hearing difficulties exhibited higher literacy levels than those in other categories of impairment. The smallest gap in average reading performance among categories of illness, disability, and impairment was found between those reporting hearing difficulties and the general population. On the whole, however, significantly low-literacy levels were found among those adults with disabilities and impairments (Indicator 36, 2003). *See also* Disabilities, Young Children with; Parents and Parent Involvement.

Further Readings: Boudreau, D. and N. Hedberg (1999). A comparison of early literacy skills in children with specific language impairments and their typically developing peers. *American Journal of Speech-Language Pathology* 8, 249–260; Catts, H. (1993). The relationship between speech-language impairments and reading disabilities. *Journal of Speech and Hearing Research* 36, 948–958; Indicator 36: Home literacy environment and kindergarteners' reading achievement. (2003). U.S. Department of Education, National Center for Education Statistics, *The Condition of Education 2003,* NCES 2003-067. Washington, DC: U.S. Government Printing Office; Kirsch, I., A. Jungeblut, L. Jenkins, and A. Kolstad (2002). *Adult literacy in America: A first look at the findings of the National Adult Literacy Survey*. U.S. Department of Education, National Center for Education Statistics, NCES 1993-275, Washington, DC: U.S. Government Printing Office; Kliewer, C. (1998). Citizenship in the literacy community: An ethnography of children with Down syndrome and the written word. *Exceptional Children* 64(2), 167–180; Koppenhaver, D., P. Coleman, S. Kalman, and D. Yoder (1991). The implications of emergent literacy research for children with developmental disabilities. *American Journal of Speech and Language Pathology* 38–44; Light, J., and A. Kelford-Smith (1993). The home literacy experiences of preschoolers who use AAC systems and of their non-disabled peers. *Augmentative & Alternative Communication* 9(1), 10–25; Marvin, C. (1994). Home literacy experiences of preschool children with single and multiple disabilities. *Topics in Early Childhood Special Education* 14(4), 436–455; Saint-Laurent, L., J. Giasson, and C. Couture (1998). Emergent literacy and intellectual disabilities. *Journal of Early Intervention* 21(3), 267–281; Weikle, B., and A. Hadadian (2004). Literacy, development, and disabilities: Are we moving in the right direction? *Early Child Development and Care* 174(7–8), 651–666; Yoder, D. E., K. A. Erickson, and D. A. Koppenhaver (January 23–24, 1997). *Literacy bill of rights*. Presented by the Center for Literacy and Disability Studies at the Sixth Symposium on Literacy and Disabilities. Durham, NC: Eric Document 407–497.

Anissa Meacham

Lowenfeld, Viktor (1903–1960)

Viktor Lowenfeld has been described as "the most influential art educator" (Chapman, 1982, p. ix) of the twentieth century, and as doing "for the drawing of children what Piaget has done for their thinking" (*Harvard Educational Review*, quoted in Michael, 1982, p. xv).

Lowenfeld arrived in the United States in 1938, having fled Austria in advance of the German invasion. While still in Europe, Lowenfeld worked with children in the Vienna School for the Blind, and had contact with Franz Cizek, an Austrian artist and educator popularly considered the "Father of Child Art." Lowenfeld lectured briefly at both Columbia and Harvard Universities before becoming a professor of psychology and founding the Art Department at Hampton Institute in Virginia. At Hampton Institute, Lowenfeld taught John Biggers, Elizabeth Catlett, and Samela Lewis, all of whom became distinguished African American artists. In 1946, after teaching for two summers at Penn State, Lowenfeld accepted a position at The Pennsylvania State University where he established a doctoral program in art education, which soon became the largest in the United States. Soon after his arrival at Penn State, Lowenfeld published his landmark text, *Creative and*

Mental Growth, a work that has been translated into multiple languages and is now available in an eighth edition, revised most recently in 1987 by W. Lambert Brittain. This, and other texts by Lowenfeld, including *Your Child and His Art* (1954), have been translated into many languages. In 1957, the National Art Education Association named Lowenfeld Art Educator of the Year. A highly charismatic teacher, Lowenfeld's students at Penn State went on to establish and teach in art education programs throughout the country, continuing his legacy and expanding his influence throughout the world.

The position that Lowenfeld articulated in *Creative and Mental Growth* maintained that children's art experiences both reflected and supported their emotional, intellectual, physical, perceptual, social, aesthetic, and creative development. Along with others of his time, Lowenfeld believed in art as a powerful, humanizing force: "The goal of art education, in Dr. Lowenfeld's words, is 'not the art itself or the aesthetic product or the aesthetic experience, but rather the child who grows up more creatively and sensitively and applies his experience in the arts to whatever life situations may be applicable'" (Michael, 1982, p. xix).

Lowenfeld also described a series of six developmental stages through which all normally functioning children were thought to progress, given appropriate encouragement and opportunity. This developmental structure indicated what parents and teachers should expect of children at various ages, and provided a sense of what children were striving to achieve in their drawings as they progressed to subsequent stages. Lowenfeld recommended a method of teaching that encouraged children to develop their own ways of using materials and media, and focused on the enhancement of ideas and impressions through motivational dialogues, in which teachers asked children questions designed to activate their passive knowledge of important experiences in their lives. Frequently criticized in recent times as being too narrowly focused on self-expression, this approach to teaching was designed to heighten sensitivity to the environment and to children's experiences within it.

Albert Einstein remarked, "In Lowenfeld's work a fine sense of understanding, systematic spirit and unprejudiced research are combined" (Michael, 1982, p. xv). Lowenfeld died in State College, Pennsylvania, in 1960. His professional papers and collection of drawings are housed in the Archives of the Pennsylvania State University libraries. *See also* Piaget, Jean.

Further Readings: Lowenfeld, Viktor (1956). *Creative and mental growth.* 3rd ed. New York: Macmillan; Michael, John A. (1982). *The Lowenfeld lectures: Viktor Lowenfeld on art education and therapy.* University Park, PA: Pennsylvania State University Press.

Christine Marmé Thompson

Luria, A. R. (1902–1977)

Alexander Romanovich Luria was a twentieth-century Russian psychologist of the sociohistorical school of thinking. A friend and colleague of L.S. **Vygotsky**, Luria continued and furthered the premises of the sociohistorical theoretical perspective after Vygotsky's premature death in 1934, adapting his work to the political and historical circumstances of twentieth-century life in the then U.S.S.R.

At the core of his research was the goal of understanding the nature of human development as a function of the social resources and historical circumstances of individuals as well as groups of people.

Luria's professional training was in psychology and medicine. He studied memory, attention, language and thought, mental retardation, brain damage, the development of fraternal and identical twins in western Russia, as well as the nature of thinking among illiterate Islamic agrarian communities in the Central Asian steppes of the early 1930s. He combined his talents and interest in the biological and neurological aspects of child and adult development with his vision for understanding development against the backdrop of historical and cultural circumstances. His goals were ambitious and broad. He lived long enough and wrote extensively about these ideas in ways that contemporary psychology and neurosciences have begun to address in recent years, particularly in a way that relates to the work of early childhood development.

Theory of Development

Luria's work, along with that of L.S. Vygotsky and A. Leont'ev, paved the way for a revolutionary view of development: one that reconciled the nature of the human brain (neuropsychology), along with mental development (psychology) across time (history), in the great variety of social and cultural circumstances (anthropology). Luria and his colleagues established three premises to this view of development that he refined over five decades of his career (Cole, 1996, p. 108).

Mediation. Development for humans is marked by the ability to create and use tools to reorganize one's interactions with others and objects. By tools, Luria and his colleagues were not only referring to objects, but more importantly, tools of the mind, namely language. Luria researched how language provides a currency for thinking, reflecting, planning, and formulating new possibilities for ourselves and others.

Historical Development. As humans, we do not "start from scratch" in development over a lifetime but rather each generation benefits from the ideas and tools of the preceding generation as they are passed on in circumstances for which the culture arranges.

Practical Activity. Understanding mental activity requires studying the particulars of daily activities of those we care to understand: both their interactions with one another over time, and how they use tools—objects and various forms of language—to get their work done.

Luria pioneered a methodology for empirical research that differed from experimental psychology with control and experimental groups but was no less rigorous. His studies of adults and children began with careful observation and documentation of their actions and talk in everyday situations followed by planned interventions attempting to remediate, or reorganize, their interactions with the world of objects and people. He then looked for evidence in his subject's responses that indicated what was amenable to change: cultural, physiological, or biological. Close observation followed interventions as he sought to document how, if at all, a person's activity was reorganized and changed as a result of the intervention.

Relevance of Luria's Work for Contemporary Early Childhood Education

Luria's work is important in contemporary educational and psychological research related to understanding the development of young children and their families from diverse backgrounds. His work reminds us to (1) seek to understand children and families from close-up involvement with them as participant observers, not arms, length detached "testing" of them; (2) understand children and their families from the premises of the important activities in their home and school life and the historical meaning of those tasks for the family and community; (3) observe closely for the tools and resources children and families use to accomplish their tasks and how they use them; (4) study closely how they make use of help and ideas offered in interventions, tracking the reorganization of their thinking from before to after to understand how people change and grow, and how the intervention might have influenced the course of that development.

Luria's work provides rich and carefully crafted empirical studies that were groundbreaking at the beginning of the twentieth century, and equally so in the twenty-first century.

Further Readings: Cole, M. (1978). *The selected writings of A. R. Luria*. New York: M.E. Sharpe; Cole, M. (1996). *Cultural psychology: A once and future discipline*. Cambridge, MA: Harvard University Press; Luria, A. R. (1976). *Cognitive development—its social and cultural foundations*. Cambridge, MA: Harvard University Press; Luria, A. R., and F. laYudovich (1972). *Speech and the development of mental processes in the child*. Middlesex, England: Penguin Books Ltd.; Luria, A. R. (1979). *The making of mind*. Cambridge, MA: Harvard University Press; Rogoff, B. (2003). *The cultural nature of human development*. Oxford: Oxford University Press.

Gillian D. McNamee

M

Malaguzzi, Loris (1920–1994)

Loris Malaguzzi was founder of the public system of preschools and infant-toddler centers in Reggio Emilia, Italy. A tirelessly innovator and influential thinker, he placed great value on practice, both for the transformation of theory and in turn the generation of new ideas.

Malaguzzi was born on February 23, 1920, in Correggio in the Emilia Romagna region of northern Italy. He moved with his family to the nearby city of Reggio Emilia in 1923, when his father assumed a post as railway stationmaster. He married in 1944 and had one son, Antonio, who became an architect. Malaguzzi traveled to many places throughout his life on behalf of early childhood education, but he remained a loyal citizen of Reggio Emilia until his death on January 30, 1994.

As a young man in wartime Italy, Malaguzzi taught elementary school in Sologno, a village in the Appennines (1939–1941) and both elementary and middle school in Reggio Emilia (1942–1947). In the meanwhile, he completed an educational degree from the University of Urbino (1946) and threw his energies into supporting the cooperative preschool movement that sprang up just after the Second World War. This movement involved the enormous efforts of women's groups as well as other citizens and carried into the early seventies, when other cities with politically progressive administrations opened municipal preschools. Inspired by ideas of (among others) John **Dewey**, Friedrich **Froebel**, Freinet, and his contemporary, Bruno Ciari, an influential activist in the city of Bologna who unfortunately died young, Malaguzzi became prominent in the progressive political circles then actively transforming Italian thinking about education and schooling. In 1951, after completing a six-month specialization course in the first Italian school psychology program at the Center for National Research in Rome, he became Director of Children's Psycho-Pedagogical Services for Reggio Emilia. In 1963, when the first official city preschool was established, he was named Director of Early Childhood Programs, a post he held for thirty years.

In the late 1960s and all during the 1970s, Malaguzzi worked with colleagues to expand the system of family-centered public early care and education programs serving children under age 6, including children with disabilities. He led the city in establishing preschool regulations that included the provision of two teachers (a coteaching team) within each classroom, as well as a special studio (***atelier***) within each school staffed by a teacher (*atelierista*) with a degree in the visual arts. These two innovations, along with continuous study and reflection on the daily experience of children (the strategy of educational **documentation**), contributed to the development of a distinctive and innovative system of early childhood pedagogy and organization now known as the **Reggio Emilia Approach**. Malaguzzi believed that creativity is a characteristic way of thinking and responding and that the growth of knowledge involves increasing the power of imagination. The adult's role is to discover and nurture all children's "expressive, communicative, and cognitive languages," sometimes referred to as children's multiple **symbolic languages.** Indeed, the 100 Languages of Children is the name of the exhibit conceptualized and designed by Malaguzzi and colleagues in the early 1980s, and that, in several successive editions, has carried the message about young children's potential and rights to many countries in the world and more than thirty-eight states of the United States.

Malaguzzi was a charismatic leader and powerful communicator. He founded Italy's National Organization for the Study and Support of Early Childhood Education, still active today, and in the 1970s and 1980s served as director of the educational magazine *Zerosix* (later called *Bambini*). As his ideas reached larger and wider audiences, the influence and significance of the Reggio Emilia experience increased. *Newsweek* magazine (December 2, 1991) rated Reggio Emilia as having the "best preschools in the world," and Malaguzzi began to receive many awards and recognitions, including the Lego Prize in Denmark (1992), the Kohl Prize in Chicago (1993), the Hans Christian Andersen Prize (1994), the Mediterranean Association of International Schools Prize (1995), the Gold Medal awarded by the President of the Italian Republic (2001), and the Nonino Prize (2002). In 1996, two years after his death, his long-time colleague Susanna Mantovani organized a conference in Malaguzzi's honor at the University of Milan called *Nostalgia del Futuro* (Nostalgia of the Future). Speakers came from all over Europe and the United States to address his influence and the legacy of his ideas. In 2006, Reggio Emilia dedicated the International Loris Malaguzzi Center "to the future, to different cultures, to ideas, hopes, and imagination."

Further Readings: Barazzoni, R. *Mattone su Mattone* (1985). Distributed by Reggio Children S.r.l. Translation *Brick by Brick* (2001); Edwards, C. P., L. Gandini and G. Forman, eds. (1998). *The hundred languages of children: The Reggio Emilia approach—advanced reflections. Second Edition*. Westport, CT: Ablex Publishing Company; Gandini, L. (1993). History, ideas, and basic philosophy: An interview with Loris Malaguzzi. In C. P. Edwards, L. Gandini, and G. Forman, eds., *The hundred languages of children: The Reggio Emilia approach to Early Childhood Education*. Westport, CT: Ablex Publishing Company, pp. 41–89; Malaguzzi, L. (1993). For an education based on relationships. *Young Children* 49(1), 9–12; Malaguzzi, L. (1994). Our image of the child: Here teaching begins. *Child Care Information Exchange*, March/April(96), 52–61. Beginnings Workshop on *Special places for children: Schools in Reggio Emilia*. Exchange Press; *A Message from Loris Malaguzzi* (1995). Video interview conducted in 1992 by L. Gandini and G.Forman on the evolution of projects. Distributed by Reggio Children S.r.l.; Mantovani, S., ed. (1997). *Nostalgia del Futuro: Liberare speranze per una nuova cultura dell' infanzia*. Bergamo, Italy: Edizioni Junior; *Not Just Anyplace* (2005). Video on the history of the Reggio preschools. Produced by Reggio Children, S.r.l.

Lella Gandini

Mann, Horace (1796–1859)

While Thomas Jefferson provided important discussions on public education and developments in European education had their immediate impact on public education in the United States, Horace Mann deserves particular credit for both establishing the American system of public education and devising its basic aims in the mid-nineteenth century.

In 1837, when asked to head the newly formed Massachusetts Board of Education, Mann was a lawyer and rising star in Massachusetts politics. From his college days, Mann had been an idealist with a religiously inspired yearning to serve and reform. And so, with service and reform in mind, Mann forsook his promising careers in law and politics for the uncertainties of a career in education.

For a little over a decade, Mann used the office of head of the Massachusetts board to reflect on what public education in the United States should mean and to lead a reform movement to establish a system that would support public education. Each year, as head of the board, Mann issued his annual reports on the state of public education in Massachusetts. By the 1850s, those reports became a blueprint and motive for making public education compulsory.

Mann defined the American public school in ways that still apply (Cremin, 1957). First, public schools meant schools for all. Public schools were to be excellent and inclusive so as to successfully compete with private institutions and thus to become the great equalizer in society. Moreover, for Mann, public schools were to be the main instruments for curing society's ills and for molding a diverse population into one common, American character defined by a common set of values.

Mann's commitment to creating inclusive schools was no less a commitment than that of the most ardent proponents of inclusion today. However, the arguments he gave then were quite different from those given today—because the context was different. Aside from diversity in social and economic class, diversity in the 1840s meant sectarian diversity within Christianity, the main groupings being Calvinists and non-Calvinists, Protestants and Catholics. It is easy for us today to ignore these categories or treat them as being trivial compared to the categories that define diversity today. However, for the American populace in the 1840s, these categories mattered every bit as much as do those used today to define diversity.

For Mann, as for many in contemporary American society, the hope and aim of public education was and is to help children learn to function well as citizens in a diverse society where group differences are respected even as common values are practiced. Therefore, for Mann, public education meant a *moral* education needed to develop children into good citizens, citizens who would insure that the new republic would thrive.

Mann also championed a broad view of public education. For Mann, public education meant liberal arts education, an education that went beyond a narrow definition of education in terms of apprenticeships and education for specific vocations. Mann's view was that all children, not just the children of the rich, should know great literature, be trained in math and science, and have experience with the arts (especially singing). In addition, all children should be taught how to live a healthy life.

But Mann was more than a moralist and idealist. He was also a practical man—as shown in the way he promoted a system that would grow and sustain his vision of public schools. That system included central oversight at the state level—to insure that local leaders did not shortchange schools to appease taxpayers. However, the heart of the system was local involvement in schools and providing training for carefully screened teachers.

Regarding local involvement, Mann argued tirelessly against selfish views of property and for views rooted in his own Unitarian Christian theology. He argued that property should be thought of as on loan to us for the purpose of caring for our neighbors, not just ourselves, and for caring for future generations as well. For Mann, our taxes and time helping local schools are sacred obligations. Mann's arguments helped establish a system of local control and oversight of schools that is still a cornerstone of American public education today.

With respect to teachers, Mann argued against the prevailing view that anyone can teach and that teaching need not require special training. Mann saw teaching as one of the most demanding professions. For Mann, not only must teachers know their subject matter, they must also know pedagogy. Furthermore, teachers must be persons with exemplary moral character, for their character serves as the mirror in front of which children practice how to behave.

Horace Mann provided American society with a new vision of public schooling, one that to a certain extent defines much in contemporary understanding of what we should mean by public education and public schools, at least with regard to essentials. Those essentials include a commitment to public education for all and to a broad and liberal education that promotes knowledge, character, and physical health. They also include local involvement and oversight of schools and having a core of trained teachers with exemplary character.

Horace Mann, and the reform movement he led, began a cycle that would become a recurrent theme in the history of American public education (Katz, 1968). Mann's idealism, his optimistic faith in the power of public schools to perfect humans and cure society's ills, led to reform but it also led eventually to disillusionment and disengagement as Mann's assumptions proved wrong. Mann assumed that all groups, including diverse groups of working class families, would welcome the kind of education he was promoting. By the 1860s, it was clear that many groups experienced compulsory public schooling as defined by Mann as an imposition, not as a means to develop and succeed. Mann's optimistic vision did not, then, match the reality and complexity of American pluralistic society.

Today, American educators wrestle with this same issue of matching a progressive, idealistic vision of public education to the complex reality of American society—particularly to the reality that families differ significantly in what they want and do not want from public schooling. Mann's legacy lies, then, more in his defining an ideal than in his providing the details needed to realize that ideal.

Further Readings: Cremin, L., ed. (1957). *The republic and the school: Horace Mann on the education of free men*. New York: Teachers College; Cremin, L. (1965). *The genius of American education*. New York: Vintage Books; Glenn, M. (1984). *Campaigns against corporal punishment: Prisoners, sailors, women, and children in antebellum America*. Albany, NY: State University of New York Press; Katz, M. (1968). *The irony of early school reform: Educational innovation in mid-nineteenth century Massachusetts*. Boston: Beacon Press.

W. George Scarlett

Maslow, Abraham (1908–1970)

Personality theorist Abraham Harold Maslow is best known for his contributions to the humanistic psychology movement, most notably his *Hierarchical Theory of Motivation*. Credited with cofounding the humanistic movement (along with Carl **Rogers**), Maslow conceptualized motivation as the human tendency to strive for a rewarding and meaningful life. Early childhood educators, who traditionally concerned themselves with children's affective development, found important support for their point of view in Maslow's theory.

Maslow was born in Brooklyn, New York, to Jewish immigrant parents. Isolated as a child, in part due to his mother's mental illness, Maslow grew up in libraries among books. Not well educated himself, his father pressured his eldest son to attend law school. After a short-lived attempt to comply, Maslow next attended Cornell University and later the University of Wisconsin, where he obtained formal training in psychology (B.A. 1930; M.A. 1931; Ph.D. 1934). Early mentors included Harry Harlow, famous for his attachment studies, and behaviorist Edward Thorndike at Columbia University, whose work had initially attracted Maslow to psychology. Maslow's excitement about behaviorism, however, subsided as he raised his two daughters—an experience that confronted him with the complexity of human behavior (Maslow, 1968, p. 55).

Maslow taught next at Brooklyn College in New York City where he came into contact with distinguished European scholars, many of whom had fled Nazi Germany. Luminaries Alfred Adler, Karen Horney, Max Werthcimer, and Erich Fromm numbered among those who shaped Maslow's intellectual growth during this period and laid the groundwork for his later humanistic views. In 1951, Maslow accepted an appointment to chair the Psychology Department at Brandeis University in Waltham, Massachusetts. Here he remained for the duration of his career. His influential book *Toward a Psychology of Being* was published in 1962.

Maslow's *Hierarchy of Human Needs*, a pyramid-shaped diagram with self-actualization at the apex, proposed that human motivation can be understood as a life quest toward fulfillment. However, basic human needs must be sufficiently well met before one could conceivably express one's unique potential. Each level of Maslow's hierarchy described these basic needs in terms of psychological tensions that one must resolve in order to move toward self-actualization. First, one's *physiological* needs must be met; *safety* needs form the second layer, followed by *love and belongingness* needs at the third. As one travels toward the top of the pyramid, the need for *esteem* and, finally, for *actualization* emerge. Those rare few who achieve self-actualization may also experience *transcendence*, a state of being where one becomes ecstatically aware of human potential in the cosmic sense. This heightened awareness, although joyous, also creates profound sadness, for, in understanding human potential in its grandest sense, one must also confront human frailty and the undeniable human tendency to bungle opportunities for growth.

Maslow's optimistic view of personality development held that children will grow in a positive direction so long as their legitimate needs are sufficiently well met. Under the right circumstances, desirable qualities of self-direction, openness to experience, trust in one's abilities, and, ultimately, creativity will emerge, allowing the self-enhancing individual to contribute constructively and harmoniously to group life. Maslow's personality theory represented a contemporary rendering of ideas introduced into early childhood education years before by Jean-Jacques **Rousseau**'s and Friedrich **Froebel**'s similar philosophies of development "unfolding" across the life span.

In the spring of 1969, Maslow took a leave of absence from Brandeis College to become a resident fellow of the W. P. Laughlin Charitable Foundation, Menlo Park, California. Here he freely pursued his passionate interest in democracy and ethics.

On June 8, 1970, at the age of 62, Abraham Maslow, having suffered a history of chronic heart disease, died of a heart attack. *Abraham H. Maslow: A Memorial Volume*, compiled with the assistance of his wife and high school sweetheart, Bertha Goodman Maslow, was published posthumously in 1972.

Further Readings: *Abraham H. Maslow: A memorial volume* (1972). Monterey, CA: Books/Cole. Conversation with Abraham Maslow (1968). *Psychology Today* 2(35–37), 54–57; Maslow, Abraham (1962). *Toward a psychology of being*. Princeton, NJ: Van Nostrand; Maslow, Abraham (1971). *The farther reaches of human nature*. New York: Viking.

Ann C. Benjamin

Mathematics

The turn of the century has seen a dramatic increase in attention to the mathematics education of young children, for at least five reasons. First, increasing numbers of children attend early care and education programs. Second, there is an increased recognition of the importance of mathematics for individuals and society. Third, there is a substantial knowledge gap in the mathematics performance of U.S. children living in economically deprived communities (Griffin, Case, and Siegler, 1994; Saxe, Guberman, and Gearhart, 1987). Fourth, researchers have changed from a position that young children have little or no knowledge of or capacity to learn, mathematics to one that acknowledges competencies that are either innate or develop by or before the pre-K years. Fifth and finally, research indicates that knowledge gaps appear in large part due to the lack of connection between children's informal and intuitive knowledge and school mathematics, and especially due to the poor development of this informal knowledge in some children (Baroody and Wilkins, 1999; Ginsburg and Russell, 1981; Hiebert, 1986). As these reasons suggest, positions regarding young children and mathematics have changed considerably over the years. Early childhood professionals increasingly acknowledge that better mathematics education can and should begin early. Even preschoolers show a spontaneous interest in mathematics. Caring for them well, in any setting, involves nurturing and meeting their intellectual needs, which includes needs for mathematical activity.

Research on mathematics has played a central role in contributing to these changing attitudes and understandings. For example, very young children are sensitive to mathematical situations and thus all have the potential to become mathematically literate. Research has demonstrated that babies in the first six months of life can discriminate one object from two, and two objects from three (Antell and Keating, 1983). This was determined via a *habituation* paradigm in which infants "lose interest" in a series of displays that differ in some ways, but have the same number of objects. For example, say that infants are shown a sequence of pictures that contain a small set of objects, such as two circular regions. The collections differ in attributes such as size, density, brightness, or color, but there are always two objects. The differences between successive pictures initially keep infants' attention—they continue to look at each picture in turn. Eventually, however, they *habituate* to the displays; for example, they begin to look at the screen less, and their eyes wander. Then they are shown a collection of three circular regions that are similar in attributes to those they had previously seen and their eyes focus intently on this new collection. Thus, the researchers know that they are sensitive in some way to *number*. This empirically established insight has convinced many that young children can engage with substantive mathematical ideas.

These changing understandings of young children and mathematics have not been without controversy, however. Over the course of the twentieth century, research on mathematics moved from a cautious assessment of the number competencies of children entering school, to a Piagetian position that young children were not capable of true numeric thinking, to the discovery of infant sensitivity to mathematical phenomenon, to the present debate about the meaning of these contradictions and an attempt to synthesize apparently opposing positions. The last phase includes a paradox: studies contradicted Piagetian positions on children's lack of ability, but supported the basic constructivist Piagetian framework. That framework has been so influential that even substantive new theories were borne in reaction to it. For example, significant experiences are often those produced by the child's own actions, including mental actions. Further, children can and do invent concepts and strategies, and, even when incorrect, exhibit intelligence. Their search for patterns is fundamentally mathematical in nature. As a specific example of the paradox, Jean **Piaget** was incorrect in claiming that early number knowledge was meaningless. Piaget was, however, accurate in describing children's construction of logicomathematical knowledge that is increasingly general and that eventually compels children to make warranted generalizations resistant to confounding by distracting perceptual cues.

Recent debates are among three theoretical frameworks for understanding young children's mathematical thinking: empiricism, (neo) nativism, and interactionalism. In traditional empiricism, the child is seen as a "blank slate," truth lies in correspondences between children's knowledge and reality, and knowledge is received by the learner via social transmission or abstracted from repeated experience with a separate ontological reality. An extension, traditional information processing theory, uses the computer as a metaphor for the mind and moves slightly toward an interactionalist perspective. In contrast, nativist theories, in the traditional of philosophical rationalism (e.g., Plato and Kant), emphasize the inborn, or early developing, capabilities of the child. For example, quantitative or spatial cognitive structures present in infancy support the development of later mathematics, and thus innate structures are fundamental to mathematical development. In this view, a small number of innate and/or early-developing mathematical competencies are privileged and easy to learn. These are hypothesized to have evolutionary significance and be acquired or displayed by children in diverse cultures at approximately the same age. Neither the empiricist nor nativist position fully explains children's learning and development. An intermediate position appears warranted, such as interactionalist theories that recognize the interacting roles of nature and nurture. In interactionalist, constructivist theories, children actively and recursively create knowledge. Structure and content of this knowledge are intertwined and each structure constitutes the organization and components from which the child builds the next, more sophisticated, structure (Clements and Sarama, in press-a).

Research from these positions reveals a picture of young children who possess an informal knowledge of mathematics that is surprisingly broad, complex, and sophisticated (Kilpatrick, Swafford, and Findell, 2001). In both play and instructional situations, even preschoolers can engage in a significant level of mathematical activity. In free play, they explore patterns and shapes, compare magnitudes, and count objects. Less frequently, they explore dynamic changes, classify, and explore spatial relations. Importantly, this is true for children regardless of income level and gender (Seo and Ginsburg, 2004). In a similar vein, most entering kindergartners, and even entering preschoolers, show a surprising high entry level of mathematical skills. For example, most entering kindergartners can count past ten, compare or relate quantities, read numerals, recognize shapes, make patterns, and use nonstandard units of length to compare objects. As mentioned, these capabilities are well established by most entering kindergartners from middle- and high-income, but by a smaller proportion of children from low-income communities. Research has shown, however, that high-quality mathematics curricula (see **Curriculum, Mathematics**) can help children from low-resource communities develop mathematical concepts and skills (see **Interagency Education Research Initiative** [IERI], as well as Clements and Sarama, in press-b). Without intervention, many of these children later have trouble in mathematics and then school in general. With support, most primary grade children can construct surprisingly sophisticated and abstract concepts and strategies in each of these topical areas.

Number and operations is arguably the most important of the main concepts that should be developed in the early childhood years because (1) numbers can be used to tell us how many, describe order, and measure; they involve numerous relations, and can be represented in various ways; and (2) operations with numbers can be used to model a variety of real-world situations and to solve problems; they can be carried out in various ways.

Early numerical knowledge associated with these concepts has four interrelated aspects: instantly recognizing and naming how many items of a small configuration ("subitizing"; e.g., "That's two crackers."), learning the list of number words to at least ten, enumerating objects (i.e., saying number word in correspondence with objects), and understanding that the last number word said when counting refers to how many items have been counted. Children learn these four aspects initially by different kinds of experiences, but they gradually become more connected. Indeed, having children represent their quantitative concepts in different ways, such as with objects, spoken words, and numerals, and connecting those representations, are important aspects of all mathematics. Each of the four aspects begins with the smallest numbers and gradually includes larger numbers. Seeing how many, or subitizing, ends at three to five items and moves into decomposing/composing where small numbers are put together to see larger numbers as patterns. Like all mathematical knowledge, knowledge of number develops qualitatively. For example, as children's ability to subitize grows from perceptual, to imagined, to numerical patterns, so too does their ability to count and operate on collections grows from perceptual (counting concrete objects), to imagined (with six hidden objects and two shown, saying, "Six . . . seven, eight! Eight in all!"), to numerical (counting number words, as in "8 + 3? 9 is 1, 10 is 2, 11 is 3 . . . 11!").

Regarding operations, even toddlers notice the effects of increasing or decreasing small collections by one item. Children can solve problems such as six and two more as soon as they can accurately count. Children who cannot yet count-on often follow three steps: counting objects for the initial collection of six items, counting two more items, and then counting the items of the two collections together. Children develop, and eventually abbreviate, these solution methods. For example, when items are hidden from view, children may put up fingers sequentially while saying, "1, 2, 3, 4, 5, 6" and then continue on, putting up two more fingers, "7, 8. Eight." Children who can count-on simply say, "S-i-x—7, 8. Eight." At this point, children in many parts of the world learn to count up to the total to solve a subtraction situation because they realize that it is much easier. For example, the story "Eight apples on the table. The children ate five. How many now?" could be solved by thinking, "I took away 5 from those 8, so 6, 7, 8 (raising a finger with each count), that's 3 more left in the 8."

After they have developed these strategies, children can be encouraged to use strategic reasoning. For example, some children go on to invent recomposing and decomposing methods using doubles (6 + 7 is 6 + 6 = 12. 12 + 1 more = 13). Primary-grade children can extend such strategies to their work with large numbers and place-value concepts. For example, they might learn first to count by tens and ones to find the sum of 38 and 47, and later learn to decompose 38 into its tens and ones and 47 into its tens and ones. This encourages the children to reason with ten as a unit like the unit of one and compose the tens together into 7 tens, or 70. After composing the ones together into 15 ones, they have transformed the sum into the sum of 70 and 15. To find this sum, the children take a 10 from the 15 and give it to the 70, so the sum is 80 and 5 more, or 85. Strategies like this are modifications of counting strategies involving ten and one just like strategies for finding the sum of 8 and 7 are modifications of counting strategies involving only one (e.g., children who know that 8 and 2 are 10 take 2 from 7 and give it to 8. So, 10 and 5. 15). We know from studies of cognition in everyday life, including adults and children selling candy in the streets of Brazil, that such strategies can be invented in supportive cultures.

To develop computational methods that they understand, children benefit from experiences in kindergarten (or earlier), including hearing the pattern of repeating tens in the numbers words and relating these words to quantities grouped in ten. First graders can use quantities grouped in tens or make drawings of tens and ones to do two-digit addition with regrouping and discuss how, recording numerically their new ten: for example, 48 + 26 makes 6 tens (from 40 and 20) and 1 ten and 4 (from 8 + 6), so there is a total of 7 tens and 4 for 74. Children invent and learn from each other many effective methods for adding such numbers and many ways to record their methods. Second graders can go on to add 3-digit numbers by thinking of the groups of hundreds, tens, and ones involved. They can subtract (e.g., 82 − 59) by thinking of breaking apart 82 into 59 and another number. Computers can help provide *linked* representations of objects and numerals that are uniquely helpful in supporting this learning (see **Curriculum, Technology**). Although some teachers and critics worry that calculators will interfere with such learning, research results consistently reveal that—used wisely, to further problem-solving efforts and in combination with other methods—calculator use is not harmful and can be beneficial (Groves and Stacey, 1998).

Geometry, measurement, and spatial reasoning are also important, inherently, because they involve understanding the space in which children live. Two major concepts in geometry are that geometry can be used to understand and to represent the objects, directions, locations in our world, and the relationships between them; and that geometric shapes can be described, analyzed, transformed, and composed and decomposed into other shapes. Initial knowledge of these concepts is not beyond the cognitive capabilities of young children. Very young children know and use the shape of their environment in navigation activities. With guidance, they can learn to mathematize this knowledge. They can learn about direction, perspective, distance, symbolization, location, and coordinates. Some studies have identified the primary grades as a good time to introduce learning of simple maps, such as maps of objects in the classroom or routes around the school or playground, but informal experiences in prekindergarten and kindergarten are also beneficial, especially those that emphasize building imagery from physical movement. Again, computers can help "mathematize" these experiences.

Children can learn richer concepts about shape if their educational environment includes four features: varied examples and nonexamples, discussions about shapes and their characteristics, a wider variety of shape classes, and interesting tasks. All are important, because concepts of two-dimensional shapes begin forming in the prekindergarten years and stabilize as early as age 6. Therefore, children need rich opportunities to learn about geometric figures between 3 and 6 years of age. Curricula should develop these early concepts aggressively, so that by the end of grade three children can identify examples and nonexamples of a wide range of geometric figures; classify, describe, draw, and visualize shapes; and describe and compare shapes based on their attributes. Young children move through levels in the composition and decomposition of 2-D figures. From lack of competence in composing geometric shapes, children who are given appropriate experiences can gain abilities to combine shapes into pictures, then synthesize combinations of shapes into new shapes (composite shapes), eventually operating on and iterating those composite shapes. Helpful experiences include making pictures and solving puzzles with geometric shapes such as pattern blocks and tangram sets.

Measurement is one of the main real-world applications of mathematics. Measurement of continuous quantities involves assigning a number to attributes such as length, area, and weight. Together, number and measurement are components of quantitative reasoning. In this vein, measurement helps connect the two realms of number and geometry, each providing conceptual support to the other. Two main concepts in measurement are that comparing and measuring can be used to specify "how much" of an attribute (e.g., length) objects possess and that repeating a unit or using a tool can determine measures.

Prekindergarten children know that properties such as mass (amount), length, and weight exist, but they do not initially know how to reason about these attributes or to measure them accurately. At age 4–5 years, however, many children can, with opportunities to learn, become less dependent on perceptual cues and thus make progress in reasoning about or measuring quantities. This involves learning many concepts, including the following: the need for equal-size units; that a line segment made by joining two line segments has a length equal to the sum of the lengths of the joined segments; that a number can be assigned to a length; and that you may need to repeat, or iterate, a unit, and subdivide that unit, to find that number (to a given precision). By the end of the primary grades, children can learn relationship between units and the need for standard units, the relationship between the size and number of units, and the need for standardization of units.

Two other areas can be woven into the main three areas of number, geometry, and measurement: algebra and data analyses. Algebra begins with a search for patterns. Identifying patterns helps bring order, cohesion, and predictability to seemingly unorganized situations and allows one to recognize relationships and make generalizations beyond the information directly available. Although prekindergarten children engage in pattern-related activities and recognize patterns in their everyday environment, an abstract understanding of patterns develops gradually during the early childhood years. Children eventually learn to recognize the relationship between patterns with nonidentical objects or between different representations of the same pattern (e.g., between visual and motoric, or movement, patterns), identify the core unit (e.g., AB) that either repeats (ABABAB) or "grows" (ABAABAAAB), and then use it to generate both these types of patterns. In the primary grades, children can learn to think algebraically about arithmetic, for example, generalizing that when you add zero to a number the sum is always that number or when you add three numbers it does not matter which two you add first.

The beginning of data analysis, also accessible to young children, contains one main concept: Classifying, organizing, representing, and using information to ask and answer questions. Children can learn to classify and count to order data, then organize and display that data through both simple numerical summaries such as counts, tables, and tallies, and graphical displays, including picture graphs, line plots, and bar graphs. They can compare parts of the data, make statements about the data as a whole, and generally determine whether the graphs answer the questions posed initially. These sorts of activities can be generated in a variety of mathematics experiences as well as more integrated curriculum strategies such as the **Project Approach** or those based on the **Reggio Emilia** approach to long-term projects.

In summary, young children have the interests and ability to engage in significant mathematical thinking and learning, more so than is typically introduced in most educational or curriculum programs. Mathematical processes, such as reasoning, problem solving, and communicating, are also critical. Children, especially considering their minimal experience, are impressive mathematical problem solvers. They are learning to learn, and learning the rules of the "reasoning game." Research on problem solving and reasoning also reveals surprising early abilities. Although the processes definitely improve, recent research claims appear valid: domain-specific knowledge is essential. However, what is then often neglected is the recognition that usually the reasoning from domain-specific knowledge simultaneously builds, and builds on, the basis of mindful general problem solving and reasoning abilities that are evident from the earliest years. *See also* Classroom Environment.

Further Readings: Antell, S. E., and D. P. Keating (1983). Perception of numerical invariance in neonates. *Child Development* 54, 695–701; Baroody, A. J., and J. L. M. Wilkins (1999). The development of informal counting, number, and arithmetic skills and concepts. In J.V. Copley, ed., *Mathematics in the early years*. Reston, VA: National Council of Teachers of Mathematics, pp. 48–65; Clements, D. H., and J. Sarama (in press-a). Early childhood mathematics learning. In F. K. Lester, Jr., ed., *Second handbook of research on mathematics teaching and learning*. New York: Information Age Publishing; Clements, D. H., and Sarama, J. (in press-b). Effects of a preschool mathematics curriculum: Summary research on the *Building Blocks* project. *Journal for Research in Mathematics Education*; Ginsburg, H. P., and R. L. Russell (1981). Social class and racial influences on early mathematical thinking. *Monographs of the Society for Research in Child Development* 46(6, Serial No. 193); Griffin, S., R. Case and R. S. Siegler (1994). Rightstart: Providing the central conceptual prerequisites for first formal learning of arithmetic to students at risk for school failure. In K. McGilly, ed., *Classroom lessons: Integrating cognitive theory and classroom practice*. Cambridge, MA: MIT Press, pp. 25–49; Groves, S., and K. Stacey (1998). Calculators in primary mathematics: Exploring numbers before teaching algorithms. In L. J. Morrow and M. J. Kenney, eds., *The teaching and learning of algorithms in school mathematics*. Reston, VA: National Council of Teachers of Mathematics, pp. 120–129; Hiebert, J. C. (1986). *Conceptual and procedural knowledge: The case of mathematics*. Hillsdale, NJ: Lawrence Erlbaum; Kilpatrick, J., J. Swafford and B. Findell (2001). *Adding it up: Helping children learn mathematics*. Washington, DC: National Academy Press; Saxe, G. B., S. R. Guberman, and M. Gearhart (1987). Social processes in early number development. *Monographs of the Society for Research in Child Development* 52(2, Serial No. 216); Seo, K.-H., and H. P. Ginsburg (2004). What is developmentally appropriate in early childhood mathematics education? In D. H. Clements, J. Sarama, and

A.-M. DiBiase, eds., *Engaging young children in mathematics: Standards for early childhood mathematics education*. Mahwah, NJ: Lawrence Erlbaum Associates, pp. 91–104.

Douglas H. Clements and Julie Sarama

Mathematics Curriculum. *See* Curriculum, Mathematics

Maturationism

Maturationism is a theoretical perspective that emphasizes the contribution of biological processes to children's development. Maturationists take the position that maturation (i.e., the process of growing from a genetic plan) is the central element in explaining how children grow and change. These theorists argue that a universal, invariant sequence of human development can be described and that factors within the genetic makeup of each individual determine the pace at which the sequence unfolds for that child. Maturationist theorists elevate the impact of nature (genetic inheritance) and downplay the importance of nurture (learning/experience) on children's developmental progression.

Maturationist thinking is most often associated with the work of Arnold **Gesell** and his colleagues at the Clinic of Child Development at Yale University. From its beginnings in 1911, the Clinic's project was to chart the developmental sequence of childhood from birth through ten years of age. Based on the concept of genetic predetermination (automatic unfolding of behavioral organizations as a function of innate biological structures), Gesell observed the sequence of development of thousands of children and described growth gradients that indicated norms for when developmental milestones would be reached across physical, emotional, and cognitive domains. Gesell and his colleagues are largely responsible for the considerable influence that maturationist thinking has had on parents' and teachers' understandings of child development.

The major principles of maturationist thinking represent the foundations of a perspective that has had a major impact on early childhood education theory and practice. Defining principles include the following: (a) biological processes, especially maturation of the central nervous system, are largely responsible for growth and change in human organisms, while environmental factors such as experience and instruction are thought to be of secondary importance; (b) each normal individual carries a complete set of human capacities, instincts, and drives, meaning that everything necessary is supplied by nature; (c) each normal individual goes through an orderly sequence of developmental milestones, and the sequence does not vary across individuals or groups; (d) each individual has a tailor-made genetic timetable that regulates the pace at which maturation proceeds, therefore a preset internal clock determines when developmental milestones will be reached; (e) the cycle of human growth is continuous and additive, so development builds on earlier development; and (f) by carefully observing the development of large numbers of children, it is possible to generate normative data that indicate when developmental milestones will be reached, and the average time when growth gradients will be accomplished can be described.

The widespread acceptance of the foregoing principles has had a significant influence on how educational researchers, policymakers, teachers, and parents think about young children's development and what that means for curriculum design, program planning, and parenting. The assumption of genetic predetermination dominated the child study field and early childhood education during the first half of the twentieth century (Hunt, 1961). Most researchers, program developers, teachers, and parents of the era believed that a child's biological inheritance essentially controlled his or her developmental progression. Environmental factors were perceived to be secondary. In Gesell's words, "No environment as such has the capacity . . . to generate the progressions of development" (Gesell, 1931, p. 211). In fact, it was widely believed that no benefit and potential harm could come from attempting to speed up children's development through instruction, practice, or pressuring children to do more than they were ready to do. The remnants of this thinking continue to have a powerful influence on early childhood education today.

The concept of "readiness" has its roots in maturationist thinking and remains an important part of early childhood discourse. **Readiness,** from the perspective of maturationist theory, refers to a point in time when an individual has reached a level of maturation that will allow him or her to learn new behaviors, skills, or concepts. Accompanying this way of thinking about readiness is the notion that expecting children to accomplish tasks for which they are not ready can cause unwarranted frustration for children and for those trying to teach them. In terms of early schooling, this translates into attempts to tailor educational experiences to match the developmental levels of children, thus allowing children to develop at their own rates and making it the job of the school to adjust to the maturation levels of the students.

Maturationists' contention that normalized patterns of child development can be described continues to dominate the thinking of many parents, pediatricians, and educators. Parents continue to measure the physical, cognitive, and social growth of their children against developmental norms established by Gesell and others. Pediatricians continue to report on young children's developmental progress in relation to normative data, so that parents are told, for example, that their child is at a given percentile for language development and so on. Program developers, teachers, and other educationists continue to design curriculum and educational activities for children based on the belief that all (or at least most) children of a certain age are at the same developmental level and have the same basic capacities and needs. The following list provides an example of growth gradients described by Gesell, Ilg, and Ames (1977, pp. 342–343) in the domain of child–child interpersonal relations.

4 years—

- Will share or play cooperatively with special friends.
- Very conversational with friends. Good imaginative play.
- But much excluding, tattling, disputing, quarreling, verbal and physical.
- More interested in children than in adults.
- May spontaneously take charge of younger or shy child.
- May have special friends of same sex.

5 years—

- Plays well with other children, especially groups kept small.

- Does not insist on having own way and does not worry about behavior of others.
- Prefers playmates of own age.
- Some are too rough, too bossy, or cry too readily to get on well in unsupervised play.
- May play better with another child outside rather than indoors.

6 years—

- Marked interest in making friends, having friends, being with friends. Uses term "school friend" or "playmate."
- Seems able to get along with friends, but play does not hold up long if unsupervised.
- Quarreling, physical combat. Each wants own way.
- A good deal of tattletaling.
- May be very dominating and bossy with some playmates.
- Much exclusion of a third child: "Are you playing with So-and-so? Then I'm not playing with you."
- Cannot bear to lose at games and will cheat if necessary to win. Also thinks friends cheat or do things the wrong way.
- Many are said to be a "bad influence" on playmates or are thought to play with someone who is a "bad influence."
- May prefer slightly older playmates

Although less common than in the past, the concept that a nursery school setting is best for young children is another legacy of maturationist thinking. Gesell, Ilg, and Ames (1977) summarized the implications of maturationist theory for educational practice in the following statement: "Parents and teachers who think that a child is so plastic that he or she can be made over by strenuous outside pressure have failed to grasp the true nature of the mind. The mind may be likened to a plant, but not to clay. For clay does not grow. Clay is molded entirely from without. A plant is primarily molded from within, through the forces of growth" (p. 12). Traditional nursery schools, which are set up more like children's gardens than academies, are designed to provide a safe, nurturing environment that allows the natural development of children to progress at its own pace. The popularity of nursery school approaches has waned as accountability pressures on early childhood programs have increased and expectations for young children's academic performance have escalated. Concurrent with these changes has been a gradual decline in the influence of maturationist perspectives.

Some of the limitations of maturationist theory include its inability to explain environmental effects on children's development, its lack of attention to individual differences among children, its excessive concern with normal development, and its lack of usefulness in guiding children's development and learning. Critics complain that maturationists' overemphasis on biological factors ignores the impact of experience and learning, arguing that genetic inheritance alone cannot adequately explain the complex processes of human development. They also make the case that individual differences are often overlooked or stigmatized when maturationist theory is applied. Weber (1984, p. 58) uses the example of the popular film series produced by the National Film Board of Canada, which characterized particular ages such as the "Terrible Twos and Trusting Threes," to make the point that normative concepts associated with maturationist thinking led to overgeneralizations that ignored differences in individual development. In addition, others have critiqued the lack of useful information available from just knowing how children compare to group norms provided by maturationist scientists. Thomas (1992), for example, summarizes, "Group averages are of limited use in explaining a child's past, predicting his future status, or suggesting what should be done to guide his development" (p. 71). These limitations may help to explain why the maturationist theoretical perspective seems to have lost much of its currency in the early twenty-first century.

Further Readings: Gesell, A. (1931). Maturation and the patterning of behavior. In C. Murchison ed., *A handbook of child psychology*. Worcester, MA: Clark University Press; Gesell, A., F. L. Ilg, and L. B. Ames (1977). *The child from five to ten*. New York: Harper and Row; Hunt, J. M. (1961). *Intelligence and experience*. New York: Ronald Press; Thomas, R. M. (1992). *Comparing theories of child development*. Belmont, CA: Wadsworth; Weber, E. (1984). *Ideas influencing early childhood education: A theoretical analysis*. New York: Teachers College Press.

J. Amos Hatch

McCormick Tribune Center for Early Childhood Leadership

The McCormick Tribune Center for Early Childhood Leadership at National-Louis University, Wheeling, Illinois, is dedicated to enhancing the professional orientation, management skills, and leadership capacity of early childhood administrators. The activities of the center encompass four areas:

- Training to improve the knowledge base, skills, and competencies of directors who administer early childhood programs;
- technical assistance to improve program quality;
- research on key professional development issues; and
- public awareness of the critical role that directors play in the provision of quality services for children and families.

The overarching goal of the McCormick Tribune Center for Early Childhood Leadership is to improve the quality of center-based early care and education programs and to serve as a model for the professional development of early childhood administrators. Through its training and technical assistance efforts, the Center equips directors with the knowledge, skills, and support they need to administer exemplary early childhood programs. Through its research and public awareness efforts, it serves as a voice for directors by advocating for better working conditions and compensation, supporting emerging leaders from underrepresented groups, and strengthening professional standards for early childhood personnel.

Funded by grants and contracts from philanthropic foundations, government agencies, and private corporations, the McCormick Tribune Center for Early Childhood Leadership's initiatives are targeted to program administrators of center-based early care and education programs. This includes for-profit and nonprofit, public-sponsored and private-sponsored, and part-day and full-day programs serving infants, toddlers, preschoolers, and school-age children during their out-of-school time. Secondary audiences include supervisors, researchers, policymakers, and trainers, as well as other current and emerging leaders in the field of early childhood and related disciplines.

Some of the Center's activities include nationally recognized director-training programs such as the Head Start Leadership Training Program, Taking Charge of Change, the Next Step Advanced Leadership Training, Coaching for Results, and Directors' Technology Training. The Center also provides training for career advisors to prepare them to mentor early childhood practitioners and for quality enhancement specialists who provide technical assistance to centers. Annually the Center hosts a leadership conference, *Leadership Connections*, for directors nationwide.

In the area of technical assistance, the Center offers organizational climate assessment using *The Early Childhood Work Environment Survey* (ECWES). Center staff also provide support for local and state quality enhancement initiatives by facilitating accreditation, assisting with the development of director credential programs, and providing technical assistance on how to use the *Program Administration Scale* (PAS) to measure and monitor the quality of leadership and management practices of center-based programs.

The Center has been a leader in providing technology support for child-care administrators including the development of Microsoft and Lotus SmartSuite technology manuals and hosting online discussion forums for early childhood administrators on its Web site (http://cecl.nl.edu).

Research conducted by the Center focuses on a wide range of professional development issues including the effectiveness of different training models, workforce turnover and compensation, and teacher qualifications and credentialing. To expand the public's awareness of the importance of strong leadership in early care and education, the Center publishes a quarterly newsletter *The Director's Link* and quarterly *Research Notes* in addition to periodic public policy reports on different professional development issues.

Further Readings: Talan, T., and P. J. Bloom (2004). *The program administration scale*. New York: Teachers College Press.

Paula Jorde Bloom

McMillan, Margaret (1860–1931)

Margaret McMillan was an educator, teacher educator, and child and family advocate who fought for children's causes and inspired legislation on the local and national levels in England. She and her sister Rachel **McMillan** founded an open-air nursery that later became the internationally famous Rachel McMillan Nursery School and Training Centre. The Centre trained the majority of the first nursery school teacher-administrators in the United States. Margaret was one of the cofounders of the British Nursery School Association, and became its first president. She and Grace **Owen** were instrumental in the passage of the Fisher Act of 1918, giving Local Education Authorities the power to provide nursery classes or schools for children between the ages of two and five years. This act encompassed many of the ideas and beliefs that McMillan had been espousing for years, including attention to the health, nourishment, and physical welfare of young children. It set standards for the cognitive and social education of children, and the staffing and administration of nursery schools.

Margaret McMillan was born and educated in the United States. The demise of her father disrupted the family's life. Her mother returned to Scotland, taking her children to live with their maternal grandparents. Margaret completed her schooling, and took positions as a governess and as a companion to a wealthy elderly woman. However, when her employer forced her to choose between socialism and speaking out or inheriting a large sum of money, she left the woman's employ to join in founding the Independent Labour Party. As an elected member of the Bradford School Board she visited many schools. She discovered a high level of curable diseases and malnutrition among the students. After ascertaining some causes of the problems, including lack of sunlight and fresh air, medical and dental care, she became determined to eliminate these causes of poor health in children. She and her sister founded clinics and an open air camp that later became known as the nursery school.

Margaret saw a need for revising the initial and in-service training of teachers, following her difficulty in finding appropriate teachers for her school during World War I. She decided to add a training center for those who wanted to work with disadvantaged children. One of the institution's distinctive features was a focus on understanding children's behavior through observation. Margaret's philosophical stance, that a nursery school teacher "helps to make a brain and a nervous system," finds its current expression in brain-based research and practice. Her declaration that the teacher of very young children must have "a finer perception and a wider training and outlook than is needed by any other kind of teacher" forms the foundation for today's early childhood teacher education standards in the United States.

Margaret McMillan's ideas were spread through her prolific writing, which included several editions of her book, *The Nursery School*, one with a forward by **Patty Smith Hill**. She was the recipient of numerous awards and government honors for her war and nursery school work. She died at the age of 70, a champion of the power of the environment and an advocate for the rights of the child.

Further Readings: Bradburn, Elizabeth (1976). *Margaret McMillan: Framework and expansion of nursery education*. Surrey, England: Denholm House Press; Bradburn, Elizabeth (1984). *Margaret McMillan: Portrait of a pioneer*. London: Routledge; Eliot, Abigail Adams (1972). Nursery schools 50 years ago. *Young Children* XXVII(4) (April), 210–211; Hewes, Dorothy W. (1998). *"It's the camaraderie": A history of parent cooperative preschools*. Davis, CA: Center for Cooperatives, University of California; Lascarides, V. Celia, and Blythe F. Hinitz (2000). *History of early childhood education*. New York: RoutledgeFalmer Publishing; McMillan, Margaret (1919). *The nursery school*. London: J. M. Dent & Sons, Ltd.; McMillan, Margaret (1921). *The nursery school*, with a foreword by Patty Smith Hill. New York: Dutton; Steedman, Carolyn (1990). *Childhood, culture, and class in Britain: Margaret McMillan, 1860–1931*. New Brunswick, NJ: Rutgers University Press.

Blythe Hinitz

McMillan, Rachel (1859–1917)

Rachel McMillan's experiences during childhood and young adulthood motivated her to enter the health field and become a sanitation inspector. She learned that poor children lived, for the most part, in deplorable conditions. She enlisted the help of her sister Margaret **McMillan** in alleviating as many of the problems as possible by advocating for such things as regular school health inspections, school baths, and nutritious school meals. As members of a socialist party, they also campaigned for women's suffrage. Rachel persuaded her sister to come to London, and together they opened a clinic in Bow in 1908 and one in Deptford in 1910. The "Baby Camp" became the Deptford Open Air Nursery. Two years later it became a nursery school staffed by "teacher-nurses." Rachel's death at the age of 58 left Margaret to carry on the work of running the Rachel McMillan Nursery School and Training Centre and advocating for young children and their families.

An important principle that governed the nursery school and its associated teacher training college was that every child should be educated "as if he were your own." A key concept was that the children should be "nurtured," which was defined as having "the all-round loving care of individuals." Another goal for the school and its teachers was to "assist parents in improving their child-rearing practices, and to develop their own potentialities." The young girls who were training to be teachers lived in the neighborhood and spent the first year of their program working at the school and making home visits in the evenings. They became friendly with the mothers and familiar with their lifestyles. This placed the nursery school work in a sociological context. The school was envisioned as a progressive influence; a research laboratory that would draw together doctors, nurses, social workers, and women of different social classes. The training college exemplified the McMillan's belief that "*preschool children should have appropriately trained well-qualified teachers.*" For this reason students took the second year of their program at the Home and Colonial College, to complete the Board of Education's requirements for a teacher training course. Both Abigail Adams **Eliot** and Edna Noble **White** studied and worked at the nursery school in the 1920s. Eliot's letters to her sponsor, Mrs. Pearson of the Women's Education Association of Boston, describe the 7:00 a.m. to 6:00 p.m. days, the schedule, and the activities. Eliot returned home to found the **Ruggles Street Nursery School and Training Centre** in Boston, and White to found the Merrill-Palmer Motherhood and Home Training School, and its laboratory nursery school in Detroit.

Further Readings: McMillan, Margaret (1927). *The life of Rachel McMillan*. London: J.M. Dent.

Blythe Hinitz

Media. *See* Children's Media

Mental Health

Mental health is a broad concept related to fundamental principles of psychological, social, and emotional development as they support positive child development. Principles of positive mental health underlie healthy development in all areas of early childhood development and are crucial to overall child well-being.

Likewise, when there is a problem associated with an area related to mental health, child well-being may be jeopardized. Children who have particular special needs may be especially vulnerable to mental health problems because of the nature of their developmental needs. In other words, a child's developmental pattern may lead to future mental health problems if there is not effective **early intervention.** At the same time, the context of a child's development may cause mental health problems, even when the child does not have particular special developmental needs. For example, a healthy child born to a parent with severe depression may develop particular special needs later in childhood if there is not effective intervention for the infant–parent pair.

The term "mental health" is often used in association with early childhood to refer to the social and emotional well-being of infants, toddlers, and young children. Although the term "infant mental health" is commonly used among early childhood professionals, the concept relates to principles of child development beyond infancy.

As a field of study, infant or early childhood mental health is a multidisciplinary field made up of clinicians and practitioners from a broad cross-section of the early childhood field, such as health care practitioners, psychologists, researchers, early childhood educators, and related service providers (e.g., speech therapists, occupational therapists, physical therapists, and social workers). Although mental health services has a connotation of pathology based on the nature, history, and stigma of mental health, the field of infant or early childhood mental health is one that focuses on the prevention of mental health problems.

The field of infant mental health is relatively new, and its beginning is often identified with the work of Selma Fraiberg (1975) and her psychoanalytic work with impaired mother–infant relationships. Since that time, there has been growing recognition of the importance of healthy relationships and social interactions to support healthy brain development and, therefore, overall development for children. Some key organizations that support the development of mental health resources, research, and practice include the following:

- **Children's Defense Fund** (CDF)
- **National Association for the Education of Young Children** (NAEYC)
- **National Center for Children in Poverty**
- National Mental Health Association
- World Association for Infant Mental Health
- **Zero to Three**

Further Readings: Fraiberg, S., E. Adelson, and V. Shapiro (1975). Ghosts in the nursery: A psychoanalytic approach to the problems of impaired infant–mother relationships. *Journal of American Academy of Child Psychology*, 14(13), 387–421.

Web Sites: Children's Defense Fund Child Welfare and Mental Health Division, http://www.childrensdefense.org/childwelfare/default.aspx; National Association for the Education of Young Children, http://www.naeyc.org/; National Center for Children in Poverty, http://www.nccp.org/index.html; World Association for Infant Mental Health, http://www.njaimh.org/world_assoc.htm ZERO TO THREE—Infant Mental Health Resource Center, http://www.zerotothree.org/imh/.

Patrice Hallock

Mitchell, Lucy Sprague (1878–1967)

Lucy Sprague Mitchell, founder of **Bank Street** School of Education, was a major figure in American progressive education during the early twentieth century. Influenced by John **Dewey,** she recognized children's need to learn through play and direct experience. A leader in the **child study movement**, Mitchell saw herself as an experimentalist. In addition, she democratized **progressive education** by spreading its ideals through teacher education and the development of children's writers.

In 1916 Mitchell founded the Bureau of Educational Experiments (BEE). This cooperative venture had four major activities: a lab school to work with children who were failing to thrive in a conventional school, analysis of the growth and development of normal children, the establishment of a sex education curriculum using nature study, and support of Caroline **Pratt**'s Play School in Greenwich Village. The BEE was the site of much observation of children and their language, and ultimately became the Bank Street School of Education. While Mitchell embraced the scientific approach of her era, she was determined that an emphasis on the whole child should not be lost in the enthusiasm for measuring and testing (Mitchell, 1953). In its education of teachers, the Bank Street School combined the scientific study of children, an emphasis upon the whole child, a curriculum built upon direct experiences and fieldwork in its lab school classrooms. Under Mitchell, the Bank Street approach emphasized dramatic play centers that would link home and school, as well as the use of field trips to provide direct sensory experience. The laboratory school at Bank Street College of Education pioneered the **developmental interaction approach** which stressed that learning grows out of the interaction among the child, others, and environment. The laboratory school was the initial model for the 1965 **Head Start** Program.

In 1921 Mitchell published the *Here and Now Story Book*, a forerunner of much of the realism seen in children's literature today. With this book, she changed the emphasis in American children's literature from classic fairy tales to stories focused on everyday experiences of children. In the preface, "What Language Means to Young Children," she stated that "young children live largely in the 'here and now' world of their own experiences" (Mitchell, 1948, p. 7). Her insistence on children's interest in everyday and familiar events ignited a conflict with the New York Public Library known as "the fairy tale war." In addition to the *Here and Now Story Book*, Mitchell authored more than twenty children's books.

Recognizing that the "here and now" movement needed authors more talented than herself, Mitchell founded the Writer's Laboratory at the Bank Street School. Here, selected students in the teacher education program participated in a writer's workshop. The Writers' Laboratory developed a distinguished crew of children's authors, including Edith Thatcher Hurd, Ruth Krauss, Eve Merriam, and most famously Margaret Wise Brown. Mitchell also collaborated with the Little Golden Books, a series of children's books sold for 25 cents a copy in the post-World War II years.

Further Readings: Antler, Joyce (1987). *Lucy Sprague Mitchell: The making of a modern woman*. New Haven, CT: Yale University Press; Mitchell, Lucy S. (1953). *Two lives: The* *story of Wesley Clair Mitchell and myself*. New York: Simon and Schuster; Mitchell, Lucy S. (1948). *Here and Now Story Book*. Rev. ed. New York: E.P. Dutton.

Susan Hall

MI Theory. *See* Multiple Intelligences, Theory of

Mixed-Age Grouping in Early Childhood Education

Mixed-age grouping in early childhood education is defined as "placing children who are at least a year apart in age into the same classroom groups in order to optimize what can be learned when children of different as well as same ages and abilities have frequent opportunities to interact" (Katz, Evangelou, and Hartman, 1990, p. 1). Mixed-age grouping is also known as heterogeneous, vertical, ungraded, nongraded, family grouping, and cross-age tutoring. In the current literature, the terms multiage grouping and multiage classroom appear more often than others.

Educating children in mixed-age groups has a long and uneven history in the United States. According to Stone (1996), the practice emerged out of necessity, in the one-room schoolhouse of the nineteenth century. It has been reconsidered periodically for various reasons such as during times of rapid expansion of public education enrollments and small school consolidation in the 1940s and 1950s. Briefly reintroduced during the reemergence of interest in progressive education in the mid-1960s and early 1970s, interest subsided again when the "back-to-basics" movement provoked concern with school achievement and standardized testing. Today, mixed-age grouping is accepted in many sectors of the educational community as a viable alternative way of **grouping** children for learning.

The actual extent to which mixed-age grouping is practiced is difficult to ascertain but, as evident in the number of publications, meetings, and internet-based information available, it appears that interest in it remains fairly strong worldwide (Ball, 2002). It should also be noted that approaches to early childhood education that emphasize the concept of community, such as Maria **Montessori**, Steiner (**Waldorf Education**) as well as the **Project Approach**, recommend mixed-age grouping of children in the classroom.

Discussion of the potential risks and benefits of mixed-age grouping often proceeds from one of three perspectives: as (1) an innovative practice, (2) an alternative to standard practice, or (3) a reflection of the preference of those involved. Although the selection of alternative educational practices is possible in some settings, in many developed countries as well as in rural or developing communities, mixed-age grouping is in fact the only option available (UNESCO, 1988). Most of what is known about the practice of mixed-age grouping comes from studies conducted in contexts of preference rather than necessity. It is conceivable that the experiences of students and teachers in mixed-age groups within a context of necessity are different from those of their counterparts in contexts where the practice has been chosen out of preference. Understanding of the characteristics of both contexts, preferential as well as obligatory, is needed to arrive at a complete understanding of the phenomenon.

Sociological Factors

Certain characteristics of contemporary society provide the background for recommending mixed-age grouping in early childhood education. First, the demographic trend of fewer children per family leads to early childhood experiences deprived of frequent opportunity for mixed-age interaction within the family. Second, children spend increasingly longer periods of time in the company of peers starting at an increasingly younger age. Most classes are composed of same-age peers as it is common practice that early childhood settings place children in groups according to strict chronological criteria. Furthermore, most state licensing regulations governing preschool and child-care institutions are specified according to the ages of those being served. In this sense, children have increasingly large proportions of experiences with same age peers for extended periods of time. Employing mixed-age grouping in early childhood education can provide opportunities for young children to come into contact and interact in a context that is characterized by diversity of knowledge, ability, and experience, much like a natural setting for human development.

Discussion about the philosophical and practical nature of mixed-age grouping, including benefits and risks, usually takes two different perspectives: application and research. Teachers and other educational practitioners with firsthand experiences with mixed-age classes tend to be enthusiastic about its benefits. One of the rationales often cited by supporters of mixed-age practices is that putting children together in mixed-age groups emulates real life, creates conditions resembling natural environments and leads to learning more and feeling better about classroom experience. Numerous anecdotal references, school-based reports, classroom evidence, and internet sites attest to the high regard for mixed-age grouping by those who practice it.

Those who recommend the adoption of mixed-age grouping in early childhood education today base their position on principles of individual development, the interactive nature of learning structures, principles of teaching young children as well as assessment, retention and promotion practices. Two international organizations are devoted to the promotion of mixed-age grouping; the Multi-Age Association of Queensland in **Australia** (see Volume 4) and the Jenaplan Schools Association that, while based in the Netherlands, represents mixed-age schools in various other countries. In North America state initiatives such as those implemented in Kentucky, Oregon, and British Columbia promote the idea of universal mixed-age and nongraded schooling for young children.

Individual Development

Age segregated or age-graded approaches to grouping children in preschool and primary school settings are justified on the normative assumption that all children of a given age are more like each other than they are like younger or older children at least in terms of development and capability. However, this normative assumption ignores what we know about how children actually develop and learn. In an era of increased attention to individual needs and aptitudes, it is questionable to subject children to schooling experiences that are narrowly defined, focused on whole group instruction, and indifferent to the wide range of individual differences typical of a group of young children.

Learning Structures and Mixed-Age Tutoring

Individual characteristics, variations in development, and experience comprise the rich context within which interacting and learning from peers contributes to human development. The zone of proximal development as formulated by Lev **Vygotsky** along with the experimental work conducted in this area in the last twenty-five years supports the idea that mixed-age grouping provides an appropriate social context for cross-age tutoring. The teacher's role in fostering a climate in which both tutor and tutee benefit from the interaction is crucial to the success of the practice.

Additional support for mixed-age tutoring comes from understanding the role of modeling processes on teaching and learning in group settings. Having opportunities to observe and interact with more capable peers who can exhibit more mature, higher levels of organization in their behavior is a potential benefit for younger children (Gaustard, 1994). For the tutor the benefits can be seen in the effort to organize and represent material already mastered to an even more integrated conceptual level as the need will arise, and from having to develop critical and higher order thinking skills. For the tutee, the opportunity to observe, model, and interact with more capable peers enhances learning by optimizing the breadth, or the cognitive distance between interacting peers, of the zone of proximal development.

Principles of Teaching Young Children

All aspects of development during the first seven or eight years of life are characterized by a wide range of individual differences. By providing children with the opportunity to interact with peers who vary widely in their competences and abilities, early childhood classrooms can become more responsive to individual differences than classrooms organized along strict chronological criteria. The heterogeneity of a mixed-age class also is likely to reduce the teachers' temptation to conduct whole-group instruction and to have all the children in the class at the same levels of achievement. Children in mixed-age classrooms can also benefit from the continuity of their relationship with caring adults that enhances the quality of their experience.

Assessment, Retention and Promotion

Retention, promotion, and **assessment** of progress take on different meanings in the context of mixed-age groups from the standard same-age context. The expanded notion of what individual development means, given the wide range of competences found in young children, reduces the pressure to make school-placement decisions along single grade narrow achievement criteria. According to McClellan, mixed-age grouping could be considered a "lifeline to children at risk" in that it can promote strong social competence development and improved self-concept, both important prerequisites for adapting to the demands of school.

Other scholars, however, caution against the assumption that mixed-age grouping works as an inherently effective practice and that the definition and purpose of it largely determines the degree of benefits it yields for students (Kinsey, 2001). Simply mixing the ages in grouping young children does not guarantee the potential benefits. Instead, developmentally appropriate practices, cooperative learning structures and integrated approaches to curriculum must all be employed as tools that work well with mixed-age grouping (Katz, 1995). The teacher has a major role in setting the stage for the benefits to occur and the potential risks to be minimized.

As a practice focused on continuity, community, and interaction, mixed-age grouping seems highly appropriate as a context for fostering life-long disposition to learn and democratic education. In mixed-age groups, the emphasis is placed on community as much as individual development.

Research Studies

Research evidence about the value of mixed-age grouping in early childhood education focuses on two types of questions. What are the effects of this practice on students? Which pedagogical factors account for positive effects of mixed-age grouping? These pedagogical factors might include organizational factors and teacher preparation.

Recent reviews of research on the effects of mixed-age grouping on student performance have examined studies drawn from different age and grade levels and including matched comparisons of multigrade vs. single grade classrooms as well as random assignment studies. Evidence of cognitive and noncognitive effects were analyzed and overall findings suggest that, at least in the cognitive development domain, students from mixed-age classrooms do not differ significantly from students in the single-age classrooms. In the area of noncognitive development, differences were found between the two groups that were not considered significant and did not necessarily contribute to achievement. It is difficult, however, to generalize these conclusions to younger children given the considerable methodological differences among the studies reviewed (Veenman, 1995, 1996). At the least, there is no evidence to suggest that student learning in mixed-age groups suffers as a result.

In another review of the same literature, Mason and Burns (1996) interpret research evidence in a way that does not favor mixed-age classrooms. Even though they agree with Veenman's conclusion that the noncognitive effects were larger than the cognitive effects, they argue that overall a negative albeit small effect was found for the mixed-age grouping. In particular, the overall quality of teaching was found to be lower than in the single-grade classrooms. Mason and Burns point out that some of the ill effects of poor instruction resulting from decisions to create mixed-age classrooms for administrative purposes were offset by the selection of strong students to be in these classrooms. Evidence from longitudinal studies (Pavan, 1992) further suggests that for some children the experience of mixed-age interaction must be long-term before any effects can be observed.

Combined, such studies suggest that the effectiveness of mixed-age classrooms depends on a number of characteristics such as instructional grouping structures, classroom management, and peer tutoring (Guiterrez and Slavin, 1992). Time, funding, as well as administrative support seem to be crucial for the success of mixed-age classrooms. Because teaching in a mixed-age group setting requires "unlearning powerfully held notions about how children learn" (Miller, 1994), the teacher is embarking on a task that has the potential to initiate significant change within the individual and within the school. Such efforts require the support that administrators and principals can provide in order for teachers to successfully experiment with the myriad of changes that likely follow in other areas. The association between mixed-age grouping and an openness to change and inquiry is when an organizational plan becomes a philosophical decision.

Future Directions

Mixed-age grouping in early childhood education is an example of a potentially good practice in need of extensive detailed research. This is an instance in which informal evidence of the value of mixed-age groups gathered from practitioners tends to be positive and they practice this form of grouping with enthusiasm. In contrast, research studies that can analytically and systematically document the processes involved are difficult to carry out. Part of the difficulty is due to the fact that performing randomized experiments, which could provide cause and effect indications, would be unethical as well as impractical. In addition, it seems that teachers of mixed-age classrooms are implementing a variety of other teaching and interacting practices that can compound the effects of the group's age composition. In other words, many different variables appear to be at work in the mixed-age grouping phenomenon.

Most of what is known today comes from work carried out in classroom settings of children in beginning elementary years. A research focus for the future might focus on the effects of mixed-age grouping practices on younger children and their experiences in child care and "educare" settings. Given the persisting demographic trends, children could potentially benefit from spending some of their group care time in mixed-age groups. Although this is common practice in early childhood services in other cultures, for example, Italy (Gandini and Edwards, 2001), to date there are no known studies documenting the benefits or risks of such practice.

Our interpretation of the information available this far is that one should not employ a reductionist perspective of "unpacking" the process-product elements of this practice. Instead, it would most likely be helpful if the focus of research efforts is on understanding the mesosystem of classroom ecology. Research on mixed-age grouping should focus on the complexity and richness of the interactions of children of different and same ages fostered in an educational environment that values relationships in a community of learners.

Further Readings: Ball, T. (2002). The nongraded continuum. Free to learn. *The Journal of the Multi-age Association of Queensland*; Both, K. (2003). Jenaplanschools in the Netherlands and their international relationships: An overview. October 2002. *Wingspan* 14(November), 16–27; Gandini, L., and C. Edwards, eds. (2001). *Bambini: The Italian* *approach to infant/toddler care*. New York: Teachers College Press; Gaustard, J. (1994). Nongraded education: Overcoming obstacles to implementing the multigrade classroom. *OSSC Bulletin* 38(3/4); Katz, L., G. (1995). The benefits of mixed-age grouping. Urbana, IL: ERIC Digest; Katz, L. G., D. Evangelou, and J. A. Hartman (1990). The case for mixed-age grouping in early education. Washington, DC. NAEYC; Kinsey, S. (2001). Multiage grouping and academic achievement. Urbana, IL: ERIC Digest; McClellan, D. (1994). Multiage grouping: Implications for education. In P. Chase and J. Doan, eds., *Full circle: A new look at multiage education*. Portsmouth, NH: Heinenman, pp. 147-166; Pavan, B. N. (1992). The benefits of nongraded schools. *Educational Leadership* 50(2), 22-25; Stone, S. J. (1996). *Creating the multiage classroom*. Tucson, AZ: Good Year Books; Veenman, S. (1995). Cognitive and noncognitive effects of multigrade and multiage Classes: A best evidence synthesis. *Review of Educational Research*, 65(4), 319-381; Veenman, S. (1996). Effects of multigrade and multiage classes reconsidered. *Review of Educational Research* 66(3), 323-340.

Demetra Evangelou and Lilian G. Katz

Montessori, Maria (1878–1952)

The lifetime efforts of Maria Montessori influenced the worldwide shift from rigid authoritarian methods of parenting and education toward those that considered the needs and interests of each individual child.

Maria Montessori was born in the Italian province of Ancona on August 32, 1870. Her father was a government official who moved the family to Rome when she was five. Her lifetime can be viewed through historical periods. She was born the year that Italy became a united country with a strong feminist movement. In 1896, she became the first woman graduate of the University of Rome medical school. A month later, she was featured in many newspapers as Italian representative at the Women's International Congress in Berlin. Upon her return to Rome, she opened a private practice as a physician, taught in women's colleges, and became involved with other endeavors. When she began to work with institutions for "deficient" children, she developed a program based upon the writings of Jean-Marc Gaspard Itard, Johann **Pestalozzi**, Friedrich **Froebel**, and others. It was designed to satisfy children's inner needs for learning as integral to the development of individual personality and their accomplishments soon gained widespread attention. (Stevens, 1913, p. 7).

After the worldwide depression of the 1890s, some apartment complexes for low-income workers in Rome were rehabilitated. A "children's house" for daytime supervision was included in one of them. When Montessori became its director when it opened in 1907, she continued experimenting with ways to facilitate children's learning through self-activity. Within months, articles describing the unique "Casa dei Bambini" appeared in popular magazines and newspapers. This began a lifetime of publications and worldwide lectures, as detailed in biographies by Lillard (1996), Kramer (1976) and others.

Although she spoke only in Italian, Montessori gave ten well-attended public lectures in American cities in 1913, organized a demonstration class, and presented papers at the San Francisco World's Fair and the National Educational Association conference in 1915, and returned for more lectures in 1917. During these visits, she made friends with such notables as Alexander Graham Bell and the daughter of President Woodrow Wilson.

Despite this initial welcome, interest in her system was temporary in the United States. University faculty and other professionals either ignored her work or wrote negative criticism, with a book by William Kilpatrick (1914) having a devastating effect. Classroom teachers adopted some materials and techniques, but saw her method as simply another version of their Froebelian **kindergarten**. Her complex beliefs were couched in flowery Italian, not the scientific terminology that was becoming popular with psychologists, and translations were often inaccurate. Another problem was that she spoke only of her own new concepts, which meant that her inclusion of active outdoor play, art, and music were not recognized. Although the first Montessori schools in the United States were opened by women who had studied with her in Italy, the focus was often upon the didactic materials rather than her entire philosophy.

Montessori also fell from public favor because, like many feminists, she wanted to be a mother without marital restrictions. With the collaboration of Dr. Montesano, a colleague at the Orthophrenic School, son Mario was born in 1898. He spent his childhood with a foster family and in a boarding school. She had no siblings, but she introduced him as her adopted nephew when he accompanied her to California in 1915. Despite this, acceptance of Montessori's methods can be attributed to her son. By the 1920s, when Mario recognized her inability to manage financial affairs, he became her business manager. He scheduled their activities and developed commercial production of her didactic apparatus. In 1929, he organized the Association Montessori Internationale (AMI) and he coordinated global activities from its Amsterdam office until his death in 1982. His son and other family members continue that mission.

Preoccupation with World War I was an additional reason that Montessori was ignored in the United States. However, in 1917 she opened a research institute in Spain and in 1919 began a series of training courses in London. Mussolini persuaded her to coordinate an Italian educational program in 1922, but increased emphasis upon Fascism caused her to move back to Spain in 1934. When the Spanish Civil War erupted two years later, the Montessori family was evacuated on a British naval vessel. She opened a training center in the Netherlands in 1938, then conducted courses in India during the World War II years of 1938 to 1940. Her book on *The Absorbent Mind* was written after observing the contrast between the impersonally rigid infant care in Europe and the close physical contact maintained by Asian mothers. She returned to India in 1947 to open the Montessori University in Madras. Her last public address was in 1951, when she attended the International Montessori Congress in London. After decades of moving from place to place, she acquired an apartment in Amsterdam, which is now the AMI headquarters. It was about this time that someone asked her where she considered her home to be. Her often-quoted response was "My country is a star which turns around the sun and is called Earth."

After Montessori returned to Amsterdam, her previous efforts toward peace education were intensified. There was a standing ovation when she spoke at the **United Nations Educational, Scientific, and Cultural Organization** (UNESCO) in 1949, expressing again her belief that civilization depends upon children being given their rightful place in society while learning to fit into it. She was nominated for the Nobel Peace Prize in 1949, 1950, and 1951. At the time of her sudden death in 1952, she was scheduling further travel to promote peace.

From 1913 onward, many concepts promoted by Montessori were integrated into parental practices and early childhood programs in America. These include active involvement by the child, self-selection of materials, self-pacing within a structured environment, and the role of facilitative adults instead of authoritarians. The resurgence of interest in Montessori schools began in 1958, with the first one in Greenwich, Connecticut. Nancy Rambush (1962/1998) was a leader in the effort to adapt the original European version of Montessori education to one more appropriate in America. It emphasized the role of parents and introduced other materials to supplement those of traditional Montessori schools. Her goal was to advance the system, and she correctly described the result as phenomenal. Nienhuis Montessori publications and materials continue to serve public and private schools worldwide. In addition to accredited and self-designated Montessori schools and teacher training programs functioning around the globe, her ideas about peace education, sensitive periods, and play as the child's work have been verified by countless research studies.

Further Readings: Association of Montessori International (AMI) (1970). *Maria Montessori, A centenary anthology*. Amsterdam: AMI. Available online at www.montessori-ami.org; Kilpatrick, William Heard (1914). *The Montessori system examined*. Cambridge, MA: Riverside Press; Kramer, Rita (1976). *Maria Montessori*. New York: G.P. Putnam's Sons; Lillard, Paula P. (1996). *Montessori today*. New York: Random House; Montessori, Maria (1949). *The absorbent mind*. Madras, India: Theosophical Publishing House; Rambusch, Nancy (1962/1998). *Learning to learn: An American approach to Montessori*. Baltimore: Helicon/New York: American Montessori Society; Stevens, Ellen Yale (1913). *A guide to the Montessori method*. New York: Frederick Stokes.

Web Site: For reprints of early publications, see the North American Montessori Teachers' Association Web site, www.montessori-namta.org.

Dorothy W. Hewes

Montessori Education

The Montessori Method, sometimes described as Montessori Education, is named after Maria **Montessori** and is based on her beliefs and practices first utilized in her *Casa dei Bambini* (Children's Home) in 1907 in the slum tenements in Rome. This method is based partially upon educational experiments with children with mental disabilities that originated in the work of Jean-Jacques **Rousseau** and the adaptation of those methods to aid the development of normal young children. Montessori's pedagogical approach was no doubt influenced by Montessori's medical training, and the desire of the Association of Good Building in the Quarter of San Lorenzo (the Quarter of the Poor) in Rome to reduce vandalism in their tenement buildings and promote hygienic education.

Montessori had both great respect for children at her "Casa" and also high expectations of them. Children were expected to present themselves on time, groomed and with clean clothing and could be expelled if they appeared unwashed, in soiled clothing, were incorrigible, or had parents who, through bad conduct, were perceived as destroying the educational work of the institution

(Montessori, 1912, 1964). Her goal was to create a prepared environment in which children have the freedom to explore and to pick and choose those things with which they wanted to work, thus fostering independence (Hainstock, 1997), without committing any rough or rude act. This was not initially to be a collective classroom with children seated in rows, but a place in which children were helped to become individually engaged, and focused on their individual lessons. She termed this approach to education *discipline through liberty*.

Montessori had a number of beliefs that guided her educational innovations, the most important of which assigned primacy to the period from birth to six years of age, when the development of character occurred. Montessori felt that many *defects*, including speech deficits, become permanent if not addressed during *sensitive periods*, a term borrowed from the Dutch biologist Hugo DeVries and referring to a special sensitivity for a particular developmental trait. The time between three and six years of age, at which time the child forms and establishes the principal functions, was such a sensitive period to Montessori. She observed that young children are capable of long periods of concentration and use learning materials repeatedly. She devised sets of sequenced learning materials that guide children toward reading, writing, understanding place value in mathematics, geometrical shapes and a geographical recognition of the continents and nations. While concentrating, children's movements become refined and coordinated, leading to increased self-discipline.

Montessori lessons were to be brief, simple (stripped of all that is not absolute truth), and objective (presented in such a way that the personality of the teacher would disappear) and the job of the teacher was to prepare the lesson, to deliver it, and to observe carefully the child's interaction with materials, adjusting her preparation and delivery based upon the child's response to it, quietly offering limited guidance, and preparing children for the next activity. Among the recurring features of her approach to teaching was an emphasis on a prepared environment, the use of didactic materials, and what she referred to as the "Three Period Lesson."

Montessori had specific ideas about the context in which children's learning should take place. School was to be a *prepared environment* in which a child is able to develop freely at his/her own pace, unhindered in the spontaneous unfolding of his natural capacities, through the manipulation of a graded series of materials designed to stimulate the senses and eventually the thinking, leading from perception to intellectual skills (Kramer, 1976). The classroom was designed so that a child can access the Montessori materials easily, freely selecting and replacing them without the need of adult assistance, once they have been properly introduced to them.

The educational method the teacher(s) employed in this prepared environment was based upon the presentation of *didactic materials* that attracted the spontaneous attention of the child, and contained a gradual gradation of stimuli. Many of these materials are *self-correcting*. For example, if a child tries to place a Knobbed Cylinder in the wrong hole, the child gets immediate feedback from the cylinder that the hole selected is too small or too large. The child experiments until the correct hole is selected, a term Montessori referred to as *auto-education*. Materials in Montessori's didactic system were originally manufactured by the House of Labour of the Humanitarian Society at Milan, and starting in the 1920s through collaboration with Albert Nienhius, by Nienhuis Montessori in Holland.

Materials were often presented initially in three stages, and Montessori adapted this *Three Period Lesson* technique from Edouard Seguin. In the first stage, for example, the child might be presented with two colors, red and blue, both of which appear face down on a mat. The teacher would turn over the first color tablet and say, "This is red" and repeat the same way for the blue tablet. The second stage is intended to help the child recognize the object that corresponds to its name. Here the teacher might say, "Give me the red one," and then, "Give me the blue one." The third stage focuses on recognition of the name that corresponds to the object. The teacher shows the child the red tablet and asks, "What is this?"

There are generally agreed to be four major pedagogic categories in her method. The *Exercises of Practical Life* include those that have to do with the care of the child's own person and those that are concerned with the care of the environment. Exercises included washing, polishing, sweeping, ironing, pouring, and brushing. The original intent was to help children learn how to keep themselves and their environment clean, what Standing (1957) called the "domestic occupation for young children." These have now come to mean activities related to real life that offer opportunities to develop coordinated fine movements, logical sequence, functional independence, and grace and courtesy.

The *Sensorial Activities* utilize concrete, mathematically precise materials that isolate each quality perceived by human senses. Activities with these materials offer opportunities to classify and refine sensory perceptions while developing abstractions, memory, and exactness. The aim is refinement of the differential perception of stimuli by means of repeated exercises. One well-known example is the pink tower, where young children place increasingly small cubes on top of bigger ones. Often Montessori would isolate one sense (e.g., sight, by use of a blindfold) to heighten other senses, and incorporated whispering and *solemn silence* in her approach.

Language Activities include materials centered on vocabulary enrichment, spoken-language skills, writing, and reading. The Sandpaper Letters, an alphabet composed on individual sandpaper capital letters pasted on pink, painted boards, were used to introduce individual letters to children.

Numeration Activities use concrete, sensorial-based materials that offer interactive experiences with numbers, numerical relationships, and the foundations of the decimal system. The Golden Beads (small beads made of plastic or ceramic, and arranged individually as a unit, as a bar of 10, as a square of 100, and as a cube of 1,000) are a classic example of such a numeration material.

Although many associate Montessori's work with the period of early childhood, Montessori came to recognize the unique learning capabilities of elementary and middle-grade students. She created an integrated curriculum incorporating anthropology, astronomy, biology, chemistry, geology, geometry, history, literature, mathematics, and zoology that is now used in early and some upper-elementary programs. The first Montessori public elementary school program was established in 1965 by Nancy Rambusch in Cincinnati. Others have adapted her methods to teaching children in the home (Hainstock, 1997).

Early criticisms of Montessori's method were that she minimized the role of the adult in preparing what children would discover in the classroom as well as minimized the effect of the relationship between teacher and child. This was perhaps a natural reaction by outsiders to observers of a teacher who appears to have less control because her influence is less obvious than in traditional classrooms. Another, perhaps more justified, criticism was that in an attempt to keep the method "pure," both Montessori and her early followers maintained a tight control on the model's dissemination.

Continuing criticisms include a perceived lack of spontaneity and creativity in classrooms, insufficient time for social interactions, materials that are too restrictive, an overemphasis on "practical life" activities, an approach that is outdated, and concerns about transitions and adjustments by children moving from Montessori to public school classrooms using other approaches. Ironically, given that her programs were desired for children of poor families, contemporary critics point to the fact that the predominately private Montessori schools are only appropriate for or at least available to well-to-do families.

In spite of these controversies, and well over 100 years after the first *Casa dei Bambini* was opened, Montessori's method endures and several teacher training programs and Montessori Children's Houses continue to flourish. There are an estimated 3,000 private Montessori schools and several hundred primary and/or lower elementary programs, as well as several upper-elementary programs in public schools, in the United States. There are also nearly twenty Montessori education graduate programs in the United States and training programs in nineteen other countries. Many features of the approach that Montessori developed have become embedded in early childhood classrooms and incorporated by manufacturers of materials for programs for young children. She played a major role in influencing society's image of children as different from adults. She put forth persuasive arguments that children learn through play, that early development has an impact on later development, that there is much to be learned from careful observation, and that it is often better not to intervene when a child begins to struggle with a material. She contributed to our understanding that scale is an important feature of materials and furniture for children, that educational materials may facilitate development, and that intrinsically interesting and self-correcting materials may sustain attention. And finally, Maria Montessori believed strongly that schools must be a part of communities and parents should be involved in their children's education.

Further Readings: Edwards, C. P. (2002). Three approaches from Europe: Waldorf, Montessori, and Reggio Emilia. *Early Childhood Research and Practice* [Online], 4(1); Edwards, C. P. (2006). Montessori's education and its scientific basis. Book review of *Montessori: The science behind the genius* by Angeline Stoll Lillard. *Journal of Applied Developmental Psychology* 27(2; March/April), 183–187. Hainstock, E. (1971). *Teaching Montessori in the home*. New York: Random House; Hainstock, E. (1997). *The essential Montessori: An introduction to the woman, the writings, the method, and the movement*. New York: Plume; Kramer, R. (1976). *Maria Montessori: A biography*. Chicago: University of Chicago Press; Lillard, A. (2005). *Montessori: The science behind the genius*. New York: Oxford University Press; Montessori, M. (1949). *The absorbent mind*. Madras, India: Theosophical Publishing House; Montessori, M. (1964a). *The Montessori method*.

New York: Schocken. First published in English in 1912; Montessori, M. (1964b). *The secret of childhood*. New York: Ballantine. First published in English in 1936.

Michael Kalinowski

Moral Development. *See* Development, Moral

Mothers

Motherhood is a role experienced by many women throughout the world. In the United States alone there are an estimated 80.5 million mothers; as such, mothers comprise well over a quarter of the entire U.S. population. While there are many commonalities among mothers, differences also exist, for example, in the age of motherhood, rates and timing of employment, and with whom parenting responsibilities are shared. Differences also exist across historical and cultural contexts, and in the individual and society's interpretations of motherhood. However, every group has some basic tenets that help to define the role of mothers.

The age at which women become mothers varies broadly. Some women bear children as adolescents, while a growing number of women in their forties and fifties are now able to bear children because of advances in reproductive technologies. From 1970 to 2002 the average age of U.S. women at the birth of their first child rose from 21.4 years to 25.1 years. In the last twelve years the birth rate among teenage mothers (ages 15–19) decreased by 30 percent, accompanied by a 31 percent increase in birth rates among women aged 35–39 and a 51 percent increase for women aged 40–44. These changes in birth rates among teenage mothers and women aged 35–44 could explain the increase in the average age of a U.S. woman when she gives birth for the first time.

In the United States, the numbers of teenage women having children started declining well over ten years ago; many have attributed the decline in birth rates among this population to welfare reform that was enacted in 1996. **Temporary Aid to Needy Families** (TANF) contains provisions that serve to reduce teenage pregnancy and dependency on welfare. In order to receive cash benefits under TANF, for example, a teenage parent must live with an adult over the age of 21 and attend school or job training. These provisions were included because of research findings indicating that teen mothers who live with their own mothers appear to benefit economically and cognitively from this arrangement. These findings are consistent with patterns of multigenerational living that have characterized family lives for centuries in diverse cultures around the world. In the United States, teen mothers who live in a multigenerational setting generally obtain more schooling than teen mothers who live in other arrangements. However, researchers have also found that this multigenerational arrangement may at times be a source of stress and conflict.

As has been the case throughout history, motherhood is associated with and influenced by features particular to the social and cultural context. In many industrialized societies, mothers find themselves trying to negotiate their careers or employment status in combination with motherhood. This particular negotiation is different from what is experienced by mothers in agrarian or traditional societies. Many women decide to stay home with their infants, if it is economically possible, and other women divide their time between work and home, working either part-time or full-time. Over the last 30 years, rates of maternal employment in the United States have increased dramatically. In 1976, 31 percent of mothers with children under the age of 1 were participating in the labor force. However, in 1998, 59 percent of mothers with children under the age of 1 were participating in the labor force. In 2004, 55 percent of U.S. women who had given birth in the last twelve months were either employed or looking for a job. Upon deciding to return to work, mothers must contend with arranging care for their young children, adapting to their role of motherhood, and attempting to balance their work and family life.

Research on the impact of work demands on a mother and the impact of these demands on the child has led to numerous changes in parental leave taking policies after the birth of a child as well as changes in policies limiting the amount of work hours. Parental leave policies in different cultures convey distinct interpretations of the maternal role, the mother–child relationship, and female participation in the workforce. For example, in Norway, a mother can take up to a year's leave and receive 80 percent of her salary, and in Mexico mothers can take up to twelve weeks and receive 100 percent of their salary. In the United States women can take up to twelve weeks of unpaid leave. As for policy changes in work hours, in 2000, France adopted a 35-hour workweek to help facilitate a parent's negotiation of work and family life. Since mothers often are considered a major influence on their children's development, some people (researchers, policymakers, religious organizations, family members) express concern that maternal employment puts children's development at risk, since these young children would be cared for by nonmaternal caregivers.

According to the National Survey of America's Families (NSAF), as of 2002, about three quarters of infants and toddlers of working mothers in the United States are in some form of child care. Child-care settings range from informal care by a relative to formal center-based care. About 39 percent of infants and toddlers are in care for an average of twenty-five hours per week. Although a debate exists around the effects of child-care participation on the development of young children, research has found that the quality of child care is correlated with cognitive, language, social and emotional developmental outcomes in young children (NICHD Early Child Care Research Network, 1998, 2000). However, the family exerts a much greater impact on children's development than does child care. Mother's perceptions of their experience at work, as well as the amount of earnings, also appear to impact their children's development. A mother's negative perception of her work experience and low earnings can lead to increased stress and difficulty managing the household. A positive perception and higher earnings can foster maternal mental health and enable participation in high-quality child care.

The sharing of parenting responsibilities also creates a demarcation for many women entering motherhood. Some women share the responsibilities with a spouse or partner while other women share the responsibilities with other family members (e.g., grandmother, aunts, siblings), and some women bear the sole responsibility of caring for their child. The number of single mothers has increased from 3 million in 1970 to 10 million in 2003. Rates of single fatherhood have also increased over this time. Of family groups in the United States that include children, about 26 percent have a single mother as the head of the household. About three quarters of all single parents are employed; therefore these parents are highly dependent on informal and formal child care. Young children of single mothers spend an average of thirty-four hours in child care, eleven hours more than the young children of two-parent families. About 46 percent of families headed by a single mother with a child under the age of 5 live below the poverty level. Researchers have found that children living in **poverty** are more likely to develop emotional, cognitive, and behavioral problems than children living above the poverty line.

Despite the age at which women become mothers, their employment status, or with whom child care responsibilities are shared, a major component of motherhood is adaptation to a role that is in constant flux as the child develops, as well as a conceptual adaptation to society's expectations. As children develop, caretakers must constantly adapt to the child's developmental needs. What a child needs from his mother as an infant varies from what that child needs as a toddler or adolescent. Because of this fluctuation in the child's needs, the maternal role is a developmental process, with both stability and a need for flexibility and change.

Motherhood, in a societal context, is also in a state of flux. Conceptually, society's expectations of motherhood in the United States are constantly debated. Although en masse, working mothers and single mothers have existed in the United States for generations, the general expectation for women traditionally has been marriage and, once pregnant, remaining at home to raise children. In the past, women who wanted to pursue a career had to abandon the prospect of becoming a parent. In some respects, this separation of career and parenthood for women has changed dramatically in the last 40 years. Policies have been enacted in order to support women's pursuits of both careers and motherhood (e.g., Pregnancy Discrimination Act—outlawing discriminatory hiring practices because of pregnancy, Family and Medical Leave Act—providing a 12-week unpaid leave for eligible caretakers). Conversely, women have also been criticized for choices related to careers and motherhood. Many women, still, find balancing family and employment roles challenging yet rewarding.

Motherhood takes place alongside other roles that women play, both at home (e.g., spouse/partner, daughter, sibling), in the workplace (employer/employee), and in other social contexts (e.g., friend, volunteer). While most women thrive in all of these roles, balancing motherhood with other activities, roles, and expectations is complicated and at times stressful. Societies differ in the supports (both formal and informal) that are provided for mothering. Formal supports (e.g., U.S. Family and Medical Leave Act) have enabled women to become mothers while also continuing their participation in society. These formal supports, along with many informal supports provided by family and friends, also serve to provide women with information, material goods, and services (e.g., **Women, Infants and Children** [WIC], **Child Care and Development Fund**), and emotional support in her mothering role. Child-care services, **parenting education** programs, parenting support groups, and help from friends and family are important in supporting mothers and their children. When women have sources of social support (emotional, informational, tangible/material) they are able to be more effective and fulfilled as parents.

Many theories of child development emphasize the role that mothers have in their children's development. Sigmund **Freud**, for example, highlighted the mother–infant relationship as the "prototype of all other love relationships." Human infants are dependent on caregivers for a very long time. Typically, mothers play a primary role in meeting an infant's biological and emotional needs. John **Bowlby** and others focused on the **attachments** that infants form to their mothers as an important component of personality development and adaptive functioning. While there are many influences on children's development (including family environment, genetic/constitutional and social context), research has shown that positive development of children is facilitated by maternal sensitivity, empathy, emotional availability, and reciprocal interaction. Several factors influence a mother's manner of interacting with her child, including the way in which she was parented, and her current circumstances and support for her as a mother. While the circumstances of motherhood vary across societies and contexts, mothers hold an important role in all societies, serving to nurture, educate, and increase the life chances of the next generation.

Further Readings: Barnard, K. E. and L. K. Martell (2002). Mothering. In M. H. Bornstein, ed., *Handbook of parenting*. 2nd ed. Mahwah, NJ: Erlbaum, pp. 3–26; Caudill, W. (1974). A comparison of maternal care and infant behavior in Japanese-American, American and Japanese Families. In William Lebra, ed., *Mental health research in Asia and the Pacific*. Vol. 3. Honolulu: East-West Center Press, pp. 4–15; Dye, J. L. (2005). Fertility of American women: June 2004 current population reports. U.S. (P20-555). Census Bureau, Washington, DC; Harkness, Sara and Charles Super, eds. (1996). *Parents, cultural belief systems*. New York: Guilford Press; Kamerman, S. B., M. Neuman, J. Waldfogel, and J. Brooks-Gunn (2003). *Social policies, family types, and child outcomes in selected OECD countries*. OECD Social, Employment, and Migration Working Papers (No.6). Archived at http://www.oecd.org/dataoecd/26/46/2955844.pdf.; NICHD Early Child Care Research Network (1998). Early child care and self-control, compliance and problem behavior at twenty-four and thirty-six months. *Child Development* 69, 1145–1170; NICHD Early Child Care Research Network (2000).The relation of child care to cognitive and language development. *Child Development* 71, 960–980.

Claudia Miranda and M. Ann Easterbrooks

Multicultural Education. *See* Antibias/Multicultural Education

Multiple Intelligences, Theory of

Multiple intelligences theory (hereafter referred to as MI theory) was named and developed by Howard Gardner, a professor of cognition and education at Harvard University. Introduced in his 1983 book, *Frames of Mind*, Gardner's theory challenges the views of intelligence as measured by **intelligence quotient** (IQ) and as described in Jean **Piaget**'s universal stages of cognitive development. Arguing that human intelligence is neither a single entity nor a unified set of processes, Gardner (2004) maintains that there are several distinct, relatively autonomous intelligences. Individual intellectual profiles reflect varied configurations of these intellectual capacities.

Gardner (1999) defines intelligence as "a biopsychological potential to process information that can be activated in a cultural setting to solve problems or create products that are of value in a culture." Describing it as a potential, Gardner emphasizes the emergent and responsive nature of intelligence, further differentiating his theory from conceptions of intelligence as fixed and innate. Whether a potential will be activated depends in large part on the values of the culture in which an individual grows up and on the opportunities available in that culture. Development of the intelligences is influenced simultaneously by species and individual biological dispositions, environmental factors, education, and personal effort. These activating forces contribute to the expression of a range of intelligences across cultures and among individuals.

Gardner began rethinking the nature of intelligence by examining the range of adult end-states valued in diverse cultures around the world. To identify abilities that support these end-states, he examined research from numerous disciplines, including biology, neurology, psychology, and anthropology. He then formulated eight criteria for identifying an intelligence, including neurological evidence, traceable evolutionary history, and the use of an encoded symbol system. Gardner (1999) argues that, because intelligences are used to solve real-life problems, the measurement of intelligences must also be based on the functioning of abilities in diverse real-life situations. For Gardner, the criteria developed to identify intelligences are one of the most important contributions of his theory.

To date, Gardner has identified eight intelligences: Linguistic, logical-mathematical, musical, spatial, bodily-kinesthetic, naturalistic, interpersonal, and intrapersonal (see Gardner [2004] for a full description). Although linguistic and logical-mathematical intelligences have been emphasized in psychometric testing and school settings, no intelligence in the MI framework is inherently more important than the others. Gardner does not claim that this roster is exhaustive or that the particular delineations among the intelligences are definitive. Rather, his aim is to establish support for a pluralistic view of intelligence. With the identification of intelligences based on eight empirically oriented criteria, the roster will be reviewed as new findings are reported.

Intelligence and Related Constructs

Intelligence in the MI framework relates to, as well as differs from, the psychological constructs of process, domain, style, and content (Gardner, in press). In terms of process, the intelligence itself is not a process; rather it is a *capacity* to process certain kinds of information in certain ways. Each intelligence operates with processes carried out by dedicated neural networks, and each has its attendant psychological processes, such as logical-mathematical or interpersonal processing.

Although related, the concepts of intelligence and domain are readily distinguishable. Intelligence refers to biological and psychological potentials within an individual. Domains are bodies of knowledge valued and applied within a culture.

An intelligence may be deployed in many domains. For example, spatial intelligence may operate in the domains of visual arts, navigation, and engineering. Similarly, performance in a domain may require the use of more than one intelligence. For example, an effective teacher relies on at least linguistic and personal intelligences.

Style and intelligence are fundamentally different psychological constructs. Style refers to an individual's characteristic and consistent approach to organizing and processing information; for example, a person can have an impulsive or playful style. MI theory is not a stylistic theory; rather, a person's intellectual profile reflects his or her computational capacities to process various kinds of content—for example, spatial, musical, and person-related—in the environment. While the psychological literature regards styles as relatively stable attributes of the individual and evident across a wide range of situations, MI theory suggests the possibility that style is a domain-specific construct as well.

According to MI theory, an intelligence is sensitive to specific contents, but is not itself a content. For example, logical-mathematical intelligence is activated when individuals operate on quantities, written numbers, and scientific formulas. These intellectual operations, however, entail more than content of numbers and formulas. MI theory contends that different intelligences are geared to different contents and there are no general capacities such as memory, perception, or speed of processing that necessarily cut across content areas. This conceptualization distinguishes MI theory from other pluralistic views of intelligence that claim mental faculties function similarly in all content areas and operate according to general laws.

Validation of the Theory

Since the introduction of MI theory in 1983, much research has been done in the fields of cognition, education, and neuroscience, either explicitly investigating MI theory or conducting studies related to its claims. Recent neurological research provides convincing data that linguistic, mathematical, and musical processing are cognitively and neurologically distinct; indeed, as Gardner speculated earlier, each of these faculties itself consists of dissociable components (Gardner, in press). In educational studies, researchers are finding that, when a wide range of abilities are assessed, children are more likely to show uneven profiles of strength and weakness than a uniform level of general ability (Chen and Gardner, 2005; Chen and McNamee, 2005).

MI theory can be validated further by evaluating its application in educational settings. Numerous reports indicate that MI theory has given teachers and parents more accurate perceptions of children's intellectual potentials as well as more specific methods for supporting and developing these potentials. Recently, Kornhaber, Veenema, and Fierros (2003) studied forty-one elementary schools across the United States that had applied MI theory to school-based practices for a minimum of three years. All these schools reported improvements in standardized test scores, student discipline, parent participation, or the performance of students with learning differences. The majority linked the improvements to MI-based interventions.

MI Theory and Early Education

MI theory can serve as a conceptual framework for implementing developmentally appropriate practice in early education. MI theory defines **intelligence** as a potential; the driving force of developmentally appropriate practice is to inspire all children to achieve their highest potentials. Three requirements for implementing **developmentally appropriate practice** are knowledge about children and their development, subject matter and curriculum goals, and teaching and assessment. In each of these knowledge areas, MI theory can be used to help teachers achieve the goals of developmentally appropriate education.

Knowledge of children and their development. Development of what many refer to as the "whole child" is a well-established concept in U.S. early education. MI theory contributes to a more differentiated understanding of this development (Chen and Gardner, 2005). Knowledge of children in the MI framework goes beyond describing general cognitive, social, emotional, and physical growth to identify a wider range of more specific developmental potentials. Because each intelligence reflects particular problem-solving features, information-processing capacities, and developmental trajectories, knowing about one area of a child's development does not generalize to knowledge of another area. In-depth understanding requires a careful review of each child's intellectual profile—his or her proclivities, strengths, vulnerabilities, and interests. Although all normally developing children possess all the intelligences, from early on they exhibit different strengths and have distinctive profiles. Strength in one intelligence does not necessarily predict strength in another.

Development from MI's perspective is domain-specific and contextual (Gardner, in press). The development of young children's intellectual abilities is tied to specific bodies of knowledge and skills and is not based on general cognitive structures that operate across domains. Strengths and weakness exhibited in a child's intellectual profile may change over time. Development is also contextualized. Specifically, intelligence develops among individuals when they interact with others, use cultural tools, or engage in activities. To foster young children's intellectual abilities, MI theory suggests that early childhood educators attend to cultural values and tools, community goals, and the child's motivations.

Knowledge of subject matter and curriculum goals. Early childhood **curriculum** is inclusive; activities in the areas of language, **mathematics**, music, visual arts, and movement are included weekly, if not daily, in most preschool classrooms. However, their significance for the development of young children's minds is not typically deemed equal. Language and reading are the top priorities for learning. For MI theory, the development of multiple intellectual potentials in young children requires extensive exposure to a wide range of areas. Developing varied symbol systems is the foremost task during the early years. Limited exposure to some areas decreases possibilities for young children to express themselves with diverse tools and to develop their potentials to the greatest extent. It also reduces the likelihood of discovering interests and abilities that parents and teachers can nurture at a young age.

Early childhood teachers are often trained as generalists. They learn to integrate a range of content areas using themes and project-based approaches to teaching. An MI-based approach to curriculum development invites teachers to use multiple entry points to promote children's in-depth exploration and understanding of topics and concepts essential to early learning and development. MI theory is not and should not be the goal of early childhood curriculum. Instead, this framework should be used to assist teachers in organizing curriculum around essential topics, in supporting children's learning of key concepts and skills in relation to these topics, and in promoting the development of multiple intellectual potentials supported by multiple symbol systems (Gardner, 1999).

Knowledge of teaching and assessment. Early childhood teaching has been known for its play-based, emergent, and constructivist techniques. MI theory differentiates the **pedagogy** of early teaching by emphasizing building on children's particular strengths and using them to build bridges to other areas of learning. In contrast to traditional approaches that focus primarily on children's deficits, teachers in MI classrooms also attend to areas in which a child excels. Teachers invite children to participate in learning tasks that further develop their strengths in ways they are motivated to pursue. Teachers also give children opportunities to use their strengths as tools to express what they have learned. Teacher support for children's strengths contributes to a positive self-image and an increased likelihood for success in other learning areas. The strategy of building on children's strengths has also proven effective in helping children identified as at-risk for school failure (Chen, Krechevsky, and Viens, 1998).

Effective teaching requires appropriate uses of **assessment**. Assessment based on MI theory is consistent with the principles of developmentally appropriate assessment advocated by many early childhood educators. The primary purpose of assessment is to aid development and learning, rather than to sort, track, or label. Features of appropriate assessment include on-going observation in the classroom, **documentation** of children's behavior when engaged in meaningful activities, and linking assessment results to teaching and learning processes. Of particular importance to MI-based assessment is the identification of children's strengths. This is accomplished by sampling a wide range of abilities in the assessment process. Project Spectrum and Project Bridging are two examples of assessment systems designed to capture diverse intellectual strengths in young children (Chen, Krechevsky, and Viens, 1998; Chen and McNamee, 2005).

Since the publication of *Frames of Mind* in 1983, MI theory has become widely recognized in the fields of developmental psychology, cognitive psychology, and education. The theoretical emphasis on concepts of diversity, equality, possibility, richness, and expansion confirms beliefs about children as individuals that many educators hold and practice. MI theory also provides educators as well as parents with language to describe children's distinctive intellectual profiles; and supports calls for mobilizing resources to help individual children reach their highest potentials and to enrich their contributions to society. *See also* Curriculum, Mathematics; Curriculum, Music; Curriculum, Physical Development; Curriculum, Visual Art; Development, Language.

Further Readings: Chen, J.-Q., and H. Gardner (2005). Alternative assessment from a Multiple Intelligences theoretical perspective. In D. P. Flanagan, J. L. Genshaft, and P. L. Harrison, eds., *Beyond traditional intellectual assessment: Contemporary and emerging theories, tests, and issues*. 2nd ed. New York: Guilford, pp. 77–102; Chen, J.-Q., M. Krechevsky, and J. Viens (1998). *Building on children's strengths: The experience of project spectrum*. New York: Teachers College Press; Chen, J-Q., and G. McNamee (2005). *Bridging: Assessment for teaching and learning in early childhood classrooms*. Chicago: Erikson Institute; Gardner, H. (1999). *Intelligence reframed: Multiple intelligences for the 21st Century*. New York: Basic Books; Gardner, H. (2004). *Frames of mind: The theory of multiple intelligences*. 20th anniversary ed. New York: Basic Books; Gardner, H. (in press). *Multiple Intelligences: New Horizons*. New York: Basic Books; Kornhaber, M., S. Veenema, and E. Fierros (2003). *Multiple Intelligences: Best ideas from research and practice*. Boston: Allyn & Bacon.

Jie-Qi Chen

Music Curriculum. *See* Curriculum, Music

N

NACCRRA. *See* National Association of Child Care Resource and Referral Agencies

NAECTE. *See* National Association of Early Childhood Teacher Educators

NAEYC. *See* National Association for the Education of Young Children

NARA. *See* National Association for Regulatory Administration

NAREA. *See* North American Reggio Emilia Alliance

Narrative

From birth, the world of babies and children is organized by scripts that reflect familial and cultural child-rearing patterns. It could be said that babies join and change the story of a family. When children begin using language they use it to organize the world. This typically takes a narrative form. As they begin to engage in sociodramatic play they act out scripts from their everyday lives that reflect events they seek to understand. Parents and early childhood educators use stories, both oral and written, to impart information, lead children into literacy, and help children cope with difficult issues in their lives. They also tell stories because it is a natural and enjoyable component of child rearing.

Narrative is a fundamental component of early cognitive and emotional development. As the child enters a particular culture he begins to understand and adopt scripts that form his understanding of himself in the family and larger society. Language, that used by adults and older children to guide him as well as that he uses to reflect on his own activity, begins to structure his understanding and memory. As he develops the capacity to pretend, he uses such play to act out stories that represent various aspects of his life. This can be simply arranging blocks of various size in a way that represents family members, acting out bedtimes rituals, or replicating the actions of television superheros. By the time he reaches school he brings with him highly developed, but culturally varied, ways of describing his world (Heath, 1983).

Throughout the world families and communities transmit information about how to behave, how to survive and who to remember through various forms of story telling. And the literatures of the world's cultures include narrative tales that chronicle the history of civilization from the beginning of time to the birth of the most recent member of the community. The folklore of a society is often captured in the stories that are told to children.

The role of early childhood educators in supporting development and learning is characterized by both explicit and implicit use of narrative. The transition of a child from home to child care literally involves adding to the child and family's story. A new set of characters and setting enters the child's life. This can be done in a manner in which both parent and caregiver attend to the child's capacity to weave new elements into his story, giving him words and scripts through which he can understand his new surroundings (e.g., "Your cubbie is where you put your coat when you first come in, then you go to the sand table. Daddy comes after we play outside."). Such scripts provide consistency and security. They also provide the framework in which he constructs his understanding of how the world works.

Children's narratives themselves play a large and established role in the early childhood classroom. A book corner with clearly displayed books, a dramatic play area with dress-up clothes, and manipulatives with which children can act out events of interest and imagination are typical in a developmentally appropriate preschool classroom. Teachers read a wide variety of children's books to children both at circle time and in small groups. Narratives represented by these books cover the range of interests of young children from retelling ancient myths to addressing daily concerns like separation and going to sleep, and from imparting basic information to sparking children's imagination. Early literacy activities including reading chapter books, reading aloud and silently, and writing become more prevalent in the early elementary grades. Teachers, in providing materials for play as well as in selecting reading content, should be sensitive to the cultural characteristics of the families and communities they serve. In the development of writing children are asked to tell of what they know and what they have experienced; they become writers of stories.

A notable curriculum innovation that is deeply grounded in the use of narrative is the storytelling method described by Vivian Paley (1990). She maintains that children use stories to help understand what they are most interested in, "nothing less than truth and life." Through the telling of stories children learn to organize both their cognitive and affective lives. Caregivers join this process by transmitting the valued stories of the culture as well as the ways stories are created within the culture. *See also* Development, Language; Language Diversity; Play as storytelling.

Further Readings: Bruner, J. (1990). *Acts of meaning*. Cambridge, MA: Harvard University Press; Heath, S. B. (1983). *Ways with words*. Cambridge, MA: Cambridge University Press; Nelson, K. (1989). *Narratives from the crib*. Cambridge, MA: Harvard University Press; Paley, Vivian (1990). *The boy who would be a helicopter: The uses of storytelling in the classroom*. Cambridge, MA: Harvard University Press; Sutton-Smith, B. (2001).

Emotional breaches in play and narrative. In A. Goncu and E. Klein, eds., *Children in play, story, and school*. New York: Guilford Press.

John Hornstein

National Association for Regulatory Administration (NARA)

The National Association for Regulatory Administration (NARA) is a U.S.-based, nonprofit organization for human care licensors. Chartered at Tulane University in New Orleans in 1976, NARA was founded on principles arising out of the scholarship of Norris Class. That scholarship helped licensors understand the conceptual and legal foundations of their profession and established the theoretical basis for licensing on which NARA's education efforts continue to build.

NARA's members formulate and enforce laws that set standards and protect vulnerable populations, including children in all forms of out-of-home care. Their responsibilities are intensive and technically demanding. Most are employed by governments in states, provinces and native nations in the United States, Canada, and the European Union.

NARA's goal is to promote regulatory services that support its vision, "consumer protection through prevention," and its focus is the advancement and dissemination of knowledge related to regulatory administration. NARA's key activities focus on effective regulation and on education and professional recognition for licensors.

An annual licensing seminar serves as a forum for networking and knowledge exchange. That conference regularly attracts licensors from jurisdictions throughout the United States and Canada, and a variety of other countries. In addition, NARA provides consultation to licensing agencies in all areas related to regulatory administration, including the drafting of child-care licensing rules. NARA also delivers formal regulatory training based on its *Licensing Curriculum* and other educational materials. Approved NARA consultants and trainers have successfully completed contracts across the United States and in Canada and abroad.

NARA sets standards for excellence in licensing through activities like the publication of a licensor code of ethics and position statements on topics such as the privatization of regulatory functions. NARA also adds to the growing body of knowledge about licensing and other regulatory processes by sponsoring and publishing its own research. To support these initiatives, extend the tradition of inquiry and honor the memory of one of its founders, NARA has established the Norris E. Class Lecture and Research Fund.

As an advocate and voice for child care licensing, NARA cooperates with other organizations, including the National Child Care Information Center, **National Association for the Education of Young Children** (NAEYC), National Child Care Association, Child Welfare League of America, Healthy Child Care America's Back to Sleep Campaign, and AAP/APHA/MCHB/HRSA initiatives related to *Caring for Our Children*. NARA is recognized as a Strategic Partner by *Child Care Information Exchange Magazine*.

NARA's executive director and members of its board of directors respond to direct requests for technical assistance from state licensing agencies and others.

Since January 2005, NARA has been responsible for developing and publishing the annual child-care licensing studies, previously published by The Children's Foundation in partnership with NARA. NARA also disseminates information to support technical assistance in the licensing area through the *NARA Licensing Newsletter*, and maintains a website at www.naralicensing.org.

Licensors play a key role in the provision of early care and education. Out-of-home care must comply with licensing laws enacted by governments to protect the health and safety of young children and establish a foundation for program quality. Through tiered quality initiatives and other measures, licensing systems are increasingly playing an expanded role as mechanisms for supporting providers and raising program quality. In fulfilling its vision, NARA assists licensors as they professionalize their activities and take steps to improve their ability to prevent harm to children and safeguard their future.

Further Readings: Colbert, J. (2002). *Regulating dimensions of quality in early care and education: a review of the research*. Conyers, GA: NARA; Gazan, H. (1997). *Emerging trends in child care regulation*. Conyers, GA: NARA; Koch, P., and N. Scalera (2001). *The case against privatizing human care licensing*. Conyers, GA: NARA; *NARA Licensing Curriculum* (1988; revised edition 2000). Conyers, GA: NARA; Stevens, C. (1995). *NARA code of ethics*. Conyers, GA: NARA.

Judith A. Colbert and Pauline Koch

National Association for the Education of Young Children (NAEYC)

The National Association for the Education of Young Children (NAEYC) is the largest and most influential organization of early childhood educators in the world. NAEYC has approximately 100,000 members and a national network of nearly 350 local, state, and regional affiliates. Since 1926, NAEYC and its members have been leading and consolidating the efforts of individuals and groups working to achieve healthy development and constructive education for all young children.

NAEYC members include teachers and administrators in child care, preschool, **kindergarten**, elementary school, **Head Start** and other programs for young children. NAEYC members are also higher education faculty, trainers, state agency officials, parents, policymakers, and others committed to improving the quality of education for children from birth through eight years of age.

NAEYC leads efforts to raise the standards for early childhood education programs, and works with educators and programs around the country to help them achieve higher standards. The organization provides the following services aimed toward these goals:

- *Early Childhood Program Accreditation*—NAEYC established and operates a national voluntary accreditation system to raise the quality of early childhood education and help families and others identify high-quality programs. To earn NAEYC Accreditation, programs meet professional standards in areas such as staff qualifications, curriculum and child-to-teacher ratios. There are now more than 10,000 NAEYC-accredited programs, serving more than 900,000 young children and families. Families can search for NAEYC-accredited programs in their communities through the NAEYC Web site.

- *Professional Development*—NAEYC provides educators and early childhood professionals with the information and education services they need to help more children get a great start. The NAEYC Annual Conference draws more than 25,000 people from around the world for workshops and seminars on research, policy, and practices in early childhood education.
- *Resources*—NAEYC publishes ***Young Children***, an award-winning journal for early childhood educators, as well as ***Early Childhood Research Quarterly***. The association also produces books, videos, brochures, and other materials to bring the latest strategies and research to teachers, families, and others working to support the development and education of young children. Many NAEYC resources are available through the association's Web site at, www.naeyc.org.

Further Readings: National Association for the Education of Young Children (NAEYC) (2001). *NAEYC at 75: Reflections on the past, challenges for the future*. Washington, DC: NAEYC.

Mark R. Ginsberg

National Association for the Education of Young Children (NAEYC) Academy for Early Childhood Program Accreditation

The **National Association for the Education of Young Children** (NAEYC) administers the nation's oldest and largest voluntary accreditation system for early childhood programs serving young children, the NAEYC Academy for Early Childhood Program Accreditation.

The 1980s were a time of dramatic growth in the field of early childhood education. Women were entering the workforce in significant numbers and the number of single-parent families headed by women was also growing. Both these factors helped to create a demand for full-day, full-year child care. At the same time, the United States Congress was considering the Federal Interagency Day Care Requirements that would have created national standards for child-care programs. President Reagan eventually vetoed this legislation, which ended this possibility. State child-care regulations varied dramatically from state to state which added to the uneven landscape of program quality. In response to this situation, NAEYC decided to establish voluntary national standards for program quality in the context of a process by which programs could achieve that quality.

In 1985, NAEYC launched its early childhood program accreditation system in order to impact the quality of early childhood programs on a national level. NAEYC Accreditation is delivered through the association's NAEYC Academy for Early Childhood Program Accreditation (the NAEYC Academy).

During its first few years, the growth of NAEYC Accreditation was steady and constant. In the early 1990s, however, both private and public support for accreditation grew substantially. States began to offer higher reimbursement rates to accredited programs. Private groups such as the American Business Collaborative provided funds to programs to support their achievement of accreditation. These and other initiatives directly affected the number of programs pursuing accreditation in general, and NAEYC Accreditation in particular.

As a result, in the NAEYC Academy's first two decades, demand for accreditation grew beyond expectations and the system was almost outstripped by the demands placed upon it. In 1999, the NAEYC Governing Board realized that not only had its accreditation system outgrown its original structure, but that early childhood education and the accreditation system itself needed to be reexamined and positioned for the next twenty years, so the future impact could be as great as that of the first twenty years.

The Board established the National Commission on Accreditation Reinvention to conduct a comprehensive review of its accreditation system. The Commission was asked to recommend changes that would prepare the association's accreditation for the future and continue to offer early childhood programs a vehicle for improvements in program quality.

At the conclusion of its two-year appointment, the Reinvention Commission made ten recommendations to NAEYC's Governing Board. The intent of the recommendations was to strengthen and restore the reliability, accountability, and credibility of NAEYC's accreditation system by redesigning it:

- To establish NAEYC Accreditation as a standard-bearer for program excellence.
- To improve program accountability for families and others.
- To focus NAEYC's accreditation system on programs for children from birth through kindergarten.

Following approval by the NAEYC Governing Board of the reinvention commission's recommendations, it appointed a Commission on NAEYC Early Childhood Program Standards and Accreditation Criteria. This second Commission's recommendations on early childhood program standards and accreditation performance criteria were approved by the NAEYC Governing Board in spring 2005.

The Governing Board also appointed a Council for NAEYC Accreditation, to work with the NAEYC Academy on policy changes to support the delivery of the new accreditation system. The NAEYC Council is accountable to the NAEYC Governing Board and also has as part of its responsibility to monitor the new system's performance.

NAEYC Academy is in the midst of implementing the reinvented accreditation system. There are over 10,000 accredited programs that serve over 800,000 children. Many of the reinvention commission's recommendations have now been established as NAEYC Academy policies or procedures. NAEYC's early childhood program accreditation system was completely reinvented and fully operational in the fall of 2006.

Kim Means

National Association of Child Care Resource and Referral Agencies (NACCRRA)

The National Association of Child Care Resource and Referral Agencies (NACCRRA) was formed in 1984. NACCRRA's earliest mission statements described the organization's two main goals: to promote the growth and development of quality child-care resource and referral (CCR&R) services, and to exercise national policy leadership to build a diverse, quality child-care system with parental choice and equal access for all families. NACCRRA continues to balance its dual purposes to serve its membership and to highlight the child-care needs of the nation's children and families.

Child-care resource and referral agencies provide a range of services to parents, child-care providers, and their communities. CCR&R has its roots in the following:

- Federal legislation (Community Coordinated Child Care in 1967–1969, and the Dependent Care Grant in 1984)
- National support efforts (The Ford Foundation (1978); Wheelock College Summer Seminars (1983); and Work/Family Directions & IBM (1984)
- Telephone messages from parents and communities to early childhood programs throughout the nation

These efforts were attempts to respond to questions about quality child care, for example, Where is it? Who is providing it? How do I pay for it?

NACCRRA was created by a show of hands at a meeting during the 1984 Annual Conference of the **National Association for the Education of Young Children** (NAEYC). A 1997 history of NACCRRA describes the progress of the new organization, which was incorporated in 1987. Under its energetic board of directors, the group's national office was established in Washington, DC, and Yasmina Vinci was hired as first executive director in 1993, with Linda K. Smith becoming the second executive director in 2003.

Almost two decades after its founding, NACCRRA continues to focus on the needs of the nation's children and families through membership services, family support information, and community development by providing strategic planning, research and policy activities, and innovative partnership practices.

NACCRRA's strategic planning activities created the following:

- A regional structure that captures geographical differences and similarities and provides the basis for Regional Institutes.
- Membership categories for agencies and individuals and multiple benefits.
- An Annual Policy Symposium, which started in 1989 and includes The Day on the Hill, when NACCRRA members meet with their state congressional delegations.
- NACCRRA Counts!, which started in 1994 and creates statistical reports.
- NACCRRA Live!, which started in 1994 and sets up teleconference calls among members.
- Quality Assurance, an accreditation process for CCR&R agencies that started in 2002.

NACCRRA's research and policy advocacy events helped create the following:

- The **ABC Bill**, 1988
- The first of annual NACCRRA Policy Agendas and a U.S. Senate Hearing on Quality Child Care, 1994
- The National Doll Campaign, 1995

NACCRRA'a partnerships among colleagues include the following:

- The Family to Family Project, which became Child Care Aware in 1990 (see www.childcareaware.org)
- April 19th Group—organizations speaking with one voice on child care, 1993; continuing with Child Care NOW Coalition, 2005
- Healthy Child Care America, 1994
- NACCRRAWare, Web-based child care searches, 2001
- Better Baby Care, 2001

- NRex, Web-based NACCRRA Resource Exchange, 2001
- Parent Central, 2004
- U.S. Department of Defense Operation Child Care, 2004

The selected NACCRRA publications listed below are available online at http://www.naccrra.org.

Further Readings: *The Daily Parent*. (A bimonthly newsletter on topics of interest to parents of children in child care distributed to NACCRRA member agencies who in turn make it available to the parents in their service area); *NACCRRA Link* (2005). Quarterly membership publication; National Association of Child Care Resource and Referral Agencies (1997). *NACCRRA at ten: A Commemorative history of NACCRRA*. Washington, DC: NACCRRA; National Association of Child Care Resource and Referral Agencies (2005). *Nurturing children after national disasters: A booklet for child care providers*. Washington, DC: NACCRRA; *Technical Assistance Papers (TAP)*. Occasional papers on significant early care and education topics.

Edna Ranck

National Association of Early Childhood Teacher Educators (NAECTE)

The Association of Early Childhood Teacher Educators was founded in 1977 at a meeting led by Michael Davis at the annual **National Association for the Education of Young Children** (NAEYC) conference in Chicago. The fifteen original founders were: Helen Canady, Beth Casey, Michael Davis, Stephanie Feeney, Doris Fromberg, Verna Hildebrand, Marlis Mann, Marjorie Ramsey, Clare Rodney, Judith Schickedanz, Robert Smith, Bernard Spodek, Jean Sword, Phil Wishon, and Mary Elizabeth York. In 1980, "National" was added to the name. Members are primarily domestic and international early childhood teacher educators at four- and five-year colleges and universities and those who subscribe to the purposes of the organization. In 1986, student memberships were recognized.

NAECTE was formed to promote the professional growth of its membership, advocate for improvements in early Childhood **teacher education**, facilitate the interchange of information and ideas about research and practice among its members and other persons concerned with the education of young children, and provide a communication network on early childhood teacher education issues. Through its journal, conference program, resolutions, position papers, and other publications, NAECTE helps generate an ongoing knowledge base of the field of early childhood teacher education. In addition, NAECTE collaborates with other professional associations, such as NAEYC, **American Associate Degree Early Childhood Educators** (ACCESS), and ATE on issues of early childhood teacher preparation, training, credentialing, and the establishment of standards for basic and advanced teacher education programs. NAECTE has developed position statements and cosponsored position papers on issues of early childhood teacher preparation, certification standards, and ethics.

A sixteen-member governing board composed of elected officers and representatives of ten regions of the United States conduct the business of the association. In 1983, the first state affiliate was formed in Alabama, followed since then by twenty-two other state affiliates. Regional and affiliate meetings are held annually and semiannually. NAECTE national conferences are held twice a year, usually near the date and location of the annual fall NAEYC conference and the summer professional development institute. The first stand-alone conference was held in June 2004, in Baltimore, Maryland. NAECTE cosponsors with publishers three annual awards: Outstanding Early Childhood Teacher Educator, Outstanding Early Childhood Practitioner, and Outstanding Dissertation.

The association's newsletter, the *Bulletin*, evolved into a full-fledged internationally recognized, quarterly, refereed journal in 1989. ***The Journal of Early Childhood Teacher Education (JECTE)*** publishes original manuscripts, book reviews, research reports, position papers, letters to the editor, information on association activities, and essays on current issues and practices in early childhood teacher education. In 1996, the NAECTE Web site was established (naecte.org) and offers membership information and news about the activities of the organization. In 1998, the NAECTE Foundation (NAECTEF) became incorporated as a tax exempt 501 (c) (3) organization with three primary goals: advocate for improving early childhood teacher education; support research on early childhood teacher education; and provide scholarships to potential early childhood teacher educators. The NAECTE archive materials are located in the Rare Books Department at Indiana State University, Terre Haute, Indiana. *See also* Race and Ethnicity in Early Childhood Education; Teacher Certification/Licensure.

Kathryn Castle

National Black Child Development Institute (NBCDI)

Founded in 1970, the National Black Child Development Institute (NBCDI) has remained steadfast in its mission—"To improve and protect the quality of life for children of color and their families by giving every child a chance." With a focus on early childhood education, child welfare, elementary and secondary education, and health, the Institute accomplishes this mission by serving as a vital information resource to all individuals who work directly with children and by providing direct services at the local level through its nationwide affiliate network.

Over the years this mission to protect and improve the quality of life for children through the age of 14 has benefited millions of children through accomplishments such as the following:

- Conducting a landmark study on children in foster care which resulted in subsequent progressive national policies;
- Advocating successfully for progressive adoption policies and subsidies that permitted older and single parents to adopt;
- Working successfully to create public policy and influence legislation that directly affects the lives of African American children by testifying before Congress on every significant child-care bill from the Comprehensive Child Development Act of 1970, the Personal Responsibility and Work Opportunity Reconciliation Act of 1996, the School Construction Act of 1999 to the Consequences for Juvenile Offenders Act of 1999 and orchestrating a special hearing on parenting in 2000;

- Working to gain public support to provide access to universal early care and education which has become a priority for governors in more than half of the states;
- Promoting publicly supported quality child-care programs for mothers who were entering the workforce in increased numbers, resulting in the enactment and special allocation of funds by a substantial number of states for child care;
- Implementing and expanding a community-based nationwide intervention/prevention program entitled Entering the College Zone from five to twenty five cities to get more disadvantaged middle-school students on the college track;
- Providing leadership to agencies like the National Institutes of Health (NIH) to decrease health disparities; and
- Building and nurturing partnerships with organizations ranging from the National Education Association (NEA), the National Council of La Raza (NCLR), **National Association for the Education of Young Children** (NAEYC), the National Association for the Advancement of Colored People (NAACP) and a number of corporations like United Parcel Service (UPS), Proctor and Gamble (P&G), State Farm Insurance Companies, and government agencies like the National Institutes of Health (NIH).

Through the years, NBCDI has made tremendous strides to improve the lives of children by raising its profile in the market place to become the leading voice for children of color through the following core program areas:

- The Early Years and Parenting—*Love to Read Early Literacy Project*, *The Parent Empowerment Program*, a parenting education curriculum; *African American Parents Project*, a partnership with the National Institutes of Health that published the *Helping Children Cope with Crisis Guide*; and *SPARK: Supporting Partnerships to Assure Ready Kids*
- The Middle Years—*Entering the College Zone* to increase the number of disadvantaged students who enter college
- Community Mobilization—*The National Affiliate Network* with groups in over thirty cities

Further, NBCDI's Annual Conference is one of the leading professional development gatherings for those working to improve the lives of children, youth, and their families. Every year thousands of educators and professionals from around the country in early care and education; elementary and secondary education and administration; child welfare and youth development; research; and local, state, and federal policy convene to gain knowledge and acquire skills needed to ensure a quality future for all children and youth. For thirty-five years, Evelyn K. Moore has served as President of NBCDI.

Web Site: National Black Child Development Institute, www.nbcdi.org.

Stacey D. Cunningham

National Center for Children in Poverty (NCCP)

The National Center for Children in Poverty (NCCP) is the nation's leading public policy center dedicated to promoting the economic security, health, and well-being of low-income families and children in the United States. Founded in 1989 as a division of the Mailman School of Public Health at Columbia University, NCCP is a nonpartisan, public interest research organization. Using research to inform policy and practice, NCCP seeks to advance family-oriented solutions and the strategic use of public resources at the state and national levels to ensure that the next generation of families will be economically secure, healthy, and nurturing, and have children who thrive.

NCCP put the issue of young children in poverty on the nation's conscience with the publication in 1990 of *Five Million Children—A Statistics Profile of Our Poorest Young Citizens*. In the ensuing decade, NCCP demonstrated what a difference a state makes to the economic and emotional well-being of young children through its biennial publication: *Map and Track: State Initiatives for Young Children and Families*. NCCP's 1999 book: *Lives on the Line: American Families and the Struggle to Make Ends Meet*, shattered stereotypes by describing the every day struggles of ten individual families.

As NCCP entered its second decade, the focus has expanded to include the plight of low-income families living on the edge, often a paycheck away from poverty, and the most vulnerable in society: infants, toddlers, and their families facing multiple risks for negative child development, challenging behaviors, and lack of success in school. NCCP believes that public policies can make a difference. Just as innovative policies dramatically reduced poverty among the elderly, so too can they improve the future of our nation's children and families.

NCCP works to address the following challenges, using knowledge gained from research:

- Make work pay
- Provide nurturing environments for preschoolers while their parents work
- Secure adequate health care for our nation's families
- Lift up the most vulnerable among us

NCCP addresses the specific needs of policymakers, practitioners and advocates, and the media. For policymakers, NCCP provides the right information to make good decisions, as they seek solutions to promote the health and successful development of children. For practitioners and advocates, NCCP highlights emerging challenges and offers insights about how to turn research into practice. For the media, NCCP works to uncover facts, identify trends, and analyze policy developments. This effort helps the media report on the realities faced by low-income children and families in the United States and make the links between poverty and a wide range of social issues, such as early childhood development, **immigration**, and mental health.

NCCP's Web site, www.nccp.org, provides the following tools, topics, and resources to put research to work for children and families.

- *Fact sheets* provide up-to-date state, regional, and national demographic information as well as rapid analyses of emerging issues.
- *Issue briefs* synthesize research, policy analysis, and on-the-ground knowledge in ways that help move state and local agendas. Topics include family economic security, early care and learning, health and mental health, and early childhood development.
- *State date tools* include the *Family Resource Simulator* to calculate family resources and expenses as earnings increase, taking public benefits into account; *State Profiles* for information on policy choices, demographics, and economic condition; and *Data Wizards* that allow users to build custom tables and compare states.

- Other online resources include NCCP's hosting of Early Care and Education *Research Connections*, which provides policymakers and researchers with easily accessible information about research, datasets, and instruments, and offers user-friendly syntheses and fact sheets to improve early care and education.

Web Site: National Center for Children in Poverty, www.nccp.org.

Carole J. Oshinsky

National Coalition for Campus Children's Centers (NCCCC)

The National Coalition for Campus Children's Centers (NCCCC) is an organization that advocates for and works collaboratively with university-based child-care centers and laboratory schools. The history of the NCCCC is closely linked to the history of university laboratory schools as well as the changing nature of women's roles in the workforce. In the first half of the twentieth century, early childhood programs at institutions of higher learning primarily took the form of laboratory schools. Typically, they were half-day preschool programs associated with teacher education or related academic programs. During the 1960s, two significant changes in the climate of higher education in our country affected campus children's programs. The community college system expanded, and there was a large increase in the number of adult students. Many of these were women and single parents who needed care for their children when they attended classes, and the activist climate of the era encouraged these students to demand **child care** on campus.

In the late 1960s, Rae Burrell was a student-parent at the University of California at Riverside who chaired a parent cooperative there. She saw the need for an organization to support the campus child-care movement, and applied for and received a grant from the Robert F. Kennedy Foundation in 1970. As a result, a not-for-profit organization called the Robert F. Kennedy Council for Campus Child Care was initiated. The primary goal of this organization was to promote quality child care on college and university campuses. Within a short period, a group of child-care professionals began to meet informally at conferences. As more people became involved, the focus shifted to include more professional issues, and Ms. Burrell moved to Washington, DC and coordinated several conferences there. Subsequently, annual conferences were held on college campuses and issues related to program administration and the **curriculum** also began to be included in conference agendas.

By the end of the 1970s grant money from the Kennedy Foundation was no longer available and the name of the organization was changed to the National Council for Campus Child Care. The advisory group became increasingly eager to assume more control, and when Ms. Burrell resisted, they broke away and, under the leadership of Harriet Alger at Cleveland State, a new organization began to take shape called the National Coalition for Campus Child Care (NCCCC). By 1981, NCCCC was asserting itself professionally, at **National Association for the Education of Young Children** (NAEYC), and with a growing membership and annual conference. In 1983, NCCCC was incorporated as a dues paying organization and a permanent office was established at the University of Wisconsin-Milwaukee.

By the late 1980's, as the focus shifted again from advocacy to education, NCCCC was recognized as a leader in the campus child-care movement and received a contract to study CCNY's sixteen campus child-care centers and another to assist the Milwaukee Area Technical Colleges. NCCCC also began to publish fact sheets, conference proceedings and special topics, and a leadership series to support the management needs of its membership and campus care directors.

In the 1990s, there continued to be a national focus on women's issues, an increase in nontraditional students on campuses, and continued concern about the quality, affordability, and availability of child care. Child care on campus took many diverse forms and children now ranged from infants through school age. Centers were administered by academic departments, human resources, student services, or other entities. In order to address the complexity of issues emerging, the Board engaged in a strategic management process to identify a plan of action. In 1996, the name was again changed to the National Coalition for Campus Children's Centers (still NCCCC) to better reflect the breadth of models. A home page was developed, a discussion listserv (CAMPUSCARE-L) begun, and a quarterly newsletter initiated. In 1997, 501(c) 3 status was attained. Todd Boressoff, Advocacy Committee Chair, coordinated legislative visits during the 1997 annual conference in Washington, DC; and as a result of his leadership, S. 1151, the campus based child-care bill, was introduced to the Senate, cosponsored by Christopher Dodd, Olympia Snowe and Edward Kennedy. This has led to significant federal funding for programs serving children of college students.

Further Readings: Alger, Harriet (1995). The American family: Taking a new look at myths and realities. Cedar Falls, IA: National Coalition for Campus Child Care. Available online at http://www.campuschildren.org/pubs/amerifam/amfam1.html; Kalinowski, Michael (2000). Child care. In National Association of College and University Business Officers. *College & University Business Administration*. Washington, DC: pp. 20–55; National Coalition for Campus Children's Centers, http://www.campuschildren.org/pubs.html#PubText; Thomas, Jane (2000). Child care and laboratory schools on campus: The national picture. Cedar Falls, IA: National Coalition for Campus Child Care. Available online at http://www.campuschildren.org/pubs.html#PubText.

Michael Kalinowski and Jane Thomas

National Committee on Nursery Schools (1925–1931)

Teachers College Professor Patty Smith **Hill** organized the National Committee on Nursery Schools out of her conviction that nursery schools needed to remain professionally led and grounded in research. Nursery schools grew in number from 3 to 262 between 1920 and 1930. Noting this increase, Hill organized three meetings in 1925. In May, she invited twenty-five individuals to the first meeting to discuss whether to form a new association for nursery schools. Attendees included Abigail **Eliot**, Edna Noble **White**, Helen Thompson Woolley, and Grace Caldwell. At this gathering, Hill appointed Lois Meek (Stolz) chair of the committee for subsequent meetings. At a later meeting, members decided to hold a public National Committee on Nursery Schools Conference in Washington, DC, in February 1926. The purpose of nursery schools and their role within public education were discussed at the conference as well as ways in which nursery schools could contribute to parent education, health, and family welfare.

A second conference was held in New York City on April 22–23, 1927, and had at least 295 in attendance from multidisciplinary backgrounds (Hewes, 2001, p. 36). A third conference convened in Chicago in 1929 where members decided to press forward to form the National Association for Nursery Education (NANE now **NAEYC**). Lois Meek (Stolz) supported the name, claiming "we did not know whether there would always be nursery *schools*, but we knew there would always be *education* for preschool children" (Stolz, 1979). Utilizing her office at the American Association of University Women (AAUW), Lois Meek (Stolz) continued as Committee Chair of the National Committee for Nursery Education until 1931. Rose Alschuler was secretary-treasurer of the Committee and donated $500 to maintain Committee operations (Beatty, 1995, p. 178). The Committee published "Minimum Essentials for Nursery Education" in 1929 and later developed a constitution and bylaws for NANE.

Further Readings: Beatty, Barbara (1995). *Preschool education in America: The culture of young children from the colonial era to the present*. New Haven, CT: Yale University Press; Hewes, Dorothy (2001). NAEYC's First Half Century: 1926–1976. In *NAEYC at 75, 1926–2001. Reflections on the past, challenges for the Future*. Washington, DC: NAEYC, pp. 35–52; Lascarides, V. Celia and Blythe Hinitz (2000). *History of early childhood education*. New York: Falmer Press; Stolz, Lois Hayden Meek Papers (1979). *An American Child Development Pioneer: Lois Hayden Meek Stolz*, interview conducted by Ruby Takanishi, Bethesda, MD: National Institutes of Health, National Library of Medicine, History of Medicine Division, pp. 72–73.

Charlotte Anderson

National Council for Accreditation of Teacher Education (NCATE)

The National Council for Accreditation of Teacher Education (NCATE) is a voluntary professional accrediting agency that has established rigorous standards for high quality educator preparation. NCATE implements a performance-based **accreditation** system in which colleges of education provide evidence that their candidates know the subject matter they plan to teach and are able to teach it effectively so that students learn. As a part of accreditation expectations, institutions must develop an assessment system that collects and analyzes data on applicant qualifications and on candidate and graduate performance, and they use that information to improve their programs.

Teachers prepared at NCATE institutions are ready to help all students learn. These teachers know the subject matter, demonstrate knowledge of effective teaching strategies, reflect on their practice and adapt their instruction, can teach students from different backgrounds, have been supervised by master teachers, and can integrate technology into instruction.

Seven hundred of the nation's colleges of education have chosen to seek the agency's approval. States (forty-eight out of fifty) formally accept NCATE accreditation, and the U.S. Department of Education has determined that NCATE meets Congressionally mandated criteria for accreditation agencies. Two-thirds of the nation's new teacher graduates are from NCATE accredited institutions.

NCATE's partnership with the states has integrated state and national professional standards for teacher preparation. The states see NCATE as a resource in standards development and implementation. A majority of states have adopted or adapted NCATE's unit (college of education) standards as their state standards for teacher preparation. NCATE's fifty state partners have adopted NCATE's national professional content standards (math, science, early childhood education, etc.) or have aligned their state content standards with NCATE's standards.

The National Association of Early Childhood Education is one of 33 national professional/policymaker member organizations that support NCATE. NCATE recognizes **National Association for the Education of Young Children** (NAEYC) standards for early childhood education and adopts them for use in the professional accreditation process. Teacher preparation institutions that have early childhood education programs use NAEYC standards as a core for the design and delivery of their programs. Members of NAEYC serve as reviewers for NCATE. These individuals review and rate program reports from teacher preparation institutions with early childhood education programs in states that have adopted the NCATE program standards. (States that have not adopted the NCATE program standards use standards closely aligned with the profession's program standards). The reviewers' decisions on the quality of the early childhood education programs at an institution undergoing NCATE accreditation feed into NCATE's Standard 1 on whether candidates have the knowledge, skills, and dispositions to help all children learn.

Web Site: National Council for Accreditation of Teacher Education, www.ncate.org.

Arthur E. Wise

National Education Goals Panel (NEGP)

In 1989, President George H.W. Bush and the Nation's Governors announced six national education goals and a National Education Goals Panel (NEGP) composed of policy leaders was established to monitor the nation's progress in meeting the goals. Fostered by concern that the nation's educational progress was not meeting international standards and by a movement toward greater accountability, the goals were designed to uplift American education and to give focus to areas of needed progress. Indeed, the goals were widely publicized and served as the foundation for President Bill Clinton's and Secretary of Education Richard Riley's Goals 2000 legislation.

The first of these goals—*"By the year 2000, all children in America will start school ready to learn"* (Department of Education, 1995)—visibily moved school **readiness** and early childhood education onto the national agenda. Although **Head Start** and other early childhood programs had been in place for decades, with the advent of the goals a new national recognition of the importance of children's early experiences to their later school success was legitimated. For the first time, national goals firmly linked early childhood to kindergarten through grade twelve education. Adding further weight and visibility to the readiness work, structural mechanisms like the Goal 1 Resource and Technical Planning Groups were formed to carry out the NEGP's charges surrounding readiness. The Goal 1 Resource and Technical Planning Groups made four primary contributions to the school readiness debate: (1) advancing readiness as a condition of individuals and institutions; (2) focusing on the conditions needed for children to be ready for school; (3) discerning the dimensions that constitute school readiness; and (4) highlighting the critical role of schools in school readiness.

Readiness as a Condition of Individuals and Institutions

Irrespective of whether the renewed focus was on readiness for school or readiness to learn, historically the onus for readiness was placed primarily on the child. To counter this view, the NEGP Goal 1 Resource and Technical Planning Groups adopted a broadened conceptualization of readiness, in which readiness is regarded as a condition of institutions and individuals. This conceptualization interpreted readiness as the match between the readiness of the child and the readiness of the environments that serve young children. This more contemporary understanding of readiness acknowledged that the sources of readiness are not only the child's emotional, cognitive, linguistic, and social abilities, but also the contexts in which children live and interact with adults, teachers, and other community members. To impact a child's school readiness, therefore, multiple contexts including families, schools, neighborhoods, and early childhood settings must be involved.

Readiness Conditions

Given this orientation, it is not surprising that a second contribution of the Goal 1 Resource and Technical Planning Groups was to focus on the array of contextual conditions necessary for children to be ready for school. Aided by the goals themselves, the Goal 1 Resource and Technical Planning Groups sought to build on the following three objectives that accompanied the goals.

(1) All children will have access to high-quality and developmentally appropriate preschool programs that help prepare children for school;
(2) Every parent in the United States will be a child's first teacher and devote time each day to helping each parent's preschool children learn, and parents will have access to the training and support parents need; and
(3) Children will receive the **nutrition**, physical activity experiences, and health care needed to arrive at school with healthy minds and bodies, and to maintain the mental alertness necessary to be prepared to learn, and the number of low-birth-weight babies will be significantly reduced through enhanced prenatal health systems.

Using these objectives, data were collected to measure the nation's progress in creating opportunities for young children to develop and thrive, prior to school entry. This emphasis shifted the focus to include inputs as well as child outcomes as measures of readiness.

The Dimensions of School Readiness

A third contribution of the work of the Goal 1 Resource and Technical Planning Groups was to clearly specify the elements or dimensions of school readiness. The Goal 1 Technical Planning Group Report on Reconceptualizing Children's Early Learning and Development, after reviewing and synthesizing decades of research, offered a conceptualization that recognized the wide range of abilities and experiences upon which early learning and development rests. Their work, now widely accepted and used, suggests that early development and learning embraces five dimensions: (1) physical well-being and motor development, (2) social and emotional development, (3) approaches toward learning, (4) language development, and (5) cognition and general knowledge (National Education Goals Panel, 1991). Conceptualized by an expert panel for use in policymaking, this work offered a solid definition of school readiness and its underlying dimensions.

School's Role in Readiness

Given the importance of focusing on learning contexts and the institutions that impact early learning, the Goal 1 Resource and Technical Planning Group also sought to define precisely what was meant by a "ready school." This emphasis was a necessary response to the increasingly common call for children to be ready for schools and schools to be ready for children. To clarify this call for ready schools, the NEGP convened a Ready Schools Resource Group who, drawing on previous work defining successful practices for elementary schools, identified keys to ready schools (Shore, 1998). Properties of ready schools include: smoothing the transition from home to school; striving for continuity between early care and education programs and elementary schools; helping children make sense of their worlds; fostering a full commitment to the success of every child and teacher; using approaches that have been proven to raise achievement along with a focus on results; and underscoring the fact that schools are part of communities.

Further Readings: Kagan, S. L. (1992). Readiness, past, present, and future: Shaping the agenda. *Young Children* 48(1), 48–53; Lewit, E. M., and L. S. Baker (1995). School readiness. *The Future of Children* 5(2), 128–139; National Education Goals Panel (1991). *Goal 1 Technical Planning Group Report on School Readiness*. Washington, DC: NEGP, pp. 10–11; Shore, R. (1998). *Ready schools*. Washington, DC: National Education Goals Panel; U.S. Department of Education (1991). *America 2000: An education strategy*. Washington, DC: U.S. Department of Education; U.S. Department of Education (1995). *Goals 2000: A progress report* Washington, DC: U.S. Department of Education.

Sharon Lynn Kagan

National Even Start Association (NESA)

The National Even Start Association (NESA) was formed in 1997 to provide a forum to meet the unique needs of Even Start Family Literacy providers. NESA is a membership organization that includes program administrators, professional and paraprofessional staff, and other interested parties who support the purposes of Even Start Family Literacy.

The mission of NESA is to provide a national voice and vision for Even Start Family Literacy programs. NESA works to accomplish its mission focused on the following three broad goals:

1 Ensure the continuity and quality of NESA leadership.
2 Generate awareness and support for Even Start Family Literacy Programs.
3 Provide professional services that support high-quality literacy instruction in Even Start Family Literacy programs.

NESA addresses its goals through a variety of activities. NESA provides assistance to its members for the development of State Chapters and on-going support for their operation. NESA has a variety of professional development activities. NESA conducts an Annual Conference that focuses on each component of family literacy—early childhood education, parenting education, and interactive literacy and adult education. NESA Academies annually bring current research in the field of family literacy to a single focus area in a research-to-practice format. NESA provides intensive training through *Keys to Quality*, a series of three-day workshops focusing on explicit content areas and designed to be presented within the specific context of Even Start Family Literacy. NESA publishes a peer-reviewed journal, the *Family Literacy Forum*, twice a year. The *Forum* provides articles that are accessible to practitioners in the field of family literacy and that connect practice with research. The research presented not only addresses issues that are relevant to instruction and program design, but also raises questions for further consideration.

Sue Henry

National Head Start Association (NHSA)

The National Head Start Association (NHSA) is a private, not-for-profit membership organization dedicated exclusively to meeting the needs of Head Start children and their families. The association represents more than 1 million children, 200,000 staff, and 2,700 Head Start programs in the United States.

Project **Head Start** began as a part of America's historic War on Poverty in 1965. Within the first ten years, supporters of Head Start had formed four affiliate organizations that represented the needs of Head Start directors, parents, staff, and friends. Directors were the first to unite (1973); they invited parents to develop a parents' association (1974); and parents, in turn, urged staff to band together (1975). Head Start friends soon followed. Each group had a different perspective but a common mission. On June 7, 1990, the four affiliates united to speak to Congress with one powerful voice. Collectively, the affiliates became The National Head Start Association.

NHSA's mission is far reaching. The association provides support for the entire Head Start community by advocating for policies that strengthen services to Head Start children and their families; by providing extensive training and professional development to Head Start staff; and by developing and disseminating research, information, and resources that enrich Head Start program delivery.

From planning massive training conferences to conducting research and publishing a vast array of publications, including the award-winning *Children and Families* magazine and the peer-reviewed research journal, *Dialog*, NHSA is educating early childhood professionals. NHSA led the way with distance training through its satellite television network, HeadsUp!, and the NHSA Academy offers college credit through self-study and off-site courses.

NHSA's 130,000 active members represent Head Start agencies; state and regional associations; commercial and nonprofit organizations; and individual parents, staff, and friends. NHSA has successfully defended the First Amendment rights of Head Start parents and staff, launched major voter registration campaigns, and proved through scientific research that Head Start increases the well-being and likelihood of success for the nation's underprivileged children and their families.

Further Readings: *Children and Families: the Magazine of the National Head Start Association* is published quarterly by the National Head Start Association. 1651 Prince Street, Alexandria, VA 22314. ISSN-7578; *NHSA Dialog* is a peer-reviewed research journal published annually by the National Head Start Association. 1651 Prince Street, Alexandria, VA 22314. ISSN 1089-2583.

Elizabeth Kane

National Institute for Early Childhood Professional Development

Early in its history, the **National Association for the Education of Young Children** (NAEYC) recognized the need for a coordinated, cost-effective training system for early childhood educators and administrators. In 1992, with the help of a grant from the Carnegie Corporation of New York, NAEYC launched its first National Institute for Early Childhood Professional Development. Since its inception, the National Institute has become an annual event that has grown from a gathering of several hundred people to more than 1600 participants. Those attending the Institute include teacher educators, program directors and administrators, policymakers, principals, researchers, curriculum and instructional coordinators, teacher mentors and coaches, advocates, early childhood specialists in local and state departments of education, and educational consultants and trainers.

The underlying goal of the National Institute is to improve early childhood services by enhancing the quality of professional preparation and training provided for individuals who care for and educate young children from birth through eight years of age. NAEYC's National Institute is designed to deepen understanding of the expanding early childhood knowledge base, help to develop skills that improve professional preparation and practice, and sharpen the ability to use effective, active learning approaches for adults. Each year, NAEYC's National Institute focuses on a new theme that represents current trends and relevant topics within the profession. Past themes have included, "The Early Childhood Profession Coming Together," "Nurturing Leaders through Professional Development," "Transforming Ideas into Action," "Building Professional Partnerships," "Exploring Difference-Building Strengths Together," and "Learning from Assessment."

The event is composed of sessions, networking opportunities, cluster groups, and other settings, all of which are planned to include diverse topics and interests.

During the Institute, attendees can choose from over one hundred sessions and workshops presented by established leaders within the field. Additionally, interactive learning opportunities allow participants to reflect on the day's sessions, raise issues, and share their own reactions with colleagues. They also provide the opportunity to network and exchange ideas with individuals who are showcasing effective approaches to professional development, high-quality early childhood programs, and new research.

NAEYC's National Institute for Early Childhood Professional Development provides a unique setting in which one can learn and share with colleagues from across the country and around the world. This environment fosters teamwork, nurtures each individual's professional development, and encourages future leadership within the field. The event continues to grow and improve, each year challenging the original goals and the changing and unique needs of the profession. For more information on NAEYC and the National Institute, see www.naeyc.org.

Marilou Hyson and Kamilah Martin

Naumburg, Margaret (1890–1983)

Margaret Naumburg, a prominent figure in the "new schools" movement in the United States for six decades, was the founder of Walden School. The curriculum of this psychoanalytically based New York City educational program emphasized the creative arts and the social sciences, while fostering the development of mathematics and science skills through innovative developmentally appropriate learning experiences. In her middle years, Naumburg utilized insights gained from her study of psychology, her work in psychiatric hospitals, and her school curricular and administrative experiences as the bases of the art therapy and art education courses she developed and taught at New York University, and later at the New School for Social Research.

Naumburg received her baccalaureate degree from Barnard College, where she studied with John **Dewey**, beginning a lifelong educational dialogue. She received a diploma from Dr. Maria **Montessori**'s first training course for English-speaking teachers, spent a summer exploring the Organic School with Marietta Johnson, and did postgraduate work at Columbia University. She studied Dalcroze Eurhythmics, F. Matthias Alexander's Physical Co-ordination, Alys Bentley's Correlated Movements and Music, and Dr. Yorke Trotter's Rhythmic Method of Teaching Music and incorporated aspects of these methods into the school curriculum.

Lillian Wald of the Henry Street Settlement provided the setting for Naumburg's first Montessori class. In October 1914, when Naumburg decided that a more eclectic curriculum would respond better to children's needs, she and a friend opened the nursery school class that became The Children's School. Naumburg and her colleagues, including Margaret Pollitzer, Elizabeth Goldsmith, Alvie Nitscheke, Cornelia Goldsmith, and Hannah Falk developed, assessed, analyzed and honed the school's philosophy and curriculum. Walden School, renamed in honor of the democratic tradition of the New England Transcendentalists, was built on psychoanalytic principles; attention to the balanced development of children's physical, emotional and intellectual powers; and a curriculum that evolved from the needs of the children and promoted learning by personal experience. The students benefited from courses taught by such well-known figures as Ernst Bloch (music), A. A. Goldenweiser (anthropology), and Lewis Mumford (English).

The visual arts program, directed by Naumburg's sister Florence Cane, drew praise from educators, parents, and writers. In addition to enhancing the environment with two- and three-dimensional art works, the children were intimately involved in decorating their school walls and furnishings. Older children painted walls, doors, and room dividers for their younger schoolmates as well as themselves. Some of the students' artwork was displayed in New York City art galleries.

Naumburg was a prolific writer. Her early works include articles about **Maria Montessori**, the Gary, Indiana schools, Eurhythmics, and **progressive education**. Later works on education describe the founding and development of Walden School, its philosophy, curriculum and intellectual roots, and the physical and affective environment it provided. Naumburg also wrote several of the earliest art therapy texts in the United States.

Margaret Naumburg's life and work demonstrated a consistency of purpose and philosophy. She utilized her knowledge of and talents in the creative arts, psychology and psychoanalysis, and writing, to enhance the lives of children. She did this through her work with schizophrenic and psychoneurotic children and young people in art therapy. She left a lasting legacy to the field of early childhood education by founding and directing Walden School, and creating a faculty and staff of individuals who carried its progressive, creative ideas throughout the country and the world, into history and into action.

Further Readings: Beck, Robert H. (1958–1959). Progressive education and American progressivism: Margaret Naumburg. *Teachers College Record* LX, 202–203; Hinitz, Blythe Farb (2004). Margaret Naumburg. In Susan Ware, ed., and Stacy Braukman, asst. ed., *Notable American women: A biographical dictionary: Completing the twentieth century*. Cambridge, MA: Harvard University Press, pp. 462–464; Hinitz, Blythe Farb (2002). Margaret Naumburg and Walden School. In Alan R. Sadovnik and Susan Semel, eds., *Founding mothers and others: Women educational leaders during the progressive era*. New York: Palgrave, pp. 37–59; Hutchins, Amey A. (December 2000). Biography. In *Register to the Margaret Naumburg Papers*, Special Collections, Van Pelt-Dietrich Library. Philadelphia, PA: University of Pennsylvania; Lascarides, V. Celia, and Blythe Farb Hinitz (2000). *A history of early childhood education*. New York: Routledge/Falmer Publishing; Naumburg, Margaret (1928). Naumburg, A Challenge to John Dewey. *The Survey Graphic* 60(September 15), 598–600; Naumburg, Margaret. (1928). *The child and the world: Dialogues in modern education*. New York: Harcourt, Brace and Company; Naumburg, Margaret (June 25, 1930). The Crux of Progressive Education. TMs pp. 1–6. Naumburg Papers, Box 15 Folder 835 [published in *The New Republic* 63,145]; Naumburg, Margaret (1913). Maria Montessori: Friend of children. *The Outlook* 105(December 13), 796–799; Naumburg, Margaret. The Walden School. In Guy Montrose Whipple, ed., *Twenty-Sixth yearbook of the society for the study of education: Part I: The foundations and technique of curriculum-construction*. Bloomington, IL: Public School Publishing Company, pp. 333–334; Rosenfeld, Paul (1924). *Port of New York*. New York: Harcourt, Brace and Company, Inc.; reprint 1961, Urbana, IL: University of Illinois Press.Rubin, Judith (1983). DAYENU: A tribute to Margaret Naumburg. *Art Therapy* 1(1 October), 4.

Blythe Hinitz

NBCDI. *See* National Black Child Development Institute

NCATE. *See* National Council for Accreditation of Teacher Education

NCCP. *See* National Center for Children in Poverty

NCLBA. *See* No Child Left Behind Act

NHSA. *See* National Head Start Association

NHSA Dialog

The *NHSA Dialog* is a journal devoted to the presentation of research-to-practice studies relevant to the early intervention field. Papers published in the journal focus on the well-being of children and families from economically disadvantaged environments and effectively integrate research findings and application.

The need for this type of connective research is critical to achieving positive and appropriate change in child and family policy. Knowledge of child development assists policymakers in making significant decisions concerning the security, health, and growth of children and what actions will effectively impact the problems and their solutions. The *NHSA Dialog* is a translational journal that provides a forum in which to present and discuss research and, in turn, to make a useful contribution to positive child and family outcomes.

The *NHSA Dialog* was envisioned to be a vehicle for promoting closer collaboration among practitioners, researchers, and policymakers interested in child development and early childhood intervention. The mission was to produce a high-quality, peer-reviewed journal that would be relevant to the broader early childhood community. That translated into long discussions with each potential author about how to use lay language to explain their findings, searching together for applications to real-world problems facing practitioners, and exploring with them how their results might be relevant to policy decisions. In 1999, the *Dialog*'s first peer-reviewed issue was published.

At the same time, other ways of enhancing the written exchanges of ideas were explored. Through the creativity of a dedicated staff, including Gregg Powell, Ph.D., the then **National Head Start Association** Director of Research and Evaluation, Faith Lamb-Parker, Ph.D., Editor, and Katherine Rogers, Assistant Editor, two sections were added to the first peer-reviewed issue: Dialogue From the Field, and Ask *NHSA Dialog*, becoming regular sections of each subsequent issue.

"Dialogue From the Field" became the section where professionals were able to express opinions and ideas, share passions, describe innovative curricula, and relay information about current research efforts. The essays were unsolicited and represented a broad spectrum of disciplines.

In "Ask *NHSA Dialog*," researchers and practitioners were solicited to pose interesting and relevant questions that then generated lively on-paper discussions about important issues for the field. Sometimes several people would answer a single question, revealing a diverse array of opinions. Short bios were included with the names of participating professionals to help readers better understand the points of view expressed.

Currently, the *NHSA Dialog* is published once a year and continues in its mission to provide essential, peer-reviewed research to the **Head Start** community, including researchers, administrators, policymakers, and practitioners. Manuscripts cover a wide range of topics relating to issues of children and families, including child health and mental health, family support and self-sufficiency, parenting, and policy issues.

Tara N. Weatherholt, Faith Lamb-Parker, and Barbara M. Burns

No Child Left Behind Act (NCLBA)

On January 8, 2002, President George W. Bush signed into law the No Child Left Behind Act (NCLBA) of 2001. NCLBA changed the federal government's role in kindergarten through grade 12 education by requiring U.S. public schools to describe their success and effectiveness in terms of students' attainment of academic standards and performance on standardized tests. The Act contains the President's four basic education reform principles: (1) stronger accountability for "guaranteeing" results, (2) increased flexibility and local control, (3) expanded options for parents, and (4) an emphasis on teaching methods that have been "quantitatively" proven to work (http://www.nochildleftbehind.gov/next/overview/index.html).

Among these four reform principles, "accountability" is considered as the most critical aspect. According to the U.S. Department of Education, an "accountable" education system involves several steps:

- States create their own standards for what a child should know and learn for all grades. Standards must be developed in math and reading immediately. Standards had to be developed for science by the 2005–2006 school year;
- With standards in place, states must test every student's progress toward those standards by using tests that are aligned with the standards. Beginning in the 2002–2003 school year, schools were to administer tests in each of three grade spans: grades 3–5, grades 6–9, and grades 10–12 in all schools. Beginning in the 2005–2006 school year, tests were to be administered every year in grades three through eight in math and reading. Beginning in the 2007–2008 school year, science achievement must also be tested;
- Each state, school district, and school will be expected to make adequate yearly progress toward meeting state standards. This progress will be measured for all students by sorting test results for students who are economically disadvantaged, from racial or ethnic minority groups, have disabilities, or have limited English proficiency;
- School and district performance will be publicly reported in district and state report cards. Individual school results will be on the district report cards; and
- If the district or school continually fails to make adequate progress toward the standards, then they will be held accountable, and federal support will be withdrawn.

Significance for Early Childhood Education

Although the focus of the No Child Left Behind Act was on primary and secondary education, there are indications that its emphasis on test-driven accountability and quantitative definitions of outcome and impact may be carried over into early childhood education by federal and state governments. For example, several states (e.g., Ohio and Florida) already have developed preschool standards even in the subject area of social studies in line with primary grade content standards. Because states and school districts are busy working toward meeting the expectations of the NCLBA law, narrowly defined teacher accountability based on standardized content and quantitative assessment has become a politically and economically important matter to a much greater extent than previously. Early childhood teacher education programs are being asked to assess whether program content covers the state standards, and to make sure prospective teachers are familiar with the standardized state test, in the name of teacher accountability.

The No Child Left Behind Act has also resulted in additional federal legislation and mandates. In April 2002, three months after passage of the NCLBA, President Bush announced his early childhood Initiative ***Good Start, Grow Smart***. This led in July 2003 to the **Head Start** Reauthorization and Program Improvement legislation, H.R. 2210, which included funding for a new assessment tool for testing 4 year olds. Concern has been expressed within the early childhood field that a standardized "one-size-fits-all" assessment tool completely ignores the diverse learning circumstances children from low-income families face.

In June 2002, the U.S. Department of Education released a report to the Congress, entitled *Meeting the Highly Qualified Teachers Challenge*, which indicated that teacher education programs are not producing the quality of teachers needed to support NCLBA. Citing a single study, the report concludes that teacher education does not contribute to teacher effectiveness. Critics of the report have countered that the study cited is only one of the fifty-seven empirical research studies recently synthesized by Wilson, Floden, and Ferrini-Mundy (2001, 2002), all funded by the U.S. Department of Education. Critics also note that the conclusions of many of the reports differ "fundamentally from those of other reviews [funded by the U.S. Department of Education] of research on teacher preparation . . . " (Cochran-Smith, 2002, p.379). Illustrative of this inconsistency are the specifications regarding "qualified teacher" within the new law. Public Law 107-110, NCLBA section 2131 (a) National Teacher Recruitment Campaign, authorized a national teacher recruitment that would include assisting "high-need" local educational agencies. Noting that high-poverty school districts are more likely to employ teachers on waivers than more wealthy districts, the Secretary's Report defines a highly qualified teacher as one who has obtained state certification from various alternative routes or passed the state teacher licensing examination and holds a license to teach in that state (U.S. Department of Education, 2002, p. 4 and p. 34). While it has been acknowledged that alternative routes to certification offer the possibility of bringing highly qualified teachers into high demand and high-poverty school districts, critics (Cochran-Smith, 2002) also warn that the new definition of qualified teachers has the dangerous potential of instantaneously transforming unqualified teachers into qualified teachers.

Thus, not only is teacher quality narrowly defined by the Secretary's Report, student achievement is also limited to test scores. The No Child Left Behind Act requires that the standardized test results included in the annual reports of the states and school districts be used to compare achievement between students of different groups. The underlying assumption of the NCLB and the Secretary's Report is that new, "tougher" standards will ensure that no child is left behind. The concern of many educators is that rather than "leveling the playing field," comparison with such tests will, if anything, leave historically disadvantaged children even further behind as support is withdrawn from low performing schools. The irony of NCLB is its role in heightening attention to what remains, for the United States, a fundamental conflict over how to provide high-quality and equitable public education for all children.

Further Readings: Cochran-Smith, M. (2002). Reporting on teacher quality: The politics of politics. *Journal of Teacher Education* 53(3), 379–382; Hyun, E. (2003). The No Child Left Behind Act of 2001: Issues and implications for early childhood teacher education. *Journal of Early Childhood Teacher Education* 24(2), 119–126. Available online at http://www.nochildleftbehind.gov/next/overview/index.html; U.S. Department of Education (June 2002). *Meeting the highly qualified teachers challenge: The secretary's annual report on teacher quality*. Washington, DC: U.S. Department of Education, Office of Postsecondary Education; Walsh, K. (2001). *Teacher certification reconsidered: Stumbling for quality*. Baltimore, MD: Abell Foundation. Available online at http://www.abellfoundation.org; Walsh, K. (2002). The evidence for teacher certification. *Education Next* 2(1), 79–84; Wilson, S., R. Floden, and J. Ferrini-Mundy (2002). Teacher preparation research: An insider's view from the outside. *Journal of Teacher Education* 53, 190–204; Wilson, S., R. Floden, and J. Ferrini-Mundy (2001). Teacher preparation research: Current knowledge, gaps, and recommendation, A research report prepared for the U.S. Department of Education. Seattle, WA: University of Washington, Center for the Study of Teaching and Policy.

Eunsook Hyun

North American Reggio Emilia Alliance (NAREA)

The North American Reggio Emilia Alliance (NAREA) is a network of educators, parents, and advocates seeking to elevate both the quality of life and the quality of schools and centers for young children. The history of this organization is rooted in the work and ideals of many dedicated individuals in the United States, Canada, and Mexico, all of whom have been inspired by the municipal early childhood programs of **Reggio Emilia**, Italy. These individuals visited the schools in Reggio Emilia, and carried back images and narratives about this powerful system of education based on a philosophy that values the potential of all children to think, learn, and construct knowledge. The first visitors returned to Reggio Emilia over and over again, leading delegations of colleagues. Supported by educators in Reggio Emilia and North America, they hosted the traveling exhibit from Reggio Emilia, *The Hundred Languages of Children*, organized conferences and courses, opened their schools for study and dialogue, and published articles and books, creating a vast network of learning inspired by the Reggio Emilia approach to early childhood education.

Beginning in the summer of 2000, a group of these educators met regularly and in November 2002 NAREA became an official organization. NAREA currently has a membership of over 500 educators representing communities across North America. NAREA's mission is to build a diverse community of advocates and educators to promote and defend the rights of children, families, and teachers of all cultures through a collaboration of colleagues inspired by the Reggio Emilia philosophy.

As an organization, the work of NAREA encourages the diversity of membership within the organization to include individuals from a full range of social, economic, and cultural communities. NAREA serves as a conduit for dialogue and exchange with Reggio Children and other international organizations that promote the rights of young children. The organization strengthens access to professional development initiatives and resources through communication tools. NAREA works to strengthen professional relationships among members by facilitating collaboration and exchange and creating professional development initiatives that are responsive to the needs and requests of members.

The benefits of NAREA membership include opportunities for communication and collaboration through several vehicles. Members have access to a Web site created and maintained by NAREA to provide information, resources, and a forum for the exchange of experiences and ideas among individuals interested in the Reggio Emilia approach to early childhood education. Members also receive the official periodical of NAREA, *Innovations in Early Education: The International Reggio Exchange*, a periodical by the Merrill-Palmer Institute, Wayne State University, quarterly. Members participate in meetings focusing on current issues in education with the support of educators from the schools of Reggio Emilia.

Inspired by the ongoing work in schools for young children in Reggio Emilia and their forty-year history of quality education, and along with a network of alliances worldwide, members of NAREA envision a world where all children are honored and respected for their potential, their capabilities, and their humanity.

Further Readings: North American Reggio Emilia Alliance, http://www.reggioalliance.org; Reggio Children, http://www.reggiochildren.it.

Lori Geismar-Ryan and Ellen Hall

Nutrition and Early Childhood Education

Nutrition is one of the most important components in the health of young children, and poor nutrition can have a negative impact on several aspects of childhood health and development including learning. Undernutrition, often resulting from **poverty** and hunger, can lead to protein and/or energy malnutrition or a multitude of vitamin and mineral deficiencies. Although several nutrition efforts have focused on undernutrition, many countries are now faced with the alternative form of malnutrition—overnutrition. Children suffering from overnutrition and associated poor lifestyle behaviors are at an increased risk for **obesity** and chronic diseases including diabetes and cardiovascular disease. Worldwide trends in childhood overweight and obesity suggest that by 2010, using International Obesity Task Force definitions, 46 percent of school-age children in the

Americas will be *overweight* and one in seven will be *obese*. However, this issue is not limited to children in the Americas. By 2010, 41 percent of children in the Eastern Mediterranean, 38 percent of European children, 27 percent of children in the Western Pacific region, and 22 percent in Southeast Asia will be *overweight*, and one in ten children in the Eastern Mediterranean and European regions will be *obese* (Wang and Lobstein, 2006).

Recently, a national survey found that 66 percent of 2- to 4-year-old children consumed a diet that "needed improvement" and 8 percent consumed a diet that was classified as "poor." Only 26 percent of children in this age group maintained a diet that was classified as "good" (Lin, 2005). There are several factors that have contributed to the current eating patterns of young children. Families have listed financial constraints and lack of knowledge regarding food preparation and storage as barriers to healthy eating (Hampl and Sass, 2001). Socioeconomic status greatly influences the types of foods families purchase. Lower-socioeconomic families are often at nutritional risk because they may not be able to purchase the proper types or amounts of food to support the growth and development of young children. For example, fresh fruits and vegetables are not regularly purchased by these families because they are perishable and perceived as more expensive. Fast food restaurants have become a growing concern in the American food culture because many fast foods are high in fat and/or sugar. Fast food restaurants are often attractive to parents of young children because they provide a cheap and quick source of food that their children often enjoy. Interestingly, fast food restaurants are more prevalent in lower-socioeconomic areas. An individual's cultural identity also influences their food intake. For example, milk consumption is traditionally lower in African, Asian, and Mexican American cultures. Not only does an individual's cultural identity influence their eating patterns, it can also influence their outlook on weight and health. Some individuals, such as Africans, Latinos, and Native Americans, view thinness with disease and overweight with health and beauty.

Healthy children between the ages of 2 and 6 years are recommended to eat in accordance with the Food Guide Pyramid for Young Children (1999) and the Dietary Guidelines for Americans (2005). The foundation of a healthy diet consists of whole grains, fruits, and vegetables along with regular consumption of low-fat and nonfat dairy products, lean meats, and beans. The guidelines provided below were designed for Americans, but they provide basic information that can be used to facilitate healthy eating patterns in all children. Young children should consume the following foods on most days:

- 6 servings of grains [one slice of bread, 1/2 cup of rice, or 1 ounce of cereal] of which half, or at least 3 servings, should be whole grain products
- 3 servings of vegetables [1/2 cup of raw or cooked vegetables or 1 cup of raw leafy vegetables]
- 2 servings of fruit [1 small piece of fruit, 1/2 cup of canned fruit, or 3/4 cup of 100 percent juice]
- 2 servings of dairy products [1 cup of milk or yogurt or 2 ounces of cheese]
- 4 to 6 ounces of lean meat, fish, poultry, or alternatives [e.g., peanut butter or eggs]

In addition to the specific guidelines above, other recommendations have been provided to help guide the development of healthy eating patterns in children.

For example, although 100 percent fruit and vegetable juices can contribute to fruit and vegetable needs, most needs should be met by consuming whole foods rather than juices; therefore, the intake of juice should be limited to 4 to 6 ounces per day (AAP, 2001). Also, children should consume a limited number of foods that are high in fat and/or sugar. The term "sugar" refers to caloric sweeteners including sucrose (table sugar) and high fructose corn syrup (HFCS). Foods high in fat and/or sugar (e.g., cake and chips) contribute calories to the diet, but they are low in nutrients such as vitamins and minerals. Therefore, these foods should not make up a large component of a child's diet. It is also recommended that children over the age of 2 years consume low-fat dairy options to reduce total and saturated fat consumption.

Beyond basic serving recommendations, it is imperative to address the appropriate means of providing food to children. When working with children, it is important to provide a variety of healthy options to the child. If a child is only provided cookies and chips, this is what the child will eat. However, if a child is provided healthier options, the child is more likely to maintain a healthy diet. It is the caregiver's responsibility to provide a child with food options, and it is the child's responsibility to determine what and how much to eat (Evers, 1997). To help prevent overeating, research indicates that children should be allowed to serve themselves or be provided small serving sizes (Orlet, Rolls, and Birch, 2003). Also, adults should encourage children to eat healthy foods without pressuring them to do so. Rather than forcing or bribing a child to eat a full serving of a new food, simply encourage the "one bite rule." Children are born with an apprehension to new foods, and it may take five to ten exposures to a new food before the child accepts the new food. In addition, children are born with a preference for sweet and salty foods; therefore, foods with other flavors may take more exposure before they are accepted. Although it is recommended to limit the intake of foods high in sugar and/or fat, these foods should not be restricted from the child's diet (Birch and Fisher, 1998). If the base of a child's diet consists of healthy options, moderate consumption of appropriate amounts of less healthy foods is acceptable and will contribute to a healthy eating pattern later in life.

Within the school environment, teachers can promote healthy eating through a number of avenues. Teachers can encourage their schools to adopt a policy that provides children with healthy foods. Teachers can also address healthy foods in the classroom. A classroom garden can be beneficial in discussing food origins, sanitary food practices, and nutritional content. Teachers can also provide children the opportunity to try new foods. Healthy foods can be incorporated into classroom lessons or a "tasting party" can be offered for children. When providing foods to children in the classroom, early childhood educators must avoid common allergens (e.g., eggs, cow's milk, wheat, soy, peanuts, tree nuts, fish, and shellfish) and foods that may cause choking (e.g., grapes). If it is not possible to incorporate foods into the classroom, try other food related activities such as making placemats or teaching children to set a table. Finally, teachers can promote healthy food intake among children by acting as good role models.

Teachers can also provide families with helpful information about healthy eating within the household. For example, teachers can encourage family meals. Eating as a family is beneficial because family meals are typically planned and therefore more nutritious than meals eaten on the go. It is also beneficial to include young children in the food purchasing and preparation processes as much as possible. For example, teachers can propose that families allow the child to pick a fruit or vegetable for dinner, perhaps as a part of a curriculum project connected with a community garden or other sources of local produce. Also, families can be encouraged to limit eating during sedentary behaviors such as watching television. Foods consumed during sedentary behaviors are often of little nutritional value, and children are often unaware of how much they are consuming during sedentary time. Teachers can also encourage parents to act as good role models. Adults can promote healthy eating behaviors by practicing appropriate eating patterns. Finally, specific programs such as **Women, Infants, and Children** (WIC), **Head Start**, and Food Stamps are available to provide valuable resources to eligible low-income families.

Eating patterns begin during the preschool years, and it is imperative to promote healthy behaviors during this important developmental period. By promoting healthy eating, early childhood educators can have a significant impact on the health of children immediately and over the life span.

Further Readings: American Academy of Pediatrics (AAP) (2001). Policy statement: The use and misuse of fruit juices in pediatrics. *Pediatrics* 107, 1210–13; Birch, L., and J. Fisher (1998). Development of eating behaviors among children and adolescents. *Pediatrics* 101, 539–49; Evers, C. (1997). Empower children to develop healthful eating habits. *Journal of the American Dietetic Association* 97, S116; Hampl, J., and S. Sass (2001). Focus groups indicate that vegetable and fruit consumption by food stamp-eligible Hispanics is affected by children and unfamiliarity with non-traditional foods. *Journal of the American Dietetic Association* 101, 685–687; Huettig, C., S. Rich, J. Engelbrecht, C. Sanborn, E. Essery, and N. DiMarco et al. (2006). Growing with EASE: Eating, Activity, and Self-Esteem. *Young Children* 61, 26–31; Lin, B. (2005). *Nutrition and health characteristics of low-income populations: Healthy Eating Index*. Agriculture Information Bulletin, 796–91; Orlet, F., B. Rolls, and L. Birch (2003). Children's bite size and intake of an entree are greater with large portions than with age-appropriate or self-selected portions. *American Journal of Clinical Nutrition* 77, 1164–70; USDA (1999). *Food Guide Pyramid for Young Children*. Available online at http://www.usda.gov/cnpp/KidsPyra/; USDA (2005). *Dietary Guidelines for Americans*. Available online at http://www.healthierus.gov/dietaryguidelines/; Wang, Y. and T. Lobstein (2006). Worldwide trends in childhood overweight and obesity. *International Journal of Pediatric Obesity* 1, 11–25.

Eve Essery, Nancy DiMarco, and Shannon S. Rich